Fred Steiner
6283 ELDORADO AVE.
NIAGARA FALLS

905 358 5233

D1283417

CORVETTES CANADA

It's action stations for the *Fergus* port depth charge crew.

CORVETTES CANADA

CONVOY VETERANS OF WWII TELL THEIR TRUE STORIES

MAC JOHNSTON

John Wiley & Sons Canada, Ltd.

Library and Archives Canada Cataloguing in Publication Data

Johnston, Mac
    Corvettes Canada : convoy veterans of World War II tell their true stories / Mac Johnston.

Includes index.
ISBN 978-0-470-15429-8

    1. Corvettes (Warships) 2. Naval convoys—Canada—History—20th century. 3. World War, 1939-1945—Naval operations, Canadian.
4. Canada. Royal Canadian Navy—History—World War, 1939-1945.
5. World War, 1939-1945—Personal narratives, Canadian. I. Title.

D779.C2J64 2008   940.54'5971   C2007-907464-2

Production Credits
Cover and interior text design: Michael Chan
Typesetting: Tegan Wallace
Interior photo-imaging: Jason Vandenberg
Front Cover Photos
    Top left: Courtesy Doug May
    Top middle: RCN photo, courtesy Frances O'Brien
    Top right: Gilbert Milne, RCN, Courtesy Vic Martin
    Bottom: RCN, courtesy Wally Charbonneau
Back cover photo: Courtesy Georgie Cameron
Printer: Friesens

John Wiley & Sons Canada, Ltd.
6045 Freemont Blvd.
Mississauga, Ontario
L5R 4J3

Printed in Canada

1 2 3 4 5 FP 12 11 10 09 08

To the men who went to sea in corvettes

A crew member chips away at the ice-encrusted *Brantford* after a severe spray storm off Newfoundland.

CONTENTS

Artist Burnie Forbes mimics the pose of the Queen of Hearts in his *Wetaskiwin* gun-shield logo.

INTRODUCTION

To the casual observer, World War II was won on land, but the key to victory was actually the Battle of the Atlantic. It was control of the seas that allowed the Allies to fight on land in Europe, and in the air.

Canada played a significant role in this struggle by building and sending to sea a large number of small escort vessels known as corvettes which were crucial in keeping open the Atlantic lifeline so that weapons of war, fuel, food and clothing could be conveyed to the United Kingdom, the base from which Europe was eventually wrested from the control of Adolf Hitler's Nazi Germany.

This was the longest continuous battle of World War II. On the one side were the hunted — merchant ships sailing in convoys protected by warships. On the other side were the hunters — German submarines known as U-boats. The German goal was to sever the ocean supply lines and strangle the U.K. into submission. As it developed the U-boats were not only hunters, but the hunted as well. Similarly, the Allied warships were not only the hunted, but, along with aircraft, the hunters of U-boats.

How better to tell the story of this epic struggle than in the words of many of Canada's participants — the corvette sailors themselves. This means the ratings in the lower decks and the officers in the wardroom, for both views are necessary to put the picture in perspective. It must be noted that this book is distinctive for the amount of space it devotes to the experiences of the men in the lower decks, who have been overlooked in most literature.

I gathered the memories of all these veterans in three ways: 1) a correspondence campaign in which I wrote more than 1,900 letters to veterans seeking their stories and elaboration on specific items; 2) telephone interviews; and 3) personal interviews.

Underlying all this, of course, there was considerable background reading and archival research, particularly at Library and Archives Canada and the Directorate of History and Heritage at National Defence Headquarters in Ottawa.

In reviewing the original *Corvettes Canada*, eminent Canadian naval historian Marc Milner of the University of New Brunswick wrote: "Johnston has woven the memories of 250 Old Salts from 50 different ships and the history of the wartime Royal Canadian Navy into a tight fabric, one that is both entertaining and extremely valuable. If you have never read anything on the Canadian navy's part in the Battle of the Atlantic, start with this one; if you've read everything that's already available, you will find this one a gem."

This book has been updated and expanded since the first printing in 1994. More than ever it is a well-researched collective memoir that will entertain and inform you not only about the Battle of the Atlantic, but also other significant Canadian campaigns, including the Battle of the St. Lawrence and the Mediterranean.

I believe the veterans' accounts and my research combine to provide an accurate portrayal of our corvette navy, with typical Canadian modesty and humour. That said, the book is not a definitive history of Canadian corvettes. I did not explore policy decisions in great detail. I describe the big picture only to the degree needed to understand the framework and situations in which corvettes were created and operated. One result of going where the men's memories took me is that a number of corvettes are mentioned only briefly, a number of events are covered only in passing, and some may be absent entirely.

Words alone are seldom enough, and so a photographic treasure unfolds in these pages, bringing that interesting era to life. This is what it was like: Most of the photos come from the veterans themselves and many are being published for the first time.

There is a bibliography for those readers interested in exploring our naval history in more depth, but there are no footnotes because this is a popular history aimed at a general audience. Instead, attribution of sources is embedded in the text where appropriate.

MJ
Ottawa, Ont.
August 2007

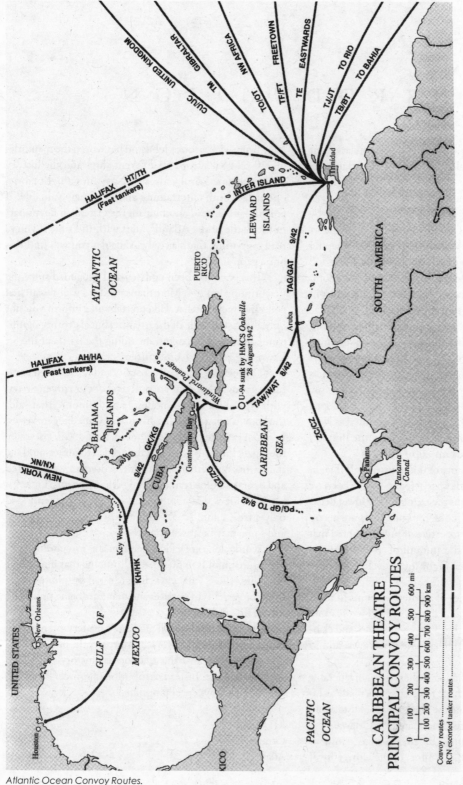

CARIBBEAN THEATRE
PRINCIPAL CONVOY ROUTES

Convoy routes ....
RCN escorted tanker routes ....

0 100 200 300 400 500 600 mi
0 100 200 300 400 500 600 700 800 900 km

Source: No Higher Purpose: The Official Operational History of the Royal Canadian Navy in the Second World War, 1939-1943, Vol. II, Part 1, Maps on pages 409, 424B, 599, National Defence, 2002. Reproduced with the permission of the Minister of Public Works and Government Services, 2008.

Atlantic Ocean Convoy Routes.

TO UK/UC
UNITED KINGDOM
TM
GIBRALTAR
TO/OT
NW AFRICA
TF/FT
FREETOWN
TE
EASTWARDS
TJ/JT
TO RIO
TB/BT
TO BAHIA

Trinidad

HALIFAX HT/TH
(Fast tankers)

INTER ISLAND

LEEWARD ISLANDS

PUERTO RICO

9/42
TAG/GAT
Aruba

ATLANTIC OCEAN

SOUTH AMERICA

HALIFAX AH/HA
(Fast tankers)

U-94 sunk by HMCS Oakville
28 August 1942

Windward Passage

BAHAMA ISLANDS

Guantanamo Bay

TAW/WAT 8/42

ZC/CZ

CARIBBEAN SEA

GK/KG
9/42

CUBA

NEW YORK
KN/NK

Key West

KH/HK

GZ/ZG

PG/GP TO 9/42

Panama
Panama Canal

UNITED STATES

GULF OF MEXICO

New Orleans

Houston

MEXICO

PACIFIC OCEAN

ACKNOWLEDGEMENTS

Many people were generous with their time and assistance in the four years I devoted to researching and writing the original Corvettes Canada, first published in 1994. In updating and expanding the manuscript for this second edition, I was once again fortunate to receive the assistance of a number of World War II Canadian naval veterans and their family members, as well as friends.

The number of photos has also been significantly increased this time to better depict that era. Moreover, the photos used in the first edition were all returned and most were no longer available due to the relentless march of time and the passing of many veterans. Therefore, the biggest challenge was to gather photos. Internet searches, personal contacts and several hundred hours on the phone bore fruit in the rich treasury of photos that appear in this book. My thanks go to all who assisted in this endeavour, particularly Morley Barnes, Bev Bate, Francois-Xavier Beaulieu, Roy Bergren, Colleen Blueman, Georgie Cameron, Carol Campbell, Wally Charbonneau, Art Chinery, Joyce Claggett, Alf Cockburn, Burnie Forbes, June Hawkins, Hoot Gibson, Victor Large, *Legion Maga-zine*, Vic Martin, Doug May, Frances O'Brien, William John Quinsey, Lisa Piercey, Tahirah Shadforth, Howard Trusdale and Christine Webster.

Individuals who provided assistance for the original book in a working capacity included W.A.B. Douglas, Carl Christie, Roger Sarty, Marilyn Gurney, Phil Lebel, Max Corkum, Vern Howland, Dan Wheeldon and Mike Newell. Organizations which were co-operative included Library and Archives Canada, the National Defence Directorate of History and Heritage, Maritime Command and the Canadian Naval Memorial Trust.

Family, friends, veterans, Legionnaires and others who pitched in include Jack Muir, Morgan McGaughey, Vern Murphy, Tina Klein, A.G.S. (Tony) Griffin, Marc Milner, Terry Banghart, Doris Williams, Ronald Harrison, Rod McDonald and the late Anthony Stacey, Barry O'Brien, Louis Audette and Frank Plant.

I am indebted again to my editor, Don Loney, ever positive and encouraging.

And, as before, I enjoyed the unstinting support and assistance of my wife, Sue.

Trillium officer Barry O'Brien.

CHAPTER ONE

"THEY DIDN'T EVEN HAVE UNIFORMS FOR US."

CANADA WAS A NATION unprepared for war in 1939. On land, at sea and in the air this dominion of 11,000,000 people lacked significant standing forces and equipment. There was no question, however, that Canada would stand with Great Britain, as she had in World War I. There were, however, many questions about the precise nature of Canada's role as World War II loomed.

The British and Canadian governments took control of merchant shipping in late August 1939, just prior to the eruption of hostilities on September 3. Just as in World War I, merchant ships sailing alone would be vulnerable to German surface raiders and submarines, so convoys were again organized to provide some measure of protection. Transatlantic convoy HX 1 sailed from Halifax on September 16, 1939, guarded by the Canadian destroyers *Saguenay* and *St. Laurent*.

Cut off from Europe and far removed from its dominions and colonies, Britain was very dependent on North America for materiel, goods and foodstuffs. The sea lanes to the United Kingdom became so vital they were the object of a six-year struggle known as the Battle of the Atlantic, the longest continuous battle of World War II.

Though Canada is a trading nation and more than 60 percent of our exports travelled by sea at that time, the Royal Canadian Navy wasn't capable of providing adequate protection for shipping. In fact, the RCN consisted of only 13 ships: six destroyers, five minesweepers and two training vessels. The permanent navy had a strength of 1,819.

In addition, the three naval reserve bodies together produced about 1,800 more personnel. The Royal Ca-

nadian Naval Volunteer Reserve had developed a small presence across the country since its formation in 1923, while the Royal Canadian Naval Reserve, also formed in 1923, offered immediate seagoing experience in the form of about 700 "NR" men who came from the merchant marine. On the West Coast was the small Fishermen's Reserve, formed in 1938 to help protect British Columbia in the event of war.

Anticipating the advent of war and the need for fleet expansion, RCN brass had included four types of ships — destroyers, anti-submarine patrol vessels for coastal work, minesweepers and motor torpedo boats — in the 1939 naval estimates, but funds were deemed insufficient and the estimates were cut even before presentation to Parliament.

When Canada declared war on Germany on September 10, 1939, the ill-prepared navy had only a rough plan for expansion. Significantly, it did not include vessels designed for convoy escort on the Atlantic. Envisioning a service along the lines of Britain's Royal Navy (RN), RCN brass failed to grasp the gravity of the submarine threat and that Canada could contribute most effectively by building and manning a large number of ocean escorts.

This book's focus is the anti-submarine patrol vessel originally intended for coastal defence. Once war erupted, key considerations for the government were that this ship be inexpensive and easily built by Canadian shipyards not accustomed to naval vessels. It also had to carry a small crew. Other important factors were a need for seaworthiness, good acceleration, manoeuvrability, speed, asdic (sonar) capability, endurance and watertight subdivision. The RCN was sadly lacking in technical knowledge; radar, a new development not available in Canada, was not included in the requirements.

In fact, the tiny RCN had few resources and relied on Britain for actual ship construction plans, just as it had relied heavily on the RN for training and support since the RCN's formation in 1910. The vessel envisaged for Canada's anti-submarine escort role was the improved "halcyon" or Bramble-class sloop. Though capable of anti-submarine escort, it had been used mainly for minesweeping by the RN. The sloop had two engines and two propellers and was, for its 815-ton size, heavily armed with two 4-inch guns.

Instead, Canada suddenly committed to building the Flower-class corvette. Cost and timing were the reasons, though one simply cannot overestimate the timing factor: the corvette blueprints arrived in Ottawa at precisely the opportune moment.

At the end of August 1939, a Canadian Manufacturers Association mission returned from the U.K. after studying war production. As Gilbert Tucker, Canada's first official naval historian, has recorded, the mission left information about shipbuilding with the National Research Council which, in turn, gave the material to naval headquarters in Ottawa on September 13, 1939. Included were plans for the corvette and the Bangor-class minesweeper, a scaled-down and cheaper version of the Bramble.

The RN had placed its first corvette order on July 25, 1939, with the Yorkshire firm Smith's Dock Co. which had also produced World War I sub-chasers. Based on the Smith's Dock whalecatcher *Southern Pride,* the new design was, in fact, originally called "patrol vessel, whaler type" because certain characteristics were desirable for hunting either whales or submarines: seaworthiness, manoeuvrability and rapid acceleration.

Canadian naval authorities quickly compared the corvette to the Bramble sloop. The corvette had only one engine and one propeller as well as one 4-inch gun. The corvette wasn't as fast, but it was deemed fast enough. Its endurance wasn't as great, but was seen as sufficient for its coastal escort mission. The corvette was equal to the sloop in its ability to carry asdic and minesweeping equipment.

In sum, the corvette was less capable but cheaper. It was easier to build and so could be constructed in quantity at a faster rate. There was a sense of urgency that's hard to imagine today. Only five days after the corvette plans reached naval headquarters, a revised naval construction program was put to the federal cabinet on September 18, 1939, and approved in principle the following day. Canada got the Flower-class corvette and also the Bangor minesweeper.

The War Supply Board created by the federal government determined that Flowers and Bangors required the same construction facilities. As a result, some shipyards would build both vessels. The first contracts let by Canada in early 1940 called for 28 corvettes to be delivered before the close of the 1940 navigation season by 12 shipyards — five in the St. Lawrence region, three on the Great Lakes, one in the Maritimes and three on the West Coast. These were to be followed within a year by 36 more corvettes. Ten of the 1940 corvettes were intended for the RN and, in a quid pro quo, two larger vessels, Tribal-class destroyers, were to be built in the U.K. for the RCN.

Britain's wartime prime minister, Winston Churchill, gave corvettes the label "cheap and nasties" and the Canadian experience bore this out. Contract prices varied with the shipyard, but initially $530,000 per vessel was common and $540,000 was the maximum in central Canada. On the West Coast, this climbed to $606,000 because of higher labour and transportation costs. In most cases, small price adjustments were made to reflect changes in specifications.

* * *

Ships must have sailors, so in Canada's nine provinces the navy joined the Canadian Army and the Royal Canadian

Courtesy Georgie Cameron

While all Canadian warships had a maple leaf painted on their funnels, *St. Thomas* bore the symbol in triplicate.

Air Force in pursuing the stream of teenagers and young men about to volunteer for the service of their choice. The army and the air force brought their wartime enlistees into their main body. The naval recruits, however, were put into the RCNVR for the war and so it provided the overwhelming majority of the RCN's manpower.

While all Canadian naval ships would have the maple leaf painted on their funnels [smokestacks] and all sailors would wear Canada badges on the shoulders of their uniforms, the distinction between sailors of the permanent navy and the wartime volunteers was reinforced when, rather than being given the RCN's straight stripes on the sleeves of an officer's uniform to indicate rank, the sleeves of VR officers contained distinctive wavy stripes. Thus the "VR" boys became known as the Wavy Navy, a phrase popularized by the song *Roll Along Wavy Navy, Roll Along*. The first verse goes like this:

Roll along, Wavy Navy, roll along
Roll along, Wavy Navy, roll along
If they ask who we are
We're the RCNVR!
Roll along, Wavy Navy, roll along

Of course, such distinctions were not on the minds of new enlistees. Take W.J. Roberts of Thunder Bay, Ont., who served in the corvette *Oakville* in 1941-42:

I joined the navy in September 1939. I was very interested in electronics and was on my way to getting my ham radio licence; also, I was repairing radios for a local concern, which stood me in good stead when I joined as a telegraphist. Myself and a few friends who also joined were on our way to Halifax.

We arrived at Montreal's CPR station and had to wait about four hours to catch a CN train to Halifax, so we went to a show to kill time. I remember parts of it well; it was a story about storms at sea and it gave me a lot of second thoughts about going to sea.

Eventually we got to Halifax in an old colonist car that still had gas lamps. We detrained onto Barrington Street where we had to march to the dockyard — a few miserable miles in the rain, as I recall.

There someone took us to the barracks where some uniforms and a blanket were thrown at us. We found a place on the floor to sleep. The next day we went through barracks routine and then I got into code class and drills.

Ralph Shideler of Saint John, N.B., who served in the corvette *Wetaskiwin* from 1941-43, enlisted November 6, 1939, at Esquimalt, B.C.: "I was the sixty-sixth person to enlist there. At basic training they didn't even have uniforms for us, just the big bulky naval coveralls. Then after six weeks it was into wireless school for training in navy radio."

The war was on. The need was great. Time was of the essence. Everything was rush, rush, rush. As the navy swelled in size, shipyards expanded rapidly, but materials and skilled labour were scarce. Deliveries were late. Only 13 corvettes were commissioned in Canada in 1940 and eight of them were ticketed for the RN. So great was the rush that the 10 corvettes built in Canada for the RN were commissioned incomplete.

Barry O'Brien of Rockcliffe Park, Ont., remembers the day — October 9, 1940 — that *Trillium* underwent builder's trials.

The ship had not yet been turned over to the navy and was still the responsibility of the builder, Canadian Vickers Ltd. of Montreal, Quebec.

Trillium was jammed with civilian and naval brass. Being the lowly sub-lieutenant, I was detailed to be aware of their wants and whims. As we sailed down the St. Lawrence River under the direction of a civilian pilot, an elaborate and liquid buffet lunch was served in the wardroom. Then most passengers opted to go up on deck. I'd been up since 5 a.m. and, sensing a chance to get my head down, I went below to the seamen's mess in the bow of the ship.

I fell asleep immediately, but the next thing I knew there was a resounding crash. Having just come off an armed merchant cruiser plying the Atlantic, my first reaction was that we had been torpedoed, but then I realized we had gone aground, so I rushed up to the bridge to find out where I might be needed. *Trillium* was high and dry on a shoal, unable to move ahead or astern, with her asdic dome torn off. She had a damaged propeller and some large dents in her bottom underplating.

The collective brass radioed ashore for a lighter to come out and rescue them, leaving aboard a few civilians and the ship's skeleton crew of officers and ratings. And so this is how we spent the night, with no food or drink. We were towed into drydock at Vickers, thereby delaying our commissioning three weeks.

But for running aground, *Trillium* would have been the initial corvette commissioned in Canada. As it was, she came onstream October 31, 1940, at Montreal and arrived in Halifax on November 14, following in the wake of *Windflower* which was commissioned October 20 at Quebec City and reached Halifax on October 31.

*   *   *

In the fall of 1940 there was great concern about the possibility of a German invasion of the U.K. In April, Germany had occupied Denmark and Norway. France had fallen that summer. Italy had entered the war on Germany's side. The United States was still neutral. So there was an urgency to get the 10 RN corvettes to the East Coast before the Great Lakes and St. Lawrence River froze up and were closed to navigation for the winter. Nature did not cooperate and winter arrived early.

"I was drafted to *Spikenard* in the Davie Shipbuilding Yard at Lauzon, Que. We broke shale ice all the way down the St. Lawrence on the way to Halifax in early December 1940," recalls Harry Carson of Dartmouth, N.S., who served in her as an able seaman asdic operator in 1940-41. "The messdecks were situated forward and the roar of the breaking ice was comparable to having your head inside a steel drum with someone beating on the drum with a hammer."

Others had it as bad, or worse. "*Mayflower* and *Eyebright* left Montreal in early December, 1940, for Halifax. The ice on the St. Lawrence was so thick that we required two icebreakers to accompany us. The two corvettes were in touch with one another by radio telephone until we reached Quebec City when it broke down," recalls Ken Hedley of Guelph, Ont., leading telegraphist in *Mayflower* in 1940-42. "From then on, I used a flashlight to converse, by Morse code, with *Eyebright* — and it was cold on that open bridge.

"Once we hit the Gulf of St. Lawrence, the ship, with its rounded bottom, bobbed and rolled like a cork. Many flaked out, seasick in the messdeck with a bucket at hand.

The only trouble was that when the ship rolled, the buckets overturned and spilled their contents. We had to pick up our meal at the galley and take it forward to eat in the messdeck — not too successfully with the odour from the overturned buckets."

Even the first corvette was not 100 percent. "I was one of the crew that brought *Windflower* to Halifax from Quebec in October 1940. She was not quite finished so we had to sail her on one boiler," says a member of her commissioning crew, David Wilson, a stoker petty officer from Dartmouth.

To prevent *Fennel* and *Bittersweet* from becoming icebound, they were sailed and towed from Sorel, Que., to Liverpool, N.S., with *Fennel* being damaged en route and repaired at Quebec City. After further work, they were commissioned in January 1941.

Ships of this class of RN corvettes were named after flowers, giving rise to the popular description Flower-class corvettes. The 10 built and commissioned incomplete here as His Majesty's Ships (HMS) were, in order of commissioning: *Windflower*, *Trillium*, *Hepatica*, *Arrowhead*, *Snowberry*, *Eyebright*, *Mayflower*, *Spikenard*, *Fennel* and *Bittersweet*. All were manned by Canadian crews.

*   *   *

Across the Atlantic, there had been many naval developments in 1940. German U-boats, now operating from bases in France and Norway, had success against shipping that was not well protected. Shipping losses continued even after convoys were routed north of Ireland. Britain required more escorts to provide greater convoy protection and also to compensate for warship losses. She addressed this need in part by obtaining 50 World War I destroyers from the U.S. in exchange for leasing sites for U.S. military bases. The RCN got six of these old ships to ease its shortage of vessels.

Into this maelstrom the Canadian-built RN corvettes began to set sail. On December 6, 1940, *Windflower* and *Trillium* left Halifax with convoy HX 94. The pair went to the U.K. for fitting out that wasn't completed until early March 1941. Their sister corvettes built for the RN followed as soon as they became available.

Each of these 10 RN corvettes made her initial Atlantic crossing with a dummy wooden gun fashioned by her crew, instead of the weapon that was to be her main surface armament. Four-inch guns simply weren't available in Canada, but these were desperate times and naval authorities decided the ships must be rushed to the British Isles. Concern for the Canadian crews was secondary to the Allies' needs.

Gilbert Sauve of Willowdale, Ont., a petty officer in *Trillium* in 1940-41, recalls a rough, stormy trip with a few unusual features. *Trillium* got an asdic contact that might have been a U-boat, "so the gun's crew put up a wooden gun, in case a German submarine came up to the surface." Then *Trillium*'s NR captain, Rollie Harris, had off-duty crew members sleep on the deck — in December, in the North Atlantic — the last two or three nights of the trip, Sauve remembers. This could have been a humanitarian gesture to try and ensure maximum crew safety or a desperate act motivated by fear of being held accountable for crew loss in the event the corvette was torpedoed. Either way, it was a most unorthodox way to run a warship — and a sign that not everybody was comfortable with their new naval responsibilities.

Improvisation was the order of the day. Aboard *Windflower*, the flagpole was taken down, painted black and wrapped in canvas. "It looked just like a gun," says David Wilson, who was drafted off after her first crossing.

A bad storm dispersed many of the ships and *Windflower* got separated from convoy HX 94. Then things got worse. Jim Sharpe of Victoria recounts second-hand a story he was told when he joined *Windflower* a few months later as an acting leading seaman: "The engine burned out a bottom-end bearing when *Windflower* was in mid-Atlantic, not with a convoy. One ERA [engine room artificer] spent most of the next 27 hours on his back in the bilge below the engine as others in the engine crew passed the spare bottom end to him for fitting and back out for honing in. The operation was a success despite the fact that a drifting ship rolls side-on to the wind and sea far worse than a ship under control."

When without propulsion — "becalmed" is the term from days of sail — a ship is at the mercy of the elements and extremely vulnerable to any enemy that might happen along. Fortune was with *Windflower* this trip, but Canadian ingenuity helped, as Jim Sharpe explains: "That repair task may have been impossible had it not been for the deck crew's share. They gathered all the spare canvas, including the hammock every sailor had, and stitched and laced it all together. The canvas was hoisted on the forestay to create a balloon jib to catch the wind and keep the ship stern end to the wind. This kept the roll to a minimum."

On the lighter side, Lloyd Jewers of Dartmouth, a stoker first class in *Hepatica* from 1940-42, recounts a personal incident from her fledgling stage: "The engine room branch were issued wooden shoes as they were very cool on the feet and very comfortable to wear in the hot boiler room. As I

The early corvette HMCS *Trillium* (foreground) in harbour, probably in 1941.

Courtesy Tahirah Shadforth

En route to Halifax, N.S., HMS *Mayflower* breaks ice in early December 1940 while rushing to get down the St. Lawrence River before the winter freeze-up.

went up from the boiler room to call a watch this day, I was wearing my wooden shoes. When I came back down, the first lieutenant was waiting for me and said words to this effect: 'If you ever again wear those wooden shoes and walk along a steel deck above me head, I will personally remove them from your feet and throw them overboard.'"

When *Hepatica* sailed for the U.K. with convoy HX 97 on December 18, 1940, Ernie Adams of Dartmouth was acting leading stoker: "A dummy 4-inch gun was mounted forward to hopefully frighten the enemy to death. It was made from a wooden packing crate. A davit used to hoist depth charges was the muzzle, which drooped somewhat. The entire structure was covered with a fitted canvas. We hoped it looked impressive. In addition, we were furnished with six depth charges, hardly enough for one sub contact. We were supplied with six Ross rifles of World War I vintage, presumably to fight off enemy aircraft and attempt to sink floating mines by shooting off the 'tits,' an impossible task with both ship and mine bouncing around."

Jewers remembers that first crossing well: "The wooden gun was put in place by Coxswain Angus (Ginger) Welsh, Danny Cunningham, Jack Polan and myself, along with Jimmy Cummings. The second day out, a storm came up and we did not make contact with any ship until approximately 200 miles from Scotland.

"It took us 21 days to reach Greenock. It was so rough that the cooks could not keep anything on the galley stove.

On Christmas Day we had bully beef and hard tack, and on New Year's Day we had sardines and hard tack."

Ginger Welsh of Halifax, tongue firmly in cheek, labels it "wonderful food."

Ken Hedley, in *Mayflower*, describes the manning arrangement: "We had been given to understand that we were only delivering the corvettes to Britain and that we would be returning as passengers for other duties. We picked up the rest of our crew in Halifax and began escorting our first convoy in February 1941. On the way over, the propagandist Lord Haw Haw broadcast from Germany that our convoy had left and would never reach the other side of the ocean.

"The crew rigged a dummy gun from a large wooden box and a wood boom. On the last leg of the trip, we had an asdic contact and, thinking it was a sub, dropped depth charges; with no further movement, it was decided the contact was only a wreck. When we arrived in Greenock, I was sent ashore with dollars to change into pounds sterling so that cables could be sent to our homes to let our families know we had arrived safely."

Ted Cunningham of Mason, Tennessee, an ordinary seaman in *Arrowhead* in 1940-41, says: "The wooden gun did exist and I had a picture of it at one time, but 50 years is a long time and I no longer have it. The following armament was aboard: six Lee-Enfield rifles with 100 rounds of ammo, two .45 revolvers, one Oerlikon anti-aircraft gun with 500 rounds of ammo and six depth charges."

Harry Carson talks about *Spikenard*: "After provisioning the ship in Halifax, we were 'armed' with a Lewis machine gun, six depth charges and a large wooden log mounted on the forward gun deck, under canvas, to create the appearance of a 4-inch gun — should we come upon a U-boat on the surface. On our first convoy duty we took up our station and used our asdic to sweep one section of the convoy. If we had picked up any submarine contacts, we could have carried out one attack with our six depth charges; then we would have been at the same risk as any of the unarmed merchant ships, unless we got close enough to ram a U-boat on the surface."

* * *

During this period, other corvettes were also in progress for the expanding Canadian navy. They, too, were Flower-class corvettes, but the RCN steered its own course, naming them after Canadian cities, towns and villages. On November 9, 1940, the first RCN corvette was commissioned — His Majesty's Canadian Ship (HMCS) *Collingwood* — in the Ontario town for which she was named. She arrived at Halifax on December 4. There were two HMC corvette commissionings on November 25: *Orillia* in Collingwood and *Cobalt* in Port Arthur, Ont., which is now part of Thunder Bay. On December 18, 1940, *Chambly* was commissioned in Quebec City.

Handwritten notes in a file at the Department of National Defence's Directorate of History and Heritage in Ottawa indicate *Collingwood* began "patrol and escort duties" from Halifax on December 15. It was a Christmas to remember: "She was in quarantine for 10 days on account of one rating having been found to have a contagious disease."

Les Badger of Cambridge, Ont., an able seaman asdic operator in *Collingwood* in 1940-41, recalls: "We were in Halifax on Christmas Eve all set for shore leave, only to be confined to ship over Christmas because some twit had come down with chicken-pox. Needless to say, he was not a popular fellow."

Some early RCN corvettes were the subject of experimentation. David Grimes of Verdun, Que., an able seaman in *Chambly* in 1941, explains: "In the beginning, we put in a few weeks with a professor, I think from McGill University in Montreal, who had invented some lights that, when properly installed and adjusted, were designed to blend the ship with the horizon to make the ship almost invisible.

"They said it worked okay, except that we would have to have the enemy tell us what adjustments to make to the lights. So one morning we came into port and off came the lights, all but those that were welded to the funnel."

The initial four RCN corvettes were based in Halifax and did local patrol and escort work the balance of the winter of 1940-41. Charles Scott of Armdale, N.S., served in *Collingwood* during that stretch: "She was my first ship as an ordinary seaman and it was the worst five months of my entire 28-1/2 years in the RCN. We were on antisubmarine patrol at the entrance to Halifax harbour during the winter months. It was always rough and cold and wet. In the spring of '41, I was drafted to Stadacona for a course. Thankfully, I never returned to corvettes!"

* * *

The Flowers for the RN were completed in various U.K. locales. *Spikenard* was fitted out in northern England. Joe Marston of Victoria, B.C., a 1941 sub-lieutenant, says: "After trials at South Shields, *Spikenard* moved to the ammunition dump at North Shields, just across the Tyne. Here in April 1941 we lay astern of the light cruiser HMS *Dido,* being de-ammunitioned after a stint in the Mediterranean. Ammo was lying all over the wharf and, of course, for our two nights there the port was subjected to heavy air raids.

"The raids went on all one night and hundreds of incendiary bombs rained down amongst *Dido*'s ammo. I must admit that I for one was not too happy with this. Members of the crew, organized by First Lieutenant Rod Knight, dashed around the dock, dropping sandbags on the incendiaries as they landed. I found an overhead covering on the upper deck and contented myself with watching and wishing I were somewhere else."

After workups to train their crew, many of these Flowers were briefly attached to the 4th Clyde Escort Group. One was *Spikenard*, which went on the U.K.-Iceland Run, going out to Iceland with empty convoys bound for North America and coming back with laden convoys for the U.K. Joe Marston describes Iceland: "In the spring of '41, we entered and anchored in the bay known as Hvalfjord, north of the capital city of Reykjavik. Hvalfjord was just reaching the status of being a major escort base, though truly it was a large, open bay surrounded by bleak mountains down which the wind roared with fury. Repair facilities were confined mostly to the depot ship, HMS *Hecla*, and for a short period we went alongside to effect a few small repairs, then to the oiler for bunkers [fuel]."

Harry Carson recalls a most undecorous moment from *Spikenard*'s days on the U.K.-Iceland Run:

Some parts of the corvette plans were found to be very odd and caused hardships and discomfort. The naval pipes [shaft] that took the anchor cables from the upper deck on the fo'c'sle [forecastle] down to the chain locker passed through the upper and lower seamen's messdecks.

The naval pipes were approximately 18 inches across. On other ships they were sloped so that the cable lay on the lower side of the pipes and, when secured at the top and bottom, did very little moving around when the ship was under way.

Our pipes were vertical. When the anchor cables were secured top and bottom, they hung free vertically in between. As soon as the ship started to roll and pitch, these cables continuously struck the insides of the pipes, sounding like Big Ben. Securing the cables top and bottom with block and tackle didn't take up enough slack to stop the noise. We finally got a bright idea that worked to our satisfaction: we stuffed the pipes with old rags, clothes and canvas until the clattering stopped.

Upon arrival in Iceland, we were allocated a berth and proceeded to it. The anchors were ready to let go and all hands had fallen in on the fo'c'sle. We were being watched by some large RN ships whose crews, I presume, were curious as to the seamanship qualifications of the colonials. At the order "Slip," the anchors came free, the cable roared out — and the old canvas, rags and worn-out work clothes shot about 20 feet into the air and fluttered down all over the fo'c'sle!

It was the finest thing that could have happened, for when we arrived back in South Shields, the dockyard workers burnt openings in the pipes and welded steel bars inside so that the cables were secured every few feet in a zigzag pattern. Watertight doors were bolted onto the openings and we had quiet messdecks.

* * *

Some of the other Canadian-built RN corvettes drew trans-atlantic convoy duty. On April 12, 1941, *Windflower* and *Trillium* were sister escorts to the eastbound convoy HX 117. What seemed a minor incident aboard one ship was a serious matter aboard the other.

Jim Sharpe in *Windflower*, recalls: "On this escort trip with a laden convoy, we were attacked by a four-engine Focke-Wulf bomber. The plane crossed the convoy but did little damage. Its bombs fell between the columns of ships and a near-miss landed beside a small freighter, causing it to roll badly and lose some of its deckload of lumber. It was temporarily out of commission, but caught up with us in an hour or so. One of our Canadian Flowers, *Trillium*, was strafed and a couple of people were injured."

Barry O'Brien, the *Trillium* sub-lieutenant, gives the other perspective:

We were in station on the port beam of the convoy when a lookout reported a Focke-Wulf Condor coming in low on the starboard side of the convoy. We immediately closed the convoy after action stations were sounded and I rushed to my station, which, as gunnery officer, was in charge of the twin pom-pom 2-pounder gun in the bandstand midships. This was the only anti-aircraft weapon we were fitted with, except for two World War I Lewis guns on the wings of the bridge.

The Focke-Wulf dropped two bombs that fell harmlessly between rows of the ships, but it continued flying low in our direction. When it got within range, I gave the order to commence firing. Everyone was taking aim at the attacking aircraft, including navy gunners on the merchant ships, so there was an awful lot of flak flying in all directions. When the aircraft was about over the last two rows on the port side of the convoy, it began strafing *Trillium* as we did our best to shoot it down.

The gun crew consisted of two gunnery ratings seated on the port and starboard sides of the pom-pom to elevate and depress the barrels while firing. A third rating, who stood beside me, controlled the supply of ammunition belts. Suddenly I noticed the gunner on the port side, Donald Robertson, knocked off his seat. But, grabbing his left shoulder, he climbed back on and continued firing. The ammunition rating next to me gripped his neck. He had been sliced by a piece of shrapnel.

These things happen very fast, so when the Focke-Wulf flew off to port undamaged and appeared not to be returning, I had a chance to survey the situation. Robertson was now slumped over the gun, badly wounded. The other rating hit was okay. I left one rating with the pom-pom while the ammunition gunner and I half-dragged and half-carried Robertson to the forward messdeck. It was not a pretty sight. There were 11 wounded men. Shrapnel causes blood to flow pretty freely and the messdeck was awash with blood mixed with the collection of sea-water that had come down the companion-way.

Harry Rhoades was our cook, and also doubled as sick berth attendant, having had a first aid course while with Ogilvy's department store in Montreal. He and I did our best to make the injured comfortable. I went to the bridge and detailed the situation to the captain. As we had no doctor aboard in those early days, he immediately chose the senior officer on board the RN destroyer *Boadicea*. By bosun's chair, they sent their surgeon-lieutenant over, with books and medical equipment in a canvas bag.

He surveyed the scene in the seamen's messdeck and I remember him saying: "There are two too far gone to save, eight probably will survive if they can get hospital treatment ashore soon and I will have to amputate the left arm of one if he is to have any chance of survival." The doctor then administered painkillers to the wounded.

We strapped the unconscious Robertson to the messdeck table as the ship was rolling considerably. The doctor took out a book and turned to the chapter on amputations. He then inquired who would administer the anesthetic. Nobody else volunteered, so I said I would. The patient was stripped to the waist. The operation began with our cook assisting and I acting as anesthetist. Every time the doctor took a slice or two, he would turn a page in his book. Every now and then I would be told to squirt a couple more drops of ether on the mask covering the patient's face and the fumes wafting up were making me dizzy and nauseous. As the doctor cut deeper, you could see how the shrapnel had shattered Robertson's shoulder, imbedding pieces of the grey duffel coat two or three inches into his body.

Robertson was fighting for his life, with his chest giving mighty heaves. The operation took about two hours. Unfortunately, Robertson died on the messdeck table almost simultaneously with the final removal of his arm.

The doctor left and went down to the wardroom where I found him later, lying prone on the settee. I told him he had done all he could. He answered that he was fresh out of medical school and this was the first operation he had ever performed. And if it hadn't been for the calming influence of the cook he would have panicked a couple of times, he said.

As we were close to Scotland, we left our three dead comrades to be buried by the Royal Navy and the eight wounded were sent to hospital. We couldn't remain as we were needed back at our Greenock base for a new convoy.

The *Trillium* trio lies side by side in a war-graves section of the municipal Sandwick Cemetery at Stornoway on the Isle of Lewis in Scotland's Outer Hebrides: Storeman First Class Jack Pettigrew, RCNR, age 33, of Toronto; Able Seaman Donald Morrison Robertson, RCN, age 20, of Vancouver; and Ordinary Telegraphist Clifford Hindle Greenwood, RCNVR, age 19, of St. Vital, Man.

There is a postscript. "The captain asked me for recommendations for any special performances by the crew during the action," Barry O'Brien adds. "I had no hesitation in recommending Robertson for his outstanding courage and valour; even though mortally wounded, he had climbed back on his seat and continued to fire the gun with his one good arm. I also proposed Harry Rhoades, who was a tower of strength before, during and after the operation. They were both awarded Mention in Dispatches, as was another crew member, Able Seaman Alexander Annis."

All three MiD citations simply read, "For courage and devotion to duty when attacked by enemy aircraft."

* * *

Back in Canada, activity had been under way on the West Coast. HMCS *Wetaskiwin* was commissioned December 17, 1940, at Esquimalt, B.C., followed by *Agassiz* on January 23, 1941, at Vancouver, B.C., and *Alberni* on February 4 at Esquimalt.

"We made a shakedown cruise around Vancouver Island in horrible weather. We actually became lost through mistaking lights," says Gordon Naylor of Chemainus, B.C., leading stoker in *Agassiz* in 1941-42. "Most of the crew were seasick. I wasn't seasick, in spite of never having been to sea before."

Charlie Appleby of San Diego, California, a cook in *Agassiz* in 1941, recalls:

On our first trip to sea with a crew that was mostly Prairie folk, I believe we had only eight men and the NR captain who had been to sea, none on a warship. When we headed out into the Pacific, all hell broke loose.

The stove started moving back and forth. My assistant Jock Glasgow and I leaped up and held to the crossbars on the skylight, feet on the sink. Pots, pans, dishes, everything came loose and rolled back and forth, smoke belching. There were no crossbars on the shelves to hold anything in place. The stove was not welded to the deck, and so on.

Most of the crew thought they were dying of seasickness, and water was being taken in with the high waves. We were at sea a couple of days and returned for refit. So much for training for sea duty. We had railings welded around the top of the stove, with crossbars, and used rope as well to tie the pots down.

Bill Perry of Victoria, B.C., has vivid recollections of his 1941 stint in *Alberni*. "Like many, *Alberni* was crewed by an NR officer as skipper, one or two permanent force ratings and a plethora of RCNVR ratings, most of whom were going to sea for the first time. It was indeed a comedy of ineptitude compounded by lack of experience.

"Workups consisted of a turn around the harbour to calibrate the magnetic compass, situated in a circa-1850 binnacle, followed by a shakedown cruise to the Queen Charlotte Islands by way of Prince Rupert. Most, if not all, were seasick beyond their wildest dreams. Water dripped from everything and everywhere. I recall, as a telegraphist, sitting in the wireless shack on a swivel chair bailing out the water with a dust pan as the sea sloshed around under the transmitters. The saying 'fed up, fucked up and far from home' was never more in evidence."

The major threat was on the East Coast and Ralph Shideler remembers how he got there: "I was drafted to *Wetaskiwin* as leading tel [telegraphist] in March 1941. The previous chap jumped ship the night before *Wetaskiwin*, *Agassiz* and *Alberni* sailed in company for Halifax.

"That was a beautiful trip. We stopped at San Pedro, California for a couple of days. Mary Pickford and husband Douglas Fairbanks came down to see us, as did actresses Patricia Morison, June Duprez and others."

Aboard *Alberni* was Leonard Lamb of Leamington, Ont., an ordinary seaman who recalls: "We stopped in San Pedro for fuel and supplies. It's amazing how newspapers reported seeing mines and torpedoes on board. Actually, they were depth charges and paravanes [anti-mine devices].

"While there we were the guests of Mary Pickford, June Duprez and others. The U.S. not being at war, the German Embassy did not want us ashore, but somehow these movie stars arranged for us to go by bus to this nightclub. Every table had the appropriate female host — every table of two men had one lady, every table of four had two ladies, which made for an enjoyable evening."

This was a bigger deal than the veterans may realize. Not only did it involve major Hollywood stars, but it had the potential for controversy because the United States was officially neutral. Many citizens felt it shouldn't be drawn into the European conflict and public opinion on the war was divided.

Pickford was the key. Born Gladys Smith in Toronto on April 8, 1893, she was an actress who became a huge star in silent films and was dubbed "the world's sweetheart." She married swashbuckling American screen star Douglas Fairbanks and the couple joined with legendary pantomine artist Charlie Chaplin and film-making pioneer D.W. Griffith to form United Artists Films, which became a big success. Pickford was a huge celebrity. She had fame, glamour, wealth and power. Beneath it all, Pickford was a Canadian and she was doing her bit for Canada's war effort. Other Hollywood people — British, Canadian and American — helped, either motivated by belief in the cause, self-interest or both.

Bill Perry picks up the description of the voyage at this point: "The trip to the East Coast via the Panama Canal was a memorable experience and probably made us forget our earlier days. Our saddest occasion was when we lost our ship's mascot, a mongrel terrier."

Once through the canal, the three ships went on to Kingston, Jamaica, says Ralph Shideler, for a layover of

HMCS *Wetaskiwin*, K175, was the first corvette built on the West Coast.

about four days: "A good time was had by all, no kidding — rum was 50 cents a quart." In all, the "beautiful trip" took nearly a month.

* * *

The Allied perception of needs was rapidly changing. The British, short of sailors, never did man the 10 Canadian-built Flower-named corvettes and the RCN continued to provide crews.

"The first RCN crews of these ships were called the Original Pigs' Orphans," Harry Carson of Spikenard declares. "When we were in the U.K. on pay day and tried to draw our pay, we were politely told that we were under the RCN and all that the RN could give us was a casual payment until we returned to Canada. Arriving back in Canada, we would be told that we were serving aboard a RN ship, so that we could only draw a casual payment while here."

Joe Marston says: "The ship's pay records were floating around the world somewhere and we were dependent upon the RN for advances. It was about six or seven months later before my pay was squared away."

A two-page history of *Fennel* prepared in 1972 by the Directorate of History and Heritage at National Defence Headquarters in Ottawa says simply that the manning arrangement "led inevitably to administrative confusion."

The RN was still short of bodies and the upshot was that the 10 corvettes were transferred, on a loan basis, to the RCN on May 15, 1941, and each was recommissioned His Majesty's Canadian Ship (HMCS). The corvettes-for-destroyers exchange was never consummated as such and each side ended up paying for what it ordered.

Soon *Trillium* had another run-in with the Luftwaffe,

as Barry O'Brien relates: "On May 24, 1941, we were in port at Londonderry, Ireland, and all available ships were ordered out to meet and escort a convoy coming in to Britain, as there was reported to be a large pack of U-boats protecting the *Bismarck*. [The German battleship had left Bergen, Norway, on May 18, passed through the Denmark Strait between Greenland and Iceland and broke into the Atlantic to attack Allied shipping and tie down British warships.]

"*Trillium* was held up from departing with the other escorts for some minor repairs and we sailed independently later. Just before our rendezvous with the convoy, we were attacked by a Focke-Wulf. I was the officer of the watch when suddenly I saw this dive-bomber coming straight at us out of the clouds with its four engines cut. I rang action stations and grabbed one of the Lewis guns, which I never had a chance to fire. However, the plane dropped two bombs directly ahead of us right on line, but fortunately they fell short, though close enough to blow the bows of our ship quite a few feet out of the water. The plane was obviously heading home, out of bombs and low on fuel.

"We joined the convoy about an hour later and I never saw, before or after, so many escorts guarding a convoy, led by the battle cruiser *Repulse*, plus light cruisers, destroyers, frigates and corvettes."

British forces sank *Bismarck* on May 27, 1941. If there was ever any lingering doubt, it was clear now that, as in World War I, the German surface fleet couldn't match the RN. German warships and surface raiders could no longer be regarded as the primary threat. That status was earned by the Kriegsmarine's submarines — the U-boats that had already produced Germany's best naval results.

A tiny corvette mothers her large charges along a North Atlantic convoy route early in World War II.

DND NF-1381, courtesy Legion Magazine Archives

Death of a merchant ship on the Atlantic.

CHAPTER TWO

"THERE WAS NOTHING LIKE AN ECHO TO SHAKE YOU UP."

IN THIS AGE of air transportation, we tend to overlook the fact that the greatest danger to the Allies in World War II was that Germany would sever the Atlantic Ocean supply lifeline between North America and Great Britain. If an isolated Britain fell, Germany would be in position to consolidate control over Europe. North America would be a solitude, having no practical base from which the Allies could attempt a reconquest of Europe.

This attempt to strangle Britain into capitulation was based on unrestricted submarine warfare. The seeds of the campaign were sown in World War I when Germany, bogged down in the horrific trench warfare in France and Belgium and unable to match the Royal Navy's surface fleet, realized that her only hope of victory was to cut off Britain's sea lines of supply.

Germany's principal weapon became the U-boat. She built 345 and they sank about 11 million tons of merchant shipping — 5,000 ships, most small and sailing alone unguarded — with a death toll of 15,000 merchant seamen. The campaign even reached Canadian and Newfoundland waters. The German price was 178 U-boats and 5,364 crew, a mortality rate of 41 percent. This was the first submarine war.

Unrestricted U-boat warfare was an outrage to many. It violated the Prize Rules that had governed naval warfare for centuries. These called for the raider to take aboard the crew of the merchant ship, then sail or sink the merchantman and put the merchant crew in a neutral vessel or a small boat they could sail to safety.

Submarines changed the very nature of warfare at sea. Because they were much smaller than merchant ships, submarines were vulnerable to ramming if they got too close. Submarines also couldn't hold merchant crews. Further, their surface armament was limited, particularly compared to that of warships, and torpedoes were the principal weapon. Initially there were acts of chivalry by U-boat commanders, but there were also examples of barbarity. The last 21 months of WW I were characterized by sinkings without notice and the abandonment of merchant crews and passengers.

The British tried to stem their losses by instituting convoys on a small scale. Ultimately the Allies, strengthened by the entry of the United States in 1917, won the war on land in 1918.

Debate on submarine warfare continued between the wars. Contrary to the 1919 Treaty of Versailles that formalized the results of World War I, Germany began to build a U-boat force surreptitiously after the appointment of Adolf Hitler as chancellor of the German Republic early in 1933.

Britain and Germany reached a naval agreement in 1935 establishing German surface strength at 35 percent and submarine strength at 45 percent of the tonnage of the Royal Navy, the ranking world sea power. Germany professed no interest in a naval arms race, and this pact helped mask her real intentions. In fact, the agreement spurred the process of German rearmament, which was already underway.

Then, in 1936, Britain, France and the U.S. negotiated the London Naval Treaty which encompassed a protocol banning unrestricted submarine warfare. Before the outbreak of World War II, the protocol was endorsed by 40 countries, including Germany.

The protocol contained rules for submarine warfare. The salient points were that submarines must surface before attacking and must guarantee the safety of crews and passengers. These conditions would destroy the important element of surprise and neutralize submarines as offensive weapons. In turn, merchant ships were to be unarmed and were forbidden from using their radios to alert others or seek help.

Of course, the amount of trust involved beggars the imagination. The shipping side knew that submarine commanders could not provide iron-clad guarantees for the safety of merchant crews. The attacking side could hardly forget that in World War I Britain had employed armed merchant cruisers — passenger ships turned into warships. Nor could the Germans overlook the loss of 14 U-boats to British Q-ships — armed vessels that were disguised as innocents to catch U-boats off-guard and blast them when they came close.

One school of thought is that idealism ruled in the conference room, but reality took over when World War II began. Another is that the British knew the Germans were building submarines and, unwilling to counter this threat by force, they tried to negotiate control. The result was limitations on the use of submarines at the expense of legitimization of Germany's right to have a navy of restricted size for defence of the realm.

Incredibly, neither the RN nor the RCN truly embraced a principal lesson of the first submarine war — escort vessels were essential so an extensive convoy system could be implemented to protect vital shipping. The British did not begin to build specialized convoy escorts in any quantity until the very eve of battle. Canada didn't start until after war broke out, despite the fact these vessels were smaller, cheaper and easier to build than destroyers. They should have been right up our alley. "I wonder what ship tonnage could have been saved had the RCN seen fit to build even 50 to 60 of these cheap and nasties," says Ray Burwash of Winnipeg, who served in the corvettes *Wetaskiwin*, *Buctouche* and *Agassiz* from 1940-43, much of the time as higher submarine detector (HSD). Of course, this was in an era when the Canadian government underfed the military, particularly the navy.

A.G.S. (Tony) Griffin, commanding officer of the corvette *Pictou* from 1941-43, observed the "curious reluctance" of senior officers to commit to convoy protection

as a naval staple and noted that fleet work in big ships retained priority status, adding: "There was certainly an element of snobbery involved, and anti-submarine work was not the road to promotion. It is interesting to note that in British naval exercises between the wars, there is no record of a single convoy-protection exercise. Destroyers were designed for fleet work, not at all for anti-submarine activity in defence of commercial shipping."

* * *

Karl Dönitz, who in World War I had been a young commander of a U-boat, was the leading German proponent of submarines. In 1935 he became Germany's U-boat boss.

U-boat is the English equivalent of *U-boot,* which is the German slang for *Unterseeboot,* meaning undersea boat or submarine. In turn, the U-boat corps was the *"U-Boot-waffe."* Dönitz built it from volunteers who emerged from a rigorous training program. Dönitz was involved in the building program, equipment, strategy, tactics, training — everything.

In Germany, however, the navy had never been the favoured military arm and in reality it stood third behind the army and air force. Even within the *Kriegsmarine*, the high leadership focused on surface vessels, greatly underestimating the value of submarines. So while Dönitz got an early jump on the Allies when war broke out, he did not have the overpowering undersea fleet that he had wanted.

If life is complicated, war may be its most complex element. While warships could be sunk without warning, passenger liners were off limits and the taking of merchantmen was subject to restrictive rules. At the start, the Germans sank the liner *Athenia*, although they long denied responsibility, while the British gave merchant ships instructions to send radio signals — S S S instead of the traditional S O S — to warn of submarine attacks. The British, not trusting the Germans, began to arm merchant ships. The Germans, aware of the sub-warning signals and encountering unexpected resistance from merchant ships, did not trust the British.

Relations deteriorated into unrestricted submarine warfare and U-boats became a part of the propaganda war, both the story each side told its citizens and the position each side projected to the world.

On September 1, 1939, Germany had 57 U-boats. Another 1,113 were commissioned during the conflict for a grand total of 1,170. Of these, 863 became operational. There were many types of World War II U-boats. A type would be developed, then refined; it could also be modified for a specific task such as minelaying.

As with corvettes and warships in general, when U-boats were in refit, improvements would be implemented and alterations would be made to adapt to changing conditions such as a need for additional anti-aircraft weaponry to combat increased Allied air surveillance.

Type VII was the backbone of the U-boat fleet. These diesel-electric boats could be built quickly and more than 700 were constructed, making this the largest type ever produced by any country. For their size, these boats had good offensive power and handled well when surfaced or submerged, although livability was compromised. This was the standard Atlantic boat, though it also operated in the North Sea, the Arctic, the Baltic and the Mediterranean. Six versions entered service, Variant VII C constituting the overwhelming majority with more than 600 boats. These were produced from 1938 to 1943 by a variety of yards in a number of cities.

VII C boats were 67 m (220 feet) long and 6.2 m (20 feet) at the beam [widest point]. They were 761 tons surfaced, 865 tons dived. They had a single hull with external ballast tanks. Maximum operational depth was 144 m (472 feet); minimum crash-dive time was 25 to 30 seconds and maximum fuel load was 113.5 tons. Crew size was usually 44.

These boats had five torpedo tubes, four bow and one stern, and carried 14 torpedoes, or occasionally 14 mines in lieu of torpedoes. Surface armament featured an 88mm (3.4-inch) deck gun. The original anti-aircraft weaponry consisted of one 20mm gun and one 37mm gun. As the danger from aircraft increased in the Atlantic theatre, the deck gun often disappeared and the anti-aircraft firepower was strengthened considerably. Some boats received 20mm guns in quadruple mounts, a potent weapon.

When surfaced, two diesel engines could generate 3,200 horsepower with a maximum speed of 17.6 knots. The surface range was 12,040 km (6,500 nautical miles). Dived, two electric engines could produce 750 horsepower with a maximum speed of 7.6 knots. The range submerged was 130 miles at 2 knots or 80 miles at 4 knots.

While a formidable weapon in its heyday, Type VII C had some serious weaknesses. Greatest was its slow speed when submerged. This forced these boats to travel on the surface for great distances during their long trips to and from their war stations. Prolonged surface travel increased their vulnerability, particularly to air surveillance. They also had to run on the surface frequently to get into position to attack convoys and to recharge their batteries so they could submerge when the occasion demanded it.

The North Atlantic was no picnic, particularly in the winter, and the rolling conning tower of a U-boat was a poor observation platform. Further, the early U-boats suffered from torpedo problems, which reduced their kill totals. Unreliable magnetic detonators caused the withdrawal of U-boats from the Norwegian campaign in 1940. Faulty torpedo depth regulators weren't corrected until 1942.

Second in quantity among the various U-boats was the Type IX. A larger submarine, this attack boat was noted for its long range and seaworthiness on the surface. More than 200 were built. More habitable than the Type VII, they operated in the North Atlantic, the South Atlantic, the Caribbean Sea, the Indian Ocean and the Pacific Ocean, often working alone against unescorted ocean shipping.

Seven versions saw action. Variant IX C-40 was the most common. Nearly 90 units entered service from 1940 to 1944. These boats were 76.8 m (252 feet) long and 6.8 m (22.3 feet) at the beam. They were 1,120 tons surfaced and 1,232 tons dived. They had an inner pressure hull and an outer hull that contained the ballast tanks. Maximum operational depth remained 144 m (472 feet); minimum crash-dive time was 35 seconds and maximum fuel load was 214 tons. Crew size was 49.

IX C-40 boats had six torpedo tubes, four bow and two stern, and carried 22 torpedoes. Surface armament started with a 105mm (4.1-inch) deck gun. There was one 37mm automatic and one 20mm gun for anti-aircraft work. Subsequently the deck gun was eliminated and the anti-aircraft armament upgraded significantly.

For surface running, two diesels could generate 4,400 horsepower, with a maximum speed of 18.2 knots. The rated range was 20,370 km (11,000 nautical miles). Underwater, two electric engines could produce 1,000 horsepower, with a top speed of 7.7 knots and a range of 63 miles at 4 knots.

While it did not fill the desire for a submarine that would go great distances at a decent speed submerged, Type IX provided yeoman long-range service. One still exists in

North America. Captured at sea west of Africa in June 1944 by a U.S. Navy task group, U-505 remains on display at the Chicago Museum of Science and Industry.

Admiral Dönitz's force of 57 U-boats quickly went to work when war broke out. Allied and neutral merchant ship losses in the Atlantic theatre averaged more than 188,000 tons per month in the last four months of 1939, according to official statistics. About 55 percent was attributable to U-boats, with mines claiming most of the rest.

The 1940 shipping losses in the Atlantic were more than 304,000 tons per month. U-boats accounted for more than half of shipping destroyed, while roughly equal portions were lost to aircraft, mines and surface warships or raiders.

In 1941, the assault escalated. From January through June, shipping losses in the Atlantic averaged more than 404,000 tons per month. Cause and effect came into play. To reduce the losses, British anti-submarine efforts were being improved in the Western Approaches to the British Isles. U-boats began moving farther westward out into the Atlantic to find easier targets.

* * *

With the increased losses at sea, the need for continuous escort across the Atlantic became apparent and the New-foundland Escort Force officially came into being June 1, 1941. Urged by Britain and eager to have her own distinct operations, Canada was assuming more responsibility though she had neither the fleet nor the trained crews for the task.

Newfoundland, a dominion ample in territory but scarce in population and economic resources, did not have a navy, but was a small British naval station much farther east on the Atlantic than Halifax. A new Canadian base was constructed in St. John's for the NEF.

Initially, the force's strength was four destroyers. Its bulk was seven corvettes — *Agassiz*, *Alberni*, *Chambly*, *Cobalt*, *Collingwood*, *Orillia* and *Wetaskiwin* — which left Halifax on May 23, 1941, for Newfoundland.

Albert Baker of White Lake, Ont., an able seaman in *Orillia* in 1941, recalls their May 27th arrival: "We pulled into St. John's at night, blowing and snowing. Tying up at the Imperial wharf, I shouted to an old fellow taking our lines, 'When do you get your good weather?' His answer was, 'We get a good week for horse racing.' He wasn't too far out."

Convoy escort from Newfoundland, Canada's chief naval effort of World War II, began to take shape. Local escorts would bring a convoy of merchant ships from Halifax or Sydney, N.S., to the west ocean meeting point east of

The corvette *Battleford* guards Atlantic convoy early in the war.

Newfoundland. From there, NEF vessels took the convoy on the long journey to the mid-ocean meeting point south of Iceland, where an RN local force would take over and guide the convoy on the final stretch to the U.K.

At this point, the NEF escorts would go into Hvalfjord for fuel and perhaps a brief layover if storms had not put them behind schedule. This became known as the Iceland Run. On the return portion, the escorts would go out to pick up a westbound convoy, cross the Atlantic and turn it over to the western local escort, which would handle the last leg to North American ports. The NEF escorts would then return to their St. John's base.

The NEF was quickly enlarged with RN and RCN destroyers, corvettes shifted from other duties and new corvettes coming from Canadian shipyards. Still, the bottom line was that Canada's eagerness to please Britain committed the Canadian corvettes to a mid-ocean escort role much beyond the coastal work for which they were built and much beyond the immediate capabilities of the green crews that were cobbled together.

Corvettes were not large vessels. The early ones displaced 950 tons, were 62.5 m (205 feet) long and 10 m (33 feet) at the beam. Their most identifiable feature was the short fo'c'sle, the raised deck at the bow. Because of availability, they had cylindrical boilers. Top speed was 15 or 16 knots.

Neither these ships nor the defensive system was sophisticated. *Spikenard* joined the NEF in June 1941 and Sub-Lieutenant Joe Marston sums it up this way:

The captain of *Spikenard*, like most others in those early years, had an unenviable position. He was expected to go out and kill U-boats and for this purpose he was provided with a slow ship — useful but slow — with obsolete weapons and instruments, and a crew of novices with a light sprinkling of trained seamen who had limited military training.

These early corvettes had no radar and no gyro compass, very useful devices in the detection of submarines. They did have a very early type of asdic — 123 — which was nothing to write home about, but was better than nothing.

In addition, the captains were sent off with other ships with which they had never worked and in many cases they did not know the captains of the other escorts, nor indeed had ever met them.

Communications between escorts and between merchant ships were of the most rudimentary sort, mainly light and flag signals. While all the ships possessed wireless and could key Morse code between them, the oscillations from these sets could be detected for many miles and could be used by submarines to home in on the convoy. Thus use of the sets was forbidden, except in cases of extreme emergency. Depth charges were the escorts' main weapon against U-boats. Concerted anti-submarine training was in its infancy and tactics were evolving slowly through hard experience.

Regardless of their crudity, sail they must. And before each departure of a group of merchant ships and their naval escorts, something called a convoy conference was held.

George Powell of Victoria, who commanded the corvette *Napanee* in 1944-45, explains: "Conferences were convened by the NCSO [naval control of shipping officer] of the convoy's departure port. All merchant ship masters attended with their radio officers to get their sailing orders.

"A convoy commodore and his staff would be in attendance. The NCSO would discuss the convoy's sailing orders. Convoy commodore would state what his orders would be if the convoy came under attack; for example, instructions for altering course. For signals he covered the use of flags by day and a series of coloured lights at night. This was a very complicated procedure at any time with a group of merchant ships, yet very important. We were operating under radio silence most of the time. The radio officers would meet separately to discuss their communication orders with the shore staff signals officer.

"The conference would be ended with the senior officer of the naval escort group briefing the assembly on the tactics he would employ in the event the convoy came under attack."

There's often a navy way of doing things and these conferences were no exception. Dudley King of North Falmouth, Massachusetts, commanding officer of *Arvida* in 1942-44, recounts: "The senior officer conducting the event would rarely address a commanding officer or his representative by name, but by the name of his ship. For example, he would not say, 'Lieutenant King, is your radar now fully operational?' He would say, '*Arvida*, is your radar now fully operational?'"

Murray Knowles of Halifax, in the corvette *Louisburg (2nd)* during 1943-45 as first lieutenant and then captain, summarizes convoy conferences: "Briefly, COs of escorting ships would attend and listen to the senior officer of escorts and the commodore of convoys along these lines: (a) how and what signal would be sent in the event of U-boat attack; (b) the time and date of convoy alterations of course; (c) which escorts would remain with the convoy during escort carrying out attacks on U-boats; (d) frequently during daylight the senior officer escorts would run between columns of ships passing signals as required; (e) establish the speed of convoy; (f) which escort would act as rescue ship for survivors if merchant or escort ship was sunk or torpedoed; (g) under no circumstances were ships to break wireless telegraphy silence; (h) a caution not to make smoke; and (i) a caution that no lights should be showing at night."

Convoys covered a large ocean area. In the early days a convoy would generally have between 30 and 50 merchant ships. For a 40-ship convoy, a standard alignment could be 10 columns wide, with about a kilometre between columns, for a width of 9 km. There would be perhaps 600 metres between each ship in a column. These distances were necessary for safety because, quite unlike cars and trucks, ships cannot stop or start quickly, or turn in a short distance.

Usually the merchant ship carrying the convoy commodore, often a retired senior RN officer, would be at the head of the centre column. Other merchant ships were arranged according to a number of factors. The most valuable and vulnerable, such as fuel tankers, were generally placed in the centre columns while ships with cargo such as grain would go on the outside. Also on the outside would be more expendable ships such as the many old freighters pressed into service.

A standard configuration of our 40-ship convoy would create a perimeter distance of about 22 km for the navy to protect. The escorts tried to form a protective screen, with warships concentrated ahead of the convoy during the day when submerged attacks were the main threat and on the flanks during the night when surface attacks were the challenge. The hard reality, however, was that in the early days an NEF escort group often consisted of one destroyer and four corvettes. The person in charge of convoy defence was the senior of the escort officers in command, normally the destroyer's captain.

In theory the escorts were positioned so that their asdic beams overlapped, providing unbroken coverage of the convoy perimeter. It was understood for decades that asdic stood for allied submarine detection investigation committee, a body formed near the end of World War I to develop a response to the new German U-boat threat. In recent years, it's been suggested this committee was a myth concocted to cover up the secret technological development. At any rate, the work was carried on in the 1920s by the RN. What evolved was a mechanism for detecting submerged submarines.

Roy Pallister of Guelph, Ont., who was a leading seaman asdic in *Barrie* and *Napanee* in 1945, explains: "Everyone has been in places where you could yell 'hello' and hear 'hello' come back. We are well aware that is an echo. Asdic uses the same principle, the main difference being that sound travels much faster in water than in air, almost four times as fast.

"An electrical impulse is converted into a sound wave and transmitted in the water. When this sound wave reaches an object, it rebounds. Since we know the approximate speed of sound in water, we can measure the time lapse between the transmitted signal and the received echo. This will establish an estimate of the distance to the obstacle."

Since World War II, asdic has universally come to be known by its American name — sonar, which stands for sound navigation and ranging. In fact, Pallister notes: "While asdic transmitted sound waves horizontally through the water in order to detect submarines, a modern sport-fishing sonar unit inaudibly transmits and receives sound waves vertically towards the bottom of a lake, through a small transducer fastened to the stern of a relatively small boat. Echoes on a screen show the true depth of the bottom, fish, sunken trees, weeds, etc. On the most modern sets today, one can see the contours of the bottom — humps, drop-offs and other fishy places — on a small screen. We also have the benefit of miniaturization. The whole unit weighs less than five pounds.

"By contrast, a World War II asdic set was huge, heavy and required a fair-sized ship just to carry it around. Today's small transducer was then known as an oscillator. It was fitted inside a teardrop-shaped dome bolted to the bottom of the ship.

"On larger ships such as destroyers, the dome was retractable, up and into a well in the ship's bottom. This was to prevent damage to the dome. Of course, 'housing the dome' also precluded using the asdic."

Corvettes, being bare-bones vessels, did not have a retractable dome, which meant that the dome was exposed and many were sheared off. Jack Drysdale of Victoria, an able seaman asdic operator in *Oakville* in 1942-43, says, "I think *Oakville* lost more domes than any other ship in the navy. If she wasn't striking logs, she was shearing them off in the ice packs outside Newfie."

Mounted on the bridge, above the wheelhouse and wireless shack, was the asdic hut. Inside, the frame of the magnetic compass bore a mark indicating the direction of the ship's bow. "To the left of this mark was the ship's port [red] side and to the right was the ship's starboard [green] side. Each side was divided into 180 degrees, o degrees being the bow and 180 degrees being the stern," Pallister continues.

The operator set the range at what was estimated to be the maximum effective distance, which could vary from 1,500 to 2,500 yards depending on water temperature, salinity, current and other factors. Then he would conduct a sweep by manually turning a control wheel that was mechanically connected to the oscillator on the bottom of the ship. Moving the wheel to the left to red 80, he would transmit an ultra-high-frequency sound beam, creating a ping noise and a line of light on the liquid compass. If there was no echo, he would move the wheel to shift the beam five degrees to red 75 and ping again, and so on. After going five or 10 degrees past the bow, the operator would swing the oscillator to green 80 and work his way back using the same five-degree increments.

This directional system for asdic reports was universal for lookouts too. Pallister explains: "All seamen knew this system and lookouts would give a report as 'Ship on the horizon, red 30 — three oh' or 'Aircraft approaching, green 120 — one two oh.' With this simple system, anyone hearing the report knew exactly where to look for the object.

"Because transmissions were audible, unlike today's sonar, we were required to wear earphones in order to hear them and, of course, the echo," Pallister continues. "As we needed to communicate with the bridge via voice pipe, we could not cover both ears at the same time, so we put an earpiece over one ear and the other earpiece against the side of our head, switching sides occasionally."

The set had a range recorder and a printout that could be examined and used to make a plot of an attack. Any echo

heard on the earphones would have to be classified immediately for type, distance and direction. Reading the echoes was critical and much depended on the operator's skill. Operators had to be aware of the Doppler effect, a change in pitch of the echo as the object became closer or farther away.

If it was a sub contact, action stations would be sounded and the chief of the asdic department, known as the higher submarine detector, would usually take over the set. The asdic officer would enter the picture, reporting to the captain, whose task was to position the ship over the U-boat and drop a pattern of depth charges.

"There was nothing like an echo to shake you up," says William Wainio of Thunder Bay, who served in *Trillium* in 1942-43. "Sometimes the operator would be ordered to hold and classify the contact. At other times, we would go straight to action stations. The action stations bell was loud enough to wake the dead. One could well understand the ridicule the asdic crew were subjected to by the rest of the hands when, as happened quite often, we had a false alarm. On many occasions, it was the real thing. I am sure that, all in all, the crew were happy to know that someone had his ears open while they were sleeping."

Wainio was an able seaman sub detector, a term that largely replaced asdic operator as the standard job title during the war. He describes his situation: "I was one of three asdic operators. We reported to a leading seaman HSD. At sea, we were on watch operating the asdic equipment two hours on and four off. We had a little longer break when the HSD stood a two-hour watch between 6 and 8 in the evening. On top of that, we were required to perform regular seamen's duties if we were off watch between 8 and 11:30 in the morning.

"Operating the asdic required undivided attention, listening for echoes from our transmissions and being ever vigilant for sounds. I was always happy to see my relief show up at the end of my two-hour shift. It could become quite monotonous listening to that pinging. It got so that I would even hear those transmissions when I was asleep. After two weeks at sea, we were completely drained, never getting a decent rest."

While asdic operators were generally given the nickname "ping merchants," working arrangements clearly varied by ship.

Phil George of Sault Ste. Marie, Ont., served in *Baddeck*, *Bittersweet* and *Alberni* from 1941-44, rising from ordinary seaman to petty officer HSD. He describes his 1942 *Bittersweet* service as a leading seaman asdic: "We worked two hours on and two hours off. The asdic shack also acted as a chart room for the navigator and the captain had a cot that dropped down and he often slept there at night so he'd be handy in case of enemy action. It wasn't bad working two hours on and two hours off, really. We were relieved of a lot of other duties such as cleaning ship, swabbing decks and that sort of thing."

While George was in *Bittersweet*, he encountered the enemy: "It was on my watch and I picked up a torpedo. Of course I yelled out 'Torpedo!' and switched off the sounding set and listened to the audio and so on and so forth. We evaded the torpedo, fortunately. The HSD took over the set and I don't know what happened after that, but we never did find the submarine. It seems strange that after all the training it was the only time in four years and nine months that I actually came across the enemy."

Leo McVarish of Winnipeg was an able seaman asdic in *Alberni* in 1943-44. He recalls four hours on, eight off, with the four-hour shift set up in a rotation, one hour on the set, one hour as a lookout, then repeat the process.

McVarish is among the operators to note that, "There were many other obstacles that could give an echo, such as whales, tide and water conditions, large schools of fish, rock formations, old wrecks."

Bill Kilpatrick of Scarborough, Ont., an able seaman asdic in *Amherst*, stresses that the set was dual purpose: "The asdic was also capable of listening to the engines and the turning of propellers of other ships, which was very helpful during fog or very dark nights when everything was pitch black — not a light in sight."

This "hydrophone" or listening capability is also described by Ray Burwash of Winnipeg, who says, "Diesel engines, ships' propellers, whistling from whales and even Morse code could be heard."

* * *

Initially, the Royal Canadian Navy was really just an adjunct to the Royal Navy, which remained a big-ship navy. This reliance developed between the two world wars when the Canadian government practically starved the RCN. However, particularly once World War II started, the RN helped the RCN only when it suited the RN's purposes. Sometimes the RN made demands that were certainly not in the RCN's best interest.

Equipment in general is a major area where Canada lagged far behind the U.K. and the United States. *Pictou* CO Tony Griffin elaborates: "Throughout the early part of the war when I was at sea, RCN technical equipment was much inferior to RN. We had the impression that, bearing in mind the magnitude of the Canadian responsibility in the Atlantic battle, we were treated shabbily in this respect. Moreover, we felt that our masters in Ottawa were pitiably weak in fighting our case for us, both with the RN and, more important, with our own Canadian war production people. There was no reason why the excellent British radar could not have been manufactured under licence in Canada. There had been criticism of the British for looking after their own ships first. But I never could blame them for that, considering their beleaguered position. ..."

Asdic was an example of the problem. The original 123A set in Canadian corvettes was at least a generation behind the gear of our main allies. A major shortcoming for Canadian escort vessels until they began to get the 144Q set in 1944 was the inability to gauge the target's depth. This was a critical factor because depth charges did not cause serious damage unless they exploded within 20 feet of the target. Still, asdic was an improvement that affected the struggle, although it appears that its value was overestimated by both the RN and RCN.

World War II created a constantly changing landscape in both technology and tactics. One side would develop a new weapon or tactic and gain the upper hand in some respect. The other side would inevitably attempt a countermeasure. The battle would continue. Sometimes, the balance of power would be changed and the outcome affected.

As part of this experimentation, the Germans furthered their own cause with a bold stroke — the night surface attack. HSD Ray Burwash notes: "It may come as a surprise to many to learn that U-boats generally made their attacks on the surface at night, or from fog banks. Even at this, they exposed only the narrow upper casing and conning tower to view, which made them difficult to see in any choppy sea. Asdic echo contact would be next to impossible while they were surfaced, leaving contact by hydrophone only, depending on range and other factors."

Burwash raises an important point. U-boats and other World War II submarines were really submersibles with little speed and limited endurance underwater. In the early

RCN, courtesy Legion Magazine Archives

The corvette *Sackville* during pre-commissioning trials in 1941. She has a short foc's'le and lacks an anti-aircraft gun in the rear bandstand as well as a gun shield for the four-inch gun up front.

part of the war, they operated on the surface much of the time and were actually safer there.

Admiral Dönitz, learning from Germany's World War I experiences, evolved the wolf-pack attack concept in 1935. Exercises in 1937 and 1938 convinced him it would work. When a U-boat located a convoy, it became standard procedure to report back to U-boat command by high-frequency wireless and then shadow the convoy. U-boat command would direct other subs to the convoy. Sometimes it didn't take long because the U-boats would already be in a patrol line to increase their chances of intercepting a convoy.

When the U-boats were in place, the night surface attacks began. The reaction of the convoy escorts was critical. If an escort left her station to pursue a U-boat, there would be a hole in the convoy perimeter that other U-boats might exploit, especially in the early days when there were too few escorts. On the other hand, the escort wouldn't want to let a U-boat get away.

It became RN and RCN doctrine to put the safe and timely arrival of the convoy foremost. A U-boat could outrun

a corvette on the surface, so it became practice to try to drive the U-boat underwater where it was much slower, then return to the convoy. U-boats had to be more careful with destroyers, which could achieve 30 knots and overtake them on the surface. Because a mistake could well be fatal, vessel identification by sound became important for U-boat crews.

Each side tried to break the other's naval codes and intercept messages, a task at which the British were enormously successful early on. As well, the Allies used HF/DF or "huff-duff" — high frequency, direction finding stations on both sides of the Atlantic — to pinpoint the location of the U-boat transmissions. Much later, such equipment was installed in ships. This information would be used to try and plot safe convoy routes, or reroute convoys in transit. It wasn't unlike a gigantic chess match at sea.

On this side of the Atlantic, the chess board was laid out in a room in St. John's, Newfoundland, explains Tony Griffin, who served for a time as staff officer (operations) on the staff of the Flag Officer, Newfoundland Force: "… The operations room was a big underground space with a

25-foot ceiling. One wall was metal, painted over by a huge chart of the North Atlantic. On this chart were magnetized symbols of all convoys and escort groups, aircraft support units, individual ships of all kinds: troopships, mainly unescorted because of their speed, cable repair ships, known concentrations of U-boats and recent sinkings. Also showing were current weather conditions, transmitted by escorts from strategic ocean sectors. The symbols were moved every few hours by Wren [Women's Royal Canadian Navy] watchkeepers. Opposite this wall in two adjoining glassed-in rooms were my office and that of my RCAF equivalent, a group captain reporting to the air vice marshal. It was a combined headquarters in every operational sense."

For the men out on the ocean in corvettes, escort duty was a routine influenced by elements beyond their control.

"Convoy duty, that was quite a job. Very much like a cowboy herding his cattle. Keeping them together and keeping the wolves away," says David Grimes, in *Chambly* on the Iceland Run in 1941. "Sometimes they would get scattered for one reason or another and we would have to get them back on station. If one got hit, all hell would break loose. Some of the escort ships would be dispatched to find the sub. Others were on the look out for survivors and keeping the convoy together. It was quite an experience."

Ernie Adams, who served in *Hepatica* in 1940-41: "The Newfie-Iceland trips were eventful while at sea, always rough, cold, dull weather and lots of action."

Reg Baker of Kingston, Ont., was an able seaman asdic in 1941 in *Shediac*, which departed from Sydney, N.S., rather than Newfie: "We ran from Cape Breton up the Strait of Belle Isle to Iceland, 5-knot convoys of old British tramp steamers that couldn't go any faster.

"Also, we didn't want to go any faster because we had no radar and we were passing through flows of icebergs quite often and we didn't want to ram them. This was quite a tester for one's nerves. We were also concerned about U-boats: because of the inefficiency of our asdic at times, we were quite vulnerable and felt like sitting ducks.

"Another problem was that these old ships would break down every once in a while. One would fall astern of the convoy and usually one of the corvettes would be detailed to go back and mother her. This left the main convoy more open and made it easier for U-boats to strike. We would be 17 days going to Iceland."

Orillia crewman Albert Baker emphasizes another aspect: "Convoy work was very monotonous, the same old routine. Days and weeks were often put in without too much happening, just keeping your station with the convoy in cold, damp weather. All in all, I think the weather was the greater enemy. A little run-in with Jerry broke the monotony and got the adrenalin going."

Certainly the corvette crews didn't look forward to Iceland, a volcanic island of 40,000 square miles situated in the North Atlantic. Lying east of the southern part of Greenland, on roughly the same latitude as the lower portion of Canada's Baffin Island, it was an independent state with cold winters and cool summers. The western-most country in Europe, Iceland has a population even today of only 250,000.

"Our turnaround in Iceland was usually very short," says *Trillium* sub-lieutenant Skinny Hayes. "There was nothing to do ashore there. The Icelanders, though sympathetic to the Allied cause, gave the impression that they'd rather be left alone. They were remote and rather aloof. The main city of Reykjavik had little to recommend it. We spent most of our time at anchor in Hvalfjord where supplies, some spare parts and an RN depot ship were available. This meant that we could get things fixed that were beyond the capabilities of our own people and the resources on board."

High latitudes have certain characteristics that are bound to influence people. Jim Sharpe describes a 24-hour *Windflower* layover in Iceland: "On June 21 the sun set below the horizon at 2350 and appeared again at 0012; therefore it was daylight 24 hours a day." Ralph Shideler in *Wetaskiwin* from 1941-43, says, "Iceland in the winter months was very hard on everyone with almost perpetual darkness and winter storms."

Even if bleak Iceland was no joy to visit, there was commerce for corvette crews to conduct.

"I used to buy Newfie rum in St. John's for two dollars a bottle. I would disguise the booze and trade it to American sailors, who got no alcohol. This was in Iceland, which was temperance," says Charlie Appleby in *Agassiz*. "For their part, the English received one bottle of beer a day as Iceland was dry.

"I also traded jam and tea to English army cooks in Iceland. We had lots of this to trade as there was very little eaten in rough weather. The English were very poorly fed. They would watch our ship come in and very soon they would row out for exchanges. We would get fresh bread from the English, who had a big bakery on shore."

George Auby of Yarmouth, N.S., yeoman of signals in *Sorel* in 1941-42, recalls a 1941 visit to Hvalfjord: "It seemed the whole American battle fleet was there. They had not yet entered the war and were patrolling the east coast to protect their shipping. We swapped rum for ice cream with the Americans."

Cliff Hatch of Windsor, Ont., a lieutenant in *Napanee* in 1941-42, takes us back to sea: "The Iceland convoys were small, usually 25 to 40 ships, and a large escort would be five ships at most — one destroyer and four corvettes. Sometimes we would only be three escorts. There was no radar and lousy weather — lots of fog, so the convoy would become separated and sometimes you'd find yourself escorting as few as three or four ships. Then days would be spent trying to re-form the convoy."

"Fog, indeed," says George Hedden of Hamilton, Ont., a coder in *Chicoutimi* when she worked with Sydney Force in 1941 taking convoys through the Strait of Belle Isle to meet the ocean escort: "At times we would experience fog so thick that it was difficult to see from stern to bow. On one particular trip, the conditions were so bad in the area between Newfoundland and Labrador that the entire convoy had to come to a halt. Although we could not see, we heard a ship astern of us contact an iceberg, then what sounded like the shovelling of ice off the deck. When the sun rose the next morning and the fog cleared, an iceberg of tremendous size was lying some distance off our port side."

Chicoutimi went on the Iceland run, without radar, leaving Hedden with this memory: "Another incident while sailing through foggy conditions in convoy was frightening to say the least. This wall of steel appeared out of the murk and I'll swear we were pushed aside by her bow wave. We were later to find out that it was the liner *Pasteur*."

Named after Louis Pasteur, the famous French chemist and bacteriologist, the *SS Pasteur* had been seized in Halifax harbour after the fall of France in 1940. With a British crew, she had become a troop transport. It would have been no contest in a collision: *Pasteur* was 30,000 tons and moving much faster than *Chicoutimi*, which was 950 tons.

Noting the lack of radar, and that both convoy and escorts "would be alternately and separately carrying out different zigzag courses" as a defence against U-boats, asdic specialist Ray Burwash comments: "Our only collision

protection came from foghorn signals, sharp lookouts and the towing of a very simple device called a fog buoy. This gadget consisted of a curved length of water pipe mounted on a small wooden board. When towed by a ship, it would squirt up a small column of water, like a garden hose. Our bow lookout could see this water squirting and know that a freighter could be just a few hundred feet ahead. Needless to say, it kept us on our toes as collisions at sea were not uncommon."

Joe Marston believes: "Convoy work in the fog was harder on the escorts than on the ships in the convoy in some respects. Ships in the convoy could hear the whistle signal of those about them and, in the daytime at least, could also hang on to each other's fog buoys.

"The escorts in 1941 were generally without radar. Even if they had radar, it was often out of action and would only pick up high aircraft echoes and not surface echoes. At any rate, once the escorts lost sight of the ships they were escorting through the fog, the escorts found themselves more or less in the position of being lost. Only by endeavouring occasionally to creep in slowly towards the anticipated position of the convoy to hear a recognizable whistle or catch a glimpse of a ship were they able to regain their station."

Trillium's Barry O'Brien says: "The merchant ships had a faint stern light and we used to try to keep sight of that. The fog was incredible and you'd strain your eyes. Sometimes the fog would play tricks with you and you'd hallucinate."

Ray Burwash notes that "collisions at sea were not uncommon." Ted Cunningham recalls: "At the beginning, the RN used to laugh at our efforts and quipped, 'Leave them alone and they'll sink themselves.'"

In the war's early days, the RCN was sometimes derided by the RN as the "Royal Collision Navy" or "Royal Colliding Navy." Cruel as the dismissal was, on looking back it wasn't entirely unfounded. For example, none of our first four warship losses was due to enemy action.

On June 25, 1940, the destroyer *Fraser* was lost by collision with the RN cruiser *Calcutta* during the Allied evacuation of France. On October 19, 1940, the auxiliary vessel *Bras d'Or* was lost in the Gulf of St. Lawrence, presumably by foundering. Just three days later, the destroyer *Margaree* went down after a collision with a freighter in the North Atlantic. Then, in March 1941, the armed yacht *Otter* was the victim of an explosion and fire off Halifax.

Depth-charge thrower on unidentified corvette fires a charge at a U-boat on the North Atlantic in the first half of the war.

CHAPTER THREE

"ENGINE STOPPED AND LIGHTS GLARING, BUT YOU HAD NO TIME TO THINK OF DEATH."

CORVETTE CONSTRUCTION in Canada peaked in 1941 when shipyards across the country turned out 56 Flower-class corvettes, bringing to 69 the number of RCN corvettes commissioned by the end of 1941:

Agassiz, Bittersweet and *Fennel* came out in January.

Alberni in February and *Kamloops* in March; then the bonds with Canadian communities began to grow with the flow of corvettes bearing the names of cities, towns and villages.

Chilliwack, Moncton, Nanaimo, Pictou, Rimouski and *Trail* were commissioned in April.

Arvida, Baddeck, Barrie, Chicoutimi, Dauphin, Galt, Levis, Matapedia, Napanee and *Quesnel* were May arrivals.

Buctouche, Camrose, Kenogami, Lethbridge, Moose Jaw, Prescott, Rosthern, Saskatoon and *Sherbrooke* were June additions.

Algoma, Battleford, Brandon and *Shediac* came in July, followed by *Amherst* and *Sorel* in August.

Drumheller, Dunvegan, Morden, Shawinigan and *Summerside* were September supplements.

Dawson, Edmundston, Kamsack, Louisburg, Sudbury and *The Pas* came in October.

Halifax, Midland, Oakville and *Weyburn* were November novices.

Calgary, Charlottetown, Fredericton, Lunenburg and *Sackville* rounded out the year in December.

Listing corvettes by their year of commissioning can provide a good sense of how things developed, but the navy preferred to keep track by another method — building programs. For example, the "Flower-class, 1939-40 program" eventually produced 65 vessels, 13 in 1940, then 51 in 1941 and one in 1942.

During this period, further corvette building programs were undertaken in Canada, so there was an overlap that can be confusing. The "Flower-class, 1940-41 program" covered five corvettes, one commissioned in 1941 and four in 1942. Meanwhile, the "revised Flower-class, 1940-41 program" contained 10 corvettes — four commissioned in 1941 and six commissioned in 1942.

The simplest method may be to break corvette production down by year of commissioning and major characteristics. Thus, in 1940 Canada turned out 13 Flowers, each 950 tons, with short fo'c'sle and cylindrical boilers.

In 1941, Canadian shipyards produced 51 of these 950-ton vessels with short fo'c'sle and cylindrical boilers. They constructed another 950-ton Flower with short fo'c'sle and water-tube boilers. As well, there were four 1,015-ton revised Flowers, which featured a longer fo'c'sle and water-tube boilers.

Considered superior operationally, water-tube boilers had not been available earlier, but they would become the norm in Canada's escort and minesweeper construction.

The four larger corvettes — *Calgary, Charlottetown, Fredericton* and *Halifax* — were a response to the

Courtesy Arnold Trask

The short foc's'le of the corvette *Prescott* is clear in this picture taken at St. John's, Newfoundland, in 1941 or 1942.

RCN, courtesy Wally Charbonneau

The corvette *Weyburn* flying colours, probably in late 1941 after her commissioning.

shortcomings of the original Flowers and the need to include additional weapons and equipment, along with more crew to operate them. Their longer fo'c'sle created more living space and dry quarters. Because the original bow had been too heavy, these four shared a redesigned bow with "increased sheer and flare" to make them ride better. They were 1,015 tons and 63.4 m (208 feet) long, one metre (three feet) more than their predecessors, but rated for the same limited endurance: 3,450 nautical miles at 12 knots.

Although clearly not the real answer for mid-ocean escort, these modified Flowers were the RCN's quick, cheap response. By contrast, the RN had Smith's Dock design the improved Castle-class corvette and also a larger escort that could still be built by yards not specialized in naval production. Enter the frigate, which was first known as a

"twin-screw corvette" because it had two propellers.

The RN ordered its first 27 River-class frigates in its 1940 program, with the earliest commissioning being in April 1942. The RCN did not act as quickly. Its first frigates were in the "River-class, 1942-43 program," with the initial commissioning in June 1943, the forerunner of 16 that year. Forty-four more came out in 1944, making a total of 60 RCN frigates built in Canada.

Four yards in the St. Lawrence region and one on the west coast produced these 60 RCN frigates plus 10 for the RN. All five yards had already built corvettes and four ceased doing so, while one, Morton Engineering and Drydock of Quebec City, carried on with both.

The River-class frigate was 91.8 m (301 feet) long and 11 m (36 feet) across, with a displacement of 1,445 tons, a top speed of 19 knots, a rated range of 7,200 nautical miles at 12 knots and increased armament, including two 4-inch guns. In addition to its 60 River-class frigates, the RCN got seven more from the RN in 1944 and three others of the still larger Loch-class, making a total of 70 RCN frigates in all.

With greater speed, endurance and armament, as well as increased space and better living conditions, the frigate was superior to the corvette as an ocean escort. In fact, though the RCN was reluctant to revise or cancel building programs under way, Canada might have had more frigates — and fewer corvettes — but for the shortcomings of North America's inland waterways in this era before the opening of the St. Lawrence Seaway in 1959. Great Lakes shipyards were never switched to frigate production because the locks of the Lachine Canal near Montreal prohibited the passage of frigates to the Atlantic Ocean, and a potential alternate exit route involving the Chicago Drainage Canal and the Mississippi River was also rejected as not navigable.

So, the RN switched to a proper ship for the ocean-escort job a year sooner than the RCN. Effects were felt down the line in the RCN. While many corvettes did mid-ocean escort duty, *Bangor*-class minesweepers began to enter service in 1941 and did much of the local escort and patrol work originally intended for corvettes.

* * *

The life of a corvette really began in the shipyard, where she was first met by some crew members. One such experience is related by Jack Skinner of Willowdale, Ont., who served in *Charlottetown* in 1941-42:

On completion of my leading torpedo operator's course in Halifax, I was drafted to *Charlottetown* which was being built in Kingston, Ontario. This was my first experience of going inland to pick up a ship that was just being built and I was excited. I was 19 years old and I was quite surprised when I was put in charge as the senior seaman rating, even though the draft was made up of a chief engine room artificer, a stoker petty officer, a leading stoker, and an able seaman asdic.

This would be in October 1941. We left Halifax by Canadian National Railways and arrived in Kingston about 32 hours later. We expected to be met by someone from the local naval establishment. However, no one showed up. By the time we decided we were on our own, it was 2 a.m., all the taxis that had met the train had left and the station master was closing up. We called a taxi and eventually made our way to the naval barracks, which were all locked up. We finally roused someone who told us there was no place for us to sleep there, but if we wanted to we could sleep on a harbour craft tied up to the dock. By that time, we were willing to sleep anywhere.

The next day we reported to the dockyard. We were told to find rooms ashore, which we did. For the next six weeks we were pretty well on our own. Winter was approaching and the ship had to be out of Kingston before the St. Lawrence froze. Additional crew arrived about the beginning of December. A mixture of naval personnel and shipyard people took the ship as far as Quebec City, where we tied up.

The river was starting to freeze and I remember one night the ice was jamming between the dock and the ship, straining the lines to near breaking point. However, the crew managed to loosen them sufficiently to make the ship safe. We were still in Quebec City when we heard that Japan had attacked Pearl Harbor [on December 7, 1941].

Other crew members joined *Charlottetown* in Quebec City. One was Ray MacAulay of Fredericton, N.B., who recalls: "On December 13, 1941, she was commissioned into the RCN. I remember that on leaving harbour the ship was breaking ice. Word soon went about that we could be known as the unlucky 13. Thirteen letters in her name and commissioned on the 13th day of the month."

The starboard side of *Louisburg* is iced up a bit at Pictou, N.S., in December 1941.

Stan Munro of Toronto also went aboard in Quebec City. He says: "Our captain, Lieutenant J.W. Bonner, made a fiery speech about the fact that *Charlottetown* being commissioned on the 13th day of the month only spelled bad luck for the 'Hun' or 'Japs' we would meet up with.

"We left Quebec City bound for Halifax in mid-December and had to break our way through ice on the St. Lawrence River a good part of the way. Because of some mixup, two leading telegraphists had been drafted to *Charlottetown*, so I was sent on to Saint John, New Brunswick, to pick up the corvette *Sackville*."

Jack Skinner continues the story: "We arrived a week before Christmas. As some work still had to be done on the ship, we stayed in Halifax for most of January. However, during that time we did make one trip, a patrol to protect fishing boats off the coast, as the fishermen were concerned about enemy action in the area. This trip was a most uncomfortable one, as the seas were very heavy, the weather was cold and the ship iced up. A considerable amount of water found its way into the messdecks, making for most unpleasant living conditions."

Howard Libbey of Sydney, N.S., served in *Calgary* in 1941-42: "I picked *Calgary* up in Sorel, where she was built. She was beautiful. We got away from Sorel on commissioning day, December 16, 1941, and hoped to be in Halifax for Christmas. We did okay till just before entering the Strait of Canso, when the steering engine broke down.

"Most of the engine room artificers were seasick and the one who was not was on watch. He sent me aft with a

Amherst carried twin anti-aircraft guns in her bandstand in 1941.

few tools to do what I could because, even though I was only a stoker second class, he knew I had machine-shop training. You can't imagine the mess that tiller flat was in, with oil all over and the ship rolling as only a corvette could. Between sliding and holding on for dear life, I managed to clean up a bearing and get it going again. I was a mess of oil and steam burns, bangs and bruises, but I got all the ERAs' tots of rum the next day. We finally got into Halifax on December 28."

* * *

As new corvettes were commissioned in 1941, they were quickly assigned to convoy escort without a lot of crew training. The big picture had changed focus. In March 1941, the U.S. government had approved Lend-Lease, an arrangement to support Britain that eventually provided equipment, food, clothing and many other necessities. Germany had invaded the Soviet Union on June 22, 1941. This ended the fear of an immediate invasion of the U.K., but created an ally which would need assistance that could only come by sea. The Atlantic lifeline became more crucial than ever.

In July, the U.S. began to use warships to protect American shipping en route to Iceland and other places. That same month U.S. forces relieved British forces in Iceland. President Franklin Roosevelt and Prime Minister Winston Churchill agreed on the Atlantic Charter in August and the U.S. navy took over control of operations on the western side of the Atlantic. Imagine this odd situation: Canadian escorts were now under the control of a country that was not at war. Small wonder that some described the U.S. as "a neutral belligerent."

Individually, it was a whole new world for the Canadian volunteer sailors. Phil George, who started as an ordinary seaman in *Baddeck*, remembers: "I recall wondering whether I was going to be seasick and then seeing the sight of land the first time we left Halifax in June 1941. When the land finally got below the horizon, you realized you were out on this great big body of water in this little ship and if you ever went down you would probably never come back alive. It was quite a feeling, quite a sensation, and I will never forget that."

Collectively, Canadian corvettes had a rough indoctrination in convoy escort. The prime example is the eastbound Convoy SC 42 on the Iceland Run in September 1941. It has been dissected by historians and has become one of the most famous convoys of the war.

In brief, British deciphering of U-boat disposition signals prompted a decision to reroute SC 42 in mid-ocean. In heavy seas, she plodded north to try to outflank the enemy, but was located near Greenland by *Markgraf,* a force of 14 U-boats. The convoy had only four escorts: the destroyer *Skeena* and the corvettes *Alberni, Kenogami* and *Orillia.* Although the escort was reinforced en route, by RCN and RN warships and air cover from a base in Iceland, the result was a slaughter: 15 merchant ships were sunk and one badly damaged, comprising one-quarter of the convoy.

U-Boat Command had by this time assumed a central co-ordinating function. The first U-boat to contact a convoy would radio the sighting information to headquarters and provide regular updates. As well, although it's not often mentioned, the Germans were reading British convoy messages until 1943. These two developments allowed U-Boat Command to plot the course of many convoys and direct multiple U-boats to the target, thus forming the infamous U-boat "wolf packs" that tried to overwhelm the convoy defenders. These packs were formed and re-formed frequently as opportunities arose.

The SC 42 debacle underlined a multitude of allied shortcomings. The initial escort force was too small and too weak. Individual escorts lacked training and collectively there was little continuity or teamwork. There was a dearth of sophisticated equipment and, significantly, a lack of air cover.

From that post-war overview, we narrow down to the personal recollections of crew members not party to the big picture. In *Alberni*, Leonard Lamb was an ordinary seaman: "SC 42 started out as an ordinary convoy except it was a Canadian escort only, and there were just four of us for 64 ships. This was *Kenogami's* first trip.

"About four days out, we had a terrific gale which broke up the convoy temporarily. After getting everyone together, we proceeded on a northerly course, but we knew from U-boat wireless telegraphy that we were in for trouble."

Albert Baker in *Orillia* recalls Greenland:

Here the whole scene changed. The sea calmed and there were ice cliffs off our port side. We were in a new world. The ice reached to the sky and was cloaked in fog, a sight I'll never forget. Our role was stern sweep, the watchdog for stragglers. After a rough crossing there are always a few ships with deck cargoes shifted. This one little tramp in particular kept dropping astern, listing badly to starboard with a deck cargo of lumber.

One afternoon while about four miles astern, she flashed that a torpedo had been fired at her. We dropped back, took a sweep around and returned to our station with the convoy. That evening I recall seeing black smoke pouring from her stack as she made a run to get back inside the screen, which she did.

The air along the coast was cold but sharp, not damp and penetrating like we were used to. In the messdeck things were much better with the change in weather, but not quite right. When Jolly Jack is quiet, there is something in the wind.

Eight or more U-boats attacked repeatedly the night of September 9th and into the morning of the 10th. Some U-boats penetrated the escort screen and surfaced between columns of the convoy. Merchant ships fired machine-guns at surfaced U-boats, while at night escorts illuminated the area with star shell so the U-boats could be sighted, or induced to submerge. There was an emergency change of course. The corvettes were caught between the instinct to counterattack, the desire to rescue survivors and the need to continue screening the convoy as it lumbered on. All was chaos.

Leonard Lamb recalls the initial attacks:

For the next 72 hours it was hell. Part of our job was picking up survivors and we ended up with an abundance, along with a German shepherd dog and two cats. The dog understood Spanish only, and when we dropped [depth] charges he would hide under the table in the forward mess and someone had to clean up.

We rescued survivors from the *Stargaard*, which looked like a pre-World War I freighter. As each survivor came over the side, one of us would take him into the messdeck, strip him bare, clean him up and give him dry clothing.

My survivor was a little man, I finally found out after I got him stripped. Now this is hard to believe, but I will list his clothes as I took them off: one life-belt, one duffel coat, one overcoat, one complete suit, two sweaters — out of which jumped a gorgeous orange cat, one flannel shirt and two suits of wool underwear. Many of this crew were dressed this warmly.

This man spoke very little English and I had a hard time convincing him to get in my hammock. We did this to get them out of the way. But every time I went on watch, this man would go with me and roundly curse out the enemy.

Both Leonard Lamb and Harry Gold of Thunder Bay, Ont., a stoker petty officer in *Alberni* in 1941-42, recall that a torpedo narrowly missed *Alberni's* stern. Gold wrote a three-page account in 1941. In part, it says: "I just came off watch at 2400, when we stopped again for two more survivors. One fellow had been in the water for three-and-a-half hours. He was out when we got him. The coxswain, the cook and I stripped him, dried him off and tried to put dry clothes on him. He would grab them and hang on for dear life. He was delirious. I guess he thought he was still in the water. We poured rum into him. We worked on him for more than three hours. He came around in about 10 hours. Well, I have now been up for 24 hours."

The next afternoon, Gold was on watch again: "I was back at the throttle when we heard another submarine. We dropped five cans on him, turned around and then dropped 10 more. The noise was terrific. I sure was a busy man in the engine room. I had a new man with me who had never seen action. He was quite pale when we finished."

Kenogami, credited with yeoman service in driving off U-boats and rescuing merchant navy survivors, also reported a close call.

Albert Baker in *Orillia* relates this story:

We sent our seaboat away. There had been two ships abreast. One went down in minutes, the other with a deck cargo of timber was still afloat, but settling. On this ship we left a dog we could hear barking. The captain was on the bridge with his bull-horn shouting, "Get the dog," but we passed it up for the lads in the water. Many of the seamen were holding onto pieces of timber. The bobbing lights on their lifejackets were the only way some were found.

Three Dutchmen on an upturned boat only a few hundred feet off our port quarter were shouting. Our seaboat crew intended to pick them up on a return trip after unloading its survivors. Many had to be lifted aboard while others made it up *Orillia*'s scramble nets. When we checked again, the Dutchmen had disappeared. They must have slipped off their boat. Survivors included coolies, Lascars, Dutch, Norwegian and British.

The Dutch boys took over our mess duties as we were continually closed up at action stations. The dishes were done, the mess scrubbed out and, most of all, they kept the coffee pot on. This was appreciated very much. Survivors were stretched out everywhere there was room. Some would not go below decks. This could be understood.

We got two survivors from the *Winterswijk*, which had a cargo of phosphite. They were blown clear off the ship's bridge. One had his scalp badly torn but, having no sick bay attendant, we did a good job on him in the fo'c'sle with scissors and plenty of surgical powder. He survived.

Seven ships were lost that night, and *Orillia* was sent astern to rescue survivors, beginning an adventure that earned Captain Ted Briggs both criticism and praise. Albert Baker recalls this experience:

Having the stern sweep in heavy fog, we slipped away to the tanker *Tahchee*, which had been fished [torpedoed] just forward of the engine room in a crude-oil tank.

The *Tahchee* was still smouldering. Some of the crew went aboard and managed to get the fire out. They examined the ship. While they were getting steam up in one boiler, we went back to a holed freighter nearby. We salvaged what we could, which was one pillowcase filled with different liquors and chocolate bars, four revolvers, a telescope, a crate of chickens and four machine-guns. On the tanker they found they could get 2 1/2 knots out of one boiler, so we took her in tow and managed about 7 knots in a good sea. We also took on fuel from the tanker.

Fate was with us. With 700 miles [1,129 km] to go to Iceland, fog was tight all the way and we sneaked along with our prize. We heard through radio they had given us up for lost, but we could not break wireless telegraphy silence under the circumstances.

Survivors put in many hours playing cribbage. We had one lad, Eddie Morrison from Prince Edward Island, who had been with Don Messer, and plenty of others with good talent. Survivors would be lying and sitting around the mess with a lost look on their faces, the past still fresh in their memories. Eddie would saunter into the mess with his guitar, give a few strums to call in the fold and we would start off. Survivors would sit up and listen and before long some would be singing along, and so the time passed.

After putting our survivors ashore at Reykjavik at 2 a.m. on September 15, they put our clocks ahead to 5 a.m. and said we were sailing at 7 a.m. We took on fuel, a crate of bread, bag of onions and cabbage. Our supplies were very low.

Thinking about our rough crossing weather-wise, we figured we would have a running sea on our return trip. This would make for a fast trip, but no such luck. It blew just as hard the other way. We pitched and tossed home to the "Hole in the Wall" [St. John's].

Captain Briggs was ordered to report to Captain D's office. They had a taxi with two officers to pick him up just as soon as we docked at about 8 a.m. They whisked him away. He had left the convoy off Greenland without reporting to the flotilla leader.

Here again we took on supplies in a hurry and by 12 noon we were on our way back to Iceland with another convoy without putting a foot ashore. I think it was 58 days before we managed to get ashore. Day after day of pounding and little rest makes one very slap-happy. We were sitting just looking at one another and laughing our fool heads off.

But the story does not end there. In a May 1991 conversation, Albert Baker said: "After the war, captain Briggs was persistent that we should get salvage money for the *Tahchee*. They finally allowed us salvage money and split it into shares. I got five shares, which amounted to $64."

At that, he produced a registered letter from the Department of National Defence, dated April 20, 1951, which said: "Enclosed herewith is an official cheque for $64.32 representing five shares of the salvage money awarded to the ship's company of HMCS *Orillia* for salvage services rendered to SS *Tahchee* during the period of 9 to 15 September, 1941.

"For your information, the total distribution of salvage money amounted to $4,824 divided in 375 shares on the following basis:

Lieutenant in command	30	shares
Lieutenant not in command	20	"
Commissioned officer not in command	15	"
Sub-lieutenant not in command	15	"
Warrant officer not in command	12	"
Chief petty officer	10	"
Petty officer	8	"
Leading rating	6	"
Able rating	5	"
Ordinary rating	3	"

While Albert Baker's share as an able seaman was $64, basic arithmetic leads one to conclude that Briggs' share as a lieutenant in command would have come to $386, a fair chunk of money for most people in 1951.

The principle of naval salvage is so well established that in *The Concise Oxford Dictionary* one definition of the word salvage is: "1. n. (Payment made or due for) saving of a ship or its cargo from loss by wreck or capture, rescue of property from fire, wreckage, etc.; property salvaged."

The navy reaction to the *Tahchee* incident amidst the disaster of SC 42 cut both ways. Captain D Newfoundland, who was RN Captain E.B.K. Stephens, noted it was a fine feat of seamanship, but labelled it an error of judgment that weakened the escort to SC 42. Indeed, the senior escort officer had tried to recall *Orillia*, but his message did not reach the corvette. On the other hand, the citation for the Distinguished Service Cross that Briggs was awarded in June 1942 makes it clear this action figured prominently:

Acting Lieutenant Commander Briggs, while in command of HMCS *Orillia*, displayed great initiative and tenacity of purpose in oiling at sea from the torpedoed tanker *Tahchee*, which tanker, as a result of Lieutenant Commander Briggs' excellent seamanship and ingenuity, was salvaged. This officer has rendered excellent and invaluable service with convoys generally during a long period of time.

Ted Briggs was an NR officer who commanded *Orillia* from November 25, 1940, to September 4, 1942. He was well versed in the ways of the sea. He should have known that protection of the convoy was the top priority. He knew *Tahchee*'s cargo was valuable, both in terms of importance to the war effort and monetary worth. He also knew the laws of salvage. Looking back 65 years, his decision stands out as unorthodox. It's not difficult today to side with Captain D. The convoy should have come first, not a single tanker, and *Orillia*'s departure left the beleaguered convoy even more vulnerable.

SC 42 was also notable for the first Canadian submarine kill of World War II, at least until research in the mid-1980s determined that the Canadian destroyer *Ottawa* shared in the sinking of the Italian submarine *Faa di Bruno* off Ireland on November 6, 1940. However, for more than 40 years, it was believed that the corvettes *Chambly* and

Moose Jaw earned the honour of being first with the destruction of *U-501* on September 10, 1941.

A pivotal player in the drama was Commander J.D. (Chummy) Prentice, captain of *Chambly*. It was a rarity to find at sea in so small a warship an officer of the rank of commander, which is equivalent to lieutenant-colonel in today's unified forces. A Canadian who had retired from the RN in 1938 and returned to Canada to live, Prentice provided rare experience for the RCN early in the war, which was recognized by his designation as senior officer Canadian corvettes.

Essentially, Prentice in *Chambly* had the new *Moose Jaw* and his own ship out for a training session. On receiving estimates of U-boat dispositions, he requested and received permission to come to the aid of the vulnerable SC 42. Prentice set course for a point ahead of the convoy's anticipated location. "We caught up with the convoy at night and zeroed in on the flashes of explosions when it was still over the horizon," recalls Bud Thrasher of Toronto, a signalman in *Chambly*.

A strong contact was picked up on *Chambly*'s asdic and rapidly classed as submarine. Coming from an unexpected direction, *Chambly* caught the U-boat by surprise and dropped a five-charge pattern with shallow settings because the U-boat didn't have time to dive deep. A misfire and human error caused the first two charges to be dropped close together. They apparently did the job as the U-boat was damaged and forced to the surface near *Moose Jaw*.

Working from various official reports and personal accounts from *Chambly* crew, it's possible to determine the essence of what followed, but there is a lack of agreement on a few points. The following reconstruction seems reasonable.

"When the U-boat surfaced in front of her," Bud Thrasher continues, "*Moose Jaw* opened fire with her 4-inch gun, which typically misfired. So, she used what was jokingly referred to as a corvette's main armament, the ram. However, just before she rammed the U-boat, her 4-inch gun finally fired and put a shell through the conning tower."

As *Moose Jaw* hit *U-501* a glancing blow, something very strange occurred: the German captain jumped from the conning tower onto *Moose Jaw*'s fo'c'sle without getting wet. Unprepared to stand off further boarders, *Moose Jaw*'s captain, Lieutenant Freddie Grubb, backed off, ramming the U-boat again in the process and continuing with ma-

chine-gun fire in an effort to ensure the crew did not man the U-boat's deck gun. The U-boat was losing speed and started to settle by the stern. The German crew started to abandon the vessel.

Meanwhile, *Chambly* had moved in. "We stopped and put our floodlight on the sub to see what was going on," says Joe Kalino of Montreal, an able seaman in *Chambly* from 1940-42. "Imagine, engine stopped and lights glaring, but you had no time to think of death. The order went out for the boarding party to assemble. Let me remind you that there is a picked bunch for the party if normal routine was followed, but this was anyone who jumped into the whaler."

Bud Thrasher remembers that "during the boarding operation, light was provided by our 10-inch signal projectors and eventually smaller Aldis lamps with coloured filters to provide less conspicuous light."

Joe Kalino brings us back to the *Chambly* boarding party: "Lieutenant [Ted] Simmons was in change. We got to the sub and had just boarded her when we saw the crew jumping into the sea. They had opened the sea-cocks and she was going down."

We shift to a description by Commander Prentice: "Lieutenant Simmons knocked one German overboard who tried to interfere with him and drove two more to the top of the conning tower with orders to show him the way below. They refused, making it clear that they expected the boat to sink at any moment.

"Lieutenant Simmons started down the hatch, but got stuck due to his gas mask. He took the gas mask off and started down a second time in the hope of finding confidential papers, in spite of the fact that he knew the boat must be filling with chlorine fumes. As he reached the bottom of the ladder, a bulkhead must have given way for he saw a wall of water coming towards him. He climbed to the top of the conning tower and ordered his boarding party to swim to the skiff which was lying off. The last man had just splashed into the water when the U-boat sank under his feet."

Stoker W.I. (Bill) Brown, 24, of Toronto, did not return to *Chambly* and, despite a search, his body was not recovered. On reaching the U-boat, he apparently fastened the whaler's bow line to the rail of the U-boat, then turned to other duties. In the darkness and confusion, his shipmates were left with differing impressions of how the stoker was lost. Most common is the belief that he was pulled under by the sinking sub when his feet got caught in chains or cables. A few felt he failed to make it out of the sub, or drowned while trying to return to the whaler.

While the boarding operation was under way, *Moose Jaw* went about picking up Germans. Aboard *Chambly*, says Bud Thrasher, "We lowered scramble nets over the sides and proceeded to take on board any U-boat survivors that could be located with the aid of our shielded signal lights. During the pickup, one of the Germans in the water kept shouting at us 'No light! No light!' in English. He was apparently afraid that his rescuers would be torpedoed by another U-boat."

David Grimes in *Chambly* says: "The Germans were stripped of all their clothing, which was returned to them, and were given survivors' kits that consisted of civilian clothes we carried on board for any survivors we might pick up. Most of the prisoners were in *Moose Jaw*. We had seven or eight and one officer. We kept the prisoners on the port side of the seamen's mess. Anyone who slung his hammock there was no longer able to, so that the men standing guard had a clear view of them at all times. We would stand our four hours on lookout and two hours guarding the prisoners.

"You know, they were young guys like us. We got along fine with them. No trouble at all. When they were taken off, it was like saying goodbye to an old friend."

Joe Kalino also recalls the prisoners: "They ate with us and slept with us under guard. We had sing-songs with them for the rest of the trip. They were taken ashore blindfolded to a prison camp. That night the captain called for a little celebration, which consisted of a double ration of pure tot [rum]."

Moose Jaw recovered five officers and 24 men. *Chambly* took in one officer and seven men, which would make six officers and 31 men, or 37 prisoners of war. German records indicate that 11 ratings perished, giving a crew size of 48, about normal for a Type IX C boat.

It was standard practice to reward success, although the process took many months. This U-boat kill was no exception. Foremost among the recognition were the Distinguished Service Order to Chummy Prentice and the Distinguished Service Cross to Ted Simmons and Sub-Lieutenant John Allan, all of *Chambly*, and all "for bravery and enterprise in action against enemy submarines."

Freddie Grubb, the *Moose Jaw* CO, received only Mention in Dispatches "for good service in action against enemy submarines and in rescuing survivors from a merchantman." Because he received the lowest award justifiable under the circumstances, none of his crew received recognition, says Sub-Lieutenant Cully Lancaster of North Vancouver, B.C., adding, "I joined *Moose Jaw* four months after the action with *Chambly* and there was still grumbling about the awarding of medals." In fact, Grubb, an RCN officer, lost his command within three months and was made a training officer. Apparently he was deemed not to have engaged the enemy with vigour.

* * *

Although it's beyond the scope of this book to examine closely what the Canadian government and the RCN told the Canadian public during the war, it wasn't always the truth or the full story. An example is the following 1941 report from the national news agency The Canadian Press:

Ottawa, Nov. 25. — (CP) — For the first time since this war began the Royal Canadian Navy has relaxed its rules of secrecy to credit to specific ships the known sinking of a German submarine.

MACDONALD STATEMENT

There have been reports before that RCN vessels have sent U-boats to the bottom, but Navy Minister (Angus) Macdonald's announcement last night on the North Atlantic sinking of a submarine and capture of 47 crew members by the Canadian corvettes *Chambly* and *Moose Jaw* was the only time an official statement has mentioned the navy ships involved.

The wording of a communique from the British Admiralty which was made public by Mr. Macdonald indicated the corvettes were on convoy duty when the incident occurred. It indicated, too, that the convoy got past safely.

The communique said: "HMCS *Chambly* with HMCS *Moose Jaw* in company recently sank a German U-boat in the North Atlantic.

"This successful action fought by two Canadian-built corvettes is a splendid demonstration of the protection given to convoys by ships of the Royal Canadian Navy."

After a brief description of the encounter, the news report continued: "Several weeks ago Mr. Macdonald said probably 'more than one' submarine had been destroyed by Canadian ships. Presumably this latest sinking was in addition to those he referred to earlier."

From a debacle with one saving grace, the RCN created for public consumption a shining example of naval efficiency. In reality, the RCN didn't even do a good job of notifying the Brown family. Syd Moyle of Rexdale, Ont., a *Chambly* seaman torpedoman, explains:

One of the most traumatic experiences I ever had was the culmination of the drowning of Stoker Bill Brown. Before refit leave, captain Prentice summoned me to the wardroom and said he had checked addresses and concluded that I would be given the task to visit Brown's next of kin to inform them of his demise. Apparently the navy department in Ottawa had informed his wife that he was "missing in action."

Captain Prentice instructed me to arrange a visit and tell the family the true story "unofficially." Captain Prentice didn't want them to be left with the impression there was a possibility that Bill could be alive and a prisoner of war.

After I was home a few days, I telephoned Bill Brown's widow and arranged a visit. It was an onerous mission for a 20-year-old kid. When I arrived, Bill's wife and three little children and his parents were waiting. I outlined the entire action and informed them that that their loved one was not missing but drowned. I explained at their prodding — Bill's dad wanted to hear it all — that Bill was the stoker member of the seaboat's crew and his duty was to prevent the scuttling of the sub. Like the others, he was dressed in a heavy duffel coat and was wearing seaboots. By the time our boys arrived, the U-boat captain had ordered the sea-cocks open and the process of scuttling had begun. Brown's seaboots were caught in the conning tower's chains and he was literally sucked under.

It was a very sad experience to see the whole Brown family crying uncontrollably. I was so upset

Corvettes (left) moored at Hvalfjord, Iceland, in 1941.

with the ordeal that I can't even remember arriving home. It was a wringer-washer experience for me, and it was a task that one of the ship's officers should have undertaken.

* * *

U-501 was one of the new, larger Type IX C long-range attack U-boats. Like *Moose Jaw*, the boat was on its first operational mission with many inexperienced crew members and it appears the crew was not alert enough to pick up the approach of *Chambly* and *Moose Jaw* from an unexpected direction until it was too late. Further, one German source indicates that the boat's diving depth was restricted by the captain after difficulty was experienced early in the voyage. The crew did have the presence of mind to scuttle the U-boat so it wouldn't fall into Canadian hands.

The captain, *Korvettenkapitan* (Lieutenant-Commander) Hugo Forster, had been in the navy since 1923, but was new to U-boats. The most surprising element of the engagement was that he abandoned his crew, which was a rarity in the *U-Bootwaffe*. Whether his action was caused by cowardice, momentary panic, a belief that the U-boat was too damaged to dive or fight on, or some other reason, Hugo Forster had performed abysmally. This ultimately had tragic repercussions, as explained in the book *Second U-Boat Flotilla*, written by Lawrence Paterson and published in the U.K. by Leo Cooper in 2003.

Sensing crew bitterness towards their captain, the Canadians segregated Forster for his safety. He was then sent to a British prison camp at Grizedale Hall in the U.K., where there had just been an instance of a captured U-boat crew conducting an illegal "court of honour." After being found guilty of cowardice in the face of the enemy, a German officer had died in an attempt to escape.

Not long after Forster was imprisoned in the U.K., the British got wind of a plan by the German prisoners of war to subject him to an illegal court martial. He was transferred to another camp, where he was ostracized by fellow officers. Eventually, as part of a prisoner exchange through Sweden, Forster was returned to Germany. There he was placed under arrest to face a court martial for cowardice in the face of the enemy. In February 1945, he committed suicide in his cell, using a pistol that had been smuggled in.

Courtesy Melvin Davis

Early in the war, *Kamloops* has a short foc's'le, two masts and minesweeping gear at the stern.

The *Amherst* whaler is outboard at sea in 1941.

CHAPTER FOUR

"BLOOD BROTHERS TO A CORK WHEN IT CAME TO RIDING OUT A ROUGH SEA."

WHEN GROUP *MARKGRAF* dispersed after devastating convoy SC 42, many of the U-boats headed home to replenish, but five stayed on patrol. Their next target was the eastbound convoy SC 44 guarded by five escorts — the Royal Navy destroyer *Chesterfield* and corvette *Honeysuckle*, and the Royal Canadian Navy corvettes *Agassiz*, *Levis* and *Mayflower*.

The U-boats sank four merchant ships and hit a fifth, but the torpedo did not explode. In the attack, *U-74*, a Type VII B boat commanded by Eitel-Friedrich Kentrat, torpedoed the corvette *Levis* shortly before 4 a.m. on September 19, 1941, about 120 miles east of Greenland's southern tip. E.W. (Bill) Foster of Bridgetown, N.S., a *Levis* stoker, recalls the incident:

I came off watch from the boiler room at 12 midnight. After cleaning up a bit, I went down to our mess, had a bit to eat, crawled into my hammock and went to sleep.

I think I remember a blue flash, and then coming to, but not in my hammock. At first I thought that we were upside down, as all you could hear was the steam hissing from the broken pipes that supplied heat to our mess.

I remember the awful smell of cordite or gunpowder from the explosion. I then noticed an opening in the port side, but I guess there was another on the starboard side.

As I was on the port side, I crawled along the side towards where the light was coming from. I wore nothing except summer underwear, and with all the water coming in from the rise and fall of the ship, I was soon wet and cold. I was lucky that the water was pretty flat.

I made it to the hole, but couldn't crawl up to the next deck as the side was pretty well blown, and in my bare feet that cold steel did not feel very good. I didn't want to jump in the water, so thought about my life-jacket, which was one of the Mae West types that you had to blow up. It was in my locker, so I crawled back to see if I could find it. I was unable to locate the life-jacket as it was pitch black.

I started for the hole again, when I heard Stoker [Walter] Jones yelling. He had been sleeping on the padded locker just below where I had my hammock slung. I grabbed him and, leading him towards the opening, told him I thought we could get out.

I thought we would have to jump in the water, but in crawling along the side of the mess, I found a hole up to the seamen's mess above. The hole was big enough for us to go through, but I don't know what state the mess was in as it was so dark that you couldn't see. I do remember that I saw a luminous watch going around in a circle. I suppose it was on someone's arm, but I didn't stop to investigate.

We somehow made our way out of the seamen's mess to the deck. Someone gave me a duffel coat to put on, but I was still cold. I went to the lifeboat station and was lucky enough to get in a boat before it was lowered off the side. Some had to jump in the water, but were picked up soon after. We then had to wait for one of the escorts to pick us up as the ships in the convoy don't stop. We were adrift for an hour or two as the other escort went looking for the sub.

Seven stokers were among the dead. Foster and Jones were the only two to make it out of the stokers' mess. The two were sleeping in a corner and it seems the explosion bent steel plates in such a way that they shielded that corner from the full force of the blast. Almost as miraculous was their escape in the dark over twisted steel and wreckage.

In a Canadian Press news story dated October 17, 1941, Jones is quoted as saying: "I owe my life to Foster. If he hadn't found the way out through the gap blown by the explosion, none of us would have got out. As for the others in our quarters, they didn't have time to know what happened to them."

The board of inquiry into the sinking found that *Levis* "was struck by a torpedo about 10 feet from the stem on the port side." The ship was nearly cut in two and the bow hung down into the water. It was only the second eastward crossing by *Levis*, notes Reuben Smyth of Montreal, a stoker. RCN reports indicate that the ship's asdic was not functioning. Smyth says, "When we were at sea four days, there was some wood floating in the water, so the captain went to ram it, but the corvette took a wave and the wood went underneath the ship and knocked off the asdic dome."

Wilson Coolen of Halifax, a leading stoker in *Levis*, recalls that because of the asdic problem, *Levis* was not conducting her usual screen. In fact, her degaussing gear designed to protect against magnetic mines was not working either and she was keeping a course parallel to the convoy, possibly using *Mayflower* as a protective screen.

The northern lights had lit up the sky earlier in the evening, and Coolen remembers remarking to the engineer, "'What a night for a torpedoing.' Of course, I did not mean us." It then got very dark.

The torpedo was actually spotted by *Mayflower* lookouts and *Levis* lookout Norman Fraser, but just an instant before it struck. Coolen was on duty in the engine room:

Without any warning there was this tremendous explosion. The ship seemed to rise up, then slowly settle. Of course, it being noisy in the engine room, we didn't hear anything on deck. Our engines were still going ahead. At that moment we had no orders

from the bridge. Very nerve-racking in the interim. Many things flashed through my mind. I was married in April, five months previous, and had just received word my wife was pregnant. She could very well have been a bride, mother and widow all within a year.

Things became quite hectic. We called the boiler room to shut down and also advised them to prepare to abandon ship. We then stopped and secured main engines, but left the generator on to supply lighting. Admittedly, for a brief moment, I was quite panicky. When in the engine room, you have no idea of on-deck activities.

Anyway, we went on deck as advised and found everyone at their stations awaiting final word to abandon ship. It seemed like ages in a raft, but we were rescued by another corvette. We found out that the torpedo had entered forward in the messdecks, which accounted for so many deaths: 17 killed outright and one some hours later — meaning a burial at sea, very depressing.

Evidence at the ensuing board of inquiry showed that *Levis* Sub-Lieutenant Ray Hatrick entered the seamen's mess looking for survivors: "There was a heavy smoke from the explosion and with my torch I could only see about two or three feet. As a result, I had to grope around. I found several bodies which were obviously dead and I hailed at the top of my voice and then I kept silent and listened. I received no reply."

Two seaboats were lowered almost immediately. Lieutenant Charles W. Gilding, the *Levis* captain, took charge of the first one. Two Carley floats were also used, though one drifted away and had to be retrieved by the second seaboat. *Levis* was abandoned in roughly 15 minutes by all but two officers and eight to ten ratings, who were soon taken off by a seaboat from another escort.

"We were sent to get those that we could, which was very dangerous as you were a sitting duck when stopped," says Arnold Gurney of Surrey, B.C., an RCNR stoker in *Agassiz*.

"I was sent with some others to put scramble nets over the starboard side and help these poor devils out of the water. I went down the net and had a hold of one fellow when some person stepped on my hand and we both went into the drink. God was that water cold, but we got them aboard and into warm clothes the crew supplied out of their own kits. Our captain, Lieutenant [B.D.L.] Johnson, whom I sailed under before the war, said to break out the rum for the fellows to warm them up. Well, I had a good shot of rum straight, but might as well have drank water. I was too cold for it to have any effect.

"It is amazing how everybody did their job that night. You have to give credit to these young people in their teens and early twenties who were never to sea before for their great showing and helping the survivors. This young fellow that I got aboard had just lost his brother in the air force, so we had quite a time with him. He said, 'They got my brother, but they're not going to get me.'"

Mayflower's captain, Lieutenant-Commander George Stephen, sent a seaboat back with a party to assess the damage. Their report encouraged Stephen to send a 10-man boarding party and *Mayflower* took Levis in tow at 0540. The tow rope parted at 0700, but *Mayflower* again took *Levis* in tow at 0830. On one visit, the boarders found a dazed, injured *Levis* crew member, Emile Beaudoin, a telegraphist from Quebec City. When nothing further could be done, the boarding party was withdrawn before noon.

The stern-first towing continued at between 2 and 4 knots, but finally *Levis* seemed to go down by the head and take a starboard list. *Mayflower*'s crew cut the tow rope at 1706.

Levis turned on her side and sank at 1710. "When she did go down, there was quite an explosion as the hot boilers hit the cold water," observes Ken Hedley.

"They took us to Iceland where we spent about 10 days," recalls Reuben Smyth. "I was very lucky to survive, but I still feel sorry for the ones that didn't."

Wilson Coolen also ended up in Iceland: "I spent at least 10 days awaiting passage to Canada. Of course, my wife was not aware of all this as only the next of kin of casualties were notified. I did return home around the middle of October."

The sinking of *Levis* was announced September 27, 1941, by the naval minister, Angus L. Macdonald. When some of the 40 survivors were interviewed on the way home or on their arrival, the sinking and salvage efforts became common knowledge.

There are, however, two aspects of the *Levis* tragedy that have been virtually ignored — the captain's conduct and the lack of proper provision for damage control.

Captain Gilding told the board of inquiry: "I had left the bridge 15 minutes before the torpedo hit. I was sitting in my cabin. There was quite a crash forward, the ship seemed to rise and there were great columns of water coming down over the ship. I tried to get out of my cabin, but was dazed, didn't know what had happened. I got out of my cabin and went up through the companion-way."

This took only a few seconds, then: "As soon as I got on deck, Sub-Lieutenant Ray Hatrick was the first one whom I saw when I got through the companion-way and I asked him what had happened and he said we were torpedoed. I then said, 'Abandon ship' and went on the bridge and she was down by the bow very much."

Mayflower's captain testified that the captain of *Levis* was apparently suffering from shock, but the board of inquiry was unsympathetic to Gilding in its verdict on October 10, 1941. For example, it found:

…

3) That the ship was abandoned before any attempt was made to ascertain the full extent of the damage, or any systematic search made for possible survivors.
4) That after *Levis* had been reboarded by volunteers, no effective measures were taken to reduce flooding or to shore up bulkheads, there being no damage control organization or equipment.
5) Whilst making all allowance for the severity of the shock consequent upon so small a ship being torpedoed, we consider it deplorable that such attempts at salvage as were made in *Levis* were left in the hands of comparatively inexperienced RCNVR officers. The responsibility for this must rest upon the commanding officer, Lieutenant C.W. Gelding (sic), RCNR.

The last of the board's seven points recommended that "immediate steps should be taken to provide all corvettes with adequate equipment for shoring up bulkheads, and that detailed instruction in damage control should be given before corvettes are brought into service." L.W. Murray, the commodore commanding *Newfoundland*, wrote the naval secretary that the damage control recommendation was "being actively pursued."

Commodore Murray "concurred in" the board's findings and remarked that "in leading the ship's company by leaving in the first boat, and not returning with the reboarding party," the performance of the captain "is considered far below the standard expected of a naval officer."

Although several former *Levis* crew members were still under the impression 50 years later that Lieutenant Gilding was court-martialled, a search of government files indicates he was never charged with any offence because he could offer as a defence the argument he was suffering from shock. It also appears that he was never given another seagoing command.

As much as the captain's conduct was disappointing, the actions of another officer were inspiring, though it took quite a while for recognition to come to Ray Hatrick of North Hatley, Que. In Library and Archives Canada in Ottawa, I found a file containing a senior officer's post-war handwritten notation to support a proposal that Hatrick be awarded the Distinguished Service Cross. In part, the note said: "It is considered that had the recommendation been submitted in 1941 there would have been no doubt of the award of a DSC."

The award, announced in the Canada Gazette January 1, 1946, read: "For bravery, resourcefulness and devotion to duty when HMCS *Levis* was sunk by enemy action. Lieutenant Hatrick was responsible for warning other escorts and the convoy. This officer directed the rescue of injured men from below deck, and took precautions to have all depth charge pistols set to 'safe.' The high quality of this officer's courage and devotion to duty in the face of the enemy was an inspiration and a splendid example to the ship's company. His actions were at all times in keeping with the highest traditions of the Royal Canadian Navy."

Short and undistinguished is probably a fair summation of the career of *Levis*. In May 1941, the Quebec ferry "banged into her aft end" in the St. Lawrence River, says Reuben Smyth. Then *Levis* got separated from the convoy in her first crossing, says Gordon Naylor of Chemainus, B.C., a leading stoker in her sister escort *Agassiz*.

In fact, *Levis* wasn't even fully fitted out. There was no anti-aircraft gun in her rear bandstand. She also lacked canvas dodgers on the bridge for basic weather protection, says Ray Burwash in *Wetaskiwin*, who concludes: "This sad loss gives you some idea of how grim, rushed and ill-prepared our ships were in this particular period."

U-74, a Type VII B boat commissioned in October 1940, also suffered a grim fate. It was sunk with all 47 hands east of Cartagena, Spain, on May 2, 1942, by depth charges from two Royal Navy destroyers and a Royal Air Force Catalina aircraft. The sub was on its eighth patrol and had sunk five ships and damaged two others.

* * *

There was lots of action on the Iceland Run in 1941. Ken Hedley in *Mayflower* recalls September 30, 1941: "*San Florentino* received four torpedoes. After 12 hours, 21 survivors in a lifeboat were picked up. Then 10 survivors in a second lifeboat were brought aboard. Some of the men's feet were so swollen by the water in the lifeboat that their boots had to be cut off.

"The bow portion of the *San Florentino* was still afloat, and our captain decided to sink it by gunfire since it was felt it would be a hazard to navigation. At the last moment, two men were sighted hanging on to the railing of the bow, and a boat was sent over to pick them up."

In early October, 1941, SC 48 started eastward with eight escorts, one destroyer and seven corvettes. The 52-ship convoy made a course alteration and was reinforced in stages by a total of eight more escorts. Although extremely large, the escort force of Canadian, British, American and Free French vessels was not a coordinated team and it showed. Nine merchant ships were lost, as well as two RN escorts, the corvette *Gladiolus* and the destroyer *Broadwater*.

Phil George, an ordinary seaman in *Baddeck* in 1941, recalls SC 48:

We had a huge gasoline tanker and every morning they would put it on the starboard wing. Every night they would bring it into the middle of the convoy and put an old clunker, a Greek freighter, on the starboard wing. The submarines finally caught up to us. The first night they hit that starboard wing Greek freighter. The second night they hit another freighter on the starboard wing.

We were at action stations almost continually for three days and three nights. The third night I went below, lay down on the floor, took my boots off and put them under my head as a pillow. I don't suppose I'd been there 10 minutes when we were called up to action stations again.

When I came up on deck, I saw the flash of the first torpedo hitting this tanker. A little while later, there was another torpedo, then a huge ball of flame

Amherst sends a seaboat away in 1941.

SC 48 is best known for another event — the torpedoing of the American destroyer *Kearney*. Ralph Shideler says that *Wetaskiwin* was stopped in order to pick up survivors on a very black night when *Kearney* stopped for the same purpose, not to avoid a collision with the Canadian corvette as an official American account has it. "*Kearney* turned on all her lights, cruising lights, deck lights, floodlights. She was lit up like a Christmas tree," Shideler says. "Our captain, Guy Windeyer, at once ordered engines full ahead and we got out of there, leaving men in the water, just as *Kearney* was torpedoed."

Bill Perry recalls *Kearney* from his 1941 stint as a telegraphist in *Galt*, which encountered a Force 10 gale and was forced to head into a driving sea on a trip westward from Iceland:

> Lockers were smashed. The water was three feet deep in all directions and getting worse all the time. I had bought 10 cartons of Camel cigarettes for 60 cents a carton from the U.S. destroyer *Vulcan* to take home on a coming leave. To see my fags swimming around the messdeck like so many gondolas in Venice beggared the imagination.
>
> The situation got so bad that the senior officer of the escort ordered us back to Iceland for repairs and general cleanup. We pulled alongside *Vulcan*. Also alongside was USS *Kearney*, which had been torpedoed a few days earlier but had managed to return to Hvalfjord on her own. She had a decided port list but was still able to accommodate her crew aboard.

* * *

One shouldn't get the idea that all 1941 convoys were besieged. A number crossed unscathed, some after being diverted from danger. On balance, the British breaking of the German naval code was an important factor at this stage in minimizing Allied shipping losses.

There were many influences at work. With fall came the dark season in northern climes and the opportunity to convoy the essentials of war to the Soviet Union. The British played the lead escort role, making extensive use of destroyers. Many were pulled from the Atlantic, putting more pressure on the RCN's fleet of small ships.

went right up through the clouds. When the flame came down, there was no tanker. There was nothing to be seen where that tanker was.

Amazingly, we picked up the captain and the engineering officer in a life raft. Apparently when the first torpedo hit, the captain called the chief engineer to the bridge to learn what damage had been done. They were talking when the second torpedo hit and the ship blew. They apparently had been blown off the bridge and must have come together with the raft in mid-air, because they had no idea how they got into it. The captain had a broken hip and we had a good deal of trouble picking them up.

The Americans began to play a larger role, transferring destroyers from the Pacific Ocean, but the most significant and underrated factor was the intervention of Adolf Hitler. He disregarded the advice of Admiral Dönitz and had the U-boat force virtually withdrawn from the Atlantic theatre in November 1941 to attack the British in the Mediterranean. In retrospect, this was a colossal error because the RCN was stretched beyond its capabilities and the Allies were extremely vulnerable. Of course, the Canadian corvette crews didn't know the U-boats had been withdrawn, so they had to remain vigilant.

It can be argued that the pivotal point in the war was the Japanese attack on Pearl Harbor on December 7, 1941. This brought the U.S. into the fray with a vengeance. In the short term, however, the USN yanked its destroyers back to the Pacific, so there was even more pressure on the RCN. The RN, meanwhile, had to concern itself with not only the Atlantic and the Mediterranean, but also the Pacific and Indian oceans.

When all these factors are taken into account, Allied and neutral merchant ship losses in the Atlantic theatre averaged 144,000 tons per month in the second half of 1941, less than 50 per cent of the 304,000 tons per month in the first half of the year.

* * *

Weather was a contributing factor in the RCN's second corvette loss which, because it occurred on Sunday, December 7, 1941, has long been overshadowed by the Japanese attack on the U.S. Navy at Pearl Harbor, Hawaii. *Windflower*, the first corvette commissioned in Canada, collided with the 10,000-ton Dutch freighter *Zypenberg* off the Grand Banks of Newfoundland at 9:20 a.m.

Windflower had spent the night ahead and to the starboard of convoy SC 58. "The sea was moderate but the fog was very thick, so we were proceeding quite slowly," recalls Coder Claude Arberry of Campbell River, B.C.

Jim Sharpe was repairing equipment on *Windflower*'s bridge:

The radar was working on this trip for the first time since it was installed in September 1941. The radar operator reported we were two miles ahead of the convoy, so the captain decided to turn around.

But why turn and steer straight for the oncoming convoy as a means of decreasing our distance ahead? The radar operator reported us closing the convoy. Anyway, the next reports came from the bow lookout and the crow's nest lookout, almost as one: "Ship on port bow."

At this point, the captain ordered "Hard a-starboard!" and the quartermaster responded. Conjecture and hindsight are great, but had we only swung 30 or so degrees to starboard we *may* have been missed or sideswiped, but we continued turning until we were hit broadside, about 15 feet from the stern, cutting the stern right off.

About this time it seemed prudent to go below and prepare for emergency stations, especially since the emergency bells were ringing. As I had been called to an emergency already, I was dressed in what I called my pajamas — well washed and tenderized dungarees and shirt — with no cold-weather clothing or life belt. When I arrived at my bunk, my life belt was gone. I put on my greatcoat and over that my llama coat. Then the lights went out. I was able to find my way out because the door up top was open, allowing a little daylight in.

When I arrived up top, I was right beside the gunners' stores where spare life belts were stored. The door was locked, so I grabbed the fire axe hanging adjacent to the door, popped the padlock, then went into the stores and grabbed an armful of life belts, which I proceeded to hand out to any takers. I think it was about this time the boiler blew.

From here on, there was much confusion. One poor hand was flopping around the deck with an obviously dislocated left knee. I had someone grab him under the shoulders while I took him by the left ankle and, with one hell of a yank, realigned the leg. We then checked that his Mae West was properly on and inflated, then threw him over the side.

I soon left the ship and swam clear. I didn't want to be drawn under. I swam for a skiff nearby, then saw the executive officer in difficulty, so I swam over and saw he was choking or gasping. I went behind him and slammed his back with both palms, twice I think. He coughed up some water and was back in action again. Together we swam for the skiff and joined the others, but it was useless as a boat because it had blown from the davit head when the boiler blew and so had a large hole forward and another aft.

As we climbed in, the skiff gradually sank since there wasn't enough wood to support all of us, all probably being seven or eight persons. Our Mae Wests [life-vests] kept us afloat but we kept the ruined skiff balanced under us at tiptoe depth. It kept us together and busy, and I suppose it was as a child is with a security blanket. The sea was running a very light swell and the waves would rise and fall from nose to shoulder height and that was the part that felt cold.

We started a sing-along to keep up our morale and attract attention. Other survivors gathered around, buoyed by their Mae Wests but holding onto boards from the lumber rack or other floating debris. A couple of us had decided to grow beards and hadn't shaved since Thursday so we looked rather grotesque with bunker fuel clinging to our three-day growth. That gave us something to laugh about.

William Hirst of Bridgetown, N.S., an ERA in *Windflower*, recounts the events:

The collision cut off our stern, a matter of a foot or so aft of the bulkhead to which my hammock was lashed. I was sound asleep, having come off watch at 8 a.m. I donned my pants and shirt quicker than at any time in my life. As there was no one else in the mess, I went up on deck to see what had happened.

With the stern missing and nothing to support the deck, the remaining deck plates had dropped considerably. As I tried to go to the port side, I slipped and had to grab the combing around the hatch to the electrician's workshop below. After scrambling past the hatch, I proceeded and met the captain, first lieutenant and the coxswain. When I told the captain the ship was going to sink, he said, "I don't think so." He had come aft to check.

I returned to the mess and was on my way down the ladder, just in time to see a great flood of water coming into the coxswain's cabin on the starboard side. I watched the water submerge my locker — in which I had put a large box of chocolate bars the day before. No sweets for me!

I then proceeded to look into the engine room. Seeing no one there and no water coming in, I returned to the upper deck and went to the fiddly deck because it was so much warmer there next to the stack. I wasn't there more than a minute or two when the forward boiler exploded. I remember the deck plates tearing like paper before my eyes. The explosion sent me 15 or 20 feet in the air, I would judge, and I fell into a large amount of water flooding across the deck and was washed overboard, along with two shipmates, a telegraphist [Alphonse Leroy Hare] from North Sydney, Nova Scotia, and the ship's electrician. The three of us quickly drifted away from the ship.

Having blown up my Mae West life-belt for extra protection, I spotted a sizable piece of four-by-four wood, I think from the damage control racks. Minutes later I realized my Mae West was deflated, only to find that a nail in the wood had punctured it.

I clung desperately to the wood and soon spotted one of the ship's smoke floats, which fortunately came close enough for me to grab with my right arm while keeping the wood under my left arm. The telegraphist had hold of the other end of the wood to help keep afloat. I turned around to find the electrician, with two elbows on top of a door from one of the cabins, peeling an orange, which he started to eat. When I turned back, all I could see of the telegraphist was his knees and elbows sticking up from the water; presumably he had drowned.

I then experienced two or three severe explosions, which I later learned was because another of our escorts [HMS *Nasturtium*] was dropping depth charges on the sunken *Windflower*. At that point, I was rendered unconscious, but not before I had spotted a lifeboat through the dense fog. The next I recall is coming to on the deck of the officer's mess on the freighter. Lying next to me on my right was one of the deceased seamen. The man to my left came to a short while later. Two sailors seized me immediately and found clothing for me. Being engine room personnel, I was anxious to know the temperature of the sea-water — it was 34 degrees Fahrenheit [1 degree Celsius].

On returning to the upper deck, I met the electrician who informed me he had been working at his workbench when suddenly his bench was taken from in front of him by the freighter. He just stood looking at the freighter go by. Upon speaking to other *Windflower* crew members, I was told that after launching the two lifeboats, one sank almost immediately and the people in the other boat had to move quickly to get away from the ship, which sank stern first. I was the only ERA to survive.

The board of inquiry found that in rushing up through the fog to help, *Nasturtium* obtained an asdic contact and "carried out depth charge attacks" on the sunken *Windflower*. This set off "another violent underwater explosion," apparently from the detonation of the remaining depth charges on *Windflower*'s deck.

Jim Sharpe has a distinct recollection: "A number of cod floated to the surface belly up, with two lateral fins sticking up and out. Someone said, 'There's your Christmas turkeys,' and sure enough they resembled turkeys floating on top of the water.

"Eventually a lifeboat came to rescue us. I recall being pulled into the lifeboat on top of other people and being offered a cigarette. I remember being hoisted on the end of a rope and rotating as I was hauled up then swung aboard the freighter. The next I remember, I awoke wrapped in a blanket, clean as a newborn babe and just as naked. I then had some soup and a gulp of gin from a bottle that was being passed around. All that time in the water, my outstanding reason for living was thoughts of my wife, who was pregnant with our first child since I had been home on leave in September."

The author's original inquiry to Rod Bradley of Burlington, Ont., a *Windflower* signalman trained operator, was answered by Margaret Bradley on behalf of her hospitalized husband: "He jumped overboard after discarding his seaboots. He helped a shipmate in the water, but the man was dead when they reached a seaboat. When Rod came to he was stretched out on the deck of the Dutch freighter. His feet were frozen and today his toenails are grizzle."

William Hirst continues: "The next morning around 11 a.m. we were in St. John's, Newfoundland. The entire crew were taken by ambulance to HMCS *Avalon* hospital where everyone was examined by doctors. We were handed a bar of pusser soap and turned loose in the showers. My beard and hair required numerous washings. We were then taken to the clothing stores in the dockyard and issued a complete new kit.

"One of the crew collected the mail. This included our Christmas presents, mine being a rather expensive camera from my parents. I had no place to put it except in my new kitbag. We were all sent on 30 days' leave and upon retrieving my baggage in Montreal, there was no camera to be found. We were greeted by our respective relations and numerous photographers, who insisted the four Montreal survivors have their photograph taken together. This appeared on the front page of the *Montreal Star* on the Saturday morning."

Official announcement of the loss had come on Wednesday, December 10, 1941, only three days after the sinking. Twenty-three men were lost — 19 ratings and 4 officers, including the captain, RCNR Lieutenant John Price of Montreal. The boiler explosion and exposure were the principal killers, not the collision. Forty-four men survived.

The board of inquiry noted that both vessels took evasive action at the last moment, but it was too late. The board concluded: "1) The collision and subsequent sinking were caused by HMCS *Windflower*'s turning back towards the convoy and, presumably, misjudging her position with reference to the convoy."

Though the board does not dwell on it, this decision to head back into the convoy is inexplicable. It violates the tenets of good seamanship and also common sense. The correct procedure to regain touch with the convoy would have been to reduce speed and let the convoy gain on the escort.

Everything possible was done to save the ship, the board ruled, but the collapse of the after bulkhead made her sinking a certainty, though it was "greatly hastened" by the boiler explosion that resulted when cold sea-water rushed into the hot boiler. This explosion was probably the greatest single cause of fatalities.

It seems the boiler explosion was mistaken by *Nasturtium* as the sound of a torpedoing, prompting her counterattack when she got a fix on a submerged object. Regardless, the board found her beyond reproach: "14) HMS *Nasturtium*'s actions had no bearing upon the causes of the collision, the sinking of the *Windflower*, nor the subsequent loss of life. It is considered that the commanding officer of HMS *Nasturtium*, believing that the convoy was being attacked and having obtained a good asdic contact, displayed commendable promptness in carrying out a counterattack."

Ironically, *Nasturtium* was damaged by the depth charge explosions. *Zypenberg* had minor damage from the collision and both were escorted to St. John's by the Canadian corvette *Pictou*.

The conduct of *Windflower*'s crew impressed the board: "Evidence shows that in the midst of recurring disasters with explosions and escaping live steam, steadiness was displayed by both officers and men." It praised the "coolness and gallantry" of the surviving officer, Lieutenant Gilbert Fraser, and described as "highly commendable" the actions of five other survivors. Later all six received Mention in Dispatches. One is Jim Sharpe of Victoria, B.C. (In modesty that is typical of those corvette veterans who have helped to create this book, he never mentioned the award to me.)

The board had found that the *Zypenberg*'s captain "is in no way to blame and did all in his power to avoid the collision." Files in the National Archives in Ottawa reveal that the British government was the insurer of *Zypenberg*, so its agents sought damages. The Canadian government denied liability. The agents suggested arbitration. The deputy minister of justice refused, saying there was no authority for settling claims against the Crown in this manner. He advised that the *Zypenberg*'s owners should follow the normal practice of resorting to the courts — in other words, suing for damages. No reply was received and the matter was apparently dropped.

A vivid personal memory of the loss of *Windflower* is etched in the mind of Gary Flock, then a young sailor from Winnipeg, Man., who went on to become an ERA in *Forest Hill* from 1943-45: "I had just joined the navy and was asked to represent the service in a tri-service memorial at my senior high school. A school chum, Jim Condie, went down in *Windflower*. Mrs. Condie was at the memorial. I can still remember her coming up to me and hugging me and telling me that I am so young to have to go to war."

* * *

Japan's December 7th attack on Pearl Harbor caused the small RCN escort force on Canada's west coast to react, notes Al G. King of Sarnia, Ont., a coder in the corvette

Dawson from 1941-43: "We were ordered to check out many small villages and inlets on Vancouver Island's west coast. On one occasion, we entered a large inlet when a heavy fog set in. Because of our early type of radar which frequently broke down, we were fogged in for three days in this deep inlet. On several occasions our asdic dome was damaged by deadheads [floating logs]. We had to have a new one installed, thus changing our patrol plans."

* * *

Over on the Atlantic Ocean, the usual signal traffic from the Flag Officer Newfoundland Force to a convoy at sea contained an additional message for the captain of the corvette *Pictou*, Tony Griffin, who recalls: "One dark night in December 1941 in mid-ocean with tough weather conditions, a signal was received from FONF addressed to *Pictou* designated 'Personal, Important' and reading: 'One able-bodied Wren mark VII Admiralty pattern joins *Pictou*, all well.' This announced the safe arrival of my daughter, Ann. In the morning watch, I went to the bridge to see all the other escorts, their lights blinking congratulations. I thought how Kitty would have loved it. The Germans were equally capable of such light touches; when the U-boat ace Gunther Prien was at sea in *U-47* and his daughter was born, a signal from Admiral Dönitz told him of the arrival of a 'new boat without periscope.'"

December 1941 is remembered as a stormy month. George Auby in *Sorel* recollects: "We joined a convoy of ships proceeding west from Iceland and bad storms plagued us. The trough seemed to be about four miles long. Most times we were out of sight. When we'd reach a crest and start going down the other side, it seemed as if we would go straight to hell we were going that fast. As we came out of each swell, I felt much pride for this little ship."

Oakville telegraphist Charlie Matthewson of North Burnaby, B.C., says: "We ran into the worst storm that I can ever remember. The waves were like mountains, smashing over the foredeck and into the wheelhouse. This seemed to last about 24 hours and when daybreak came the convoy was not to be seen. The captain, Lieutenant [A.C.] Jones, examined the damage and decided to return to Halifax. It was enough to make repairs."

On December 12 the RCN destroyer *Restigouche*, the RCN corvettes *Agassiz*, *Amherst*, *Bittersweet*, *Chicoutimi* and *Orillia*, and the RN corvette *Celandine* left Hvalfjord,

Sailors take rifle practice from the *Amherst* quarterdeck in 1941.

Iceland, to meet a convoy and escort it to North America. Instead, the escorts ran into a monster gale and it was every ship for herself. The convoy was similarly dispersed.

Restigouche was about 125 feet longer than a Flower-class corvette, but the same width and only 425 tons heavier. When her long, narrow hull cut into the mountainous seas and the shrieking wind, the River-class destroyer took such a pounding that she was in real danger. She took on a lot of water and was forced to turn around, a tricky manoeuvre in such high seas. She reached Greenock, Scotland, on December 16 in need of a refit and didn't go to sea again for three months.

Recalling the experience as "hair-raising," Ed Fraser of Willowdale, Ont., first lieutenant in *Amherst*, notes: "We certainly were thankful that we were not aboard *Restigouche*. Corvettes were mighty uncomfortable, but they could ride out a bad storm better than a destroyer.

"As I remember, a good deal of the time we were turning over sufficient revolutions to give a normal speed of 8 to 10 knots. This was just so that we could keep her bow to the wind. Indeed, there was a great deal of damage to the upper deck. We lost at least one of our boats and some of our Carley floats. The wardroom and officers' quarters had a great deal of water to bail out, which we did by forming a bucket line.

"We kept waiting for the barometer to start rising but it did not for many hours. We finally passed through the storm centre. For a few moments, there was no wind at all. It then blew from another direction, but at least the barometer began to rise. When it was all over, our position was to the east of where we entered the storm. We had actually been blown backwards."

Gordon Naylor in *Agassiz* recalls the same storm: "The gale continued for days on end. Some days we made no progress at all. When the gale blew itself out, we set a course for St. John's, but ran short of fuel. When we were down to about 10 tons remaining, we shut down the main engine and just drifted. *Orillia* came along, whether by accident or as a result of us breaking radio silence I never did find out. She took us in tow and a couple of days later she ran out of fuel, so we lit one of our boilers and with our remaining fuel we towed her the last few miles to St. John's."

Louisburg crew members Dutchy Roman (left), Scotty from England, Terry Gallant, Hugh Merryweather.

The sea-going characteristics of corvettes became legendary and it was said they would roll on wet grass. Comparisons with their larger naval sisters were natural.

"Corvettes I am sure were unsinkable; they shipped a lot of water," says Donald McNeille of Ellerhouse, N.S., a stoker petty officer in *Strathroy* in 1944-45. "They did not cut through the swells as a large ship did, but rode right up to the crest and down the other side, with propeller in the clear lots of times. You saw them one minute and the next they were out of sight."

Morley Barnes of Mississauga, Ont., a stoker in *Kincardine* in 1944-45, says: "They rode the waves like a cork. Destroyers went through the waves rather than riding the waves. In any event, corvettes sure could take an awful lot of punishment."

Bill Ivy of Mississauga, Ont., leading telegraphist in *Sorel* in 1941-42, observes: "While corvettes were very seaworthy, they were the next thing to perpetual motion. That introduction made my time on future ships, a destroyer and a frigate, seem luxurious."

Doug Lynn of Victoria, B.C., a leading seaman in *Louisburg* in 1941-42, says, "After serving on the destroyer *Saguenay* I sure found her small, but I rapidly gained respect for corvettes after several bouts with foul weather."

Leslie McLean of Victoria, B.C., an ERA in *Port Arthur* in 1942, declares: "They were blood brothers to a cork when it came to riding out a rough sea. So, life aboard a corvette had its ups and downs, if you'll pardon the pun!"

Arnold Gurney of Surrey, B.C., a stoker in *Agassiz* in 1941, also feels strongly about the rough ride: "I always said that after serving in one of these ships I could give any cowboy a run for his money at the Calgary Stampede." And Reg Baker, who served in three corvettes, concurs: "They were great sea ships. They could stand almost anything the weather handed out, but they were like trying to ride a bucking bronco."

Ray Burwash believes, "The corvette was probably the most rugged and seaworthy ship ever built, for any navy. Most old corvette vets rated the enemy as follows: 1) a winter North Atlantic gale; 2) a summer North Atlantic gale; and 3) the U-boat.

"However, with all their moaning and groaning and with the many hardships they had to endure, each corvette

Viewed from above are *Louisburg* crew members (from left) Steve Schumneffel, Chris Protopapas, Jim Hawes, Bill Gilbert.

man had a deep or secret love affair with this particular ship. He wouldn't admit it to his mates, but it was always there. Or, if you asked him what type of ship he would choose to go through a horrendous gale in, say with some chance of going down, he would quickly say, 'Corvette!'"

* * *

Christmas often caps the year and 1941 is still remembered by some. George Auby in *Sorel* was in "Newfiejohn," as St. John's was known: "We had a few days tied up at Bowrings wharf and celebrated Christmas. One of my signalmen by the name of Johnson was the youngest on the ship and took over the duties of captain for the day. He immediately spliced the main brace [ordered a tot of rum for everyone]."

Les Badger of Cambridge, Ont., now a leading seaman, recalls being at sea in *Spikenard*: "Christmas Day was a wonderfully calm day. Overnight we had lashed a small Christmas tree to the masthead and we had a record player blasting out carols. The CO had turned the wheel over to the youngest crew member aboard and we raced towards the destroyer *Saguenay* with music blaring. We came so close that I think we could have shaken hands with her crew."

Howard Cousins of Mississauga, Ont., a leading signalman in *Algoma*, has fond memories:

This is not a tale of a typical Christmas aboard a corvette with decorations and a turkey dinner. This celebration took place on Christmas Eve and of the six Christmases I spent in the navy, it is the one that stands out most in my memory.

It had been a longer trip than usual escorting a slow convoy that was diverted far to the north in an attempt to dodge the submarine wolf packs. We had been assaulted by almost continuous gales. Wet, cold and exhausted, we entered the still waters of Hvalfjord about noon on December 24, 1941. We tied up alongside the oiler to refuel. Later, we proceeded up the fjord to the anchorage. We cleaned up the messdeck, washed and put on a change of clothes and felt a renewed interest in life. To top if off, the mail boat arrived alongside. It was the biggest delivery we had ever received, with virtually everyone getting several letters and parcels. Silence settled over the mess as all were engrossed in letters from home.

After supper, with everyone in a benign mood, we put on an extra pot of coffee and opened our parcels. Cookies, fudge and other goodies were put out on the table. We shared each other's treats and settled into a Bacchanalian feast.

A telegraphist had installed speakers in the messdeck. They were wired to the radio shack and could be hooked to the radio or a record turntable. One signalman, Dick Balsdon, was a born entertainer and a perfect mimic. Before long he was up in the radio shack playing our favourite records, interspersed with commentary and his own version of commercials for such items as gourmet restaurants, pusser's rum and ladies' lingerie.

He interrupted the program to tell us in his own voice that the shortwave radio had announced that at

Courtesy Wm. John Quinsey/Hugh Merryweather Collection

Two *Louisburg* anti-aircraft gunners with their twin .50 caliber machine-guns.

Courtesy Eleanor Cousins

Leading Signalman Howard Cousins (left) operates the *Algoma* signal projector in 1941.

8 p.m. the station would broadcast a Christmas Eve speech by President Roosevelt. Word of this must have made its way to the wardroom because we received a message asking if the officers could join us in the messdeck to hear it. In due course, they joined us and Dick's voice came over the speakers telling us he would try to tune in radio station WBFN or some such to pick up Roosevelt's speech. After a bit of static and a few squeaks and squawks — he was a good imitator — an American voice came over the speakers and introduced the president of the United States of America.

Roosevelt started talking about national affairs and the war in Europe. Then our interest picked up as he referred to "our gallant neighbour to the north." Our interest was really grabbed when he made some stirring comments about the Royal Canadian Navy. For the first time, seeds of suspicion entered my mind. Then when Roosevelt started talking about HMCS *Algoma*, our ship, I dispatched a shipmate to warn Dick that the officers were in the mess listening to every word.

Roosevelt's voice went on saying what a brave, dedicated crew the ship had, what a wonderful job she was doing and how much better a job she could do if only the officers were as good as the men. He

just started to comment on the abilities of the captain when we heard another voice in the background. There was a series of squeaks and squawks and a voice came on saying that due to atmospheric conditions, they regretted that contact with WBFN had been lost and they would go back to the musical program. After a prudent delay, Dick returned to the mess with a mischievous grin.

The end of Dick's broadcast did not end the party. The band set up — a mouth organ that carried the tune, a Jew's harp, a bass made from a mop and a washtub, and a washboard. A percussionist with a pair of drumsticks made creditable noises on the tabletop and assorted pans, pot lids and bottles. We had a lusty sing-song, irreverently alternating navy songs with Christmas carols. Some men danced gracefully with empty duffel coats or mops as partners. Eventually, stuffed with good food and also tired, but with a feeling of goodwill, we slung our hammocks and turned in to sleep the sleep of the innocent.

I expect that we celebrated Christmas Day in an appropriate manner and enjoyed ourselves, but it was the night before that we really had fun and that is the part of Christmas 1941 that is retained in my memory.

Spikenard, K198, is docked at Halifax, N.S., in 1941.

CHAPTER FIVE

"I DO REMEMBER HIM TELLING ME IT WAS SO COLD ON THE NORTH ATLANTIC, SO COLD..."

THE SCOPE of World War II changed abruptly after the bombing of Pearl Harbor. American concern and resources were focused on the Pacific theatre. In early 1942, the Allies turned to reorganizing their operations in the Atlantic. Canadian sailors did not mourn one casualty of this process — the Iceland Run.

Iceland, a neutral state under the Danish crown, was in a strategic position along the North Atlantic sea routes. After the German invasion of Denmark in April 1940, the United Kingdom occupied Iceland and established a naval base at Hvalfjord, as well as air and army bases. Canadian troops even formed part of the garrison there in 1940-41. Decidedly unsure of British survival, Iceland approached the neutral United States for protection. Eventually, the Americans were invited in. Still, in the early days, many residents of the capital, Reykjavik, were not terribly welcoming to the foreign military personnel.

One of the Canadian corvettes making the run to Reykjavik was *Spikenard*. She was an unusual ship, not least because of the tone set by her captain, Lieutenant-Commander Hubert G. ("Bert") Shadforth, Royal Canadian Naval Reserve, 53, of Vancouver.

"Shadforth was a very experienced Merchant Navy officer in Canada and was a professional West Coast marine pilot," says Joe Marston of Victoria, B.C., a *Spikenard* sub-lieutenant who was later drafted off the ship. "In addition, he was a most popular officer, very highly regarded by both subordinates and superiors. His sense of humour was legendary and the little stage acts he was capable of delivering were always in demand at parties. Faint recollections remain of a rousing party

aboard *Saguenay* while we were at anchor in Iceland in the spring of '41. It was attended by *Spikenard* and *Snowberry*. Suitably adorned with a church pennant for a surplice, Shadforth entertained with his famous act as preacher, which could always be counted on to bring the house down."

Leading Seaman Les Badger remembers the time Shadforth, the oldest man on the ship, came aboard while the popular youngest crew member, Ordinary Seaman Ted Hounsell of Montreal, was over the side on a staging painting the ship's pennant number, K198: "The captain leaned over and heckled the rating about his artistic ability. The rating irreverently responded with an 'If you can do any better. ...'

"The CO turned to me and asked if I had a pair of coveralls that would fit him. I did and brought them to him. He donned them and a toque and shinnied down the lines to the staging and went at it with a paint brush. About 20 minutes later, an RCN commander came aboard and inquired of the whereabouts of the CO. I took him to the area where the artistic endeavours were happening, and where he asked the CO what the hell he was doing. He got the same response: 'If you can do any better. ...'

"However, I took the commander, bent over with laughter, to the wardroom to await the CO's arrival."

In keeping with naval tradition, at Christmas 1941, Ted Hounsell, as the youngest crew member, was made "captain" for the day. "We put the captain's uniform on him and the sleeves came near to his knees," recalls Reg MacMillan, of Sherwood, P.E.I., a *Spikenard* stoker first class.

Spikenard, K198, is tied up at Halifax, N.S., with other corvettes in 1941.

Les Badger adds: "Shadforth was a great guy. It was one of the happiest ships in the navy. Everyone would do anything for the other guy."

Telegraphist Wilf Mills, of Mississauga, Ont., says: "We had one fantastic skipper. He could tell how far he was from shore merely from tooting the whistle and listening to the echo. He was a good man, real good."

Spikenard made her last trip from Iceland in January 1942 with ON 52. Wilf Mills recalls it well: "On our last westward voyage all the escorts took a savage beating. During the storm one of the wireless telegraphy aerials came down and guess who got sent up to splice it — out on the end of the yard-arm, no safety belt, no life preserver!"

Badger relates: "We ran into one hell of a storm. It was almost impossible to maintain any type of station-keeping

and it was every ship for herself. We read a signal from the senior officer, *Saguenay*, that the New Zealand ship *Kiwi* was in trouble and we were designated to go to her assistance."

MacMillan says: "I remember the incident with *Kiwi*. She was practically sinking; we stood by her for 48 hours."

It was in this period, says Badger, that CO Shadforth wanted the starboard seaboat brought inboard: "All ratings who were not seasick or otherwise turned to were busy, so it was myself and the Jimmy, Lieutenant Robert Hughes [of Dundas, Ont.], who put lines on and climbed out into the seaboat. Just then the mother of all breakers hit *Spike* on the starboard side and away I went. I was found rolling between the stern depth charge racks, unconscious. I have no coherent recollection of anything

HMS *Spikenard* alongside at Davie Shipbuilding in Lauzon, Que., in early December 1940.

The four *Spikenard* officers at one point in 1941 are (from left): Sub-Lieutenant Joe Marston, Lieutenant Rod Knight, unidentified and Lieutenant-Commander Bert Shadforth.

until I was talking to a medical officer in a makeshift hospital in St. John's."

Spikenard next did anti-submarine patrols down to Cape Race on Newfoundland's southeastern tip and picked up some bodies of merchant seaman from a torpedoed ship. As well, the crew claimed "a big old merchant navy raft," recalls MacMillan.

The ship was out about eight days in late January 1942, before taking on provisions in St. John's for the next eastward ocean trip with convoy SC 67. "A day or two before Spikenard was to sail, Lieutenant-Commander Shadforth came to see me in the hospital and told me the medical officer would not give me the okay to sail with the ship," Badger recalls. "The CO told me, however, that he was coming back for me and that I was still part of the ship's company."

When *Spikenard* sailed on February 1, 1942, it was not to Iceland, but to Londonderry, Northern Ireland, which had become the eastern terminus for Canadian mid-ocean escorts after they handed their convoy over to the local British escort. The Newfie-Derry Run, the most famous of all convoy routes in World War II, was inaugurated on January 10, 1942, when convoy SC 64 departed Newfoundland with an escort of the destroyer *Ottawa* and the corvettes *Barrie, Buctouche, Hepatica, Moose Jaw* and *Sherbrooke*. The escorts reached Loch Foyle on January 23. Being more southerly, this route was shorter and faster than the trip to Iceland, thus permitting better use of the limited stock of Allied escorts.

SC 67 was a small convoy of only 22 merchant ships in seven columns, with the centre column containing four ships and the other columns three ships each. The escort

stationed beyond the perimeter was six RCN corvettes. An all-corvette escort was unusual on the mid-ocean run and it appears that *Spikenard* only sailed because the intended senior escort, an old destroyer, could not. The senior officer was *Spikenard,* based on the rank and seniority of her commanding officer, Lieutenant-Commander Shadforth, who had been a Royal Navy officer in World War I.

Spikenard's sister escorts were *Chilliwack, Dauphin, Lethbridge, Louisburg* and *Shediac*. Nearing the point where the convoy was to meet the local British escort, *Spikenard* was zigzagging ahead of the convoy's starboard column at about 9:30 p.m. ship's time [2330 Greenwich Mean Time], on the very dark night of February 10, 1942.

The closest escort was *Louisburg* on the starboard side. She was very busy. While attacking a firm sub contact, members of her crew saw a torpedo pass down her port side about 800 to 1,000 yards away and strike a vessel, which was thought to be a merchant ship. *Louisburg* dropped nine depth charges, carried out an anti-submarine sweep for about 90 minutes and then returned to the convoy.

In fact, *Spikenard* and *Heina*, the second ship in the starboard column, had each been struck by a torpedo. *Heina* may well have been hit by the torpedo *Louisburg* spotted. The two explosions were nearly simultaneous, certainly no more than two minutes apart. "A merchant ship was on fire, but I don't know who got hit first," recalls Mills. "We were kind of busy at the time."

While moving on, ships in convoy observed a vessel burning fiercely for a few minutes, but the two explosions were so close in timing and location that only *Dauphin*

Taken from *Chilliwack* on February 10, 1942, this view of *Spikenard* in convoy is likely the last photo of the corvette, which was sunk about 12 hours later.

about three miles away thought two ships had been hit. Her officers felt the first one was a tanker, but they did not grasp that the other victim was *Spikenard.*

On the port side of the convoy, *Chilliwack* attacked a sub contact and at the stern *Lethbridge* remained in position. *Dauphin* came across the smoking *Heina,* now astern of the convoy, and carried out an asdic sweep for a U-boat. *Dauphin* next spent considerable time picking up 30 or 31 *Heina* survivors from two lifeboats and a raft, then stood by the crippled tanker until she sank, probably just after midnight.

Meanwhile, *Shediac,* coming up from the rear, made one attack on an asdic contact, searched further for a U-boat, then searched unsuccessfully for a second sinking victim or survivors. She finally rejoined *Dauphin* and they returned to the convoy in company.

Essentially, all the escorts were preoccupied with the matters at hand. Their primary duty was to protect the

convoy, which moved on, and they had to be alert for further action. At the time of the attack, and overnight, the other escorts couldn't raise *Spikenard* by radio, which wasn't unusual because the equipment wasn't reliable. And so the night passed.

There are conflicting statements about when the convoy was joined by the British local escort group, but, regardless, the absence of *Spikenard* was not noted until the morning. It was in daylight that the realization dawned in *Dauphin* that *Spikenard* was the other ship that had been torpedoed. The upshot was that although *Spikenard* was torpedoed at about 9:30 p.m. ship's time, it was not until 13 hours later that the British corvette *Gentian* was sent back along the convoy's course to look for her.

"It was a dark night and the seas were relatively calm," says Mills. "We were not closed up for action stations, or I wouldn't be writing this now! My action station was on the engine room telegraph [in the wheelhouse] directly above where the torpedo exploded. I was in the forecastle at the moment of impact, off duty. Some sort of premonition made me get up and dress.

"When the torpedo exploded, it destroyed the stoker's mess and the wardroom and tore upward through the bridge structure, leaving it in ribbons of steel and setting the well deck on fire. I covered my head with a coat and ran through the flames, sustaining third-degree burns on my hands, only to fall into the hole full of water. From there I climbed to the upper deck over the strips of steel to my abandon ship station, which was the port Carley float. People came up out of the stokehold. I was so stunned I couldn't get the Carley float free and someone else came and cut it loose.

"Whether there were other people in the water, I cannot tell you. All was confusion. ... We started out on a port side Carley float from the upper deck, which by this time was level with the water. We caught up with a raft and transferred to it. The convoy steamed on unaware that *Spikenard* had been hit."

Reg MacMillan was resting in dungarees and sweater in his bunk in the chiefs' and petty officers' mess aft. "She was torn in two by the torpedo," he says. "It hit under the bridge. It just blew her to pieces." Reaching the deck, he cut the rope to release the port Carley float. Three men [MacMillan, Mills and George Morrison] initially moved off in the float.

It appears that Alex Day had worked to release the raft. Later, in a letter to Bert Shadforth's brother, he explained that following the underwater explosion "I had a miraculous escape after being blown off the raft and coming to under the water going down with the ship. I made the surface, heard them talking on the float and swam to them."

The men quickly came upon the merchant navy raft that had floated free, MacMillan says. They lashed the two together and transferred to the raft since it floated higher. "You were quite a ways out of the water. It wasn't like the Carley float where you were in the water."

In all, eight men reached the raft in short order. They were: Engine Room Artificer Alex Day of Verdun, Que.; Stoker Petty Officer Harold Laabs, most recently of Fort William, Ont.; Acting Leading Seaman Russell Deans of Trail, B.C.; Stoker 1st Class Reg MacMillan of Mount Stewart, P.E.I.; Stoker 1st Class George Morrison of Pictou, N.S.; Signalman John (Jack) Whitworth of Hamilton, Ont.; Te-

Spikenard Stoker Petty Officer Hal Laabs in 1941.

legraphist Wilf Mills of Toronto, Ont.; and Able Seaman Dennis Cowan of Ottawa, Ont.

Spikenard then sank. In MacMillan's mind, her bow went down first, "but she still had way on," meaning she was still moving forward. Next there was a second explosion, this one from the aft part of the ship. It was likely caused by cold water rushing into the hot No. 2 boiler, but it might have been depth charges. No one will ever know for sure.

The whole thing happened very quickly. MacMillan believes the ship went down in two minutes. Mills estimates three minutes. The initial damage was so extensive, and the sinking so rapid, that *Spikenard* was unable to get off an emergency signal. The ship's whistle added to the chaos. "A lanyard [a rope to pull the whistle] ran from the bridge to the [smoke]stack and the mast fell across it, so the steam whistle blew continuously," says Mills. It was a requiem for the corvette.

After the second explosion, the eight men in the raft hauled aboard two shipmates suffering badly from internal injuries. They heard the shouts of others, but couldn't locate anyone else in the dark before the voices died out. *Spikenard's* final resting place is a position about 500 miles south of Iceland and 500 miles west of Ireland.

The men were not dressed for prolonged exposure to the North Atlantic in February. They were cold and huddled together for warmth as best they could. The raft contained water and some emergency provisions. "You know something," says Wilf Mills, "I hated corned beef and all that was on that raft was corned beef and sea biscuits and I wouldn't eat it." Reg MacMillan also recalls that water was the only thing consumed. The men, however, were bothered by the lack of "smokes." The only cigarettes they had were sodden.

There was little chit-chat, says Reg MacMillan. Describing Harold Laabs as a good friend, he said: "He was a little short guy. He was argumentative. He always brought me along to get him out of it, but I liked him." As for any decisions, "it was between him and Day," the two senior survivors. "There were no votes or anything like that. Laabs was a petty officer and he had a lot to say. Day was quiet."

Shortly after midnight, one of the two late additions, an acting leading stoker from Dundas, Ont., died. "Cyril Kitchen — we always called him Gus — died in my lap from internal injuries suffered when the ship blew up underwater," Mills recalls. "One of the heartbreaking times for me was when I was home on leave and his father phoned wanting to know about his son." Kitchen's body was stripped to provide clothing for the others, a prayer was said and the body was slipped over the side. This sad but necessary process was repeated about 9:30 in the morning with the death of Charles Regalbuto, a young ordinary seaman from Ottawa, Ont., who had just joined *Spikenard*.

There was no obvious panic or thought of not being picked up, MacMillan insists, even after an airplane went by on the morning of February 11th without sighting them.

From a distance, a small raft is only a tiny speck on a huge expanse of ocean, so the *Spikenard* survivors were fortunate they were finally spotted by *Gentian* and picked up late on the afternoon of February 11th after 18-1/2 hours in the raft.

Gentian's commanding officer, Lieutenant F.V. Osborne of the Royal Australian Navy, interviewed the eight survivors. "From what they told me it was immediately ap-parent that there was little likelihood of anyone else having survived. … However, I searched the area for two hours without seeing any float or any wreckage at all."

Given their ordeal, the eight survivors were in pretty good shape, although Wilf Mills, Russell Deans, Dennis Cowan and Jack Whitworth were hospitalized for treatment of burns. "All praise to the surgeons that looked after us in the hospital in Liverpool," says Mills.

Osborne concluded that most of the damage was on the port side. Fire broke out immediately. Both seaboats were destroyed. The action stations bell rang just as the ship was hit and the men up front did not hear it. Mills can agree with that, but he admits: "We [the survivors] had arranged beforehand to say we were at action stations to protect our captain, who perished, but we were not."

Osborne deduced that other ships in the convoy, and possibly the other escort vessels, assumed that the burning ship was *Heina,* but it was actually *Spikenard*. This, he felt, "accounts for the fact that it was not known until next morning that *Spikenard* had been attacked."

The Aussie also reported: "The senior rating survivor, ERA Day, told me that with his approval it was decided on the raft that Stoker PO Laabs should take charge, that he did so, and did valuable work in keeping up the men's spirits. ERA Day asked me to mention this fact."

The board of inquiry held February 20th decided that *Spikenard* and *Heina* were probably torpedoed by the same U-boat. Post-war examination of German records verified this and identified *U-136.*

"Though the explosion was undoubtedly enough to sink the ship, the fire increased the disaster by burning the bridge and wireless office, with their personnel, and one of the boats, besides contributing to other casualties," the board reported. "It seems at least possible that the fire was augmented by the drum of petrol stowed beside the mast."

Of particular importance, the board endorsed the policy of having other escorts attack U-boat contacts before undertaking rescue operations, but it also found: "No flares were provided for any boats, rafts or floats and it is our opinion that the survivors would have been rescued almost at once, and many more therefore discovered, had a flare been exhibited when an unknown corvette [*Shediac*] passed shortly after the ship sank."

Deciding that seaboats "can seldom be used" after a torpedoing, the board recommended that lifesaving rafts and Carley floats be provided for at least the whole ship's company, and that these should contain methods for drawing attention, including flares.

The report in a file at the National Defence Directorate of History and Heritage indicates that the board noted that the ship was flooded below the waterline at once, but the upper messdeck could not be made watertight because there was no watertight hatch to the flooded lower messdeck. It recommended such a hatch be installed in corvettes to improve the chances of saving ships.

The final recommendation of the board was "special mention" of Laabs "for resourcefulness and fortitude." As no award was forthcoming, it appears that the navy brass did not act on this.

At this early stage in the convoy war, maintenance was poor or worse, but ships were sent out regardless. The January 29, 1942, entry in *Spikenard*'s handwritten log in the Directorate of History and Heritage in Ottawa says, "RDF aerial carried away at sea." RDF stands for Radio Direction Finding, what we now know as radar. One file at Library and Archives Canada reads, "Replacement of this unit is beyond present capabilities of St. John's Base staff due to lack of time and facilities." A second memo says, "*Spikenard* left Newfoundland without her RDF working due to the fact that the Newfoundland fitting staff was unable to carry out repairs." In an apparent effort to underscore the significance of this shortcoming, this memo by Commander A.R. Pressey, superintendent of the Anti-Submarine Branch, concludes with the following: "Note: *Spikenard* was torpedoed at night."

Reg MacMillan recalls that, "On the day of the torpedoing, the *Spike* had no asdic, RDF or radio. Her only communications was by Aldis lamp to the other ships. ... But we were senior ship, so we stayed in position." In effect, neither her eyes [radar] nor her ears [asdic] were functioning that dark night and she was pretty close to speechless, too. Her opponents had no such handicaps.

* * *

In those days, long before the world was linked by television and the Internet, newspapers were the main medium of public communication in Canada, followed by radio and newsreels at the local theatre. When announcement of the sinking was made in Ottawa on February 19, 1942, nine days after *Spikenard* went down, it was big news in papers across the country.

The *Toronto Daily Star* was given to running large headlines. February 19th was certainly no exception. Three headlines ran the entire width of the paper at the top of the front page. The uppermost headline in thick black lettering one-and-one-half inches high was the largest. It said: "CANADA CORVETTE, 57 MEN LOST." The story on the sinking was titled "Spikenard sunk by Nazi U-Boat Ottawa reveals." Also on the front page were a list of casualties, a wide photo of a corvette and a two-column photo of *Spikenard* first lieutenant Bob Hughes, formerly a staff writer for the *Star*. On page 3 the paper published an article about life in a corvette on the North Atlantic that was, with the navy's approval, the product of a recent collaboration between Hughes and a reporter.

The Gamble family of Galt, Ont., in 1941: Elizabeth, Bill, Colleen and Jack.

The eight *Spikenard* survivors after being picked up by the British corvette *Gentian* are (front, from left): Wilf Mills, Alex Day, Harold Laabs, Reg MacMillan; (rear) John Whitworth, George Morrison, Dennis Cowan and Russell Deans.

Other coverage followed in many papers a week later when three crew members were interviewed in London on their way back to Canada on survivor's leave, and then later still when survivors were interviewed by local papers on their arrival home. In the spirit of the day, some of the coverage was bellicose. An example is the headline "Spikenard crew to make Nazis pay" in the *Montreal Star* on February 27, 1942, over a Canadian Press story containing statements that the survivors had a grudge to settle with the Germans and pledged to avenge their shipmates' deaths. "Take these clippings with a grain of salt," survivor Wilf Mills advises. "I'm afraid the reporters indulged in flights of imagination."

Most common of all was a wartime version of the standard newspaper obituary. This story in the victim's local paper would contain the news from the navy that the man was missing and presumed lost, a photo if available and information from the parents.

The *Spikenard* toll was 57 dead — all five officers and 52 men. They came from eight of Canada's nine provinces, Ontario claiming 23 and Quebec 13. Two were from the United Kingdom.

* * *

The story of a ship is largely the story of people. Dutch Davey of Sarnia, Ont., a radar operator, says: "I was drafted from *Spikenard* because a crew member I had replaced came back from being sick and requested his old ship. I was in the destroyer *St. Laurent* when *Spikenard* was reported missing and never did get information at the time."

Lorna Zigar of Newcastle, Ont., says: "My mother and I were in England when war broke out. We remained there. My favourite brother, [Probationary Steward] Dan Watts from Saskatoon, Sask., was serving in *Spikenard*.

"My brother was to leave the ship in [Northern] Ireland and come home on compassionate leave as my mother was dying of cancer. We received a wire from the navy to this effect. My mother passed away and just about a week later I received a telegram addressed to her saying Danny was missing and believed lost. Thank God she never did live to hear this. My sister visited the four injured boys in the hospital."

Mrs. Helen Higgins of Rockport, Ont., describes the reaction in her family at the loss of her brother, Able Seaman John Robert Hall of Brockville, Ont., "Our family was devastated and mother and father had a hard time accepting it. For years they wouldn't talk about Jack, and they wouldn't get in touch with the eight survivors."

Elizabeth Gamble of Galt, now part of Cambridge, Ont., was another who received a telegram. It came on February 18, 1942. The rest of her life was changed by the short message: "The Minister of National Defence for Naval Services deeply regrets to inform you that your husband John McIlveen Gamble, engine-room artificer 4/c, Royal Canadian Naval Volunteer Reserve, official No. V8328, is missing believed lost on active service."

A blacksmith by trade, Jack Gamble was born in Northern Ireland. He worked in the Belfast shipyards before emigrating to Canada. "He was a petty officer, an engineer," Reg MacMillan recalls, "a smart man, a very nice guy. He was going to be able to visit his folks in Northern Ireland."

Jack Gamble had been in the army reserve for eight years and joined the RCNVR in December 1939. At 39, he was an old-timer in a volunteer navy full of youngsters. He left a wife and two children, ages seven and five. Mrs. Gamble, one of 14 widows created by the sinking, didn't get much immediate help from the navy — the balance of Jack Gamble's wages totalled only $34.72, which was sent to her on April 30, 1942. She got a job in a textile factory and raised her two kids in the family home. She never remarried and received a widow's pension from the federal Department of Veterans Affairs. Elizabeth Gamble died in 1990 at age 88.

Les Badger recalls the sinking aftermath: "I was in the hospital in St. John's when the MO [medical officer] came and told me that the ship had gone down with all hands. I was still aboard *Spikenard* on February 14 according to my service records.

"My brother, who was HSD in the corvette *Chicoutimi*, was in the convoy behind the ill-fated one. His CO, who knew us both, told him of the sinking and that all hands had gone down with her. He was somewhat surprised when he returned to Halifax and found out I was okay. He turned up at the door of my fiancée on the eve of our wedding day, March 14, 1942, and, to have him as the best man, we had to change our plans. Talk about confusion."

Les Badger read in a naval history that there were survivors, but for 49 years he was unsuccessful in verifying this or contacting any of them. It took this author more than two years to trace all eight. For a small group they experienced much misfortune.

George Morrison of Pictou, N.S., 22, a stoker first class, died on October 2, 1942, when the car in which he was a passenger left the road and plunged down a steep embankment near Kentville, N.S.

Michael Cowan of Kingston, Ont., a World War II air force veteran, had paid several visits to *Spikenard* in port in Newfoundland. He says his brother, Dennis, an able seaman from Ottawa, "never volunteered much information about the sinking, even though he was a bit of an extrovert. It was sort of a hard subject for him. You know, it changed him for a considerable amount of time. It was a very sobering experience. He sort of got mellow for a while but that eventually wore off and he returned to his happy-go-lucky self.

"After the war, being single and adventurous, Dennis went up north with a friend. For a while he was in the mines in Northern Ontario. Then he decided to go to Great Slave Lake [in the Northwest Territories] because things were picking up there. He got into a fishing business — whitefish. He invested in nets and a snow machine [using his re-establishment allowance from the Department of Veterans Affairs]. They were doing a lot of ice fishing, putting their nets down through the ice.

"This one day they were out and they hit an air pocket under the ice. Their snowmobile went through and Dennis and another fellow were drowned. The bodies were never recovered." It was December 1951. Dennis Cowan was 32. "It was quite a shock to me," says his brother Michael. "It was a tragic thing. It was kind of ironic, after surviving the North Atlantic."

Violet Frances Day of Verdun, Que., was the wife of Alex Day, 34, an engine room artificer when *Spikenard* went down. "I put all these memories out of my mind a long time ago, in order to carry on and take care of my home and my daughter during the war years," she explains. "We were so young and knew so little about life.

"He was a man from the sea. He loved the sea. Before he was married he was around the world working on ships." But after the torpedoing, she says, "he couldn't go back to sea right away. He was a nervous wreck for a while. He used to sit bolt upright in bed at first and yell 'Action stations!' It gave me a fright. They put him ashore."

While ashore, Alex Day became an officer. A man of religious conviction, he had compassion for the families of his departed shipmates who had been told their

His Spike is on display at the Crow's Nest in St. John's, Nfld.

loved one was missing and presumed lost. "He wanted to confirm for the Griffin family of Verdun that their son [Patrick] really was dead," Violet Day explains. "We went to see the families of all those in Montreal who had men in *Spikenard*."

In a letter to Bert Shadforth's brother, Alex Day wrote: "*Spikenard* was a very happy ship due to the consideration shown the crew by her officers. Your brother, sir, did not stand on formality, but treated us all as human beings. … He was regarded with the greatest respect. We lost a man we could ill afford to lose. You have every reason to be proud of your brother."

After the war, Alex Day worked as a stationary engineer and maintenance manager. He was forced into early retirement by ill health. Suffering from cancer and Parkinson's disease, he died in August 1970 at age 63. "He was buried at sea," Mrs. Day said. "His request was that he be buried in the North Atlantic which almost got him once."

Stoker Petty Officer Harold Laabs had no next of kin in 1942 and lost touch with the other survivors. Initial research revealed only that he died in Tonawanda, New York, near Buffalo, on February 22, 1972, 30 years to the month after his ship was sunk. We now know that he visited and offered to assist the struggling widow and young daughter of his *Spikenard* buddy Chief ERA Art MacLean. It also appears that he later married and raised a family.

William Whitworth says his brother, Jack, got out of the navy in 1945 as a chief petty officer. "He never did talk much about the sinking," William says. "He did say she was hit midship and split in two. There were 10 on a raft. Two died. He said it was pretty cold."

Excerpt of Letter From Marc Shaw

Following the publication of *Corvettes Canada* in 1994, Marc Shaw of Kingston, Ont., composed a letter to the author shedding additional light on the aftermath of *Spikenard*'s loss:

April 9, 1994   Kingston, Ont.

Dear Mr. Johnston:

I felt I had to write, both to let you know how much I appreciated your research, and to give you some further information, for so much of the book was relevant to me and my family.

My grandfather, John Arthur (Art) MacLean, was acting as chief engine room artificer aboard *Spikenard* when she was torpedoed. He was only 32 at the time, married with an eight-year-old daughter (my mother), and living in Rosemount, Montreal. Even at that young age, he was a veteran sailor, having worked on the Great Lakes since about the age of 14. He had enlisted in 1940.

My grandmother never remarried. The precarious financial situation she found herself in following her husband's loss forced her to move with my mother to her own mother's home here in Kingston. Following a long history of ill health (asthma and arthritis), she died in October 1990, two months short of her 80th birthday.

After her death, an old candy box, tied up with lace, came into my possession. The contents turned out to be my grandfather's letters to her, written aboard *Spikenard*, on leave in Halifax, and from points in England and

Spikenard Chief ERA Art MacLean with wife Louise and daughter Rose.

Scotland. The letters, 34 in number, cover a two-year period leading right up to *Spikenard*'s last trip. They tell much of his life in the service and his loneliness at being separated from his family. They are chatty, by turns upbeat and melancholy, and intensely human. Most poignant of all for me were an additional five or six envelopes addressed to my grandfather from my grandmother, which never reached him. These letters had been opened and returned to sender, less the contents.

In the same box were also the letters and notes of sympathy received by my grandmother from friends, relatives and people from the service who knew my grandfather. These were also very affecting. One was from Harold Laabs, one of the *Spikenard* survivors mentioned in your book. His letter expressed his feelings at having lost his best friend aboard ship. Explaining that he had no family obligations of his own, he offered to help my grandmother and mother financially. He also offered to tell her, if she wished to know, what he knew of my grandfather's actions at the time of the sinking. He said that he was the last to see my grandfather and the last to leave the ship.

Well, he and my grandmother did meet, on a number of occasions. I don't know anything about what they discussed or what my grandmother learned. My mother, who was included in and who has fond memories of these get-togethers, believes Mr. Laabs asked my grandmother to marry him, but, owing to her own responsibilities looking after her own mother, she turned him down. At some point soon after, contact was lost. My mother and I had often wondered about trying to track down Mr. Laabs, if he were still alive. Now I know from your book that he died in 1972.

Ever since I was a child, I've been interested in the corvettes and *Spikenard* in particular and I have amassed a pile of excerpts from all the standard books on the navy and the corvettes. …What I didn't have, until now, was much of an idea as to what life aboard *Spikenard* was like. Your book has changed all that and I now feel that the gaps have been largely filled. I wish my grandmother were alive to see this book. Her recollections were few in number. When she spoke of my grandfather she tended, understandably, to dwell on the happier prewar times. Her husband's death certainly created a scar that never healed, and there was always a tinge of sadness about her. She thought of herself as a "war widow" until the day she died. Remembrance Day ceremonies were always difficult for her.

Marc Shaw

After the war, he worked 30 years for Imperial Oil, starting by painting pipeline pipe. His last job was in charge of building Imperial Oil gas stations in southern Ontario. He moved around Ontario with his work and never married. Suffering from emphysema, he retired at 55 because of his poor health. Jack Whitworth died in Hamilton in December 1984 of respiratory problems at age 65. He bequeathed his body to McMaster University in Hamilton for science purposes.

Russell Deans joined the navy before the war and "loved the sea," says his widow, Mary Deans of Castlegar, B.C. "The only way he would talk about the sinking is if he had a couple of drinks too many and then he would only talk to me," she says. "He wouldn't talk about it to others. I do remember him telling that it was so cold on the North Atlantic, so cold. … I think there was a lot that was unpleasant that he'd sooner forget." His post-war naval reminiscences dealt mostly with his service in the destroyer *Haida*. Deans served as postmaster in Castlegar for 35 years. He died suddenly in August 1989.

Some might say that Reg MacMillan lived a charmed life for he also survived the torpedoing of the frigate *Magog* in the Gulf of St. Lawrence in 1944. Following the war, he re-enlisted in the navy and retired in 1969 after 29 years service, then worked as an automotive parts counterman. Ever an optimist, he survived four heart attacks and bypass surgery, before passing away in October 1995 at age 76.

Wilf Mills served 31 years with Ontario Hydro as a stock control analyst and buyer, persevering despite tuberculosis and colon cancer. His son Douglas of Mississauga, Ont., says that his wartime experience was troubling and "steeled his resolve against the need for war." His marriage in Halifax in wartime remained strong until his death in 2001 at age 83. He was the last of the *Spikenard* survivors.

* * *

There is more to the saga of *Spikenard* and SC 67.

Under *Kapitanleutnant* [Lieutenant-Commander] Heinrich Zimmerman, U-136 completed its first active patrol with four kills — *Spikenard,* the Royal Navy corvette *Arbutus,* the Norwegian freighter *Heina* and the British freighter *Empire Comet*. On its second war patrol, U-136 sank three more merchant ships and damaged a fourth. However, upon leaving St. Nazaire, France, on its third patrol, U-136 was sunk in the Atlantic west of Portugal on July 11, 1942, by depth charges from two Royal Navy ships and a French destroyer, with the loss of all 45 crew.

On September 15, 1942, Gus Kitchen was awarded Mention in Dispatches posthumously "for bravery while serving in defensively equipped merchant ships," his assignment previous to *Spikenard*.

In early 1943, two of *Dauphin's* officers, Lieutenant-Commander Robert MacNeil and Sub-Lieutenant Chuck Rathgeb of Toronto, Ont., were presented with the Norwegian War Medal for their gallantry in rescuing the crew of the tanker *Heina* on that fateful night of February 10, 1942.

And although most sources attribute *Heina's* sinking to U-136, several now believe that the stricken tanker was hit later by a torpedo from U-591.

Courtesy Marc Shaw

Art MacLean relaxes while working on a Great Lakes boat prior to World War II.

Spikenard lives on today in both Halifax and St. John's.

In Halifax, a small handmade model of *Spikenard* resides in the Maritime Command Museum. Made for a crew member's sister in the U.K., it was brought back to Canada in 1989 by Bob MacMillan, Reg's son, who was in the crew of a Canadian destroyer which visited there.

In St. John's, the commemoration is even more personal. The downtown seagoing officers' club was reached by climbing 59 wooden steps. Thus, it became known as the Crow's Nest. Opened in January 1942 in what had been a fourth-floor warehouse, the club collected 600 or more mementoes during World War II, particularly the gun-shield logos of warships.

One memento resulted from a challenge the officers of *Spikenard* issued to the officers of *Dauphin, Lethbridge, Louisburg* and *Chilliwack:* an impromptu contest to see who could drive a six-inch spike into the floor with the least number of blows. The complication was the floor itself

— three-inch thick white pine which is "harder than Hades," says Pat Latta, a former president of the club.

The winner was Bert Shadforth. Shortly thereafter, *Spikenard* and Shadforth were lost at sea. A brass ring with the carved inscription "Spikenard His Spike" was inserted around the nail to create a memorial. When the Crow's Nest closed in June 1945, the spike and surrounding floorboard were cut out and sent to a naval officers' club in Montreal where they went on display in a wooden frame. Back in St. John's, a new piece of floorboard had been installed, complete with a circle of brass and a spike to indicate the spot of the original.

The Crow's Nest reopened in June 1946 with a broader membership and souvenirs began drifting back to St. John's. About 1967 the naval association in Montreal returned the remaining artifacts when the Montreal club closed. Today, the *Spikenard* symbol is back in its original home, only this time it's mounted on a pillar, just a few feet from the floor marker. It's not well known, but the floor spikes themselves have been filched and replaced a number of times. Still, it's all a fitting memorial to another time and His Spike has become the club's most treasured artifact.

In February 2007, the 65th anniversary of the loss of HMCS *Spikenard* was commemorated in St. John's with a program titled Three Days of Remembrance. Informally called a Corvette Wake, it was *the* event in the city with extensive media coverage. The Crow's Nest Officers' Club played a prominent role, but the long list of participants included the provincial government, the lieutenant-governor, the city, Canadian Forces Station St. John's, the shore base HMCS *Cabot,* the Naval Officers' Association of Canada and the Canadian Naval Memorial Trust (HMCS *Sackville*).

A ceremony of commemoration was conducted at the war memorial. Placing a wreath in memory of her grandfather was Tahirah Shadforth of Ottawa, whose father was less than a year old when *Spikenard* was lost. During a "make and mend" at the Crow's Nest on February 10, glasses were charged with a tot of rum. At the appointed hour, participants made a toast to *Spikenard* and her crew. A minute of silence followed. There were other weekend events and the naval white ensign was flown from flag staffs in honour of the *Spikenard* anniversary and the Battle of the Atlantic. Guests were present from across Canada, and from Great Britain and Londonderry.

LETTERS FROM ART MACLEAN TO HIS WIFE

May 13th [1941]   c/o General Post Office
HMS *Spikenard*   London Eng

My Darling Wife

Your ever most welcomed letter of April 19th received yesterday and to say I was glad to get it is putting it mildly. So sorry dear that you are not getting all my mail. I am sending you this one via airmail so I hope you get it quicker. Take note when you receive it and answer back by the same method. It seems a long time between our letters so we shall see if this is any better.

   Well anyway dear I was glad to hear that you are well, also Rose and all the rest at home. I am sure that I will hardly know Rose when I get home, which by the way is going to be some time yet by the looks of things, so dear I hope you can bear that news. I know it is hard to take but believe me dear it is no fault of mine that I am here, except that I joined up in the first place. However, it is too late to do anything about that now, so I will just have to put up with it. Anyway dear I was inquiring the other day about putting in for a Warrant Officer. If I take the exam and pass there is a slight chance of getting sent home, I hope, as this ship carries no engineer officer. Of course I am only whistling past the graveyard now. Anyway dear, my left leg is bothering me a lot lately so perhaps I will have to do it the hard way and go sick. I'm no coward dear, but what I see of this war is enough for me. I wish you could see the mess that one night of an air raid would do to these cities and towns. Words could never describe it.

   We have a lad on here from Kingston. His name is Isbell. You might know his father as he works in Anderson's. There is also a lad here from Verdun, in fact there is lads here from all over Canada.

   I don't know dear why I never hear from Mother. I wrote her often enough so when you write her just tell her that I would love to hear from her. I never saw Ted yet dear. I am after some leave [vacation] now but I am afraid that I will have to wait for a few weeks for that. Perhaps then I will be able to see him. Before when I did have a chance to see him I never had enough money. Now I have a couple of extra pounds but it isn't much use to me as I can't get the time I need to spend it, and I might add it is burning a hole in my pocket.

   In my last two letters to you dear I asked for some cigarettes and socks that you said you had. I am asking again, just in case you don't get them, and you might get this letter ahead of them seeing that it is going via airmail. By the way when you send the socks you can also put some candy in the package, Life Savers etc. Of course you know that the cigarettes are sent duty free. Send them like you sent them to Ted.

   Well my dear I guess I will have to close for now so with all of my love for you and Rose.

                                                    I remain your true loving hubby and Pal.

                                                                              Art

                                              * * *

January 29th [1942]   c/o Fleet Mail Office
HMCS *Spikenard*   Halifax N.S.

My Darling Wife

Your 3 most welcomed letters and parcel rec. within the last couple of days and I sure was glad to hear from you dear and to know that you and Rose are well. And speaking of health I am fine, in fact I will know for sure in a few minutes as the MO [medical officer] is on the ship now. He is going to examine us all, just an old naval custom I think. Anyway dear I feel swell, only once in awhile I have a slight heartburn, from overeating or something?

Well dear the parcel was swell. It came at the right moment when we were at supper. The cookies were real good. I might add that they didn't last long once they were tasted. All the boys say they were nice, only not enough of them.

This will be about the last letter that you have from me dear for a month or more so don't go and get all het up over nothing. I wrote you 4 letters since we came in but so far I never received a reply. The mail is awful slow around this place. It is like everything else.

I sure have some swell snaps to show you when I see you all dear. I would like to send them to you but I can't. Anyway keep your eye on the Toronto Star Weekly for the next month or so and you may see them there. They are about a rescue at sea. We had lots of experiences since we came out of refit.

There must be some more mail from you dear for me as you said in one of your letters something about Jess not hearing from Ottawa yet. What is he going to do, join up? Tell him to write me a line and I will give him the lowdown.

Well the Dr. was here and looked us over so once again I am fine, damn it all. I tried to tell him I was sick (I am not) but it made no never mind with him. Of course you can guess what he was looking for.

I am sitting writing here dear with a big bottle of scotch in front of me. This being our last night in port so we generally celebrate it.

Well Honey I guess that is about all the news for now, except that I love you and miss you and Rose something awful. Perhaps within this next 3 months I will be seeing you again so my dear pray and hope that is all I can say about it now.

So my dear with all of my love for you and Rose,
I remain your ever loving hubby and Pal.
Art

LETTERS OF CONDOLENCE TO LOUISE MACLEAN

Dear Louise

I can't tell you on paper how sorry I am for you and Rose to think that Arth's end came so suddenly. He was so young and full of life. But I suppose many go when war is on and they don't all come back. God does all things for the best, so maybe his end was swift and he might have been brought back a cripple and suffered a lot.

And God help you. It will be lonely but you will have to keep up for Rose's sake. Mother is willing and ready to help in any way and Johny will give you a helping in advising you if you need it. But carry on and do your best.

Love to Florence, Rose and Johny. We got Florence's letter this morning. It is a lot colder than in the beginning of the week.

Love to all from Mother

Mrs. Louise MacLean   Orangedale East, In. Co., C.B., N.S.

My Dear Louise
Just a few lines to offer you my sincerest sympathy in the recent loss at sea of your husband Arthur.

There is little to be said in a case of this kind, words seem so futile. There is, of course, the helpful and inspiring thought "He died doing his duty." I'm sure [that,] knowing that, it will help to bear your sorrows better in the years to come.

For myself, if he had to die at this time it would be the way I'd want him, I mean serving his country.

Hoping under the circumstances you and little girl are well, I am

His Father
Chas. J. MacLean

* * *

Dear Louise   Fleet Mail Office, Halifax, N.S.

I know how you feel and there is no use me saying a lot of fancy things that will not help any.

Believe me when I say I am heartbroken, and can't say anything to help.

Your loving Br-in-law
Fred
Love to Rosie, Flo and Johny

* * *

Mrs. Louise MacLean

My Dear Mrs. MacLean
I wish to offer you my deepest sympathies on the tragic death of your husband.

During the past year I have been in the closest contact with the members of the corvettes, and it was only a little over a month ago that I said mass on *Spikenard* when nearly every man went to Confession and Communion. You know these men lead a hard and dangerous life, but the terrible part of all this war is the sad lot of women like yourself who have now to carry on alone. You have the sympathy of all the barracks, but it can mean little unless it accompanies prayer. This morning on a sister ship of *Spikenard* I said mass for the repose of the souls of those whom He in His Infinite Wisdom called so suddenly. Your poor husband John was remembered, as he will be each anniversary mass which will be said every Sunday.

If there is anything that I can do to make this blow less severe, please feel free to command me.

With my full sympathy to your and his family, I am
Yours sincerely
Harold B. Murphy
(RC) Chaplain, RCNV

The corvette *Snowberry* guards starboard flank of North Atlantic convoy, probably in 1942 or 1943.

CHAPTER SIX

"I MET MY HUSBAND AT THE STATEN ISLAND USO."

THE NEWFIE-DERRY RUN, inaugurated in January 1942, gave the Canadian escorts more time in a better European port. "Londonderry was established as a U.S. naval operating base and was much more efficient than either Iceland or St. John's," says Skinny Hayes of Sidney, B.C., an officer in *Trillium*, *Kenogami* and *Guelph*. "Eventually the repair facilities, run entirely by the Americans, were excellent."

This run, which was to last nearly three and a half years — until war's end — was good for the soul, which helped crew morale. "I'll never forget my first glimpse of Ireland," notes Rod Kendall of Thunder Bay, Ont., leading seaman HSD in *Napanee* from 1941-43. "When we left St. John's, it was to all appearances still winter, snowy and cold. We arrived in Loch Foyle on a Sunday morning about 14 days later and it was spring.

"After fuelling at the tanker at Moville, unshipping our asdic dome and taking on a pilot, we took off up the Foyle River for our berth in Derry. That's when I realized why they call Ireland the 'Emerald Isle.' After the drab barrenness of Newfoundland, the green fields of Ireland were truly beautiful."

Robert MacDonald of Lower Sackville, N.B., a telegraphist in *Dundas* in 1942-43, says: "One vivid memory I have is of going up the Foyle River to Londonderry after a bleak and stormy springtime crossing of the grey Atlantic and seeing for the first time the bright green grass and newly leaved-out trees along the shore glistening in the early sunshine."

Don McGivern of Ottawa, a *Summerside* lieutenant in 1943-44, relates: "We would proceed up the west coast of Ireland and around the north shore to Londonderry. What an inviting sight it was to finally see Ireland, with its 50 shades of green, and sail up Loch Foyle, which is like a country lane where it seems you can practically touch the lovely green fields of the estates along the way."

Bern Rawle of Tantallon, N.S., a *Cobalt* stoker in 1942, recalls his first glimpse: "I came up on deck and saw the green fields with the sheep grazing and the sun shining and I was simply overpowered by the fresh smell of the land."

Commerce was conducted at Moville. Manuel Zlatin of Halifax, *Amherst*'s leading supply assistant in 1942-43, explains: "While we were refuelling, bumboats from Southern Ireland would come out to us. They would sell anything from live chickens and geese to silk stockings. They would buy anything: paint, clothes, .303 ammunition, anything of value."

Art Geizer of Halifax, N.S., *Agassiz* coxswain from 1941-45, comments: "It was known that for a few pounds of tea we could acquire three or four half-starved chickens. A few fathoms of rope could also be used for the feathered delicacy — a foul undertaking for fowl."

Jack Nash of Oakville, Ont., a 1943-45 *Owen Sound* telegraphist, says: "The Irish would sell us live chickens and would ring their necks and throw the chicken and the separated head on the deck. Ugh!"

Tom Baird of Woodstock, Ont., recalls an incident at the start of a westward trip during his 1943-44 duty as a *Regina* ERA: "Our messman comes down and says he has a good deal: 12 chickens for four pounds of tea but, alas, he has no tea as it had been traded at a Londonderry bar. On checking the cupboard, we had several cans of English coffee which no one liked, so we decided to cover the top of the coffee with tea for the Free Stater. The messman does this. We got the chickens and were on our way. Well, you would never believe how tough those chickens were. We had one of the best cooks in the navy and no way could he get those chickens tender. They must have died of old age in the zoo. I don't know who beat who, but it was a good try."

Bob Dick of Willowdale, Ont., a telegraphist trained operator in *Napanee* in 1943, recalls: "In our communications mess I usually got the fellows to chip in a couple of bucks. Before leaving Newfie I would buy and store a few things for our mess, especially mayonnaise. When we refuelled at Moville, our interest was bread, lettuce, tomatoes, anything green. We then had a great feed of sandwiches. They sure tasted super. I can still picture sitting there feeding my face beautiful mayonnaise."

From Moville, eastbound escorts took a trip up the Foyle River to Derry. Doug Murch of Cambridge, Ont., a coder in *Agassiz* in 1943-44, recollects: "My first crossing and arrival in Derry was a thrill indeed and a delicious change. We sailed up the Foyle, all escorts in line astern, with bagpipe music swirling proudly from the ship's PA system. Never did anything look so softly green and lovely as those Irish hills towering on the starboard side on that beautiful spring day."

Art Chinery of Hobart, Indiana, a radar operator in *Orangeville* in 1944-45, says: "The highlight of each trip was our arrival in Ireland. The green of Ireland and the land smells were so good after three weeks at sea and the time before that in barren St. John's. We usually followed *Chambly* in procession up the river. At a bend in the river just before we came in sight of Captain D and he of us, we passed a Wrens [Women's Royal Naval Service] barracks and the *Chambly* signalmen hoisted a huge pair of black bloomers to the masthead for the Wrens and then had to replace it within seconds so Captain D would see the proper signal."

George Van Tassel of Rockland, Maine, leading signalman in *Camrose* in 1942-43, recalls: "It was always a great sight going up the Foyle knowing that you were safe for a little while longer. The green grass and the Wrens waving to you as the ship passed the signal station at Broome Hall made one forget all the bad times, the gripes and nattering."

Paul Morse of Parrsboro, N.S., leading stoker in *Ville de Quebec* in 1942-43, recalls, "One time, one of our officers

In 1942, Quartermaster Dutchy Roman with bosun's pipe aboard HMCS *Louisburg*.

called down to the boiler room to make black smoke. He was going with a Wren who was based in a large building near a bend in the river. The wind drift was just right and she got the message — and dirty laundry on the clothesline. They eventually married."

Rodney Pike of Edmonton, captain of *Orangeville* in 1944-45, remembers sailing from Tobermory, Scotland, to Londonderry after workups in May 1944: "We picked up old George Gillespie, the Irish pilot at Moville. He took us up the river and we secured alongside our salt-encrusted sister corvettes at Jetty 10. As was the custom, I gave Mr. Gillespie a full glass of whisky."

William Anderson of Niagara Falls, Ont., a stoker in *Collingwood* in 1941-42, says: "When we started going into Londonderry, it was like money from home. We could even get ashore there, something we couldn't really do in Iceland. And in Ireland the Younger's Ale was nice and dark and tasty. To say nothing of the girls."

A rhythm developed on this run, says Art Chinery: "When we were in harbour we got a lot of shore leave and we partied as much as possible. When we sailed most of us had big heads and sour stomachs. As soon as possible we would get our heads down and sleep a little. I was always happy when I did not have to go on watch after leaving harbour.

"The ship was always very quiet for about a week to 10 days. We caught up on our sleep and generally got used to being at sea again. Then the ship would slowly awaken. We would have cribbage tournaments, bridge tournaments and much more. We'd start cleaning up our tiddlies [uniforms] for the next shore-going in either Ireland or Newfoundland. By the time we hit port, we were ready to go, go, go." William Wainio, a 1942-43 *Trillium* crew member, provides an overview of Derry, which is on the northern tip of Northern Ireland:

> The Foyle River divides the city, the Waterside to the east and Londonderry with its walls to the west. Streets run through what at one time were gates in the wall around the city. Roaring Meg, a huge cannon, is one of the few remaining mementoes of days gone by.
>
> Crews going ashore from the British, American and Canadian flotillas would hardly be classed as sightseers. They were sure to make their first stop at Cassidy's bar, which just happened to be across the street from the dockyard. From there they would disperse, making the rounds of as many bars as their wallets and constitutions could withstand.
>
> Barrage balloons at key points around the city were a grim reminder that there was still a war on. Since there was so much rain over there, joking remarks were made referring to the need for the balloons to keep the city from sinking. The city, like other places in the U.K., was blacked out at night. There were far more smokers then and perhaps it was a good thing. The lighted cigarettes prevented many collisions on the sidewalks.

Standing in front of an *Amherst* Carley float in 1942 are Alf Cockburn (right) and two mates.

Above all, Derry was a place where Canadians were welcome, especially in the pubs. Away from home for the first time, many young men had their initial experiences with booze and sex here. It was, after all, a time not only of shared danger, but also of great adventure. More than half a century later, this part of their life is long past and, probably feeling it would serve no purpose save to irritate their partner, they say relatively little about it.

Bob MacIntosh of Richmond, B.C., a stoker in *Owen Sound* and *Fennel*, recalls his 1944 introduction to Derry: "My home province, Nova Scotia, did not have drinking establishments in those days and I had my first sip of beer in a public bar my first night ashore. The pub was the Harbour View Bar and the brew was Younger's No. 3."

J.E. Schumacher of Dartmouth N.S., a leading seaman in *Amherst*, recalls when his buddy Harry Creighton

won £45 — "a considerable sum of money in 1943" — in a crap game on the destroyer *St. Croix*. "Anyway, we gleefully took off ashore, hitting every pub on the way as well as visiting the Clarendon Dance Hall. None of us ever had too much luck there with the Irish girls. They all had steady boyfriends from the American base. Anyway, we didn't care. We had a full load of Guinness and Bushmills [Irish whisky] onboard."

Garry Flock of Winnipeg, Man., an ERA in *Forest Hill* from 1943-45, relates that, as part of the effort to control venereal disease, Derry had "prophylactic stations identified by, of all things, a red light. These stations had a male attendant and facilities to cleanse oneself if you had been out with a woman."

William Wainio recalls: "At the end of August 1942, *Trillium* was one of the escorts for ON-125. On the second day at sea, over half the crew broke out in ugly red blotches accompanied by a maddening itch. Our sick bay attendant was unable to diagnose or prescribe anything for it, so we sought assistance from United States Coast Guard cutter *Spencer*. As the weather was calm and no reports of enemy presence had been received, she sent a boat over with a doctor. After checking a few of the crew, he started to laugh and mentioned something about Irish fleas.

"Apparently the crew got a bit carried away in Derry on shore leave. They started drinking Guinness as they would any other type of beer. This proved to be too rich for their blood and they broke out in hives a few days later. In a few days the symptoms disappeared. This remained a standing joke for some time and the lesson didn't require repeating."

Images of Derry abound. Asdic Operator Alf Cockburn of Don Mills, Ont., who made 40 or more crossings in *Amherst* says, "As soon as we docked, we welcomed aboard the big dairy drums of fresh milk which we would drink until we bulged."

Sid Husby of Westbank, B.C., an ERA in *Hespeler* in 1944-45, says, "When we arrived, we always headed just out of town to a place where a lady served toast, fried eggs and bacon. What a treat that was after eating powdered eggs aboard ship."

George Goodwillie of Neepawa, Man., a signalman in *Agassiz* in 1943, says: "I think the most of us enjoyed Derry. The people were friendly and it seemed that every young Irish lad could sing the old Irish songs like a bird, and were always ready to do so. Of course, there was always a price."

Jack Scott of Winnipeg, Man., an able seaman, says: "On *Trentonian*'s arrival in May 1944, a young Irish boy came aboard selling buns. He also carried a guitar and sang beautiful Irish ballads. He had a wonderful voice. He always received a few shillings from crew members and always sold his buns."

But all was not bliss. "While ashore in Derry we were hounded by youngsters looking for handouts," says George Dollis of Wellington, Ont., yeoman of signals in *Chambly* in 1944-45. "In my early days, feeling really charitable, I would give them a quarter. To my surprise they usually responded, 'Cheap Canadian bastard. The Yankees give us a dollah!' Naturally, the handouts became fewer and smaller."

Jack Nash remembers: "Londonderry was not a great place but considering the conditions and the thousands of Canadians and Americans, it wasn't too bad. We all had our favourite haunts and, of course, used the horse and buggy services extensively. I can recall a favourite trick was to take a ride back to the dockyard and then we would all jump out and not pay. It wasn't right, but at the time we thought it was fun."

J.E. Schumacher in *Amherst* recalls this mode of transportation: "At the time there were no taxis in Derry. Irish jaunting carts were used. You would sit on both sides facing outboard, hanging on as best you could, no easy task in the state we would be in. It didn't help matters that the 'jarvies' [drivers] would whip up their horses to get in as many trips as possible before all the sailors got back to their ships."

Derry was inundated with sailors. In addition to those stopping over, such as the Canadians, it had both an RN base and a large U.S. operation, which peaked at nearly 150 ships and 20,000 sailors. This offered opportunity for some, says Ron Batchelor of Maxville, Ont., recalling his 1944 stint as a leading seaman in *Brandon*: "Two items the Americans continually ran short of were film and booze. Some of our crew obliged by entering the courier business. It was most lucrative."

* * *

On the western end of the mid-ocean convoy run was Newfiejohn, the sailors' affectionate nickname for St. John's. Skinny Hayes first saw it in June 1941 while a sub-lieutenant in *Trillium*. He recalls:

It was surely a primitive naval base. It had been, for hundreds of years, a base for the lucrative Grand Banks fishing fleet. One side of the harbour was lined with fish-processing plants, piles of coal for the bunkers of steam-driven trawlers, drying racks on the sides of the hills used to dry and salt cod, and rickety wharfs now used by both weather-worn wooden Grand Banks schooners, Portuguese trawlers and already rusting corvettes and destroyers from both the Royal Navy and the Canadian navy.

There was also a repair depot ship anchored in the harbour and an old wooden hulk full of salt for the cod. The facilities were primitive and rudimentary. A small command setup had been established ashore. Stores could be provided as long as you ordered meat and spuds. Spare parts and equipment all had to be sent up from Halifax, which took a week or more.

The main link between Newfoundland and Canada was the "Newfie Bullet," a very slow steam train that ran on a narrow-gauge railway from St. John's to Port aux Basques on the southwestern tip of the island. From there a ferry ran to Sydney on Cape Breton Island in Nova Scotia and a train went on to Halifax. There was also a regular ship run from Halifax direct to St. John's, once or twice a week, which also carried supplies and passengers.

Louis Audette of Ottawa, Ont., who commanded *Amherst* for 20 months from 1942-44, says:

I grew very fond of St. John's. Shabby and old, it had something lovable about it. The harbour was superb and the magnificent entrance to it was always affectionately known as the "Hole in the Wall" because of its narrow entrance with its steep sides.

During the critical days of the Battle of the Atlantic, the mooring buoys in the centre of the harbour always held a number of damaged merchants ships: bows or sterns blown away or badly holed. Naval ships usually lay alongside on the south side or, occasionally after the dockyard was built, at the west end on the north side. Little bumboats used to ferry us across to the town at the King's Steps or elsewhere. The fare was a Newfoundland 20-cent piece but, due to confusion with the Canadian 25-cent piece, the oarsman often made an extra five cents per passenger.

In the earlier days, all ship fuelling was done from a tanker which lay in mid-harbour, but later storage tanks were installed on the south side with fuelling connections to the jetties. In the years 1942 and 1943 especially, the centre of the harbour was always crowded with ships, damaged or otherwise, made fast to mooring buoys. This crowding made manoeuvring quite tricky as there was only a narrow fairway around them.

One day as I was going to sea, steaming eastwards down the north side, a small craft propelled by an engine came out from the jetties on my port bow, steering southeastwards to go through a small opening between the moored ships. I had the right of way and held to it. Seeing my determination, the small craft promptly stopped her engines and hoisted sail, thereby acquiring the right of way. The day was really his, even if by trickery. However, I did not want to go astern on my single screw and have my ship's head pay off to starboard in the narrow fairway, so I blew five short, angry blasts on my siren and held to my course. Sooner than collide, my small friend lowered his sail, started his motor and yielded me the right of way.

Roy Pallister of Guelph, Ont., a leading seaman asdic in *Barrie* in 1945, says: "Newfiejohn had an aura all its own. There is no other place on earth like St. John's in those days. After spending day upon day at sea escorting a convoy, a ship's crew would feel the utmost relief after passing through the cliffs, entering that harbour and going to the oiling jetty. Most of them would be allowed to go ashore. Oh happy day!"

Bern Rawle, who served in *Cobalt* and *Strathroy*, says: "Unlike Halifax harbour, there is no approach. You are either in or out. On my first trip to St. John's, I remember the big tanker with a hole blown through it floating in the harbour. The hole was so big that harbour craft sometimes took a shortcut by sailing through it rather than going around."

Newfoundland was a different culture, as George Hedden of Hamilton, Ont., found while a coder in *Chicoutimi*: "In the summer of 1941 we were fortunate enough to get shore leave in Newfiejohn. While doing some sightseeing, I stepped off the curb and an automobile nearly ran me down due to my ignorance of the British system of driving on the opposite side of the road."

Amenities were lacking, Skinny Hayes recalls from his 1941-42 duty in *Trillium*: "Recreational facilities were nonexistent. A 'wet' canteen was set up ashore and there was a movie house or two."

Jim Alward of Winnipeg, Man., a telegraphist in *Sackville* from 1942-44, says: "The wets reserved for seagoing ratings was located on Water Street. Wooden tables and wooden benches were the only articles of furniture. The bottles of Black Horse ale were served without glasses. The zombie canteen on the edge of town was far more comfortable. Although rest camps were provided from 1943 to give men respite — lots of sun, good food, games, fishing and sailing — our shore authorities could have tried to provide similar amenities given to ratings in the U.S. Navy."

Roy Pallister remembers his first visit to the oiling jetty in St. John's: "For those not on duty who are allowed to go ashore, a one-lunger bumboat comes alongside and he charges 10 cents a head to take us across the harbour. He also sells screech in a beer bottle with a cork in the top. The screech is 50 cents and is the genuine article, as opposed to the liquor store screech sold today. I should have known better than to try to drink this stuff, as I can't drink much of anything without becoming violently ill. It is only through the good graces of one of my shipmates and a couple of good-guy shore patrol types that I got back to the ship relatively intact. Never again!"

The officers had something to look forward to in Newfiejohn because of one Captain D, Rollo Mainguy, explains *Amherst* CO Louis Audette: "The Crow's Nest was a remarkable and delightful place and a monument to Rollo Mainguy's ingenuity, thoughtfulness and consideration for the seafaring officers of his command. It was the fourth storey of a shabby old warehouse which had been nicely and practically rigged out: bar, fireplace, easy chairs, tables for light meals, kitchen, refrigerator and a most adequate supply of booze to warm hours ashore that could otherwise have been bleak and cheerless. One or two nights a week, ladies were allowed in. It was near the King's Wharf and access was by an outside staircase three stories high. Though hair-raising adventures on the staircase are recounted, I know of no serious injury or death. Inside, the fireplace formed the cheery central theme and the walls were covered with ships' crests, real or facetious. Gordon and Phoebe, the steward and his wife, became a part of everyone's life."

Bowmanville CO, Mort Duffus of Vancouver, B.C., says: "The Crow's Nest was a delightful haven where bacon and real eggs were manna from heaven."

Louis Audette notes Mainguy also initiated Captain D's cocktail party every Friday: "This became the great occasion for meeting everyone — the shore-going, the sea-going and the Newfoundlander."

Bill Taylor of Duncan, B.C., a *Kincardine* lieutenant in 1944-45, recalls: "I remember accompanying our No. 1 to a

Captain D's bash and when it was over and we were heading back to the ship, which involved a bumboat ride across the harbour to Bowrings wharf on the east side, darned if we didn't come across a shore patrol wagon parked but idling and with no one in it. Why walk when the opportunity presented itself to ride? We probably should have driven it only as far as the bumboat jetty, but no, once underway, we decided we might as well take ourselves down to the dockyard where we could pick up a free ride over to the east side wharfs. And we made it back to the ship without incident, or so we thought.

"We didn't get away with it as somewhere along the line our No. 1 had been recognized and later that evening our old man received a signal requesting — ordering — him to report to Captain D the next morning, accompanied by his first lieutenant. They weren't on cordial speaking terms for a while, but when the CO was appointed to command a frigate, who did he request as his executive officer? Indeed, it was our car thief."

There's more to a place than facilities. "What St. John's did have were the most wonderful people in the world," says Skinny Hayes. "They had few material things, but they were outstandingly generous and good-natured with a great sense of humour. It didn't take long for the visiting military to outnumber the residents, but there was no rancor or feelings of jealousy. The citizens were happy to share what was available with all or any of us."

Bern Rawle says: "Dear old St. John's. I always have a soft spot for Newfoundlanders. They might not have a hell of a lot, but they always shared whatever they had."

Murray Armstrong of Petitcodiac, N.B., a padre with the Newfoundland Escort Force, says: "My heart warms up still when I think of the hospitality of the St. John's homes. Many of them took the sailors into their hearts and into their homes. This was as fine a panacea as these men who braved the elements and a resourceful enemy could have."

Albert Baker, an *Orillia* rating in 1941, concludes: "St. John's was always good to come back to after a long trip. Good, lovable people. They did their best to make things enjoyable for us."

* * *

Convoy escort meant slogging back and forth across the Atlantic. Skinny Hayes, captain of the corvette *Guelph* in 1944-45 but a young officer in *Trillium* in 1941-42, recalls:

The winter of 1941 was a grim one. The weather on the North Atlantic is not good at the best of times, but in the winter and in the more northern latitudes it is pretty awful. The German Submarine Command had organized their U-boats into wolf packs and when one submarine found a convoy the remaining boats of the group were homed in ahead of the convoy for a concentrated attack. There could be up to 20 U-boats attacking a convoy of 50 or 60 ships escorted by one or two destroyers and three or four corvettes.

Coupled with that was the mid-ocean gap in air coverage. The patrol aircraft of the day could only fly out over the Atlantic a relatively short distance in support of the convoys. It was quickly established that submarines do not like aircraft flying around looking for them and they have to submerge and run on their batteries. Air cover then was most important because it vastly reduced the scope of operation of U-boats by keeping them submerged at very slow speeds during daylight. They could not easily position themselves ahead of the convoys for a decent attack.

The mid-ocean gap was a large area in the middle of the Atlantic beyond the reach of aircraft from either side of the ocean. In that area the submarines could come to the surface in daylight, out of sight of the convoy escort, steam at full speed on their diesel engines, charge their batteries and get ahead of the convoys by nightfall and attack on the surface, almost with impunity.

Most convoys were escorted by three or four corvettes whose top speed was less than a U-boat's on the surface and, if we were lucky, one or two destroyers, which were considerably faster and carried more sophisticated communications gear. Every day a long message would be transmitted by radio to all ships at sea listing all the German U-boats with their estimated positions. The navigator of each escort ship would plot the ones nearest his convoy. In that way a good estimation could be made whether your convoy had been detected, was being shadowed and/or would be attacked. It was a scary experience to look at the plot on the chart and know that as soon as it got dark some ships — maybe even yours — would have a torpedo fired at them, one or more may be hit and would probably sink and men's lives would be lost.

Various diversions were tried, sometimes very successfully. The course of the convoy would be altered after dark for a few hours so the shadowing submarines' estimated position of the convoy would be in error. This only worked, however, before a U-boat had actually made contact with the convoy. Once contact had been made, the submarine could keep in touch because the noise given off by the engines of 50 ships carried a long way through the water. In addition, there was always the one or two ships that persisted in making smoke, which could be seen through a periscope for a very long distance. It was a wearisome battle with the elements, too frequently interspersed with terror as ships all around were torpedoed and men thrown into the freezing water and left to die.

Irv Kaplan of Montreal, Que., signalman in *Arvida* in 1941-42, also recalls the winter of 1941-42: "Many ships were sunk. We were continuously at action stations and busy picking up merchant ship survivors, as well as trying to keep in station. I must admit that the U-boats had the advantage at this time."

Lloyd Jewers of Dartmouth, N.S., a *Hepatica* stoker, recalls the U-boat attack on Convoy ON 60 off Newfoundland on February 8, 1942. The bow of *Alysse*, a Free French corvette, was blown off and *Hepatica* took her in tow, then was relieved the next day by a rescue tug from St. John's. But on February 10th this tow line parted (broke). "All that held her up was the bulkhead," Jewers says. "She went around in the sea and it pushed in the bulkhead and down she went. She went with all her depth charges and her boilers had a full head of steam and they all exploded. I was in our boiler room. I thought we were torpedoed as all the gauge glasses and light bulbs broke. We were in complete darkness. I tried to contact the engine room in a hurry. When we found out what had happened, we went back to the boiler room and restarted all the equipment."

Thomas King of Chatham, Ont., an able seaman, joined *Amherst* in the spring of 1942: "We escorted the slow convoys, some only averaging seven knots. We sometimes would sail by way of the Azores, hoping to miss the U-boats. The crossing took 16 to 28 days, depending on the fog, storms and enemy submarines. I made at least 14 trips in *Amherst* [in 1942-43] and we lost ships and men on every one."

Courtesy Legion Magazine Archives

Sackville at sea off the Azores in 1942 or 1943.

An example of a difficult crossing was the westbound convoy ONS 92 in May 1942. "We had made occasional and uneventful runs on submarine contacts, but this was different," recalls *Arvida* crew member Jim Bessey of Stouffville, Ont. "It started at night. Tracer bullets were flying all over the place. You were tempted to be mesmerized as if you were watching fireworks at the CNE [Canadian National Exhibition in Toronto], not realizing they were bullets. Oil tankers were exploding. Starshells on parachutes lit up the night.

"I was a submarine detector, but my alternate duty was working in the ammunition magazine at the very bottom of the ship. With the smell of cordite, the thudding of depth charges and ships exploding, and the thought that a stray torpedo might hit the magazine, my two-hour shift seemed like an eternity."

Back at his primary work station at midnight, "I recall everyone being paralyzed as we picked up the sound of a torpedo coming directly at us. The lieutenant had my earphones on and was yelling it was going to hit us. He had a 'this-is-the-end look on his face.' The torpedo went under us without hitting the ship. Maybe he was mistaken, but we all felt born-again sailors."

In the Directorate of History and Heritage in Ottawa are comments by *Arvida*'s CO, Lieutenant A.I. MacKay, on that grim night of May 11-12 when five merchant ships were sunk: "I sighted a vessel heavily listed with one bright light burning and about a mile and a half east of her several survivors' lights. The sea was littered with wreckage and the night pitch dark. I closed the biggest group of survivors' lights and found the entire crew of *Mount Parnes* in two boats. They were screaming and yelling and everyone on our bridge, myself included, took them for Chinese, but they were Greek with four British gunners. I ordered them to put out all lights and I closed them. They were panicky and although the boats had oars no attempt was made to use them. We had to lift most of them on board, although a net was rigged and ropes thrown (to) them. They left four injured men in the boats and made no attempt to help us get them, so I was compelled to abandon the four injured men as my engines had been stopped too long for safety."

Jim Bessey remembers that many merchant seamen were in the water that night: "At about three or four in the morning we were dispatched to pick up survivors. I think this was the most heart-wrenching memory of my navy experience. Sailors from the merchant ships, little red lights blinking on their life jackets, were very difficult to see because of the dark. They were hollering to be picked up. We had scramble nets over each side of the ship for them to grab. We picked up as many as we could, but I'm sure we missed a great many others. At daybreak we picked up a few more clinging to debris. They were covered in oil.

"I can remember working mouth to mouth trying to save one of the merchant sailors — to no avail. We had our first burial at sea. (An aside: I was in the firing party and mistakenly fired my rifle when the officer said, 'Ready.' It was a little embarrassing, but that's all.) The survivors were cleaned up and given dry clothes and our ship was dispatched to Iceland to unload our guests. I would guess between 60 and 80 survivors."

* * *

The U-boat fleet was expanding rapidly. It smashed the 200 mark in the last quarter of 1941, reaching 233. This rose to 272 in the first quarter of 1942 and 315 boats in the second quarter of 1942. The impact on Allied and neutral merchant ship losses in the Atlantic theatre was incredible. From an average of only 144,000 tons per month from all causes in the last half of 1941, losses multiplied to 515,000 tons per month in the first half of 1942.

Courtesy Wm. John Quinsey/Hugh Merryweather Collection

Halifax harbour seen in April 1942 from the corvette *Louisburg*.

To put the Atlantic theatre in perspective, U-boats sank 105 ships there in 1939, then 435 ships in 1940 and 410 ships in 1941. But 225 ships went down in the first quarter of 1942 and 240 in the second quarter. In only six months, U-boats sank 465 ships in the Atlantic, surpassing the total for either 1941 or 1940.

The RCN always had more to worry about than the mid-ocean run now connecting Newfie and Derry. Much more. It had to protect feeder routes taking ships to the west ocean meeting point. Fast convoys designated with HX numbers originated in Halifax from September 1939 to September 1942, when New York became their base. Slow convoys bore SC numbers and began in Sydney, N.S., from August 1940 till August 1942. They then originated in Halifax, then New York and finally Halifax from March 1943 till war's end.

The need for protection increased sharply in the first half of 1942. *Pictou* CO Tony Griffin explains: "In late 1941 the U-boats entered into their second 'happy time' — Operation *Paukenschlag* ('beat the drum'). Or, the 'American turkey shoot' as the German crews called it." The Americans ignored British advice to adopt the convoy system as soon as the U.S. entered the war. They also failed for several weeks to black out their coastline at night. "Between mid-December 1941 and mid-May 1942, U-boats sank more than 300 ships in American waters with a total tonnage of over 2 million aggregate tons and a loss of nearly 5,000 merchant seamen," Griffin asserted. "This was the worst five-month

period of the whole war, and it was the direct outcome of the failure of the Americans to adopt the convoy system and to darken both their ships and coastline…"

This German offensive against unprotected shipping helped give rise to the Triangle Run. Loaded merchant ships would form up at Halifax's Bedford Basin. Canadian ships of the Western Local Escort Force, later the Western Escort Force, took them out to rendezvous with the mid-ocean escorts at the west ocean meeting point. The WLEF escorts would next refuel in St. John's and take a westbound convoy to New York or Boston, then bring a convoy up to Halifax to complete the cycle. The triangle, then, was generally Halifax, St. John's, New York or Boston, and back to Halifax. The Triangle Run lacked the stature of the Newfie-Derry Run, but the American ports were something else in terms of things to see and do.

Howard Libbey of Sydney, N.S., a stoker in *Calgary* in 1941-42, says: "We had a great time on that Triangle Run, especially when we could get a weekend in Boston. Saturday night was Boston baked bean night and then there was the Silver Dollar Bar that was supposed to have the longest bar in the world."

Gerald Martin of Chilliwack, B.C., a telegraphist trained operator in *Charlottetown* in 1942, says: "I got my first and only tattoo in Newfie. I didn't see much of Boston outside of the Silver Dollar Bar. I met up with some American sailors and boy what a time when they found out I was RCNVR and not RN."

Best of all was the Big Apple. "New York was a great town for a serviceman," says Jack Drysdale of Victoria, an asdic operator in *Oakville* in 1942-43. "Subway fare was a nickel. Pepsi-Cola and a hotdog were 15 cents. Tickets were obtained from the USO [United Service Organization] for stage shows, picture shows, lunches and suppers. So, you could have a dollar in your pants and have a real ball."

Al (Soup) Campbell of Surrey, B.C., a 1943 *Buctouche* crew member, says: "The sailors from the small towns on the Prairies had to marvel at the great cities in the U.S.A. One of my first stops was New York City where our captain managed a boiler clean — 10 days tied up on Staten Island. Three things come to mind. At the USO we were given tickets to see a Broadway show, *Early to Bed*. At 18, I fell in love with the live theatre. We went to Coney Island for a day and were given strips of tickets for the rides and sideshows. The American public was very generous to us Canadians. My chum fell off the Staten Island ferry and we had to stop and fish him out of the oily harbour water. Coming from Flin Flon, Manitoba, to New York City was the biggest thing that had ever happened to me."

Tony Cebulski of Oshawa, Ont., a *Norsyd* stoker from 1943-45, says: "New York was probably the best — a time to see the Empire State Building, Statue of Liberty, Stage Door Canteen [a USO nightclub], my first subway ride, Times Square, the Bowery, etc. Most of these sights were free for service personnel."

Robert MacDonald in *Dundas* visited a USO in October 1943: "A friend and I got two tickets to a World Series game at Yankee Stadium. It was very hot in New York and, having arrived by subway far too early, we decided to wait at an air-conditioned bar across from the stadium. As the only foreign sailors in the crowded bar, we were objects of friendly interest that resulted in our receiving quite a few free drinks.

"We were having a fine time and whatever interest we had in the ball game was soon lost. After a while, I noticed most of the patrons were very interested in listening to the radio. Realizing that the game was on, it struck me that someone there might want our tickets, so I asked the man on the next barstool if he wanted tickets. They were snatched from my hand and he was out of that bar in a flash. When the barkeeper asked and I explained what I'd done, he said, 'Well, I guess we're going to lose the war.' When I asked why, he replied, 'If all our allies are as stupid as you two, we can't win. You could have sold those tickets for 50 bucks to almost anyone in the bar.' He certainly was disgusted. We were pretty sad ourselves because we were, as usual, nearly broke."

S.J. Yankoski of Russell, Man., a 1943-44 *Hepatica* able seaman, says: "New York and Times Square — we really lived it up there. Ratings that had stayed on through the ship's early 1943 refit initiated us to the night life there. Who knows, maybe our next trip out could be our last."

The author's letter to Richard Hetherington, a 1941-45 *Agassiz* ERA, was answered by his widow, Adele Hetherington of Moose Jaw, Sask.:

Richard's port life was familiar to me for I was born and lived on Staten Island until I married my husband. I met my husband at the Staten Island USO the first week *Agassiz* came to New York for refit [in December 1943]. The ship stayed in port for nearly three months and then returned once every four weeks for more than a year.

On his first shore leave in New York City, my Prairie-raised husband crossed the harbour on the Staten Island ferry with his buddies and went down into the subway station, stopping at the booth for change. Before he had time to get through the turnstile, the train had come and gone with his friends on it. Although he was a person very able to fend for himself, he often remarked about this time when he felt completely lost and alone.

Servicemen in New York were given free transportation on many facilities and were shown appreciations in various other ways. They usually stopped at the USO on 42nd Street for free tickets to many shows and different kinds of entertainment as well as invitations to homes.

That refit is exuberantly recalled by Doug Murch in *Agassiz*: "One month's leave for all ship's company and 10 weeks in that paradise for servicemen — New York City! We were elated; it was everything they said and more. We were barracked with the U.S. Navy. I especially remember the food in the messhall. Even the breakfast was a banquet. No one dines like the U.S. serviceman. And still I heard complaints — but not from us! Well, New York was indeed paradise. The hospitality, the food, the entertainment was limitless. This was New York City in wartime. I cannot describe it, as words fail."

Al Campbell comments on the actual escort work: "This was my first ship and I was very scared of my abilities to send and receive signal messages while on watch. I'm very thankful that I was not on mid-Atlantic convoy duty as my first assignment. The Triangle Run was a great way to get salty and put to use our St-Hyacinthe signal training."

Robert MacDonald recalls: "We saw little action on the Triangle Run. We would hear over the air lots of other escorts engaged in defending against attacks."

Ray MacAulay of Fredericton, N.B., an able seaman, has a vivid memory: "*Charlottetown* sighted and attacked a U-boat in the early morning of April 25, 1942, while accompanying a convoy 100 miles off land. We contacted the enemy prowler and closed to 1,000 yards when it suddenly appeared fully surfaced in the light of the moon. We attacked with a 10-depth-charge pattern, followed by nine more charges. The detonating charges jammed the steering mechanism of the ship, knocked out the electrical power and put the asdic equipment out of order. By the time these defects were corrected, the contact was lost. A doubtful contact was picked up, however, and further attacks were made, but the U-boat had escaped. Still, it was agreed by all that *Charlottetown's* prompt action had saved the convoy from attack."

Action of a different sort is recalled by *Cobalt* able seaman Reid Sheppard of Sarnia, Ont.: "Only once did I ever think we might capsize. *Cobalt* left Halifax for New York with a few ships to join a convoy. Shortly after we cleared the harbour a fierce winter storm hit and for the next couple of days we iced up badly. I was on the wheel one night when we were hit broadside by a wave and listed over as far as I'd want to go, then finally righted. One's life jacket wouldn't have been much good in a sea that cold. We spent much of the time off watch chipping ice. After the first few hours we didn't see any of the ships we were escorting, but all made it to New York."

W.J. Roberts of Thunder Bay, Ont., a telegraphist, recalls a 1942 Triangle Run trip in *Oakville*: "The storm was so bad that we lost the convoy and 17 ships turned back. We were somewhere southeast of Sable Island and it was all we could do to make way into the waves, which were easily 30 feet high. I think every one in the ship was seasick except myself and a coder, Don Bond. In the wheelhouse, I had to step over other crew to get to my desk. In my off time I was helping the others. I even relieved the helmsman for a spell: it was quite an experience as you had to catch the wave going down. At some time I think the rudder came right out of the water. The navigating officer had me give him radio bearings all through the night. The next morning he said that according to my bearings we had sailed over Sable Island [south of Nova Scotia]. However, I was later vindicated when they found that the helmsman had been steering 10 degrees off course."

Canadian corvettes were also given many odd jobs as the need arose. Cliff Hatch, a *Napanee* lieutenant, says: "In the summer of 1942 *Napanee* escorted an Admiralty [RN] tug which would go out 1,000 miles from St. John's to tow in a torpedoed freighter. We did that three times without ever touching shore for six weeks. The men were really fed up, but they took it well."

Joe Kalino of Montreal, Que., an able seaman in *Chambly*, recalls that while waiting for the next convoy, his corvette would have to "go out and sweep with asdic some of the Newfoundland bays, which took a lot of patience because you were barely moving around. I think that was the worst part of our duties."

Walter Pulsifer of Powell River, B.C., *Louisburg* coxswain, says: "In August 1942 we departed Halifax to escort a small convoy to a point just east of Newfoundland where it was to join with a larger convoy and go overseas. Just as we reached the meeting point, a hurried signal diverted us to proceed in haste to Conception Bay on the Avalon Peninsula of Newfoundland because a submarine had sunk two ore carriers off Wabana, an iron-ore loading site. We made several sweeps, another corvette joined us and a thorough search was made, but no luck."

Reg Baker was a 1941-42 asdic operator in *Buctouche*: "One time in the first half of 1942 they sent us out of St. John's with two other corvettes escorting six merchant ships into the gulf south of Newfoundland. After we let them go and turned around, we were running three abreast and we were in the middle. I came up to the asdic cabin to relieve my opposite number just before 2400 hours. This chap had the earphones on and was transmitting with one hand and using a chronoscope in the other to clock the range of the transmission. It was phenomenal, far beyond the normal range of approximately 2,500 to 3,000 yards. On one transmission we heard an echo. It turned out to be a sub.

"All three corvettes altered course towards the target. At about 300 yards the captain had us fire a starshell, which is like a neon light hanging in the sky. When this thing exploded, here was Jerry coming right down between us and the ship on our starboard side. Those guys dove out of the conning tower into the sub, crash dived and disappeared. We searched the area for four hours to no avail. He either laid on the bottom or he got below our sound-wave capability because of water temperature variations. This is the way it was — frustrating, difficult, hellish. These young U-boat commanders were very efficient in evasive tactics. They had lots of nerve and would try anything. We had to be very alert and have good water conditions or they would get away from us."

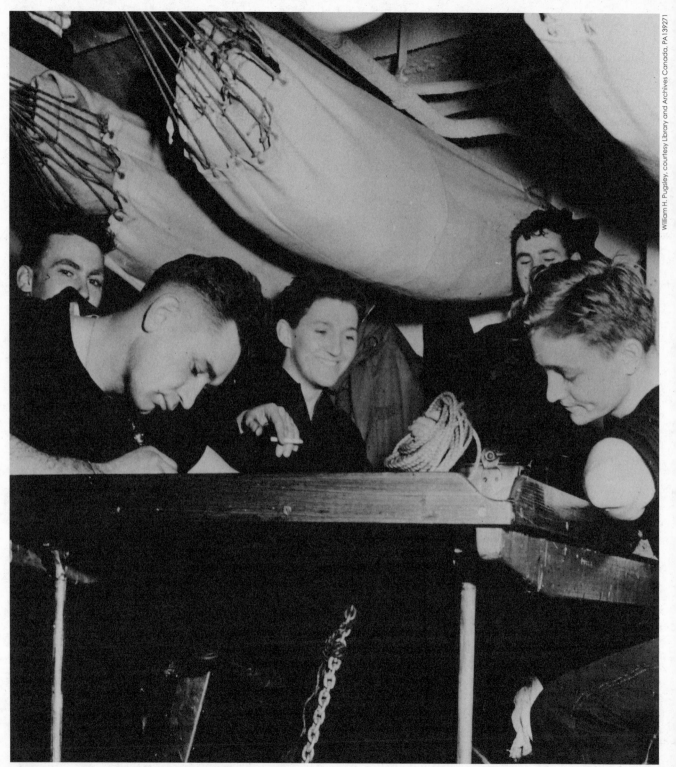

Hammocks are slung overhead in this messdeck in an unidentified corvette.

CHAPTER SEVEN

"You can imagine what a smelly, dirty-looking crew we were after a few days at sea."

THE CONCISE OXFORD DICTIONARY offers many meanings for the noun **mess**, including "dirty or untidy state of things" and "state of confusion, embarrassment, or trouble" as well as "company of persons who take meals together, especially in the fighting services" and "place where such meals are taken."

Recalling his 1942-43 service in *Fennel* as leading signalman, Bill Acheson of Orleans, Ont., comments: "If ever a term was apt and fully descriptive, it is the word 'mess' as it applied to the fore lower messdeck of a corvette at sea, in any sea, but particularly in heavy seas.

"Picture, if you can, more than a dozen men crammed into a space not much larger than an average living room in a modest home. They eat, sleep and live together with all their belongings — at best in cramped, uncomfortable conditions and at worst in a seething cauldron of filthy bilge water and debris of every description as their ship is tossed and turned by the monstrous waves of an angry North Atlantic."

Laurie Manuel of Nolalu, Ont., a stoker in *Matapedia* in 1941-42 and in *Port Arthur* in 1942-43, says: "Rough weather created many miserable conditions for crew. Heavy seas breaking over the bow would hit the lower part of the bridge and wash back under the foredeck. This meant water in the messdecks and difficulty in getting food from the galley [kitchen] to the forward end and also getting to the heads [toilets]. Wet hammocks were common. It's amazing how crews adjusted to so many tough conditions."

Leo McVarish of Winnipeg Man., was an able seaman asdic in *Alberni* in 1943-44. He says: "The seamen's mess up forward wasn't the Ritz. It was sleeping, eating

and recreational quarters all in one. It was overcrowded. Some of the earlier tenants or senior ratings were fortunate to sling their hammocks and have some kind of comfort while others were not so fortunate.

"All along the port and starboard sides and centre tables were lockers. These became the sleeping quarters for the overflow. You learned quickly of the discomforts. You had great difficulty sometimes staying put in the rolling and pitching.

"At night in the darkness of the messdeck, you could barely see the forms of humanity sprawled about amongst the swinging hammocks, trying as best they could to get some shut-eye."

Reg Baker, an able seaman asdic in *Orillia* in 1941 and in *Buctouche* in 1941-42, recalls the seamen's mess: "These short foc's'le corvettes were very crowded and there wasn't adequate room for everyone to sling a hammock, so some people had to sleep on the padded storage lockers or on the deck [floor]. Rest and sleep were nearly impossible under these conditions. Somehow we managed."

Jim Galloway of Hamilton, Ont., recalls his 1942-43 stint as an *Agassiz* seaman:

After my first crossing in July 1942, I ached all over from having to hold on or brace myself against the motion of the ship while on watch, and also off watch in the messdeck.

When trying to sleep on the foot lockers, I would have to brace myself between the messdeck table and the storage rack for shoes and hat boxes, which was situated behind the foot lockers. One arm would be hooked over the rack to keep from being pitched out on the deck.

The messdeck after a few hours at sea could have three to four inches of water swishing back and forth as the ship climbed each wave, went over the top and back down the other side. Then there was the motion from side to side to contend with as well. Certain things like knives, forks, empty fruit cans, etc. would be flung from the table. These would wash back and forth in the sea-water that came in over the lip of the messdeck doors on each side of the ship.

We were never allowed to close these doors for fear that if we were torpedoed or in a collision with another ship they would become warped or twisted and trap men inside. Both doors had heavy canvas covering the opening to prevent light from escaping during the blackout at night. Any light, even a cigarette, could be seen for miles at sea and could give away the location of the convoy to U-boats.

Although we had three steam radiators in the messdeck, they were usually shut off because the salt water swishing around would hit the warm radiators and give off sickening steam vapours. Other than being out of the wind and weather, it was only a few degrees warmer than outside.

George Kahan of Thunder Bay, Ont., an able seaman in *Oakville* in 1944-45, offers a terse assessment: "Bad at night below deck: blackout curtains, deadlights on port-holes, no air, fuel oil smell from the engine room. Glad to go out on watch even in a storm."

Ted Cunningham remembers being an ordinary seaman in his first ship, *Arrowhead*, in 1940-41: "It took some time to get used to. Our mess and sleeping quarters were in the bow, the roughest place in the ship. It was not unusual to be sitting at the mess table under an umbrella of hammocks and have two smelly feet suddenly set next to your coffee or breakfast, but you got used to it."

Recalling his introduction to *Chambly* in 1944, Howard Markle of Burlington, Ont., an able seaman, says, "Life soon settled down somewhat, if you could say getting used to riding a roller coaster and being wet, cold and miserable for 24 hours a day for two-plus weeks at a time was settling down."

Walter Pulsifer of Powell River, B.C., was coxswain in *Louisburg* for a spell in 1942: "One thing I can particularly

Four buddies in *Louisburg*'s communications mess in November 1942 are (from left): Johnny MacPhail, Bill Robinson, Gord MacLeod and Bill Gilbert. Note the "micks" (hammocks), both slung overhead and in the rack.

remember is the lack of sleep and the discomfort during the winter on the North Atlantic. Yes, lack of sleep and biting cold sure stick in my memory."

Vic Martin of Sarnia, Ont., a 1942-43 *Regina* able seaman, says, "It was a rough life. Living space was at a premium and the ship was always rolling."

George Dollis, *Chambly* yeoman of signals in 1944-45, remembers the communications mess as an area of about 24 feet by 20 feet where 13 men lived: "The most intriguing feature of all was that our mess was just above the stokers' mess and they actually had to come down our stairwell and through our cabin to reach their quarters." The communicators lacked privacy, but they did possess practicality and had "a double hotplate where a tea pot and coffee pot were kept going continuously while at sea."

It was not unusual for each mess to house some provisions and treats. Art Chinery recalls his 1944-45 stint in *Orangeville*: "Each mess had its own supply of utensils, plates, cups, coffee pot, tea, coffee, sugar, salt, pepper, bread, jam, butter, etc.

"We washed our dishes in a galvanized pail. Upon completion, the individual whose turn it was took the dishwater topside and dumped it overboard. Every once in a while we would forget to retrieve the dinnerware from the pail. Once we dumped it and saw all those knives, forks and spoons going overboard, we knew we were in trouble with our messmates. That and normal plate and cup breakage

Two sailors, one mascot and the stern depth charge rails on an unidentified corvette.

led to midnight forages to other messes to steal what we needed."

George Rickard, of London, Ont., a 1942-43 *Dauphin* signalman, recalls dishwashing: "We had our own dishpan that was placed at one end of the mess table. Hot water was drawn from the washroom above, soap, china and cutlery were added. Now came the tricky part — keeping the dishwater from sloshing over the side of the pan with each roll of the ship.

"Actually, it became rather simple. The washer would follow the same action as a compass in a binnacle. He tilted the pan's bottom edge from one side to the other with one hand, while the other hand did the washing. The dishwater was supposed to remain horizontal. As each plate or cup was washed, it was grabbed by a second messman who dried and deposited it into a rack."

A rough sea and a flooded messdeck are recalled by Mel Greenwood of Windsor, Ont., a telegraphist in *Giffard* in 1943-44: "It got so rough once that the wireless cabin on the bridge actually moved about two inches. On coming off watch at 4 a.m., I learned that the porthole in our forward mess had broken and water was pouring in. Seamen were doing their best to board it up. The water was at least eight inches deep and swishing up and down the deck. However, since it was the seamen's job to fix it, we climbed into our hammocks and let them do it. At 6:30 or so when we got up, our mess had to be cleaned up, so out with the buckets it was."

Morley Barnes of Mississauga, Ont., has a vivid recollection of 1944-45 when he was a stoker in *Kincardine*:

"Strange as it may seem, the odour still remains in my mind. The stink of these ships. I swear to this day if I was blindfolded and put on a corvette I would know where I was — by the smell.

"Think of it. About 100 men all cooped up in this tin can. Fresh water was very scarce, laundry and showers were nonexistent. Hatches and portholes remained locked for fear light would escape. Add to this burning oil, vomit from seasick personnel, rotten socks, body odour from not washing, dirty clothes, stinking garbage and you will get the drift of odour. The smell could keep you awake half the night."

Art Geizer, *Agassiz* coxswain from 1941-45, says: "We could only wash, not take a shower. That luxury was a no-no. The ship could only carry so much fuel. This was utilized to get us from A to B and also to make fresh water for the boilers. Try to imagine eating, working and sleeping in clothes that you have had on for a week or more."

Howard Trusdale of St. Thomas, Ont., an able seaman in *Fergus* in 1944-45, says: "Our engineer officer, a Naval Reserve type, had a real fetish about water, especially the chance it could be wasted. He monitored its use very effectively. He turned all water off from 0900 to about noon and then again in the p.m. Our executive officer carried a large ring with a great number of keys. Some of them were the water shutoff keys."

Bob Carson of Midland, Ont., who served in *Alberni* from 1942-44, becoming a leading seaman, recalls that the water would only be turned on three or four times a day, usually at meals, "so you had to be quick or line up to use the facilities."

Despite the lack of water onboard, beards weren't overly popular. *Agassiz* seaman Jim Galloway observes: "The salt made them stiff and uncomfortable. In winter, the spray froze on them."

Bern Rawle, a stoker in *Cobalt* in 1942 and a stoker petty officer in *Strathroy* in 1944-45, comments on personal hygiene: "We slept in our clothing while at sea because the action gong could sound at any time, giving one no time to dress. As there was always a shortage of fresh water, certainly none for showering or laundry, you can imagine what a smelly, dirty-looking crew we were after a few days at sea."

Jim Alward, a telegraphist in *Sackville* from 1942-44, made this notation: "Water in the washroom — it was

Courtesy Vic Martin

A small group of *Regina*'s crew in February 1942 (from left): Camille Lanteigne, Frank Roach, Vic Martin, Parks, Eddie Boudreau.

Courtesy Vic Martin

The Quebec members of *Regina*'s crew on April 30, 1943, are (front, from left): Patrick Pratt, Derek Asselton, Lou Proietti, Bob Dunlop; (rear) Gib Todd, C.O. Denoncourt, Mort Mortimer, George Dick, Jim Peters.

scarce and rusty. The shower was dormant for the trip. One would wash to the waist, but it was most reckless to take off everything lest the bell would go. I did not relish the prospect of standing half-naked on the bridge at my action station. Stink, therefore, was a problem."

Reg Baker has pungent memories of his two short foc's'le corvettes, *Orillia* and *Buctouche*: "Seamen in cold, damp weather were usually cold and wet and when they came off watch they would pull off their seaboots [rubber boots rolled down at the tops], strip off their wet wool socks and hang them over a heat radiator to dry out.

"This certainly did not enhance the air in the seamen's messdeck. At night this messdeck was almost completely closed up because it had to be blacked out. There was a ventilation system, but it wasn't efficient, so the messdeck would be foul at times."

Harvey Burns of Sherbrooke, N.S., a leading seaman in *Port Arthur* from 1942-45, says: "The ventilation was very poor and several of the boys had spots on their lungs. We also had two cases of scabies."

J.H. McMenamon of Burlington, Ont., a stoker in *Port Arthur* in 1942-43, attests: "Life in a corvette was very hard. You had to be young to put up with it. Living conditions defy accurate description, especially during rough weather. Remember, there was no ventilation and all portholes and hatches were dogged down [latched] on leaving harbour."

Corvettes did not come with laundry facilities. John C. Grant of Dartmouth, N.S., a 1942-43 *Regina* stoker, recalls: "Laundry was done in a bucket using a toilet plunger as an agitator. When down in the engine room, we sometimes dried it on the hot pipes."

Glenn Martin of Prince Albert, Sask., a 1944-45 *Arrowhead* ERA, says, "We had to do our own laundry in a tub, with a plunger."

Herb Turner of Sorrento, B.C., an ordinary seaman and radar operator in *Rosthern* in 1944-45, recounts: "We had to put our clothes into a bucket, add some cold water, then turn some steam into the bucket and in that way do our washing. When Ross Wilson became our captain and saw how primitive things were, he was quite surprised. It was not long before a washing machine was installed in the washroom. He evidently bought it with his own money. He had been an Eaton Department Store manager before joining up. He was a very understanding man. We all thought a lot of him."

Bern Rawle recalls: "We slept in hammocks and were each issued two blankets that soon became stiff with dirt. "I remember that eventually arrangements were made for our blankets to be laundered while in St. John's and my reaction was, 'My word, this navy is getting pretty good.'"

Thomas King of Chatham, Ont., an able seaman in *Amherst* in 1942-43, says, "We had a terrible time shaving and trying to wash our clothes in that sea-water. We never felt clean and longed for that day or two on shore leave to have a good shower and real food. If it was your duty watch when you hit port, you were out of luck and stayed on board."

Ken Hedley of Guelph, Ont., who served in *Mayflower* from 1940-42, recalls the early days: "The buzz was that corvettes were only for use in coastal waters and that life aboard these small ships was so harsh that one would be drafted off after six months' duty."

The six-month time limit was a myth, but living arrangements changed considerably during the war as initial design shortcomings were identified and the early ships were slowly modified. Lessons learned were also applied to the construction of new corvettes, so they became more habitable, but they certainly could never be called comfortable.

One reason is that new equipment was added throughout the war and crew size increased to operate it. This required more crew space, of course. Crew size was seldom constant. The very early corvettes appear to have had an initial crew of 54 to 58, but the precise number could depend on available manpower. At war's end, the newer, larger corvettes could have a crew of between 100 and 105. These totals include officers, with five being the general rule early in the war and seven the norm at the end.

Generally speaking there were five messes: one for chief petty officers and petty officers; another for stokers; a large one for seamen; a separate one for communicators such as coders, telegraphists and signalmen; and a miscellaneous mess for odds and sods, such as two cooks, the sick berth attendant, the victualling assistant and the two stewards who served the officers.

A ship at sea is a 24-hour-a-day operation. A general overview of how living and working fit together comes from Skinny Hayes who progressed from sub-lieutenant in *Trillium* in 1941 to lieutenant in 1942, to first lieutenant in *Kenogami* in 1943 and commanding officer in *Guelph* in 1944-45:

The daily routine at sea was only varied by the weather, sea conditions and enemy activity. The officers lived amidships in a couple of cabins and the wardroom, which was the officer's mess. The executive officer, the second in command, had a cabin to himself. The other officers shared a four-berthed cabin. The Old Man, the captain, lived in a larger cabin one deck up. The men lived in various messdecks around the ship and slept in hammocks, except for the senior chief and petty officers, who had bunks.

Most everyone on board kept a watch of some kind, either as a lookout, signalman, officer of the watch, coder, radio operator, submarine detector or helmsman, or in the engine room or boiler room as an engine room artificer, oiler, electrician, and so on.

In the earlier ships, the galley was right aft so all the food was cold by the time it got along the upper deck to the messdecks. … We had little refrigeration so vegetables and meat spoiled quite quickly. Almost nothing was frozen so canned food was all that would last for any length of time.

Outside of watchkeeping, most of the daily routine involved keeping the ship clean and the gear operating efficiently. Most of the ship's company not on watch went to work in their various departments or messdecks between 0800 and 1200. After the noon meal, which was the main meal, most people slept, read or did hobbies. Their time was their own. Those people who did not keep watch generally worked in their departments all afternoon.

There obviously were some communal activities, such as card-playing, most of which was done in the 'dog watches' between 1600 and 2000. There was no public address system, so announcements and orders had to be relayed around the ship by a bosun's mate going around to each part of the ship in turn, blowing a bosun's call — a small, shrill whistle — to get attention, then shouting out the order or message.

The messdecks were generally damp, crowded, smelly and sometimes cold living spaces. The officer's cabins were much better and there was always the wardroom to use as a sitting place.

The weather and sea conditions were the constant concern. Fuel in sufficient quantities was not a major worry for corvettes, although it certainly was for the destroyers. The weather, though, was always the worry. Good weather, light winds, clear skies and periods of moonlight meant submarine attacks. On the other hand, storms and fog meant less enemy activity but more discomfort in already pretty primitive living conditions and, at the worst, heavy damage to life, limb and ship's equipment. Added to this was the occasional encounter with ice. Heavy ice formed on the upper decks of ships in the cold northern latitudes when spray swept over the decks in the winter months. In summer, icebergs drifted across the shipping lanes in the western Atlantic.

George Rickard says: "We tried to follow a daily routine, both at sea and in port. Messdeck cleanliness was cardinal. The deep red linoleum had to be scrubbed, tables wiped down and crumbs dug out along the edge of the tabletop and side rail. Gear had to be tidied up and items along the racks put in order. When officer's rounds [inspection] took place, most of us were required to leave the messdeck.

"Being a signalman, if off duty I was required to check signal halyards, restore bunting [signal flags], clean up the flag deck, check out the Aldis signal lamp [for signalling in Morse code] and do any paint chipping and touchups.

Getting fresh air behind the *Amherst* funnel on a nice day in 1942 are asdic operator Alf Cockburn (left) and telegraphers Lloyd Robertson and Vokes.

If the weather was bad, then it was at the messdeck table with the CBs [confidential books], making amendments and deletions to our code books from the material received at the SDO [signal distributing office] in St. John's."

Max Corkum of Halifax was a lieutenant in *Moose Jaw* from 1943-45, before moving to *Huntsville* in which he became first lieutenant. He later became the first commanding officer of the restored *Sackville*, the sole remaining Canadian corvette. She is maintained by a public trust as a floating museum in Halifax, with the cooperation of Maritime Command of the Canadian Forces, today's Navy.

"Living conditions for all ranks were far from ideal, although officers lived better than sailors from the standpoint of space," Corkum says. "We all ate the same food from the same galley.

"Water was at a premium at sea. Since the corvette was driven by steam, even though we could make some water from sea-water, it was necessary to conserve the water in our tanks as much as possible. The showers were only turned on at sea for short periods. It came down to going for long periods without a proper wash. So long as I was able to stay dry, I did not change my clothes very often. In port, it was a different story: We could use as much water as we wanted."

Bill Winegard of Guelph, Ont., who later became president of the University of Guelph, a member of Parliament and federal cabinet minister, advanced from the lower decks to the wardroom, serving as a lieutenant in *Saskatoon* in 1944-45.

"My memories of corvettes are centred about being wet, cold, cramped and at times dirty," he says. "Life was more pleasant for me aboard *Saskatoon* because, by that time, I was a commissioned officer and our quarters were significantly better than those which I had become accustomed to as a rating. It was more pleasant to crawl out of a bunk and step on a reasonably dry deck, even in a storm, than it was to climb out of a hammock and inevitably step on to a deck wet with a mixture of salt water, Carnation evaporated milk and sometimes broken crockery."

Hal Pickering of Cochrane, Ont., was another who was commissioned from the ranks, becoming a sub-lieutenant in *Halifax* in 1944-45. "The wardroom facilities were much more comfortable than messes of previous ships that I served in from 1941 in the lower deck," he says.

Hall Tingley of Galiano Island, B.C., recalls the setup when he was a sub-lieutenant in *Louisburg* in 1942: "Living conditions were sparse, but adequate. I shared quarters in a very small cabin, upper and lower bunks, with Sub-Lieutenant Dick Wright, a native of Montreal and a good type. The first lieutenant, R.A. Jarvis, occupied a single cabin, as did our captain, Lieutenant-Commander Frank Campbell. Our navigating officer was the final of five officers."

Jack Shirley of Oakville, Ont., describes conditions when he was a sub-lieutenant in *Chilliwack* in 1942-43: "We were two to a cabin with curtains on the bunks so the off-watch person would not be disturbed. We never undressed at sea, just took off our outer clothing. Water was short so we did not shave at sea. We ate the same food as the crew, maybe perked up a bit by the wardroom steward."

There was some resentment of the privileges that went with the heavier responsibilities of officers.

Bruce Crickmore of Don Mills, Ont., a coder in *Port Arthur* in 1942-43, comments: "Speak of the mess, that term sure was apropos — 20 young men living in quarters which nowadays would precipitate riots in our jails. What was disheartening was the fact that two stewards waited on five officers who were apportioned more room than 20 ratings living next door in hammocks. And we all had volunteered. When trouble is shared, the burden seems lighter."

Jim Alward of *Sackville* says: "On small ships, especially on corvettes and minesweepers, conditions for officers were relatively primitive, but only relatively. In a corvette, six officers were attended by two stewards who served them their meals, made their bunks and sent out their laundry while we were in port. Officers were often able to shower at sea and wear clean clothes."

Corvette living conditions left a lasting impression. J.E. Schumacher, a leading seaman in *Amherst* in 1943, says: "The short foc's'le corvette was a diabolical arrangement if ever there was one. Nothing could have been conceived to have made a seaman's life more miserable if He had permitted it. Stink and fumes were always present from the paint locker located right forward. There was a lively violent motion right up in the nose."

Doug Murch, *Agassiz* coder, observes: "It is difficult to describe the heaving, rolling, pitching and staggering chaos that is a corvette messdeck in rough weather. The constant swaying of hammocks, the creaking and groaning of bulkheads and equipment, the clatter of smashing crockery in the cupboard, the spilled food on decks, ratings wearily going on and off watch or rushing madly to action stations for depth-charge attacks was a kind of nightmare. All this took place in the eerie dim blue lighting that was the only illumination provided."

David Grimes of *Chambly* remarks on the dishes: "A rack secured to the forward bulkhead [wall] had two rods to keep the plates in. However, it was open at the top front, so when the ship pitched the plates would rise up and come shooting out of the rack on to the deck and smash. We would end up with very few plates. When you came off watch, you would have to use a plate left by the fellows ahead of you. You could wash it if you were fussy, or just put your food on it and eat.

"Of course, eating was a bit of a problem, especially keeping things on the table. You had to hook your finger in the handle of your cup and wrap your arm around your plate. This held things in place, but it didn't always stop what you had on the plate or in the cup from moving around. Some fun."

Jim Willett of Lantzville, B.C., recalls "abominable" conditions during his stint as a stoker in *Dauphin* in 1941-42: "In heavy seas the china dishes were smashed to bits within 24 hours of leaving port. Why we were never provided metal plates and cups, I will never understand.

"When your watch was finished and you returned to your hammock, you were assailed with the vile stench of unwashed bodies, stale cigarette smoke, the smell of eggs being fried on a metal ashtray that was used and reused alternately as an ashtray and a frying pan, time and again.

"Then your ears were assailed with the insistent noise of the anchor chains smashing against the bulkheads as the ship was tossed about in the huge waves that are ever-present in the North Atlantic, summer or winter."

Courtesy Eleanor Cousins

The weather-beaten *Algoma* enters the Foyle River in February 1942 after an Atlantic crossing.

Bill McCallum of Port Perry, Ont., was a stoker in *Strathroy* in 1944-45: "Because a corvette is always rolling and pitching, a lot of your energy goes into remaining vertical or in one place. Thus you are always tired and sleep whenever you can.

"In the boiler room there is no place to sit. The best you can do is to lean against the escape ladder, which is nearly vertical. Of course, the motion in the boiler room is not as great as on deck, since the boiler room is right over the keel and pretty well centred fore and aft."

Bill Munro of Ottawa, a telegraphist who served briefly in *Snowberry* in 1943, says: "In the wireless cabin, not only was there water on the floor but also the operator's stool was not secured to the floor. In rough weather you had to hold on to anything you could to keep from falling off the stool. With one hand you were writing and with the other holding on for dear life."

Labelling the life "very strenuous in rough weather," Chuck McFadden of Hamilton, an able seaman in *Giffard* in 1943-44, says, "You hung on with both hands at times."

Others agree. "When the weather was heavy at all and you had to move from one end of the foc's'le to the other, you swung from one stanchion [post] to another, basically. It was quite a chore just to move around," says Phil George, who served in *Baddeck*, *Bittersweet* and *Alberni*.

"Moving around the ship was a nightmare," says Morley Barnes of *Kincardine*. "You were constantly banging into things. Outside, you would hook yourself to a lifeline, for fear of being swept overboard."

Archie Marsh of Abbotsford, B.C., was a leading seaman in *Regina* in 1943-44, *Matapedia* in 1944-45 and *Nanaimo* in 1945. He reflects: "To be always hanging onto a stanchion or bracing yourself became most tiresome, but to relax for a moment could be a problem as the ship would lurch high on a wave, then drop into a trough with a thunderous crash. Seconds later we would start the elevator ride again, up to a high angle then the shattering crash as another huge wave would rush over the ship with such force I often wondered if we would founder. It was quite scary at the time and very nerve-racking."

Drawing from a personal diary, Howard Cousins gives us a perspective of life at sea during his stint as leading signalman in *Algoma* in 1941-42:

The ship was your home and the weather had a direct effect on the degree of comfort that home provided. When the wind and seas built up, the comforts of your home were virtually nonexistent. As the ship rolled and pitched, you were thrown around continuously, not daring to move without holding fast to something. The bridge was wet with spray, and sometimes solid water.

The highly developed storm gear we have today was not available then. An oilskin coat worn over a duffel coat, a sou'wester on your head and seaboots on your feet was the rig of the day. In theory, the oilskin coat overlapped the tops of the seaboots. In practice, the wind whipping around the bridge caused the skirt of the coat to lift and flap. Before long water had seeped into your boots and soon your feet were wet and cold. Water also found its way down your neck. Some of us wore a towel around our neck, but before long the towel became soaked and water trickled down your chest and back.

A corvette on the crest of a wave could have one-third of the forward portion clear of the water. As the ship rolled and dropped down into the trough, it was almost a free fall. The poor blokes in the forecastle felt virtually weightless; anything on the lockers, shelves and tables, including your meal, frequently floated off. When the ship smashed into the back of the next wave, it felt as if the ship had been dropped on concrete.

Drawing meals from the galley was awkward, to say the least. The galley was located aft of the wheelhouse and the duty messman had to collect the meals for his mess on a tray, then carry that tray along the open deck to the forecastle. With no hand available to hang on with, seas breaking over the side and down from the break of the forecastle, it was a perilous trip. Some meals did not make it.

I remember one occasion when the messman, having successfully made the trip, proudly stood at the head of the table as someone removed the oilskin protecting the food. The messman was starting to boast how good he was when the ship fell rapidly over the crest of a wave. When the ship was brought back up with the usual jolt, the messman and our food were thrown across the deck.

Bad weather also invoked the laws of physics in the basic act of getting into your bed, which was a hammock suspended from steel rods on the deckhead. To get into your hammock, you grabbed the rod and swung yourself up and in. Timing was essential. If the ship was lifting to a sea, it was virtually impossible to push yourself off the deck, let alone swing up into the hammock. On the other hand, if you waited until the ship was falling off the crest, a slight push of the toes was enough for you to float effortlessly up to the hammock.

Everyone's job became more difficult under bad weather conditions. The helmsman had his work cut out to keep the ship somewhere near the prescribed course. Stokers and engine room artificers were constantly threatened with physical injury as they moved about carrying out their duties. The cook often gave up and resorted to sandwiches. The lookout was brought down from the crow's nest and joined us on the bridge, which was but small comfort.

Like everything else, signalling had its problems. To operate the 10-inch signal projector, you stood on a small platform at one wing of the bridge, trying to hang on, operate and train the projector. At times this was impossible and we resorted to a hand-held Aldis lamp.

On one occasion, I was on the starboard wing of the bridge endeavouring to acknowledge a signal from the senior officer of the escort when the ship rolled heavily to port. I tried desperately to grab the canvas dodger, missed and fell to the ice-covered deck. I slid feet-first, with ever-increasing speed, down the steeply sloped deck until my feet crashed into the officer of the watch. He suffered a badly bruised and painful ankle, which fortunately was not broken, probably because he was wearing heavy boots.

No, home was not a place of comfort in bad weather, which did have one good thing going for it — there was very little chance that the convoy would be troubled with submarine attacks.

Fortunately, there were breaks in the gales. During the night the wind might drop and by morning the ship would be sliding easily over long swells.

Then, the first thing to be done was to make our home livable again. Everyone available turned to. This wasn't in response to an order from authority, but was a spontaneous act to better our lot. The vents on the deck were uncovered, portholes opened, odds and ends picked up and stowed.

We then went at it with water, soap and scrub brushes. The lockers were lifted out and the area under and behind them thoroughly scrubbed.

Arguments, bitching and beefing gave way to good-humoured banter, proper meals were served, the heads could be used with a certain degree of comfort and life settled down to a comfortable routine.

At the end of his recollections, Cousins typed a note: P.S. — On rereading the description of life in bad weather, it sounds pretty grim and it probably was. To put things in perspective, however, I recall that after the war my mother, in all innocence, asked, "Of all the horrors of war, what was the worst?" With no hesitation, I answered, "Writing letters."

* * *

With space so scarce in corvettes, its efficient use was important. A few corvettes had a mix of bunks and hammocks in the lower decks, but the vast majority relied on hammocks to make the most of cramped quarters. This meant that lower deckers often took adversity lying down — and became grateful for it.

A hammock became commonly and affectionately known as a "mick." A sailor in his mick was in his own little world, for his canvas cocoon insulated him from the goings-on.

George Rickard remembers the routine: "After the noon dinner we were not required to work as we had to stand night watches and we usually needed to catch up on sleep. It also gave us a chance to relax in our micks and read a *Reader's Digest* that was tucked under our hammock mattress along with a collection of socks and underwear."

Doug May of Sardis, B.C., a telegraphist in *Kincardine* in 1944-45, comments: "When not on watch or cleaning ship, the favourite pastime was getting your head down. We became inured to noises and activities around us. I can remember one time when we were on a gunnery shoot with the 4-incher. I slept right through it in my hammock even though the gun mounting was above me and I was separated from it all by only the deck plates."

"Where you slung your hammock was determined when the crew went aboard," says Moose McGill of Courtenay, B.C., a stoker in *Kitchener* in 1942-43. "You would look around and see a good spot; for example, not over a table but near the gangway for quick exit in an emergency. Hammocks were quite comfortable to sleep in, even in extremely rough weather."

Telegraphist Wes Johnson of Ottawa joined his first ship, *Kincardine*, on June 1, 1944, five days before her commissioning: "They told us to take a spot and sling our hammock and that would be your place as long as you were aboard the ship. Well, I guessed that the best thing was to sling my hammock as close to a companion-way as I could, so that if anything happened I would just go up the stairs and over the side.

"Of course, it was the wrong thing to do, as I found out later when I realized I had my hammock slung right over the magazine, which was about 20 feet below me and had tons of explosive — depth charges and ammunition. I didn't worry at all then about self-preservation because I realized that if we got hit by a torpedo I wouldn't know what had happened.

"Also, with my hammock right next to the companion-way, everybody who passed by gave me a friendly slap on the ass. I made the wrong move. That was the greenhorn coming aboard."

If you joined an existing crew, hammock space was hard to come by, says H.J. Taylor of Belleville, Ont., a coder in *Agassiz* from 1942-44 and in *Tillsonburg* in 1944-45: "You had to be aboard for at least six months before you could get a place to sling your hammock. In the meantime, you slept on the lockers or the deck when it was really rough."

Telegraphist Doug May's *Kincardine* watch card.

That experience was shared by Bob Carson in *Alberni*: "It was six months before I got a hammock space."

Art Chinery recalls one of the laws of the messdeck from his 1944-45 experience in *Orangeville*: "Hammocks had to be stored each morning in the rack in the centre of the seamen's messdeck. We were not allowed to sling them until late in the day.

"I found sleeping in hammocks very comfortable and there was no problem of being thrown out during rough weather. They were also warm, especially on cold winter nights. Every night at sea I would fall asleep planning on how I was going to escape that messdeck if anything happened."

Chris McGregor of Vancouver, B.C., a telegraphist trained operator in *Orangeville* in 1944-45, says, "We slept in hammocks, which I believe were superior to bunks. No one rolled out of a hammock in a heavy sea and when the messdeck was cool or cold, a hammock was really quite cosy."

Don Lindberg of Thunder Bay, Ont., a telegraphist trained operator in *Louisburg (2nd)* from 1943-45, simply says, "Hammocks were the best way to sleep as one was always level and secure in bad weather."

Howard Trusdale of London, Ont., remembers his 1944-45 experience in *Fergus*: "Each man had been issued a hammock and most slept in them. You swung up into it, then the ship's motion was taken up by the mick. We learned early to put our slicker [raincoat] over the hammock because in cold areas the warm moist air of the mess would condense on the cold deckhead and the drops formed fell onto our blankets. It took a long time for the blankets to dry and the slicker saved the bother.

"A properly lashed hammock was supposedly able to keep a man afloat for a few hours," Trusdale adds. "How one would get the hammocks out in an emergency was never explained."

An insensitive shore bureaucracy once prevented Murray Collins of Sault Ste. Marie, Ont., an able seaman in *Port Arthur* in 1943-44, from using his hammock: "On one trip from Halifax to New York, my hammock ropes broke so when we landed back in Halifax, I went to the stores for replacements. On the dot of 1600 hours, the stores doors were closed in my face. With no new ropes, I made the next trip sleeping on locker cushions under our mess table. Needless to say, after several days and nights between slopped food, salty sea-water and vomit, my sweater could stand by itself."

* * *

Corvette men had a hard time putting their troubles behind them when they went to the heads — the seaman's latrines.

Jim Alward comments: "There was a very heavy iron door that seemed to weigh a ton as the ship rolled while we were entering or leaving. Those who were not strong enough to withstand the pressure were in danger of losing fingers. After Tiffy [the sick berth attendant] nearly lost the tip of his index finger, they took off the door."

George Rickard also recalls that the heavy iron door "had the ability to crush one's fingers as it suddenly swung shut during a sharp roll of the ship."

John Parker of Woodstock, Ont., an able seaman in *Algoma* from 1942-44, says, "And try to go to the heads in a heavy sea. The door was so heavy the heads were a makeshift air-raid shelter."

W.J. Roberts, *Oakville* telegraphist in 1941-42, says two things scared him — the stability of the ship in a gale and the "armour plate door" on the heads: "Someone would fail to latch it and if that thing caught you on a swing, it could wipe you out."

Bottoms up, the adventure is just beginning. Max Corkum, who spent most of his corvette time in *Moose Jaw*, explains: "In the officers' heads, the toilet of course went over the side, the port side to be exact. The storm valve at the exit did not work, so whenever the ship rolled down to port, the water would rush in. This would send a blast of air up the soil pipe, which would spray water, or whatever, from the bowl all over your bottom. The trick was to rise up from the bowl every time there was a roll to port.

"The same situation would occur in port when a harbour craft went close by, creating a wake on the port side. This would always be a surprise because when you were in the heads you would be unaware of the presence of boats around the ship. On one occasion in port, we were entertaining a group of Wrens and one went up to the heads. Suddenly, we heard screams coming from that area. All the locals laughed because we knew why."

Jim Alward recalls his stint in *Sackville*: "At night when one groped through the blackness of the heads, he prepared himself for the cold Atlantic as it rushed up the outlet pipe.

One fellow from Winnipeg was literally inundated with a rush of water up the pipe. In a sense, the ocean flushed him out of the heads."

Donald McNeille, a stoker petty officer in *Strathroy* in 1944-45, remembers, "There were four or so toilet seats, open, no privacy at all, just like the outside backhouses of old farmhouses. The sea-water flowed through underneath you all the time you were sitting, which gave you a real good rear-end wash and a half-frozen behind, so one did not linger any longer than required."

In today's computer parlance, the heads were not "user friendly." They also necessitated a dirty job but, surprisingly, it was not despised. William Wainio, *Trillium* rating, explains: "It fell upon the new ordinary seamen to be assigned the prestigious task of 'captain of the heads' for perhaps a month or two. This consisted of keeping the water closets [toilets] and washrooms clean. This was done on a daily basis, both in harbour and at sea.

"While it would appear to be as low as one can get, it had its advantages. The captain of the heads was not required to do any other ship's chores, apart from maintaining his action station. In harbour, when his housekeeping was completed, he was free to go ashore. I had the privilege of this honoured position for two months."

* * *

Irreverence was a characteristic of language aboard ship, but there were limits. Tony Griffin, 1941-43 CO, in *Pictou* explains: "No record of wartime life in the navy could be complete which omitted reference to the f-word, without which the entire Allied war effort would have ground to a halt! The word insinuated itself into every sentence, even into words, such as abso-fucking-lutely! It became so prevalent that the use of it had to be curbed in harbour when guests were in the wardroom; the crew were told that it would be a punishable offence to use the word on the upper deck in that situation. One afternoon in St. John's, with guests in the wardroom, 'Where's the fucking paint pot?' came in loud and clear. 'Take that man's name.' The offender was put in the rattle and duly appeared before me.

"He confessed right away and I awarded him three days' restriction of leave. 'On cap, about turn, quick march.' As he marched off, he was clearly heard to say in a stage whisper 'Three fucking days for one fucking *fuck*.' The solemnity of the occasion was broken; there was general laughter. I called him back and suspended the sentence, telling him that next time it would be something more. ..."

Relaxing in the welldeck of *Louisburg* in July 1942 are (from left) Dick Keenan, Brock Parsons, Nick Robinson, Buck Buckley.

Courtesy Wm. John Quinsey/Hugh Merryweather Collection

The corvette *Barrie* in rough seas on the North Atlantic, probably in 1944.

CHAPTER EIGHT

"IF YOU WANT REAL TOUGH, TAKE LIFE ABOARD A CORVETTE WHILE SEASICK."

THE ROYAL CANADIAN NAVY struggled for much of World War II to produce enough trained sailors for all the new ships of the various classes and types it put to sea. To maintain operations, the navy took a tough approach to that age-old bane known as seasickness, which generally had a greater effect on smaller ships. So even though a large number of volunteer sailors were affected, especially in corvettes, only the worst cases were reassigned to a larger ship or given shore jobs.

The vast majority of corvette crew members toughed it out. This has generated many vivid memories. One who made the adjustment is Doug Clarance of Gabriola, B.C.:

The four years I spent in the navy were the most significant of my life. In that time I think I grew more in both experience and conditioning than in any other time in my life. Unfortunately, I do not regard my 18 months in *Regina* as the best period of my career as a naval officer.

I joined the navy as a green recent graduate from senior matriculation in a Vancouver high school. After a brief four-month training at HMCS *Kings* in Halifax, I joined *Regina* in 1942. I felt I looked the part as a sub-lieutenant, if not able to act it. The thing that got me off on a poor footing, in my analysis, was motion sickness.

I was seasick beyond all measure. In fact, although I weighed about 180 pounds, being six-foot-four I was skinny. And yet I lost as much as 10 pounds a trip. I would be seasick the full journey. When you are seasick, you really don't give a hoot about much of anything and I found it extremely difficult to be really interested in my job, although I did my darnedest to do it. Needless to say, this did not win me a good position in the eyes of the crew. I suspect they regarded me as typical of the 90-day wonders who became officers who were more or less incapable and useless as far as they were concerned.

This was coupled with the fact that the captain did very little to give his junior officers a proper understanding of the conduct becoming of an officer. Certainly he did not set an example any of us cared to follow.

A new captain [Harry Freeland] was appointed that fall and he began to whip the ship into some sort of order. The sea was calmer and my seasickness started to get better, yet it got to the point where the captain told me that if I did not improve and lick my problem he would have to ask for a shore appointment. It was so important because he expected the ship to be appointed for overseas duty and he wanted to be sure that he had competent officers. So I proceeded to eat most of my meals three or four times until something stayed down. I got to the point where I overcame my seasickness, after the first day at sea, and became relatively capable, I think.

Doug Murch remembers when *Agassiz* headed from Halifax to nearby St. Margaret's Bay for sea trials in April 1943:

I was sitting with the guys in the forward messdeck when the rolling and pitching started and quite unexpectedly this horrible feeling of nausea came over me. I recall someone saying, "Quick, give him a piece of dry bread!"

In no time I was up the ladder and throwing up over the side. I spent the entire voyage lying in the scuppers under an old greatcoat with bouts of on-and-off throwing up, wondering what in hell I had gotten myself into and what was going to happen to me. Throughout this nightmare other ratings were slipping and sliding along the sloping deck, stepping over me as if I were just a heap of old clothes. The scary part was that nobody gave a damn.

Seasickness is no joke and nothing to be ashamed of. Lord Nelson himself suffered from it. Many sailors suffered from it in varying degrees.

I was in abject misery for the first two days of each and every trip. You had to stand your watch regardless. Nausea and vomiting being non-stop, you carried a bucket: soiling the messdeck was an absolute no-no. There was no sympathy — only a grudging tolerance of the seasick rating.

While sick I developed a super-sense of smell which made the stale air of the messdeck intolerable, and oil fumes from the engine room were even worse. These odours, normally quite acceptable, just turned my stomach inside out. My way of dealing with this was to spend my off-duty hours wedged into a remote corner of the rail by the wheelhouse, with the salt air and spray in my face, which brought a measure of relief.

After two days of this, a miracle occurred. My appetite and ability to eat somehow returned and I was okay, except in extremely violent weather when the nausea would return to some degree. Life aboard a corvette was tough, but if you want real tough, take life aboard a corvette while seasick.

George Auby was yeoman of signals in the advance party that picked up the corvette *Sorel* in the shipbuilding city of Sorel, Que. He remembers that in August 1941 more crew came aboard at Quebec City, and *Sorel* headed for Halifax: "As soon as we hit the swells of the Gulf of St. Lawrence everybody was sick except the captain, yours truly and a Newfie wheelman. The Old Man asked if I could cook and the Newfie volunteered. He cooked up a pot of potatoes which he dumped on the wardroom table, skins and all. On the bridge the subbies [sub-lieutenants] had to share one bucket, taking turns. All were glad to see hard ground again."

Henry Kozlowski of Laval, Que., an able seaman, recalls that he was one of a small group of replacements who joined *Arrowhead* at Quebec City in August 1944. "When we left for Halifax, the St. Lawrence River was calm. As we approached the Gulf, the sea became choppy and some of the replacements became sick. The rails were our only hope and were used for two to three days. Some of us could not reach the rails on time and had a go on the deck. We were given a bucket and a mop and told to clean up the mess. That didn't exactly help matters. Food intake was scarce the first few days. We ate mostly toast, which we held down, but as time went by we graduated to more solid food. Mind you, one of the replacements was a cook and he had a go at the rails as well. Seasickness is nothing to laugh at: it can make a man wish he were dead."

Howard Markle was an able seaman when he joined *Chambly* at Jetty 5 in Slackers (Halifax) one evening in 1944. "The next morning I was dutifully chipping paint on the foc's'le and enjoying my first views of the harbour and Dartmouth. The gentle swells from the passing harbour craft were, however, somewhat disconcerting. The sickness that I was beginning to feel concerned me greatly as I envisaged myself a victim of chronic seasickness. Having heard that seasickness was not considered a reason for staying ashore, I began to regret that I hadn't volunteered for the army. I must have looked a tad out of sorts and the leading seaman in charge sent me to sick bay where, much to my relief, I was diagnosed as having measles and shipped off forthwith to Camp Hill Hospital in Halifax."

Bob MacIntosh joined *Owen Sound* as a stoker in 1943: "Finally we went to sea, after three weeks in Halifax harbour. St. Margaret's Bay was our destination, which wasn't very far, but it took us into the open sea and the land swell. A few of the crew were seasick, but not I. I was quite proud that I found my sea legs so soon.

"Three weeks later we were sent to Newfoundland. We left Halifax in a howling gale that only got worse each day. This was a heavy sea, the heaviest during my seven years at sea. The waves were easily 40-footers, perhaps more. We were nearly there and I still hadn't lost my cookies, although I had felt some nausea.

"It was my turn to help with the dishes after dinner and I was drying while my partner Gordon Lawrence was washing them in a pail. He was feeling pretty tough and was quite green looking as he held the pail of dishes wedged between his feet. He was sitting down with his head over the pail when he let go, right into the dish-water. That did it for me and I lost my supper right there. We both saw the humour of it and carried on, mopping up the mess and feeling better."

* * *

Newfoundland comes to mind often when the subject is seasickness. George Rickard was a raw signalman when *Dauphin* left St. John's late in the summer of 1942:

I was on the bridge as a standby at the flag locker on leaving port. Soon the quartermaster piped duty watch to sea stations and at the same time we hit the land swells. That was it. Down off the bridge over to the lee side to join about a dozen others in spewing our guts out into the Atlantic. I wormed my way over to the hatch and descended into our messdeck and the comfort of my hammock. Items were being tossed about by the motion of the ship and the air seemed to float around in chunks. Back up the ladder and out into the fresh air. There, under the foc's'le, I heaved up until nothing came but green bile. A real salty able seaman heading for the forward messdeck made the comment that it wouldn't do me any harm, but if I brought up a red ring to push it back down my throat as that would be my asshole.

Knowing that I would eventually have to go on watch as duty sig, I had put on seaboots, a handknit turtleneck sweater supplied by the IODE [Imperial Order Daughters of the Empire] and my life jacket. I knew of one spot on the upper deck that would provide a reasonable amount of protection from the weather as well as a bit of warmth. This was the raised area around the funnel, which was called the fiddly deck. With a Coke and a pocketful of crackers, it seemed to be the only spot for any relief from the agony of retching. Here for days in, days out, nights in and nights out, I lived, working my way to stand duty on the bridge as required, knowing that I had a job to do and was not along for the ride. Eventually I got over my seasickness and soon became as salty as the rest.

Jim Galloway recalls his first trip to sea. He was an ordinary seaman when *Agassiz* left St. John's on July 7, 1942:

The ship began to rise and fall with the long, rolling waves. The sardines I had for lunch started to swim around. I laid down on top of the foot lockers. My first watch was on the bridge as lookout on the port side. The first lieutenant was on the same watch. Each time I would remove the binoculars from my eyes, he would growl at me, saying I had to make continuous sweeps from dead ahead to 90 degrees on the port side.

My eyes were aching, as were my arms from holding the binoculars up. It got to the point I could see very little and be sure of it. The motion of the ship climbing up and down each rolling swell got my stomach heaving. The next thing I knew I was throwing up all over that corner of the bridge.

The first lieutenant called me a few choice names and ordered me below to get a bucket and rags to scrub the bridge clean. I fully understood I should clean up the mess I had made, but to scrub all the bridge gratings while at sea seemed more punishment than fit the crime. The other lookout offered to help me, but he was told off and directed to sweep my sector as well as his own. I went below and got two buckets and cleaning equipment. I spent the rest of the dog watch scrubbing with one bucket and throwing up in the other bucket.

On leaving the bridge, I was completely demoralized, cold and sick. In the messdeck, the smell of food made me sicker. I went back outside to stand at the break of the forecastle, throwing up over the side from time to time. When I returned to the messdeck, I laid down on the foot lockers and slept until time to go on watch again. I took a bucket with me. I used it a lot, I might add.

Howard Cousins in *Algoma* says: "The worst place to sail from was Newfie. As soon as you poked through the harbour entrance, the Narrows, you were in the middle of the Atlantic Ocean. At times it was with feelings of trepidation that the lines were cast off and the ship eased down the harbour into the teeth of a gale. We knew that in a few minutes we would be hanging on grimly while sheets of spray swept over the bridge. There were occasions we sailed

Unidentified corvette with winter ice on her bow.

under conditions that in normal times would cause a ship's departure to be delayed until the weather moderated."

Alf Cockburn of Don Mills, Ont., an asdic operator, came to *Amherst* in Halifax in August 1941 shortly after she was commissioned: "Our first real activity was to approach Bermuda to pick up and escort a troopship of Canadian soldiers from Bermuda to Botwood, Newfoundland. The trip was uneventful but rough and I was so seasick that I contemplated hiding out somewhere in Newfoundland for the duration. However, once we docked I forgot all about such intentions and was never seasick again."

John Hunter of Vancouver was an able seaman in 1943: "I had served seven months in a Fairmile [a 112-foot motor launch] working out of Gaspé before I was drafted in December 1943 to the corvette *Fennel* in St. John's. It had taken me a few trips to get used to the motion of the motor launch, but this was a new experience. I think I ate supper that night, but know that a few days passed before I had another meal. We had to go to the galley to collect our meal on trays. We had to pass the boiler room and the smell of steam and hot oil killed any appetite I might have had.

"My action station was loader on the twin Bofors [an anti-aircraft gun], a new experience. In my state of health, it was fortunate I wasn't called upon to help defend us. I have jokingly said that for the first half of the trip I was too sick to eat and for the last half I could hardly move for hemorrhoids. When we arrived in Derry I was sent to hospital for a week or so, then on to *Niobe*, the RCN manning depot in Scotland."

Telegraphist Bob Dick joined *Pictou* in 1942: "I well remember the day I was drafted as within a few hours I was out in the Atlantic on my first convoy. That evening was my first action stations at the stern depth charge rails. Watching that stern going up and down didn't please my stomach and I did my share of six meals a day — three down and three up. I was glad to see us going through that gate at St. John's."

George Hollins of Kirkfield, Ont., was an ERA in *Midland* from 1943-45: "My first watch at sea was in the boiler room. I was responsible for the oil-fuelled fire, nozzles and pumps, the draft to prevent smoke, and the water level in the sight glass — high up from the steel plate deck laid in the keel. Seasickness quickly reduced me to crashing stations — read 'laying down on the catwalk alongside the boiler where the smell from the bilge and fuel oil only made survival worse.'"

Gordon Naylor of Chemainus, B.C., a leading stoker in *Agassiz*, relates an incident that reflects the peculiar sea-handling characteristics of a corvette: "On convoy in 1941 we rammed a Newfoundland fishing trawler in fog at night. We recovered the entire crew. They made the passage to Iceland and back with us. One of the trawler crew said he had intended to go to Halifax and join the Canadian navy, but after being seasick most of this trip, he had changed his mind."

* * *

Food could be a barrier for newcomers. Tom Baird relates an incident from his *Regina* days: "After sea trials at Pictou, N.S., in December 1943, we got sailing orders to proceed to Halifax. This was a first time at sea for almost all the crew. Only a few from the original crew and a couple of officers remained after our refit. It turned very rough.

"I shall never forget the first supper. The menu was pork chops, mashed potatoes, gravy, creamed corn, raisin pie and coffee. Well, quite a few did not get to the table and some who did sure did not stay long. Our chief ERA was right in his glory. He sure could eat those pork chops. I asked the chief why they served pork chops and creamed corn. He said that menu sorts the men from the boys. If they can handle that, they will be good sailors."

Owen Sound telegraphist Jack Nash says: "Our trip from Quebec City to Halifax in December 1943 for the beginning of serious training was something else. Of the 90 or so people aboard, I would estimate that 80-plus were seasick, including myself. It was the first time most of us had seen the ocean and it was quite an introduction. I never saw it rougher in the next two years.

"I always remember the cook did chicken for supper and the food was taken in trays to the various messdecks. When we got to Halifax there was chicken all over the decks as the trays spilled and no one was well enough to do anything about it. I remember my legs were so weak after two days of throwing up that I could scarcely make it down the gangplank in Halifax. We eventually got used to the motion."

Old hands were sometimes less than considerate. From his 1944-45 service in *Trentonian*, Jack Scott of Winnipeg, Man., recalls a young seaman named Red who struggled with seasickness: "One day when it was fairly rough, we had bacon and eggs for breakfast. Red was making a real attempt to eat his meal and all was going well until some clown stuffed bacon rind up his nostrils and then called,

'Hey Red!' Red took one look, put his hand over his mouth and rushed to the heads."

Similarly, Albert Maskell of Willowdale, Ont., a signalman in *Fennel* and *Hepatica*, recalls "old sea dogs sucking on pieces of salt pork in front of new recruits in really rough weather."

Recurring seasickness was a routine for some. Jim Bessey of Stouffville, Ont., who served in *Arvida* and *Lethbridge*, comments: "Every trip for the first 12 to 24 hours. A miserable feeling. I envied the old salts."

C.J. McDonald of Medicine Hat, Alta., was a seaman in *Oakville* in 1943-44: "I was sick all the time at sea. I enjoyed being out at sea, except for the seasickness — a hell of a lot worse than a hangover."

Sorel yeoman of signals George Auby relates: "It was my duty to check the funnel party, a group of seven to nine chronic seasick sailors who, come hell or winter, spent all their off-duty time outside, aft of the funnel. These men seldom ate and would not enter a mess. We had the occasional request for a loaf of bread. Needless to say, many had boils on their rear-end from sitting on hot boiler plates. This kept the sick bay tiffy busy."

With seasickness being so prevalent, and so debilitating, sailors tried a raft of things to find an antidote. There was, however, no universal cure, but some sailors did find a personal remedy.

William Anderson, a stoker, was drafted to *Collingwood* and introduced to the stokehold the day after consuming a few pints of Oland's brew: "There I was in front of a big cylindrical boiler about 15 feet in diameter with three roaring fires and the uptakes [chimney] vibrating like all get out. A very scary place for a seasick jeep. The leading hand made me drink lime juice, which he had in a stone jug, and did everything possible to keep me occupied and hating him every second.

"On completion of that watch we went up top just in time for up spirits, the daily rum ration which the leading hand made me down in one gulp. I really didn't know if I was going to blow up or just lose all my hair, but within 20 minutes I felt hungry. I ate some lunch, plain potatoes, and went aft and hung around the quarterdeck all afternoon. I was never sick again, with one exception."

S.J. Yankoski was a gunnery rating in *Hepatica* in 1943-44: "I had my share of seasickness. It is one of the worst feelings you could have. One winter night when I was sick, I rolled out of my mick. Smitty, the leading seaman

from Vancouver, asked where I was going. I said, 'I have the midnight watch.' He said, 'You get back into your mick. I'll take your watch.' I had a good sleep and did feel better.

"Finally I was old enough to have my tot of rum and I believe it was that tot that cured my seasickness. To this day I have stayed with my Pusser's."

Another solution was found by Garry Flock who left the 5,675-ton armed merchant cruiser *Prince Robert* to go to the 970-ton *Forest Hill* in 1943: "I could not keep anything down. Our cook suggested I eat raw turnip. That had cured him. By golly, it worked for me, too."

Herb Turner of Sorrento, B.C., was a radar operator in *Rosthern* in 1944-45: "I was fortunate I was not seasick very often, except for the times when we had to sail too soon after having partaken too much of the spirits. The best thing to do was stay outside and get as much fresh air as possible, but in the winter on the North Atlantic, the weather was too severe for that. The next best thing was to get your head down until your next turn to stand watch."

A trip to the naval doctor in the Halifax dockyard didn't solve the problem for Jim Galloway: "I had lost a lot of weight being seasick and not being able to keep food in my stomach. It was a miserable way of living. I did not want to be drafted ashore as medically unfit. I decided I was going to be a sailor or die in the attempt."

Galloway found no comfort sleeping on *Agassiz*'s lockers, so the next stop in Greenock, Scotland, he bribed a dockyard worker with two pounds sterling and a carton of cigarettes. In return, he got an iron hook welded to a bulkhead in the seamen's mess. This allowed him to sling his mick, using a stanchion to anchor the other end. On the next trip across the Atlantic he climbed into his mick at every opportunity: "The food stayed down. For several days I just gloried in getting into my hammock and shutting my eyes so I could not see the motion of the ship. No matter how bad the seas got and how much the ship bucked, rolled, twisted and pitched, I was never ever seasick again.

"I was so thankful for the work that the dockyard man did that when we again put into Greenock I looked him up and gave him the news and another carton of cigarettes. I never regained all the weight I had lost, but did put a few pounds back on and I felt great."

Jack Bagnell of Truro, N.S., an able seaman, was drafted to *Port Arthur* in October 1942 when she was in Halifax: "We left the next day to go overseas. From here to Newfoundland, it was just like sitting in your living room.

We stayed in Newfoundland overnight and headed out the next day. An old Greek freighter broke down. The waves were so high that when we were up on top of one, you could almost see down her funnels. I became some seasick. I couldn't hold my head up. My buddy, Quance, got me some raisins. 'Eat 'em, eat 'em all,' he said. So I shoved as many as I could down and I stopped getting seasick."

Ray MacAulay of Fredericton, N.B., was an able seaman in *Charlottetown* in 1942 on the Triangle Run — Halifax, St. John's and Boston or New York: "I do recall some rough water, lots of seasickness, wet clothing and no place to dry it. One storm all the crew were sick. The only thing I could get to stay with me was raisins."

Bill Acheson was leading signalman in *Fennel*: "I was never a good sailor, even in a larger ship. The seas on the Triangle Run in the winter of 1942-43 turned my stomach and food into instant and complete strangers. On occasion I could manage hard tack and a mug of tea. On other occasions, of all things, a bottle of Coke — for a nickel no less, at the ship's canteen — would settle my queasy stomach."

Bill McCallum of Port Perry, Ont., was a stoker in *Strathroy* in 1944-45: "Once in the navy my sole ambition was to go to sea. My only fear was that I might get seasick. Luckily for me, when I was about to go to sea our ship was moored next to HMCS *Midland*, an older corvette in which my brother was serving. He said that he got sick on the first day out of port, but then everything was okay after that.

"He advised me to eat as often as possible and never pass the fanny, the name given to a large breadbox in every mess that was stocked with bread, jam, honey and margarine. I followed his instructions, never once was sick and gained 10 pounds the first week."

* * *

Not everyone could manage. In Library and Archives Canada I found a memorandum written in December 1941 by Gus Miles, commander D *Halifax*, to the commanding officer Atlantic coast. The subject was a corvette officer who shall remain nameless: "It has been necessary to ask that this officer be relieved from HMCS *Louisburg* because of continued seasickness. This is the only fault of which his commanding officer complains, and it is recommended that he be appointed to a larger ship rather than to permanent shore duty."

Corvette veterans recall their less fortunate shipmates. Jack Scott of Winnipeg, Man., an able seaman in *Trentonian*, says: "On a trip from Halifax to Londonderry in April 1944, an ERA on his first ship was seasick before leaving the gates of Halifax and remained sick for the trip. Unable to eat, his condition worsened and they took him off the ship in Londonderry on a stretcher. I hope they flew him home eventually. He sure was no sailor."

Bill Ivy of Mississauga, Ont., was leading telegraphist in *Sorel* in 1941-42: "I remember two of my sparkers [telegraphists] who were plagued by seasickness. One, an unsung hero, was so sick we didn't see him in the mess for the whole trip, about 18 days. As soon as we left harbour, he found a corner on the upper deck near the funnel, wedged himself in and slept in a nest of duffel coats.

"He stood his watch, though, in the stuffy, smoky air of the wireless cabin, with a gash bucket between his knees, hanging on with one hand while copying monotonous four- and five-figure groups of Morse code broadcast to all ships and hardly ever addressed to your ship.

"He and others who were seasick didn't receive much sympathy from their shipmates, who would tell them in their worst moment that if they felt something come up that was round, with a hole in the middle like a Life Saver, to swallow quick or it would be all over for them. This poor fellow was drafted ashore mercifully after the return trip across the Atlantic."

Harold Miles of Halifax was a stoker petty officer in *Kincardine* in 1944-45: "I recall one of our cooks tied himself to a fire hydrant on the quarterdeck and laid there for the whole trip from Londonderry to St. John's. It's a wonder he survived as he was washed over by some of the waves that always came over the deck in bad weather. He was taken off when we came into port, and that was the last we saw of him."

Sid Husby was an ERA in *Hespeler* in 1944-45: "We had one poor guy who always got sick when we went to sea. He wouldn't go down to the crew quarters. He slept, and ate when he could, in the passageway between the two entrances down to the engine room. The crew brought his food to him. He was a little guy and we felt sorry for him because he just couldn't hold his food down. When he was found in the scuppers at the stern of the ship covered by the waves coming aboard, the captain said that's enough of that. When we came into port he was drafted off the ship, and we heard he never went to sea again."

Noble (left), Norman and Parsons hold lunch for the *Regina* crew in 1942 or 1943.

CHAPTER NINE
"ONE DOLLAR PER DAY PER MAN AT SEA."

"RUDIMENTARY" is a charitable description of the food served to corvette crews. Food supplies were drawn from naval stores by a crew member known as the victualling assistant (VA) or, increasingly as the war progressed, by the supply assistant.

Hewlett White of Agincourt, Ont., VA in *Collingwood* from 1942-45, makes the point that the "health and happiness of the crew" was directly affected "by the variety and quality of food that the VA stocked for an ocean run. Our busy time was while we were in port. It was the responsibility of the VA, in co-operation with the senior cook, to prepare a menu for each trip, making sure there were sufficient quantities of supplies.

"The day our stores arrived at shipside, the duty crew unloaded the carrier. There was never any lack of help, particularly when fruit was coming aboard. We always ordered an extra case as we knew that one would be dropped on deck."

His namesake Albert White of Windsor, Ont., a 1942 *Rosthern* able seaman, confirms: "When we were loading supplies in port, we would get some fruit or canned items and put them in our lockers in case of bad weather at sea."

VA Hewlett White continues: "Corvettes operated under the central messing system where all foods were prepared in the ship's galley. Officers and crew had the same menu. We had to see that the galley received the proper amounts for each meal. The staples — bread, tea, coffee, milk — were distributed from our storeroom at stipulated hours each day.

"The VA was required to keep a rigid account of all foods dispersed. We were subject to an inventory each time we arrived in our home port. We were also required to report a cost per man per day. That cost varied and was very high during our sea days but averaged out from the reduced amount of food we used in port."

Ivan McCabe of Regina, Sask., leading cook in *Orangeville* in 1944-45, says: "Our victualling used to run about one dollar per day per man at sea. That was considered pretty expensive." He, too, notes the cost was lower when the ship was in port because many men would be ashore at least part of the time.

Laurie Simpkin of Halifax, N.S., the VA in *Hepatica*, 1940-41, comments on conditions: "When we left Halifax in December 1940, we had no refrigeration, so we could only carry about a week's supply of fresh meat and vegetables." The meat was stored in a beef screen, "a large locker, solid metal halfway up four sides, with a metal screen on all sides to allow a free flow of air to pass over the contents."

Carrying a large slab of beef from the beef screen midships to the galley aft was no easy chore. Getting dry stores to the galley could also be difficult, Simpkin says: "If I had to get a sack of flour, I had to wait for the ship to dive into a wave and when the ship came up, I had to grab the sack, dash up the ladder and hope to get all the way up — or else land on my fanny, most times with the goods on top of me."

Ken Hedley, in *Mayflower* from 1940-42, says: "Refrigeration was nonexistent and meat was kept in a wire cage on the deck. After a few days of salt-water spray and air, the meat became quite high."

Jim Sharpe of Victoria, B.C., HSD in *Windflower* from 1940-42, recalls: "There was no refrigerator on board. Fresh quarters of beef and sides of pork were hung in beef screens on the upper deck. Fresh vegetables and fruit, when available, were also hung in similar 'rabbit cages.' These cages were covered with canvas in an attempt to divert the rain, wind and salt spray.

"This situation was not all bad, although during warm summer days things didn't last too long, especially the meat. The first couple of days the cook was able to cook roasts, but after that he would cut away the exposed portions and salvage enough for stew. During most of the year, the fresh meat could be made to last maybe 10 days. Spuds and other root vegetables, eggs and 'canned dog' — any canned meat — were our staples."

Dietary deficiencies were sometimes a problem. Morley Barnes of Mississauga, Ont., a 1944-45 *Kincardine* stoker, recalls: "Several sailors got scurvy, myself included. I still have the spots on my body. This, of course, is caused by lack of fresh fruit and vegetables. Later we did get some [vitamin] pills and they did help. Scurvy is an unusual disease. Your various joints swell and you develop a sore, almost like a boil. It's these sores that leave their mark."

The need to demagnetize the ship combined with the lack of refrigeration had a further negative impact. Garry Flock of Winnipeg, Man., a 1943-45 *Forest Hill* ERA, explains: "We had a degaussing line encircling the ship. It was electrically charged to protect the ship against magnetic mines. This line emitted a bit of heat and was a great place for cockroaches to hide. We used condensed milk. One of us poured some out one day. What came out? Why, a cockroach — drowned. Thereafter, we always stuck a match into the pierced holes."

John Parker of Woodstock, Ont., recalls mealtime from his 1942-44 *Algoma* service: "'Pass the corn syrup.' Plop, plop — out come the cockroaches first. It was the same from the condensed milk."

It was the norm to make the most of what was available, like it or not. Albert Baker, *Orillia* able seaman, recalls the Iceland Run in 1941: "Anchored out in St. John's harbour was a damaged ship with its hold full of mutton from Australia. The authorities left it there for use by our escorts. Jerry would have done us all a good turn if he had sunk it.

"For several trips it was still there and we would load up with this mutton, hair and all. The first few days out we would have roasts or chops. The cook would do a good job of it. Then it would start to turn and the rush was on

to get rid of it. We would have lamb stew for breakfast, dinner and supper.

"Finally, the captain threatened the supply assistant that if any more of that mutton came aboard, he'd go overboard with the meat. We survived, but it was not uncommon to hear the 'baa' of sheep on a quiet night on watch."

Sometimes supplies were borderline. Ivan McCabe aboard *Orangeville* says: "Eggs were always old. We put them in a pot of water and if they floated, we threw them away."

Aboard a corvette, the two cooks were key people. Hewlett White is succinct: "The food was as good as the galley staff. *Collingwood* was fortunate to have excellent cooks."

Skinny Hayes, an officer in *Trillium, Kenogami* and *Guelph,* observes: "Cooks varied considerably. Some ships even had a good one or two. Most didn't. I don't think naval cooks got any training in cooking."

Charlie Appleby, of San Diego, California, a cook in *Agassiz*, comments: "I had been in the restaurant business in Winnipeg in the 1930s. This counted for nothing and got me in trouble, I was so upset with the way food was handled and wasted: potatoes peeled hours before cooking, and so on. I was always told to 'do it the navy way.' Saturday inspections in cooking school — their name, not mine — were at 1130, with the noon meal at 1200. The officer would inspect with white gloves. We used coal stoves and the stupid ass would feel in the ash-bin. If his hand got dirty, extra duty for all and they threw out everything: cleansers, soap, towels, anything in the galley that had been used. A terrible waste. They were all old RCN men in charge and they were what spoiled the service…"

Bern Rawle recalls 1942 when he was a *Cobalt* stoker: "In those days the food was pretty terrible. Part of the problem was that the cooks were untrained. Many of them had apparently signed on inland as cooks with the understanding they could transfer to another branch on arrival at the coast. This, of course, never happened, so the poor chaps did their best but produced some pretty horrible stuff."

George Auby in *Sorel*, says: "I would like to mention the hardships of being on a corvette included badly or uncooked food. At this date it is easy to realize that very few men are natural chefs and these men with little training did their best to supply the hunger needs of roughly a hundred men."

Jim Russell of Riverview, N.B., a 1943-45 *Calgary* cook, says: "Cooking aboard a corvette wasn't all sunshine. The galley was small and hot, especially during blackout hours as all the portholes and hatches had to remain closed. There was only an oil stove to cook on, which wasn't very reliable. Pots were secured on top of the stove by iron rods. When it became really rough, the ship rolled so bad that even large pots could only be partially filled. For example, when cooking a roast the fat would spill out and sometimes catch on fire."

Ivan McCabe aboard *Orangeville*, one of the last and largest corvettes, says: "We were right on the upper deck aft of the funnel. The galley was about eight foot by 12 foot. We worked in tropical shorts and running shoes most of the time, it was so darn hot. We had a coal-fired stove and an oven on each side of the firebox. There was a flat iron railing around the outside of the stove-top. It had slots and we put flat iron bars in these to lock pots in place. In rough weather you had to be careful what you cooked."

Charlie Appleby notes: "The galley, being amidship, had the least movement and it was sometimes wild. You could look out the skylight and see waves. All the pots tied to the stove continued crashing and banging with the waves. Even using only six or seven inches in the bottom of three-foot-deep pots, they would still slop over on the stove. We had no air-conditioning, not even fans, and at sea it was blackout with no ventilation. It could be 120 degrees or more.

"The galley was a meeting place and as men were relieved from duty they would head for it. Hot tea, coffee and kye [chocolate] were ready most of the time. My assistant Jock Glasgow and I would keep our eyes out for younger sailors who didn't show and try and get them to take some nourishment. It wasn't always easy."

Like everyone else, cooks had to respond to any call to action stations, notes Jim Russell, and if depth charges went off while the ship was not going fast enough, "the resulting concussion would shut off the flame on the stove or turn on a water tap on the sink and when you returned you would have a mess to clean up."

Appleby took a different tack: "When action stations came we cut the oil line to the galley — goodbye cakes or whatever and run for your station."

Jim Russell gives us a glimpse at his job: "For breakfast we served hot cereal, which was called mush. One easy break-

Louisburg Cook McBride, Steward John McAuley and mascot.

fast to prepare was bacon and tomatoes, which was called red lead and bacon. The cook got a ribbing about that meal. We also used a lot of powdered eggs and powdered milk. All the meat was frozen and had to be thawed overnight for cooking the next day. For dessert, we made pies and puddings or had canned fruit. The officers and crew all got the same meals, so you caught hell in all directions."

Ray Scalzo of Winnipeg, Man., a 1943-44 *Arvida* able seaman, got a brief cook's-eye view: "At one point, the cook was sick. One of the other boys and myself were elected to take over. Both of our dads were chefs. I guess they were hoping that some of their talent had rubbed off on us. We were both Italian, so you guessed it: we made spaghetti and meatballs! You never saw anything like it. We were fighting the waves, the sauce was slopping back and forth in the pot, spills were on the stove and the meatballs were slightly burned. By the time we got to serve it, the boys were so hungry they got it all eaten up without too many complaints."

Art Geizer, the 1941-45 *Agassiz* coxswain, says: "I generally felt sorry for the cooks because they took verbal abuse from a lot of new entry sailors who, for the most part, had never seen salt water. They expected the same as mom cooked. Can you imagine preparing a meal while standing on a rolling deck, with pots and pans on a hot stove? Under such adverse conditions, they did a marvellous job."

Not everyone was always understanding. William Bizruchak of Winnipeg, Man., a *Brantford* able seaman, recalls his first visit to New York City: "This day Manny Malton, the ship's cook from Winnipeg, really got the crew worked up. For some reason, Manny boiled a good beef roast for supper instead of roasting it in the oven. This was too much to bear. Shortly after supper, if you could call it that, some of the crew gathered outside the galley. When Manny came out, they grabbed him and threw him overboard. On his way down, we could hear him yelling, 'I can't swim! I can't swim!' But I knew that he was a very good swimmer because prior to his enlistment he was a part-time lifeguard at the town of Winnipeg Beach in Manitoba. After we pulled him out of the water, Manny and ourselves had a good laugh and all was forgiven."

Generally, though, cooks wouldn't have too much trouble gathering testimonials about their contributions. Jim Shurrie of Stratford, Ont., a 1944-45 *St. Thomas* ERA, says: "We had a good cook, so that means a lot." W. Leo Johnson of Winnipeg, Man., a 1944-45 *Orangeville* leading seaman, says: "We had an excellent cook, which makes for a happy ship. Ivan McCabe became a restaurateur in Regina."

Jack Scott of Winnipeg, Man., a 1944-45 *Trentonian* able seaman, says: "There is no doubt in my mind that the worse job at sea is that of a cook. The cooks were given very little praise for their efforts and long hours on duty."

Albert Baker of *Orillia* comments: "The cooks should get a medal of their own. There is no way they could possibly please everyone, but they did it very well under the circumstances."

Doug Murch of *Agassiz* says, "The cooks, I thought, were obliged to perform under incredible conditions." Jim Simpson of Prescott, Ont., who served in *Arvida* and *Sackville*, adds, "No doubt that corvette cooks were unsung heroes."

Heroes, yes. Saints, not necessarily. Max Corkum of *Moose Jaw* remembers making allowances for a cook who often got drunk and into trouble ashore in Milford Haven, Wales: "On one occasion, he ripped out the plumbing from a pub, and on another he threw a brick through a store window. The police were usually very good. All they wanted was the cost of repairs and then no charges were pressed. He usually came to me for the money he required. I would give it to him, as he would always pay it back. He was a good cook and good ones were hard to find."

Even when the weather allowed the cooks to prepare hot meals, the short foc's'le corvettes presented a challenge. Each mess would send a man — called the duty messman or cook of the mess — to the galley with a large pan to get the food for 10 to 12 people. Jim Alward of *Sackville* com-

ments: "I would be served the rations at the galley and then I would proceed down the short ladder to the break in the foc's'le. Here it became tricky because as sheets of water slopped down in a rough sea, one had to stand astride [balanced], wait for the right moment and run past the canvas break to the ladder leading down to our mess. Inevitably, meals drawn were sometimes nearly awash in salt water."

Herb Turner, a 1944-45 *Rosthern* radar rating, recalls: "If the sea was running high and the green ones were coming over the foc's'le, the food would sometimes get drowned with salt water, or be lost because the person carrying the pan would not be able to stay on his feet."

John Parker, a gunnery rating, recalls his 1942-44 *Algoma* experience: "The trick was to go with the flow and try to dash into the mess before a big green one [wave] would pour down from the foc's'le, or, if it was windy, to try to save the pan from being blown overboard. It happened more than once."

Assessments of the food vary. Tom Jackson of Halifax, N.S., a 1942-43 *Regina* stoker, says, "The food was super — and lots of it."

Bill St. Clair of Didsbury, Alta., a 1942-43 *Port Arthur* stoker, has this assessment: "Our food was never that bad. We never went hungry. It was never like mother's, but it was filling."

Bob Carson says, "Food was, I suppose, adequate to sustain life, but very crudely put up."

Bern Rawle, who served in *Cobalt* and *Strathroy*, says: "I remember something called fried egg which was actually an egg boiled in fat. Then there were the sausages which, by some process I have never understood, were burned black on the outside but were raw inside. A dish called 'red lead and bacon' had apparently originated in the Royal Navy as fried tomatoes and bacon, but it was transformed into almost raw slices of bacon floating in tomato juice. You may have heard the saying, 'God sends the food, but the Devil sends the cooks.'"

Skinny Hayes recalls: "When the weather was rough most people in corvettes got seasick because of the violent movement of the ship. This in turn meant no meals or cold meals — Spam and sandwiches, or worse. Almost nothing was frozen, so canned food was all that would last for any length of time."

Leslie McLean of Victoria, B.C., ERA and Chief ERA in *Port Arthur*, says: "On a fairly calm day the meals were

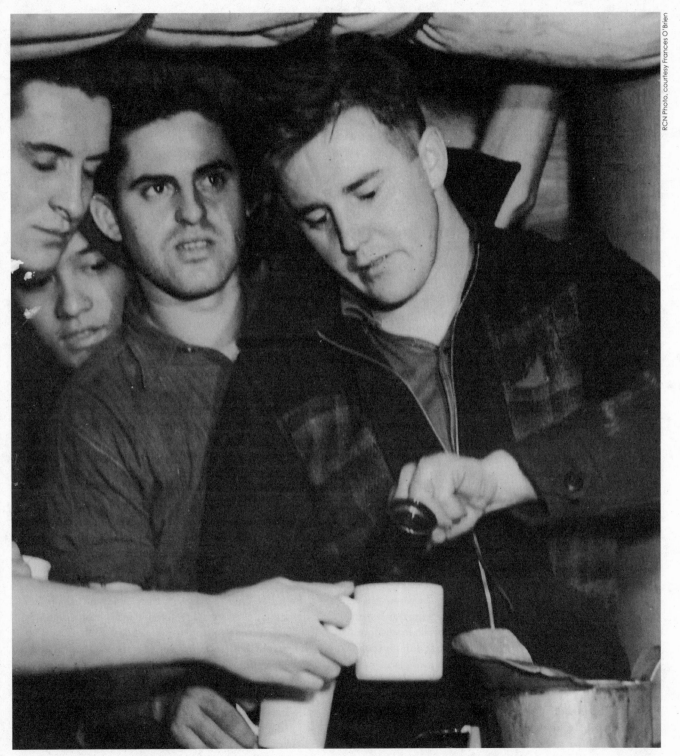

RCN Photo, courtesy Frances O'Brien

The daily rum ration aboard *Long Branch*.

good and came down to the messdeck in fairly good shape, but in a rough sea it was catch as catch can and quite often it came in a can.

"One time we were tied alongside in Halifax taking on supplies. About 10 cases of something had been loaded aboard when we were ordered to the St. Lawrence where the enemy had sunk a ship. Well, we hunted for that damn sub for a whole week without any luck. After a few days we were running short of supplies, but the Old Man was so intent on finding that sub he wouldn't put in [to a port]. It was then we found out what was in those cases. Yep, it was corned beef. There is one thing I'll say for our cook: he knew how to serve up corned beef in a good many ways. We never did find the sub."

Howard Trusdale, a 1944-45 *Fergus* able seaman comments: "All in all, meals were good, but obviously not all were popular. On one occasion we were issued sauerkraut and wieners. Now sauerkraut is an acquired taste and there was only one guy aboard who had it. By coincidence he was from Kitchener [which has a large German population]. As we returned to our table nearly everyone scraped their kraut on to his plate. He ended up with a pile just a little lower than the Matterhorn. I think he ate it all."

George Hollins says sauerkraut and wieners "became known as dog vomit and, as often as not, was thrown over the side."

Other meals could also be unpopular. Donald McDiarmid of Calgary, Alta., who served in three corvettes, recalls his 1943 *Camrose* stint: "Harry Dawson, the first lieutenant, loved — repeat, loved — kidneys, so an ample supply was always taken aboard. His love of kidneys was shared by very few of the officers and crew."

Dutch Davey was a leading seaman radar in *Arrowhead* in 1942-43 under Lieutenant-Commander Edgar Skinner: "When our captain wanted smoked kippers for breakfast, everyone had smoked kippers for breakfast. I've never had any since."

Albert Baker recalls: "One victualling quirk was that the captain had a love for kippers, which many of us had very little use for. Unfortunately, these did not spoil. We usually scrounged something to take their place."

Jim Alward remembers: "When we reached the U.K. we had kippers for breakfast. I refused to eat them because I had never had kippers for breakfast."

Ted Cunningham, a 1940-41 *Arrowhead* seaman, says: "The food was good. The sea air and the tot of rum at 1130 each day made you eat even if you weren't hungry. I had

some trouble getting used to kippers, herring and red lead and bacon for breakfast."

Armour Weir of Cleveland Heights, Ohio, an *Oakville* asdic rating, recalls his first trip to Newfiejohn. It was in March 1942 and a freighter was anchored outside St. John's harbour with a big hole in her bow. "For breakfast that day we had kippered herring," he says. "The only ones who ate it were the guys from the Maritimes and myself."

Doug Murch says: "There was one thing I came to thoroughly detest — cold storage fried eggs. These things, oily and grey in colour, turned up many mornings for breakfast."

The food had a lasting influence on some sailors, according to Bill Kilpatrick: "The fresh milk didn't last too long when we left port. Then we were faced with powdered milk. The powdered milk of today isn't too bad, I believe. Of course, I never have had powdered milk since the war."

Jack Nash of Oakville, Ont., a 1943-45 *Owen Sound* telegraphist, says, "I swore off Jell-O when I was discharged."

Fred Drew of Sherbrooke, Que., a 1943-45 *Forest Hill* able seaman, says: "We had many boiled eggs and today I will not eat them."

Adele Hetherington of Moose Jaw, Sask., replied on behalf of her late husband Richard, an *Agassiz* ERA: "My husband got very tired of hearing some sailors complain about the food. He said they were probably fed better than they were at home. However, there were some foods I could not serve him. The macaroni and cheese I made was never to have tomatoes mixed with it and canned meats were a no-no. I also had to learn to make New England-style clam chowder."

Meal preparation often went beyond the cooks and the VA. "I peeled a lot of spuds," recalls Raymond Rochette of Sainte-Foy, Que., a 1942-44 *Calgary* able seaman. "Sometimes the stokers would steal some for their provisions. It makes me laugh to think of that today." Bob Carson in *Alberni* also remembers the potato peeling: "As we were 90 people, it took a bag a day." Bread was a corvette staple. Max Corkum in *Moose Jaw* and *Huntsville*, comments:

One thing that always amused me was the way we had bread delivered in the U.K. We were issued what was known as the national loaf. It was grey and quite moist. It did not take long to turn mouldy.

The bread would arrive in a horse-drawn, two-wheeled cart with an open frame like a big basket. The cobblestones were covered with dry horse manure. As the horse trotted and the wind blew, the dried residue would blow all through the open cart — and over the bread, which was not wrapped.

Upon the cart's arrival at the side of the ship, all hands would lay down their paint brushes. Painting in the navy was continuous whenever there was nothing else going on. The sailors would form a sort of bucket brigade from the ship to the cart on shore. The bread was then passed hand to hand to the storage area in the ship. Each loaf was therefore handled by all the painty hands of the sailors. Is there any wonder that we looked forward to the mould so that the outside of the loaf could be cut off?

Jim Alward says: "Our bread was stored in the fiddly locker and therefore was exposed to the wet of the upper deck. The locker became the ideal place for mould — 'fluff' — to grow daily. The cook of the mess had to cut the fluff off, but within a week the fluff won."

Doug Murch recalls: "Bread turned mouldy after a few days at sea. We simply cut away the mould and used the rest. The 'usable' portion got smaller each day until the bread supply ran out."

Sid Husby, an ERA in *Hespeler* in 1944-45, recalls: "The bread we took to sea from St. John's was brought aboard in huge wicker baskets. It was good and fresh, but after a few days we were eating a small square in the centre, having cut off all the mould on the outside. The captain eventually asked if anyone could make bread, and an upperdeck sailor said yes. From then on, his duty was making bread and little else, and did he love that."

Garry Flock remembers cutting away the mould and adds: "Sometimes as a treat our cook would bake bread. What a lovely smell pervaded the ship."

Howard Trusdale says: "The bread didn't really keep that well, especially that which we took aboard in Ireland. Possibly they didn't use preservatives. As a result, most tables pooled a little money and bought fresh bread from the civvy bakers in Derry. It was still reasonably fresh when the issue stuff could be used as a weapon. On occasion the cook baked bread. We could tell how mouldy the flour was

by the cinnamon content he used to mask the taste. It didn't appear to hurt any of us."

Art Geizer remarks: "We would take a bag of Canadian flour to the naval bakery in Derry and they would bake about two-thirds of it for us and the rest would be for services rendered. The black bread issued us in Derry was not too palatable. It weighed at least three times ours."

Harvey Cooke of Dartmouth, N.S., a 1941-42 *Arrowhead* stoker, says: "Bread did not last. The pleasure was reaching Northern Ireland and trading tea and coffee to the Irish boatmen for huge loaves of home-made bread and jam or honey, which we stored for later use at sea."

Aboard Port Arthur, some crew members developed another solution. Bill St. Clair explains: "The food I missed most at sea was fresh milk and bread. When we got fresh bread in port, we used to take it down in the stokehold and dry it out on top of the boilers. Then when we wanted fresh bread, we would dunk it in a pail of water and put it in the oven for a while. It would come out fresh again. Our cooks never made bread at sea. The captain smelled ours one night when he came off watch and asked where the hell we got the fresh bread, so we gave him some."

When the bread was gone and rough weather prevented the preparation of meals, the common substitute was something impervious called hardtack, which prompted comments from many veterans.

Phil George, who served in three corvettes, remarks: "The hardtack is well named. It's very hard."

Archie Marsh, who sailed in three corvettes, too observes: "These biscuits looked like large dog biscuits. I don't know what ingredients they contained, but they must have been mixed with cement. Soaking in hot water or cocoa would not soften them."

George Hollins says: "A chisel and hammer would be adequate tools to split this large, round, one-inch-thick biscuit into bite-sized chunks. Even then, the density being equivalent to the specific gravity of marble, you had to soak it for 15 minutes in a scalding hot cup of cocoa. Or, better still, 120-proof pusser rum."

Reg Baker, another three-corvette man, comments: "You would think they came out of a cement mixer. We stood them on edge and tried to split them in two with our dirks [large jack-knives], if you didn't cut your fingers off first. We then toasted these halves and buttered them and put strawberry jam on them. This seemed to suffice our bodies."

Don Cameron of Oromocto, N.B., a 1944-45 *St. Thomas* stoker petty officer, says, "My specialty was to split these biscuits and fry them in butter. They were delicious." Albert White says, "One biscuit with a glass of water would last a person all day."

Rounding out the biscuit brigade are two more fans. Bill Kilpatrick says, "We could always fall back on hardtack. I actually grew to like it." Doug Murch adds, "Strangely enough, I liked the hardtack."

* * *

Corvette crews often became enterprising where food was concerned. Lloyd Jewers of Dartmouth, N.S., says: "On the way to Halifax in February 1942, *Hepatica* arrived off Beaver Island. I'm from that area. As we came up all the fishermen were out and I recognized one of the boats as Willie Volger's, so I asked the officer of the watch to pull up to Willie and get a meal of fish. Willie could not believe it was me, and we had the best mess of fish that was available."

Hewlett White, *Collingwood*'s VA, recalls: "There was one occasion when we were two days out of Halifax that the skipper decided to drop a pattern of depth charges as an exercise to make sure every crew member knew the routine. It had been many months since we had occasion to drop them in combat. The result was a sea of sparkling cod. Orders were given to lower two sea-boats to gather up some of the kill. Yes, we had all the fish we could eat for dinner that night."

Ivan McCabe of *Orangeville* recalls: "The sonar would go to work and pick up a school of fish. We'd drop a depth charge and the fish would be stunned. We had a long-handled net and brought them in. The boys would go to work and clean them and we'd have a feed of fish." This would occur "perhaps every second trip," he says.

Leonard Lamb, a 1941-42 *Alberni* ordinary seaman, recalls a fowl experience: "In March of 1942, we knew upon reaching Newfie that we would be paid and it was Joe Driscoll's 21st birthday. So while laying in Moville, Ireland, we acquired for the celebration a big white goose from one of the bumboats. Alas, it was an Irish goose that flew overboard on St. Patrick's Day and the seagulls had the feast."

Harold Miles, a 1944-45 *Kincardine* stoker petty officer, also had his feathers ruffled: "One time some of the boys from my mess somehow obtained two geese in Londonderry, got them aboard ship and kept them down in the tiller flats [the steering compartment]. I can't recall exactly how many days we had them, but our first lieutenant found out and told us to get rid of them as they were making a mess. I think some of the officers used to keep their trunks and suitcases there.

"Anyway, another fellow and myself took on the job of getting rid of them. We decided we would have a nice roast goose dinner, so we took them out on the upper deck and used the cook's chopping block. We were in harbour when we did this. When we plucked them, the feathers floated all over the ship, for which we were given hell and told to clean up the mess. Well, I helped do the dirty work, but when it came to the feast, I was on watch in the boiler room. When I came off expecting to get a drumstick, or more, the other members of the mess had eaten all but a couple of wings. To say I was disappointed is putting it mildly."

The resourcefulness in acquiring food knew few bounds. Tom Baird in *Regina* says: "In the chiefs' and petty officers' mess our cupboard was always loaded. The steam line to the steering engine went through the storeroom. We always made sure one of the joints on this line would spring a leak. It was necessary to fix this leak after supper so the boys could raid the stores for extra supplies such as jam, sugar, tea and coffee. When we repaired one joint, we always eased off a couple of bolts on another so it would let go shortly. Our officers never caught on so our cupboard was never bare."

William Bizruchak of *Brantford* remembers one caper:

We were tied up in New York City. This particular evening, being hungry and daring, the seamen's branch decided that some thick steaks would be in order. We could not open the lock on the large freezer door on the starboard side of the seamen's mess, so, after some thought and hard work we managed to remove the pins from the hinges. There were a lot of happy faces as we were sliding the door out.

Then it happened. We all heard the bosun's whistle outside the seamen's mess. That meant the nightly inspection. I never saw action stations with such speed. There was no time to replace the pins in the hinges, so some of the men stood at attention with their backs to the heavy freezer door, holding it from falling forward.

In walked the lieutenant and the leading seaman. I'm sure there were a lot of prayers said quietly in that minute. A moment after they left, the supply rating walked into the mess and headed straight for the freezer door. He unlocked the lock and pulled on the door. It came down on top of him and the only thing that saved him from falling into the miscellaneous mess below was the handrail on the floor protecting the opening.

We lifted the door off him, helped him up and couldn't make out whether he was crying or laughing, or both. After a short conversation, we did promise that we would not try to borrow any more steaks and he assured us that if he could spare any steaks at any time, he would do so. All is fair in war and we did win the war.

Len Leier of Swift Current, Sask., a 1944 *Owen Sound* communications rating, recalls: "The locks on the VA's locker and the wireless cabin were the same, although they used different keys. We noticed that the VA was going down and bringing up canned fruits and whatnot for the officers all the time, but the ratings never seemed to get any. We decided that we were going to do something about it. When the VA went down one time, we took his lock off and put ours on from the wireless cabin. After he left, we removed our lock, went in and liberated some of the stores, then put his lock back on. We were having fruit juice for quite a while after that."

His shipmate, Jack Nash, also remembers that foray: "We actually stole the VA's keys and helped ourselves to some goodies, particularly canned fruit. We believed the VA was selling our rations to the Irish Free Staters, so we felt justified in helping ourselves."

With household rationing in effect across Canada, there was public demand for a wide variety of goods and foodstuffs. George Hollins recalls that during his *Midland* stint: "One of the stokers with friends in Halifax regularly smuggled tea and sugar ashore by securing a bag around each knee, well concealed by his bell-bottom trousers. He just walked past the RCMP and shore patrol stationed at each exit from the naval dockyard in Halifax. I never saw them stop and search any navy personnel. No such surveillance existed in St. John's."

Ivan McCabe says: "Cooks could get away with anything and usually did. I remember if we were short, we'd

sell 25 pounds of tea for 25 pounds sterling in Ireland." Bartering had its own idioms, says McCabe: "'Have you got a rabbit?' — a little something to dicker with. The cook never had to worry about his share of rum. We always had rum for small favours."

It seems only natural to compare what you have with what others have. Carl Halstead of Winnipeg, Man., a 1942-43 *Morden* telegraphist, says: "Naturally we all beefed about the food, but I believe if we all had six months or so with the Royal Navy as I had, we would have toned it down."

The wartime ideal was American. Leo McVarish says: "We always got the best of food whenever we pulled into U.S. ports."

Irv Kaplan of Montreal, a 1941-42 *Arvida* signalman, recalls: "We had an American Coast Guard cutter in our group one convoy and during a particularly bad storm we had to make for Iceland where we tied up alongside a depot ship. We visited the cutter, *Spencer*. Imagine, they had ice cream, fresh fruit, even bread freshly baked onboard. Of course, they were a regular naval ship with proper facilities."

Convoys contained merchant ships from many countries carrying crews of various nationalities. Albert Baker remembers: "The Russians had a little different system from us. They carried their meat alive, butchering it as it was needed. On one occasion in a heavy fog, daylight was just coming in and I could hear roosters crowing and sheep baaing. We had been keeping station on a Russian ship and the sound carries in a fog." It was also common for Greek freighters to carry meat on the hoof, particularly goats.

Within the Canadian navy's mid-ocean fleet, it was the common perception — and the reality — that the food and living conditions were better on the larger ships such as destroyers and escort carriers.

"Corvette duty was tough, dangerous and totally devoid of the simplest of creature comforts," says E.M. Fox of Boca Raton, Florida, a 1943-45 *Arvida* coder. "Quarters were extremely confined and possessed only the barest of necessities, only those mandatory for getting the job done. As a matter of fact, the navy gave 'hard layer's pay' for corvette duty. In layman's jargon, that was extra remuneration for this difficult and uncomfortable duty."

This RCN recognition of corvette hardships is mentioned with pride by some veterans. "We sure earned our 25-cents-a-day hard layer's pay in *Amherst*," says Alf

RCN, courtesy Wally Charbonneau

Weyburn shows a bit of wear in May 1942.

Cockburn, who guesses that he made more than 40 crossings in her from 1941-43. The amount seems trifling today, but back then it meant something because the starting pay for a rating was $1.10 a day. The amount went up with experience, training, rank and trades qualifications.

Looking back 50 years through the telescope of time, corvette veterans offer varying assessments. Rod Kendall, *Napanee's* 1941-43 HSD, says: "Living conditions could be very grim. Corvettes were very seaworthy little ships, but in rough weather they took on a lot of sea-water, especially with the original short forecastle. It's amazing what you learn to put up with. After a few trips we took the good with the bad as a matter of course."

Charlie Bridle of Winnipeg, Man., a 1943-45 *Owen Sound* signalman, says: "It was easy to forget the difficult living conditions. Even these evoke strong, happy memories."

Rick Collins of Victoria, B.C., who served in *Brantford* and *Chambly*, observes: "Like all people are prone to do, we remember the good times, but believe me the bad far outweighed the good. The worst of all was the living conditions and believe me there is no one that can describe what it was like and cover everything, particularly in the short foc's'le ones. The powers in Ottawa at the time would say the corvettes were ideal for the type of work they were doing, but they didn't have to sail in them.

"There was no fresh water or decent hot food after a few days at sea. The weather was foul. We could never seem to get our clothes dry and living space was restricted. Add to this being on watch four hours on, four hours off for days on end. This did not lead to happy or efficient crews.

"I've been told that the average age of those at sea was 26 in the wardroom [officers] and 20 in the lower decks [ratings]. It makes sense to me because if we had been older, I don't think we could have stood up to it."

Bern Rawle says: "I rather hesitate to go too much into this because much of it is unbelievable. No one today can begin to understand living conditions in the early corvettes. Even those who visit HMCS *Sackville* today in Halifax see a ship that is restored along the lines of one of the later, improved models. In my experience, any attempt to tell the truth simply was an invitation to a chorus of ridicule and derision. For this reason, I never talk of those days and tend to relegate that whole period of my life to a past that is best forgotten."

Jim Willett, who served in *Dauphin* and *Louisburg*, says: "As I look back now and realize the positively horrifying conditions we lived under, day after day, month after month, I do wonder why more sailors did not go AWL [absent without leave]. Thinking about it, I guess we were young and tough, having been a product of the Depression, and we were conditioned to accepting living standards totally unacceptable by today's standards."

Scott Sanders of Brampton, Ont., a 1943-44 *Giffard* leading seaman, says: "Living conditions left much to be desired, but when one thinks about it, most of us had just come through the Depression so we were used to hard times. We were glad sometimes to have anything to eat — even hardtack and syrup! There was some grumbling here and there. Most of all, we were resigned to the fact that nothing else could be done."

Bob Carson in *Alberni* observes: "All in all, living conditions were lousy to say the least, but a favourite saying at that time was 'There's a war on, you know.'"

New Westminster, at anchor in 1942, was built at Victoria, B.C.

CHAPTER TEN

"WARTIME AT SEA IN THE ATLANTIC WAS CERTAINLY A FAR CRY FROM THE RELATIVELY QUIET TIME IN THE PACIFIC."

ELEVEN CORVETTES were commissioned by the Royal Canadian Navy in 1942. *New Westminster* and *Regina* led the way in January, followed by *Timmins* in February, *Vancouver* in March and *La Malbaie* and *Moncton* in April. *Brantford*, *Port Arthur*, *Ville de Quebec* and *Woodstock* came in May, and *Kitchener* in June.

Moncton was the last 950-ton corvette with short foc's'le and cylindrical boilers to close out this type at 65 vessels. Four of the other 1942 corvettes were 950 tons, with short foc's'le and water-tube boilers, ending this type at five vessels. The remaining six 1942 corvettes were 1,015 tons with extended foc's'le and water-tube boilers. They completed a group of 10 revised Flowers. Together, these three types totalled 80 Flower-class corvettes over three years, with 13 ships in 1940, 56 in 1941 and 11 in 1942.

Although the rate of corvette construction had slowed in 1942, the RCN manning policy remained illogical. Commander J.D. Prentice, the senior corvette officer afloat in 1941-42, notes in one report that as soon as men were trained, they were taken from the operating ships to man new construction: "*Chambly* had 259 officers and men borne on her books in 1941 and 1942, nearly five times the number of her original complement."

Leo McVarish in *Alberni* comments: "Unfortunately, as new corvettes and minesweepers were being commissioned, a ship's crew that had the experience of working together as a team were continually being drafted to other assignments that disturbed the working performance of most ships' routines. ... This arrangement, unlike that for the destroyers whose crews were almost permanent, did not always make for an efficient ship's company as many ordinary seamen hadn't yet tasted the spray of sea-water on their lips. This all took time and this turned out to be one of the problems in the Canadian navy."

Jack Tice of Hamilton, who spent three-and-a-half years in *Mayflower* and *Lindsay*, says: "Usually a refit occurs about every 12 months. One sidelight of a refit is the rotation of crew members. I went through three refits in one ship, *Mayflower*, and sailed with a new crew each time. It causes me some confusion today because I try to remember with whom I sailed after each refit."

Those regulating manning policy in Halifax stubbornly clung to their ways to the detriment of efficiency. In anti-submarine warfare, as with troops on the ground, you can't have good execution without teamwork and continuity. A crew must practice and perform together so that its response becomes swift and sure when action is required.

The operations brass wasn't much better. Groups were not left intact so the ships could get on-the-job training together to improve their efficiency. William Wainio says: "While I served in *Trillium* from 1942 refit to 1943 refit, we were assigned to A-3 group, which was a combined Canadian-American operation with the U.S. Coast Guard cutter *Spencer* as senior officer. We worked together nearly a year, but the rest of the escort complement were constantly changing."

To be fair, the demands on limited escort resources were many. And sometimes the demands seemed to sprout like green grass after a spring rain. One such time was 1942.

In wartime oil is an absolute necessity not only for the army, navy and air force, but also for industry. In those

113

Courtesy Vic Martin

Amid the debris from the sinking of the *Alexander McComb*, the corvette *Regina* rescues survivors off Boston in June 1942.

days, Canada imported much of its crude oil from the United States and South America for refining here. In peacetime the supply was secure and Canada's storage facilities were not extensive. In wartime extra storage capacity was needed because the crude oil that moved by sea became vulnerable. Being short of escort vessels, however, the Allies did not strengthen shipping protection until they had no choice.

Oil tankers were always a particular target for U-boats. By aggressively extending the war to North American shores and the Caribbean Sea in early 1942, the German navy discovered easy prey — and created a shortage of oil in Halifax and the U.K.

This caused the Allies to initiate fast tanker convoys between Trinidad and Halifax. Most of the escorts came from Halifax Force. Much of this work was done by RCN corvettes, with *Sudbury* and *The Pas* starting in May 1942. *Hepatica* and *Snowberry* joined in June. *Fredericton, Halifax* and *Oakville* were added to the force in July. Most of the runs were now between Halifax and Aruba. Before this Caribbean assignment ended in late summer, this duty also involved convoys linking Trinidad, Aruba and Key West, Florida.

In the view of *Oakville* able seaman Reg Adams of Scarborough, Ont., "Our Caribbean convoys were a picnic after the Atlantic runs."

Halifax crew member Charles Clarke of Winnipeg says: "We were issued tropical gear — shorts, gun-shirts, helmets and black knee-high stockings. Most of the crew wore shorts on watch so we all had nice tans. With our white clothes and tans, we sure looked tiddly when we went ashore."

Leading Seaman Ted Percival of Sidney, B.C., recalls: "I am from Winnipeg and aboard *Halifax* I became friendly with another Winnipegger, Ward Putnam. We each had a girlfriend in the Peg and we decided to put our girl's initials on our backs with medical sticky tape, let the sun tan our lily-white bodies and, of course, leave our girl's initials on our back! Others followed our lead. ... And, yes, we did marry those girls."

Percival says *Halifax* had teak decks that had to be holystoned, which is scoured with soft sandstone. "A real advantage of wood decks is they don't get overly hot in the tropics and most of us went around barefoot," he recalls.

There were other climatic adjustments. Clarke says: "We would have to wet down the depth charges with salt water to keep them from sweating." He also recalls that awnings installed to provide shade didn't stand up too long. It was too hot to work in the afternoon. And, despite canvas wind-catchers to get air down to the engine room and the stokehold, "the stokers didn't have it as good as the upper-deck crew. It was so hot they used to change shifts more often." But up on deck, "the night watches were something to remember, 70 degrees in shorts — no shirts or shoes."

Oakville asdic operator Armour Weir says: "Our first stop was Aruba, a parched-looking place, and all you could see was oil tanks and a refinery. I learned from an American soldier that a U-boat had shelled the island that February."

The route sometimes took the Canadian corvettes to Cuba. "We used to go to the U.S. naval base at Guantanamo Bay and get our supplies," says Charles Clarke. "The

Yank sailors had the best of everything. We could buy a box of 50 Havana cigars for a dollar and cigarettes were 10 cents for a pack of 25." He also remembers that Key West, Florida, "was a great port for a leave," and "when we went to Trinidad rum was about 90 cents a quart bottle, so we sure had some great parties."

Coder Bernard Breslow of Côte St-Luc, Que., recalls a suspenseful trip when a German spy captured in South America was transported by *Sudbury* from Port of Spain, Trinidad, to Halifax: "He was quartered in one of the officers' cabins and under armed guard day and night by two intelligence officers with sidearms. While the spy was on deck getting fresh air, there would be a couple of ratings with rifles and orders to shoot him if he decided to jump overboard."

Oakville was the lone RCN corvette to gain any real recognition for the Caribbean duty. While escorting the 29-ship convoy TAW 15 in the Windward Passage on August 28, 1942, she sank *U-94*.

The U-boat had been spotted by a U.S. Navy plane which released four depth bombs and a flare. *Oakville* rushed up and dropped five depth charges without asdic contact. The U-boat was forced to the surface and a duel in the dark ensued, with *Oakville* ramming the U-boat three times, smashing it with 4-inch shells and raking it with machine-gun fire.

When the captain brought *Oakville* alongside, Sub-Lieutenant Hal Lawrence of Victoria, B.C., and Stoker Petty Officer Art Powell of London, Ont., became a two-man boarding party by jumping directly down onto the Type IX C boat. They shot two Germans and drove several others overboard. While Lawrence went inside the U-boat, Powell guarded more Germans escaping the sub. When the boat started to go down by the stern, Lawrence came back up. Just before the boat went under, the two Canadians took to the water with the rest of the Germans. The American destroyer *Lea* recovered Lawrence and Powell, as well as 21 survivors, while *Oakville* ended up with seven, including the captain, *Oberleutnant zur See* (Lieutenant) Otto Ites, who had sunk 14 ships.

There was much worthy of credit in *Oakville*'s action. There was the offense: determined leadership, quick depth charge work, seamanship in the manoeuvring and ramming, skillful gunnery, courage in clearing the breech of the 4-inch main gun after a misfire, the danger of the boarding

attempt and the capture of prisoners. There was also the defence: prompt and resourceful action in controlling serious damage and flooding, which saved the ship from sinking.

These two dimensions guaranteed the number of awards would be greater than usual, but a file at Library and Archives Canada shows that *Oakville*'s captain, Lieutenant-Commander Clarence King, recommended 17 crew members for recognition. This figure, which did not include the skipper, was impossibly high as King, a World War I veteran, should have known. In the end, 10 awards were presented, with the Distinguished Service Order for King, the Distinguished Service Cross for Lawrence, and the Distinguished Service Medal for Powell and David Wilson, the stoker petty officer on watch when the aft boiler room flooded. The remaining six were awarded Mention in Dispatches.

Unrewarded was Charles Gowdyck, an asdic rating whose action station was at the bottom of the ship with three watertight hatches closed above him. Says Reg Adams: "Nobody thought about poor Gowdyck until about a half-hour after it was over and we rushed down to open the hatches to let him up."

Gus Miles, Captain D Halifax, assessed the *U-94* episode: "In my opinion, HMCS *Oakville* was undoubtedly correct in ramming the submarine to ensure his destruction and the taking of prisoners is in accordance with Admiralty policy which encourages this for the purpose of gaining intelligence. The commanding officer … and all his officers and men deserve the greatest credit, not only for their successful action which lasted approximately 45 minutes, but also for bringing their damaged ship safely to Guantanamo unassisted."

Rear-Admiral G.C. Jones added this comment: "I fully concur with the remarks of Captain D. The spirit and dash displayed by HMCS *Oakville* was worthy of the highest traditions of any service."

The daring of the U-boat fleet was also demonstrated during this engagement. While *Oakville* was battling *U-94*, a second boat, *U-511*, attacked convoy TAW 15 from the port side vacated by *Oakville*, sinking two tankers and damaging a third before slipping away.

RCN corvettes with the U.S. Navy were next assigned to escort convoys from Guantanamo, Cuba and Key West, Florida, to New York City. *Sudbury*, *The Pas*, *Fredericton*, *Snowberry* and *Halifax* began this work in September, while *Lethbridge* joined in November and *Oakville* in December after she was repaired. The corvettes worked for varying periods until the assignment ended in March 1943.

The implementation of a convoy system to protect the Allied oil lifeline deprived the German navy of easy targets and in late summer of 1942 its main focus shifted back to the North Atlantic from the Caribbean. The increased protection for oil shipments did, however, spread the Allied forces a little thinner.

* * *

Another battle had broken out at home — the Battle of the St. Lawrence. The U-boat onslaught in the Gulf of St. Lawrence began in May 1942. It was just another part of the ongoing redirection of the German offensive to the areas of best opportunity.

Canadian naval authorities anticipated this development but did not deploy significant forces in advance to nip it in the bud. They had limited resources and set other priorities, with mid-ocean convoys, coastal shipping and the Caribbean oil convoys heading the list. The government and the navy also faced pressure from the U.K. and the U.S. not to pull corvettes off mid-ocean duty. And the naval brass all along had the fallback position that they could close the Gulf to ocean shipping.

The issue was further complicated by divisive political implications. In an April 27, 1942, national plebiscite, the electorate was asked to release the government from its promise not to send overseas those men conscripted into the army for home defence. In an effort to woo voters in reluctant Quebec, where World War II was widely regarded as a British war, Prime Minister Mackenzie King had publicly pledged to give priority to defending Canada's shores and waters. The question, and therefore the government, was strongly supported in eight provinces, but soundly rejected in the ninth, Quebec.

When the Gulf campaign began in May, a number of factors favoured each side. Foremost for the attackers, who would come up the St. Lawrence River to within 175 miles of Quebec City, was the inability of the defenders to detect submerged U-boats. "Conditions in the St. Lawrence made the asdic equipment unreliable," explains Dave Jeffreys of Cardiff, Wales, a *Charlottetown* lieutenant in 1942. "Different densities and temperatures of layers of fresh and salt water brought havoc to the transmitted beam. The enemy became well aware of our difficulties and would approach a

convoy with confidence, knowing we could not locate him, or could only do so with a large amount of luck. That's what our lives depended on."

The gulf and river were also a long stretch to defend. Although long, the area was narrow compared to the mid-Atlantic, reducing the ability of convoys to take evasive routing action. Fog sometimes allowed U-boats to operate on the surface in daytime. As well, Canada did not devise an efficient blackout system for navigational lights, so these and radio beacons could sometimes be used to advantage by U-boats.

Moreover, the British were no longer able to break the German Enigma code. New German code machines, using four rotors rather than two, were in use by February 1942, along with a new system for enciphering grid references. Canadian use of direction-finding equipment on German radio traffic was the main method of tracking the enemy.

In turn, some factors favoured the defenders. The proximity to land allowed aerial surveillance from Royal Canadian Air Force bases at Sydney, N.S., Gaspé, Que., Gander and Botwood in Newfoundland, and air training bases at Mont-Joli, Que., Chatham, N.B., and Charlottetown and Summerside, P.E.I. As well, both the phosphorescence of the gulf water and the northern lights increased the chances of detecting U-boats on the surface at night. With ports close at hand, there was a chance for respite for naval crews. Further, the need for defence was not year-round: the St. Lawrence River was frozen over in winter and closed to shipping from December to late April or May.

Bill Coates of Trail, B.C., a 1941-42 *Charlottetown* leading seaman, recalls the gulf: "We were on the Triangle Run until July 1942 after the U-boats came into the St. Lawrence River. The RCN was very short of escorts and could hardly

HMCS *Charlottetown*.

spare some of us, but we were sent to Gaspé, which would be our home base. Our duty was to escort ships from Sydney, N.S., all the way up to the narrows of the river and convoy ships from the narrows back to Sydney, where they could form up for the slower convoys for overseas."

Of course, the better escorts were used for Atlantic convoys, so, beginning in May, the Gulf Escort Force based at Gaspé was cobbled together with corvettes, minesweepers, armed yachts and 112-foot Fairmile motor launches. It totalled only 19 ships by September.

Ray MacAulay recalls: "*Charlottetown* escorted 11 convoys up or down the river. It was a very busy two months in the Battle of the Gulf. Gaspé was the port we used for fuel, food, ammunition, etc. It was a very pretty area and nice people. We sure appreciated the good shelter and rest while waiting the next escort duty."

Although a bold imposition in Canadian territory, U-boats worked alone, not in packs. The struggle was on a much smaller scale than on the North Atlantic. Although there was public concern along the shores of the St. Lawrence River and the gulf, there was still an element of innocence in a country not accustomed to war within its boundaries.

Fred Rush of Surrey, B.C., a *Charlottetown* telegraphist, recalls: "Looking back, it was quite a time. We were a bunch of green kids. I was an old man of 23 or 24. It was a holiday with pay with no thought of war. We ate good — navy style — and slept good. One day up the river to pick up our small convoy, three or four days back to Sydney and then back to Gaspé for a layover. A real holiday with pay. A very gentle time. Baseball, swimming, the usual chores cleaning and painting ship, the wet canteen and then back at it again after about seven days."

The government attempted to cloak the gulf events in a veil of censorship and selective release of information, ostensibly to prevent Germany from gaining useful knowledge. In reality, the government did not want to risk alarm and outrage, which would likely result if it became widespread public knowledge just how vulnerable shipping was in Canadian waters. Even as it was, questions were asked in the House of Commons, principally by opposition politicians from Quebec.

On September 7, 1942, the armed yacht *Raccoon* disappeared, lost with all 38 hands when torpedoed by *U-165* while escorting a convoy in the St. Lawrence River. She was the 14th ship sunk in the gulf that year.

The RCN had a shortage of escorts to protect the gulf, but also found another reason to propose its closure. Britain had requested Canadian escorts to participate in Operation Torch, the still-secret invasion of North Africa scheduled for November, and Prime Minister Winston Churchill made a personal appeal to King. The RCN brass already wanted to be part of this big show.

Only if there were a reduction in other needs could the RCN send the 17 corvettes under consideration. Contrary to King's pledge, the federal government put Allied concerns ahead of Canadian interests when, two days after the *Raccoon* disaster, Canada's Cabinet War Committee closed the St. Lawrence to ocean shipping. This was said to free up 12 corvettes. The West Coast threat was deemed to have decreased and five more corvettes were freed up. Presto, 17 corvettes were available! *Bangor* minesweepers would stand in for corvettes on the Triangle Run.

For Canada, the St. Lawrence waterway was the shortest shipping route, the cheapest and the one with the greatest capacity. Its closure was the easy way out. It was a significant decision with many ramifications, some quite unfavourable for Canada. Montreal and other Quebec ports suffered as goods bound for overseas were hauled by rail mainly to ports along the American eastern seaboard where they were loaded in freighters bound for the U.K. This, in turn, taxed Canada's rail capacity, especially the quantity of rolling stock.

It took some time after the September 9th decision for ocean shipping to clear the St. Lawrence and there was still a need for local shipping as well. Both escorts and U-boats remained active. The *Bangor,* minesweeper *Clayoquot* and the corvette *Charlottetown* were returning in tandem to their Gaspé base on September 11, 1942, at a speed of 11 knots after helping deliver convoy SQ 35 to Red Islet near Rimouski.

"Breakfast was red lead and bacon," says Gerald Martin of Chilliwack, B.C., a *Charlottetown* telegraphist trained operator. Everybody seemed grumpy. I went out on the quarterdeck with Leading Telegraphist [Edmund] Robinson, had a smoke, got fresh air and talked with the Chief ERA [David Todd of Greenfield Park, Que.], then he went below to his cabin off the starboard quarter. Rob and I proceeded up to the bridge, then to the wireless shack. I took over from Telegraphist Fred Rush and told him what was for breakfast. He moaned then took off below.

"I sat down and went over the wireless log and Rob checked the strongbox to see all books were locked up. Just then a loud explosion. Rob shouted that we had been hit by a torpedo. Everything went dead. I fell against the transmitter. We headed for the wheelhouse. Then the second one hit. We went out on the deck and tried to release the port lifeboat, but it was jammed. The Old Man [Acting Lieutenant-Commander Willard Bonner] was there and shouted, 'Abandon ship!' The stern was beginning to settle so we went over the starboard side into the water. I grabbed a line that was hanging from the lifeboat and pulled myself into it. We tried to get as many as possible in and the rest went swimming for the two Carley floats [rafts] that we let go."

Ross Duff of Kingston, Ont., a *Charlottetown* coder, recalls: "At about 0800 hours I was sharply awakened by the sound of an explosion and then by another immediately after. The blast was so extensive that it made a shambles of the messdeck and caused panic in those in the mess. There was a quick clamber to get to the ladder leading to the upper deck and we made it in record time. I reached the port side of the ship just as the captain gave the order to abandon ship.

"A seaman, 'Judy' Garland, was on deck at the life jacket locker passing out jackets to anyone who wished to take one. I didn't take time to put on a life jacket as I saw a Carley float hit the water and start to drift downstream with the current. I jumped overboard on the port side of the ship, with a number of other crew members, and started to swim as fast as possible towards the raft and to get clear of the ship. The water was oil covered and icy cold and the raft was getting away from us. It had drifted a considerable distance from the ship and when I was 10 to 15 yards from it I stopped to rest. While treading water, I turned to look at the ship. She had reared on her stern, bow in the air, and in almost vertical position she sank into the water and disappeared."

Bill Coates says, "We got the starboard lifeboat off, but the ship listed so badly we couldn't swing the port lifeboat out, so the captain told us to jump for it and do the best we could. All we had was those old Mae West life belts, but all they would do is keep your head out of the water. I was near the lumber rack where we stored the staging planks. They were two inches thick, 12 inches wide and about 10 feet long. I threw one over the side and jumped in after

it. When I got hold of it, I paddled away from the ship before it sank."

Lieutenant Dave Jeffreys says: "I was torpedoed twice in the British merchant service before the sinking of *Charlottetown*, so you see that event was just another unpleasant memory. When the torpedo struck, I was, with past experience, immediately aware what had happened. I just got to the next deck when the second torpedo struck. I made for the boat deck. On arriving there, the vessel's stern was level with the sea and everyone was leaping into the sea. There was not long to go. I immediately followed. Dressed in pyjamas and 'nowt' else, I swam away fast and eventually arrived at a Carley float."

Ray MacAulay swam to a lifeboat, which was crowded: "I was asked to swim to a float a short distance away. As soon as I got on the float, I looked for the ship. It had gone under."

At 0803 the first torpedo hit the starboard quarter, then the second one struck in the vicinity of the engine room or No. 2 boiler room, says a report by First Lieutenant George Moors. The torpedoes killed only one person, Chief ERA Todd. One Carley float was destroyed. The ship sank in three to four minutes.

One lifeboat and three floats were released and occupied, but the worst came when some of the sinking ship's depth charges exploded. It's in dispute whether the charges were set to safe or preset for a specific depth, but it's clear some men near the ship were killed, including CO Bonner, and others were seriously injured.

After the ship sank, says Ross Duff: "I resumed swimming and was almost at the raft when there were several explosions in the water. The concussions sent sharp and driving pains into my back and abdomen. I made a few more stokes, grabbed for the raft and climbed inside. There were others on the raft by this time, but I do not recall the number or their names. Those of us who were a reasonable distance from the ship suffered only severe pain and some nausea for a few days thereafter."

Dave Jeffreys says: "Hanging on to a Carley float, I felt the shudder on my legs as the charges went off. The lads lying on their tummies in the water suffered badly."

Charlottetown stoker Frank Dillon of Ottawa was using the sidestroke when the charges went off: "I went right up and down. How high? It could have been five feet or 500 feet. I doubt it was 500. It could have been 25 or 30 feet, dear knows. When I came down, I naturally went under and then came up. I swam up, I remember that. I did not lose consciousness for some reason. I did feel the pain. And I swallowed a lot of oil." He made it to a crowded Carley float. "We sang," he recalls. "I don't know if from the battle or being scared or what it was. We sang songs. Maybe we'd seen it in a movie somewhere. I don't know where we got the idea."

Bill Coates says: "I received a fractured hip and stomach pains but I was lucky the plank kept most of my body above the water. I was finally pulled into the starboard lifeboat."

Gerald Martin was in the lifeboat: "We pulled Seaman [Donald] Bowser [of Nova Scotia] into the lifeboat and he wanted us to push him back in the water. He was dying, but we held on to him and rowed with the only two oars we had. The boat was loaded and water was coming in and we kept bailing it out with whatever we had. The first lieutenant took charge as the senior surviving officer. We tried to get everyone onto the floats and boat."

The first lieutenant's report says: "Before the ship sank completely, most of the crew were in the rafts or the starboard boat. The boat had 17 men in it, but we managed to collect a few men in the water and transfer them to a float, and then go further after four more who were severely injured. This operation took up about one and one-half hours and no dead bodies were seen except that of the captain who we finally picked up and lashed to the rudder, after filling the boat with living men. The boat then proceeded in the direction of shore with the object of landing our injured men and sending small boats to pick up the men on the rafts. During this time it was quite thick and [it] seemed advisable to make shore rather than to wait for *Clayoquot* to search for us and pick us up.

"After rowing for about an hour, the rudder was torn adrift by the weight of the captain's body and he was left adrift because we could make better time and he might possibly be picked up by another ship when the fog cleared."

Ross Duff describes another dramatic moment: "Because of the heavy mist or fog that day, visibility wasn't

Charlottetown survivors in a crowded Carley float approach the minesweeper *Clayoquot*.

Courtesy Allan Heagy

too good. As we drifted in a raft and tried to stay within sight of a second raft, we believed *Clayoquot* would rescue us in short order. But, to our surprise, she came steaming through the mist at top speed and appeared to be going to plough right through those of us in her path. At what seemed like the last minute, she veered away from us and continued to steam ahead. We later learned that *Clayoquot* was following up on sonar contact with the submarine but did not complete an attack because of the number of *Charlottetown* crew in the water in the area where she would have to drop her depth charges."

U-517 captain Paul Hartwig was the architect of *Charlottetown*'s doom, and was a pivotal player in the Battle of the St. Lawrence. Though he sank nine ships in Canadian waters from August 27 to September 15, 1942, he did not see *Clayoquot* on September 11 and remained oblivious that she spent more than two hours searching for his Type IX C boat.

Clayoquot had in fact stopped to pick up survivors but aborted this effort to pursue the attacker when asdic contact was obtained. It wasn't until 1010 that she finally began to take aboard survivors from the three rafts. Ross Duff says: "It was a cold and wet three hours on that raft and most of us were numb and shivering. Even the full cup of neat rum given to me on *Clayoquot* didn't bring back much feeling to my arms and legs." Ray MacAulay says: "We were some thankful when *Clayoquot* stopped to pick us up."

Charlottetown had been six miles from shore. When *Clayoquot* reached the lifeboat at 1130, it had been rowed within two miles of shore, but it was another nine hours before the *Charlottetown* survivors were landed at Gaspé.

"It was extremely cold, that I still remember," says Dave Jeffreys. "Great kindness on *Clayoquot* and eventually we arrived at Gaspé. Looked after and fussed over so marvellously by Commander and Mrs. [Barry] German. Visits to hospital very, very distressing, lads dying from effects of depth charges."

The final count was 10 dead and 54 survivors. Two of the victims had put aside a prewar encounter: Willard Bonner had been the captain of an RCMP patrol vessel and Donald Bowser had been a rum-runner he once chased. "The respect those two had for each other was just something," Frank Dillon says. "Whenever the captain was on the bridge for action stations, or anything else, Bowser was always in the wheelhouse with the coxswain."

Another victim was John Garland, an ordinary seaman from Gallagher Ridge, N.B. Nicknames were very popular and he was dubbed "Judy" after the famous American singer. Garland was best-known among the crew as the master of Screech, the ship's mongrel mascot.

Amid the uproar following the torpedoing, Garland, who couldn't swim, stayed at his designated station handing out life jackets from a storage locker. "When captain Bonner gave the order to abandon ship and jump for it, for some reason Seaman Garland went back to the seamen's mess to look for Screech," says Bill Coates, revealing a little-known drama. "We that were close to him told him to jump, but he insisted on going to look for Screech and that was the last he was ever seen." In the pandemonium, the men were unaware that Screech was safe, having been instinctively tossed overboard by John Dillon, Frank's twin brother.

The bodies of six crew members, including captain Bonner, were never recovered. The other four fatalities were buried on land. The remaining 54 crew members went on survivor's leave when health permitted.

Evidence at a board of inquiry showed that the standard anti-submarine procedure of zigzagging was not followed by either *Charlottetown* or *Clayoquot*, supposedly because *Clayoquot* was short of fuel. In fact, her tanks were not quite that low. She had sufficient fuel to search for the U-boat and survivors for about three and one-half hours before steaming to Gaspé. Steaming a straight course would simplify the job of the German marksman.

So ended at nine months the life of the corvette with the 13-letter name commissioned on December 13. The first lieutenant's sinking report was dated — yes, you guessed it — September 13. In line with common practice, the name *Charlottetown* lived on with the commissioning of a new frigate on April 28, 1944. But in a distinct departure from RCN tradition, the frigate was given the same pendant number as the corvette, K-244.

Screech also lived on. The dog and a number of the crew ended up at the Dillon family home in Montreal on survivor's leave. "After we went back to Halifax, dad made a padded box, and shipped Screech to Judy Garland's mother," Frank Dillon says. "She wrote back and thanked him for the dog. She was very happy to receive him."

Best known of the 1942 losses in the gulf is the SS *Caribou*, a ferry that regularly linked Port aux Basques, Nfld., and North Sydney, N.S. She was torpedoed by *U-69* on

October 14 with the loss of 137 lives, including 56 service-men who were passengers.

The first round of the Battle of the St. Lawrence ended that month. Half a dozen U-boats sank 18 merchant ships and two RCN warships, and severely damaged three other merchant vessels. The attackers did not suffer a single loss. From mid-September on, greatly increased air cover and a strengthened escort force eliminated most of the easy prey, though the *Caribou* was a high profile loss. The official naval historians would have us believe that these were acceptable loss rates and the battle was not a defeat. Certainly that was not the perception of the public or the media at the time, nor of this observer today, and with ample justification. After all, the *Kriegsmarine* did maul the RCN and prompt Canada to close our main inland waterway.

* * *

Another 1942 theatre was Canada's West Coast. Among the RCN ships involved were seven corvettes commissioned at Victoria and Esquimalt, B.C., in 1941 and 1942.

Unlike the East Coast, shipping on the West Coast was not organized into regular convoys. Operating from Esquimalt in the southeastern part of Vancouver Island, the corvettes usually did 10-day patrols of local waters. Large Japanese subs were the threat.

Telegraphist Robert MacDonald of Sackville, N.B., says: "Life at sea in the World War II Pacific was fairly uneventful with a few exceptions. We did some escort work with convoys consisting of supply and troopships bound for the Aleutians. Once we were overflown by unidentified bombers which we believe now were the Japanese planes that bombed Dutch Harbor [in early June 1942].

"*Dundas* spent considerable time on anti-submarine patrol, which consisted of back-and-forth trips across Juan de Fuca Strait off Sheringham Point. This is not far from Estevan Point, which has the dubious distinction of being the only place in Canada to receive enemy shells during World War II. I was on watch when this happened and received the Morse code message from the Estevan Point civilian radio operator in the 500 kilohertz international distress frequency. The message simply stated: 'Am being shelled by surfaced Jap submarine. Am closing down.' This caused quite a commotion and *Dundas* was diverted to the area, which after a lengthy search resulted in no contact."

During this active period in June 1942, the 2,180-ton sub *I-26* crippled the freighter *Fort Camosun*, while *I-25* shelled the lighthouse at Estevan Point, on the west coast of Vancouver Island, which Prime Minister Mackenzie King called "the first attack upon Canadian soil ... since Confederation."

We excerpt from a diary kept by *Vancouver* coder Lyle Killeen of Ottawa, beginning on the fourth day of a patrol from Esquimalt:

Thursday, June 18, 1942 — Very quiet today. Wrote to Jack. Mail is to be put off tomorrow, so I'll write home. *Caraquet* is taking it into port. Got messages that subs are lurking around and we're ordered to keep a sharp look out. They're operating pretty close to shore.

Friday, June 19, 1942 — *Caraquet* left us today and took our mail. We traded a few books with her so we'll have something to read.

Messages coming in now pretty fast. A sub was spotted by aircraft in a position about 10 miles from us. The *Fort Camosun*, a new Canadian freighter, was torpedoed 40 miles away and [the corvettes] *Edmundston* and *Quesnel* were dispatched to her aid. Sub again sighted and a "can" was dropped but she got away. We got a message to go after the *Fort* too, so full speed ahead. *Edmundston* and *Quesnel* took off 50 survivors and said they need the help of tugs to save the freighter.

Saturday, June 20, 1942 — We were ordered to wear life belts all the time. Ship is in two watches now. Sun is bright. Sighted the stricken freighter. An American heavy bomber that was circling her came out and challenged us. We're to provide anti-submarine screen with *Quesnel*, and *Edmundston* is to tow. She's a 10,000-ton freighter and is loaded down with lumber, which held her up. There is a hole in her about midship where she was struck. Boat's crew went aboard to lighten her cargo, so they threw a lot of lumber off. She has a bad list to port and her bow is away down. Tug arrived and has her in tow.

Sunday, June 21, 1942 — We proceeded at about five knots and were ordered to return to Esquimalt. We're protecting her with a V-sweep formation. Estevan [Point] land station was shelled by sub and

Kelowna attacked another about 100 miles up the coast. There is definitely an established nest of them around here and we're to be ready for action and do I hope we get it. We intercepted a distress signal from Estevan during the period she was shelled, but it was cut off.

Monday, June 22, 1942 — *Quesnel* ordered to return to harbour as her supply of oil is low. *Fort Camosun* began to wallow and so we headed into Neah Bay [in the northwestern corner of Washington state] for safety. *Salvage Queen* and divers sent to pump the water out of her. We carried on to our Sheringham patrol and *Edmundston* stayed at Neah Bay.

Tuesday, June 23, 1942 — Ordered to return to guide *Fort Camosun* into Esquimalt. Joined her at 1600 [hours] and started patrol at Koitlas Point, San Juan Bay.

Wednesday, June 24, 1942 — Started our trip back to harbour making very slow time. *Edmundston* is alongside the freighter and we're carrying out an anti-submarine sweep around her. A sub was supposedly sighted by aircraft in our area so two [mine]sweepers and us made a total anti-submarine sweep. Fished off stern.

Thursday, June 25, 1942 — Arrived in at 1:30 a.m. with freighter and *Edmundston* coming in later. We tied up at ordnance. Went ashore with Greene and borrowed $5 off Lamb. Met Code at the Y and went to show. Met Bob Wales and finished his crock. Sculled around, got a watermelon and went to park to eat it. Later went to Legion and then crashed dance at Trianon. Hitched back to ship at 1:30 a.m.

Another glimpse at the West Coast experience comes from Robert MacDonald in *Dundas*:

Most wireless watches were quiet. Due to radio silence, there was little transmission work, mostly reception of the low-frequency area broadcast from Esquimalt station CKL/CKN. This was sent in Morse code at a low rate, probably not more than 15 words per minute and usually sent twice to make sure we got it. To be doubly sure, it was repeated again sometime during the 24-hour period. We also kept watch on the international distress frequencies, often hearing from the war areas in the South Atlantic, Indian Ocean, etc., when merchant ships were under attack by U-boats or surface raiders. These distress calls were prefixed by the letters S S S or R R R followed by their position, when there was time to get it out.

In September 1942, *Dundas* left for the East Coast in company with four other corvettes, *New Westminster*, *Edmundston*, *Quesnel* and *Timmins*. After passage through the Panama Canal, we switched from the Esquimalt broadcast to the Admiralty broadcast from Whitehall. It seemed all hell let loose. We sparkers [telegraphists] were quite unprepared for the fast and furious Royal Navy broadcast which ripped along at 20 to 25 words per minute with no pause between messages and nothing sent twice. In no time at all, our message log was a mess and the wireless office looked like a cyclone had struck. Until we got things under control, the leading tel, Andy Rogers, spent hours helping out the operator on watch. Wartime at sea in the Atlantic was certainly a far cry from the relatively quiet time in the Pacific.

Two corvettes, *Dawson* and *Vancouver*, remained on the West Coast. A signal containing the words "craft in water" directed *Dawson* to a specific location in a very heavy storm. "To our surprise," says Coder Al G. King of Sarnia, Ont., "we found a coastal patrol aircraft in the water, with its crew of four or five clinging to the wings. We were unable to pull alongside, but, after some futile attempts, we finally shot them a line and made it secure. We were finally able to send over a bottle of rum to warm the crew, though the first three bottles crashed, with many a tear shed. After several hours the storm abated enough to permit us to send over our whaler to rescue them. We were delighted to discover that one of the airmen was a friend of Bernie Scott, one of our coders. They had worked together in Hull, Que., before the war. A happy reunion followed."

In mid-August 1942, these two corvettes headed for the Aleutian Islands in the North Pacific. On their way, *Dawson* stopped at Prince Rupert, B.C., to take on fuel and supplies. Recalls King: "Shore leave was granted at Prince Rupert. After some hours of celebrating, several members of the crew returned to the ship in the wee hours a little the worse for wear, carrying a huge totem pole. They tied it to the mast. Dawn brought more than a hangover. A visit from the RCMP started the day. They had been notified of the stolen totem pole. Lower decks were cleared. Once the guilty parties were identified, they were ordered to return the totem pole and, to add to the indignity, they had to carry it back. Having accomplished this, we were given permission to proceed on our mission to the Aleutian Islands. Reprimands followed for the offenders."

Dawson and *Vancouver* were part of the U.S. buildup in response to the Japanese occupation of Kiska and Attu on the western end of the Aleutian's chain. The corvettes helped protect troopships and convoys of freighters, tugs and barges carrying construction materials, vehicles and supplies southwest down the chain of islands. The duty sometimes took them into the Bering Sea and foul weather was common. Major stops were at Dutch Harbor in the chain's eastern end and at Adak much further along. The area is so remote that Amchitka Island between Adak and Kiska was later used for American nuclear tests.

A few selections from Lyle Killeen's *Vancouver* diary:

Friday, August 21, 1942, Kodiak — It's typical Alaska weather and the rain is the worst I've ever seen. It comes down in sheets and sheets and it's pretty cold. I went up today with guys off all the other ships to learn American code. We rode around in station wagons and they really have a layout here.

Monday, September 14, 1942, Adak — Awakened by the noise of planes. There were two B-17s, 13 Liberators, 12 P-38s and 19 P-39s. It really was a sight and I think they're heading for Kiska to give the Japs a reception. About 1400 [the U.S. destroyer] *Humphries* came up with mail for us and it sure was a happy day. I got 12 letters. Now we have some mail and books to read.

Wednesday, September 23, 1942, Adak — Came to Kuluk Bay at 0800 and took up station on patrol again. The rest of the convoy proceeded into harbour and *Dawson* and us were left to patrol. There were four minelayers in here this time laying a minefield. The weather is lousy and the ship sure rocked plenty. The seamen lost their last plate during the rolling around, so I guess we'll have to divvy up our few. The night was miserable with rain, mist and the tossing

waves. Lots of sick complaints aboard: hernia, teeth, ears and maybe appendicitis.

Wednesday, October 28, Kodiak to Dutch Harbor — At 1830 a destroyer came whizzing out of the blue, took over our convoy and told us to conform with previous orders and return to Kodiak.

The moon came out full and we played bingo all night. The crew is a lot happier and already buzzes are flying about going home. I won a buck, then Ray and I stayed out on deck and talked until 10 in the morning.

*   *   *

Over on the Newfie-Derry Run, 1942 was a busy year with some successes amid heavy losses. Escorted by a Canadian group of two destroyers and four corvettes, the westbound convoy ON 115 was shadowed by a small wolf pack. The destroyer *Skeena* forced a U-boat to dive, and the corvette *Wetaskiwin* joined in the attack.

"We tracked it for several hours and it had gone very deep. As a result, we would lose contact at about 400 to 500 yards," recalls *Wetaskiwin* HSD Allan McConney of Uxbridge, Ont. "So, each [ship] stood by and indicated to the other just when to drop a pattern of charges. After I had reported hearing a loud explosion underwater, we saw material come floating to the surface. We sent away the seaboat and picked up some body parts and other material. The body parts we kept in our fridge till we got back to St. John's.

"As a result of this sinking, when the Earl of Athlone, who was governor general, came to St. John's to inspect various ships, he came aboard *Wetaskiwin*. As the buffer I was in charge of the piping party and had to teach two other seamen to pipe."

Teamwork and improved tactics deserve credit in the July 31st sinking of *U-588*, a Type VII C boat, with all hands. Good asdic work played an important part and, although he didn't mention it, HSD McConney was one of those decorated, earning Mention in Dispatches.

On August 3, 1942, survivors of the torpedoed *Belgium Soldier* were picked up by *Galt*, acting as rescue ship of a convoy. Able Seaman Norm Cowell of Burlington, Ont., says: "A scramble net was put over the side by the quarterdeck and I was on one end. We'd pull a survivor towards the net, a line was secured around him and the crew on-board pulled him on deck. The engine was stopped so that it would not pull anyone into the propeller. As the ship rolled to our side, we would be under water. Being after midnight and with oil on the water, it seemed an eternity holding one's breath until the roll back.

"That night three of the 33 survivors died. The next day each victim was wrapped in canvas with a weight attached. Each in turn was placed on a board, with the White Ensign on top, and a burial service was held. Then the board was raised and the body slid into the ocean from under the flag."

In early August, after bringing a convoy across the Atlantic, the escorts detached at the western rendezvous, except for *Pictou*. She screened [protected] a merchant ship that was making engine repairs and then redelivered her to the convoy. *Pictou* then proceeded independently to St. John's. Her captain, Tony Griffin of Toronto, Ont., picks up the story on August 5, 1942:

> Off the Grand Banks of Newfoundland in moderate weather, a dense fog descended, and since our radar was, as usual, defective, we had reduced speed. Suddenly we were surrounded by ships and knew we were in the middle of a convoy.
>
> In this situation, the first thing to establish is the course of the convoy and to assume the same course. Before we could do this, a very large merchant ship was right on top of us. I will always remember the image of that enormous ship towering above us and heading straight for our midships. I knew that if she struck us broadside we were finished (exactly what had happened to *Windflower*). The only hope was to take a glancing blow. So I immediately rang down: "Emergency full ahead, hard-a-port." She struck us aft on the port side with a terrifying crash and we listed 45 degrees. The ship disappeared into the murk and we never saw her again.
>
> The bulkhead at the stern was immediately shored up with timbers, but because it was now wide open to the sea, I ordered the forward compartment to be flooded to get her stern up. The damage control party then began clearing away the wreckage and in four hours, to my relief and surprise, we were able to proceed, the propeller being undamaged. When we reached St. John's, the misery and indignity of the

Courtesy Norm Cowell

In August 1942 a victim of the sinking of the merchant ship *Belgium Soldier* is buried at sea from the quarterdeck of the corvette *Galt*.

affair were, to some extent, lifted by a light-hearted signal: 'Report ETA your stern!'

At St. John's a court of inquiry was established to check into "the circumstances surrounding the collision between HMCS *Pictou* and the Norwegian steamship *Hindanger*." The court found me responsible because of "lack of co-ordination in the ship's coding and ciphering department." Meaning that I should have known of the convoy and its course and position from the nightly situation reports which were transmitted in cipher every evening from Nova Scotia to ships in the western ocean, and from Rugby, England, to those in the eastern half. For this I "incurred the displeasure of the Department."

On August 4, 1942, the crews of the corvette *Wetaskiwin* and the destroyer *Skeena* receive congratulations in St. John's, Newfoundland, for their July 31, 1942, kill of *U-588*.

I felt this deeply; but it was a fair judgment. … At the review of the inquiry, the members of the Naval Board took note of the final helm and engine orders which undoubtedly saved the ship. Moreover, they noted that, after all, I did get the ship to port. But it should never have happened."

Ironically, *Pictou* outlived the freighter. Ed Fraser of Willowdale, Ont. was first lieutenant in *Amherst* when she escorted convoy ON 127 in September 1942. "We picked up the survivors from the [torpedoed] Norwegian SS *Hindanger*," he recalls. "Only one member of the crew was lost. We then sank her [so she wouldn't be a threat to navigation]."

* * *

Much later in coming — 1987 to be exact — was credit to *Morden* for the solo kill of the Type VII C *U-756* on September 1, 1942. While the corvette was escorting SC 97 southwest of Iceland, the ship's radar detected the sub on the surface at night. Three depth charge attacks were made. *Morden's* CO, Lieutenant J.J. Hodgkinson of Verdun, Que., reported it was difficult to imagine that the U-boat could have avoided the explosions, but tangible evidence of a kill was lacking.

For 45 years it was assumed that the U-boat *Morden* attacked had gotten away, while a U.S. Navy Catalina aircraft sank *U-756*. Then British research indicated that the Catalina attacked *U-91* which escaped. *Morden* had actually attacked *U-756*, which was never heard from again.

When credit is given or revised years after the fact, it's common that many surviving crew members — now spread across the country and long out of contact with the Department of National Defence — are unaware of the change. Unfortunately, in such cases, crew members miss out on the official credit, and the handful of medals that would have followed the original action if the success had been realized.

September 1942 marked the formation of the first support groups, whose mission was to go out looking for U-boats, rather than waiting for the U-boats to attack convoys. Though in the long run this would prove to be a significant development, it did not reduce the need for the traditional close screen around convoys. To increase the amount of goods transported with limited escort resources, the size of convoys on the Newfie-Derry Run was also growing.

It remained a tough go for the escorts. Skinny Hayes says: "One of the anti-submarine procedures then in favour, when a submarine was thought to have penetrated the screen of escorts, called for all the ships in the escort to fire illumination flares outwards, then steam in towards the convoy at best speed, turn and try to catch a surfaced submarine silhouetted against the light of the flares. For some reason this manoeuvre was called a raspberry."

The *Trillium* lieutenant recalls the night of September 20, 1942, when the eastbound convoy SC 100 was attacked: "One or two ships had been torpedoed so things were obviously tense onboard most ships.

"We were carrying out a raspberry and on the run in to the convoy one of the convoy ships opened fire on us with a 20mm Oerlikon. Our 4-inch gun's crew was on the foredeck ready to shoot at the enemy. Unfortunately, three of them were hit, and one lost an eye. Hard lines when one considers we were trying to protect our assailant and he was supposed to know what was going to happen and had been looking at this same corvette zigzagging alongside him for days!"

Leading Seaman Harry Mann of Edmonton, Alta., says: "I remember one of the seamen saying, 'Look at the pretty purple balls.' Actually, they were tracer bullets and there were other bullets in between them."

Craig (Slim) Canning of Islington, Ont., a *Trillium* able seaman, has reason to remember it well: "The gun crew were all in position and had an armour-piercing shell already loaded. Orders were given to illuminate with a star shell. This meant we had to fire the first shell and reload a star shell, which we did. Suddenly a merchant ship opened fire on us. Being a gunlayer, I had been setting the sights and when shrapnel glanced off the barrel and through the sight, I was hit in the right eye. Norm Hatchwell and Frank Garness were hit in the legs, as they were loaders positioned at the rear of the gun. We fired the star shell to let our attacker know who we were.

"Aboard *Trillium*, the Old Man ordered that whenever the pain got bad we could have a tot of rum, so the pain got bad. Two days later we were transferred to the United States Coast Guard ship *Campbell* for medical attention as they had a doctor aboard. Two days after that we arrived in Derry and were taken to an American hospital. Hatchwell and Garness were released the next day and returned to *Trillium* as she arrived in port. I was released from hospital after three weeks and, until *Trillium* came back, I stayed with an uncle who lived in Derry. I returned to Newfoundland in *Trillium*, then went on to Christie Street Hospital in Toronto, my hometown, for an artificial eye. I was subsequently discharged from service."

Without the realization of her September 1942 sub kill, *Morden* was best known as the Rescue Ship, a reputation primarily earned by saving four large batches of survivors between September 1942 and May 1943. Most notable was the rescue of 194 men, women and children from the torpedoed 8,807-ton British ship SS *Winnipeg II* on October 22, 1942.

Morden telegraphist Carl Halstead of Winnipeg says: "Our CO [Lieutenant Hodgkinson] was an ex-Merchant Navy man and not one to pass up anyone. Often it was not according to the book to stop. This time the cooks deserved full marks for feeding such a lot. The CO said our crew [of 71] got fed first' then the passengers got a chance. Great stew was pretty well the menu. There wasn't room to move, but everyone made the best of it. We all parted with socks and other clothing."

A different type of rescue is recalled by two *Aggasiz* shipmates. Coder H.J. Taylor says: "After leaving a convoy one trip in late 1942, we came upon a torpedoed ship. She was loaded with lumber and had no crew, so our captain [Lieutenant-Commander B.D.L. Johnson], an old tugboat man, hooked on and we towed her all the way to the Bristol Channel at about two knots. We were sure a prime target for a sub. In about 1947, I got a cheque for 17 dollars for my share for saving her." Recalling that salvage money was divided on a share basis, Coxswain Art Geizer comments, "By a share basis, I mean that the officers got the lion's share while we got what was left over."

A corvette could even encounter danger in port. *Louisburg* was tied up at Derry on December 9, 1942, when the 1,105-ton British sloop *Bideford* approached. Budd Parks of St. Catharines, Ont., a *Louisburg* seaman, says: "Her bow crew stood at attention on her foc's'le. As she rounded the bend in the river, her steam whistle sounded. I looked up. The ship should have been steaming slightly to starboard. Instead, she was coming at *Louisburg* on a slight angle. The crew on *Bideford*'s foc's'le dove for the deck. I dove for the deck on *Louisburg*. The sharp bow of *Bideford* ripped the steel plates away like potato peelings. *Louisburg*'s side lay open from aft of the boat deck to the bridge forward, about two feet above the water line. There were some anxious moments, but no one was seriously injured."

W.R. Ransome of Sointula, B.C., a *Louisburg* cook, recalls: "There were about 10 fellows gathered at one galley door with their pans. These doors were all Dutch type, with the top half open and the bottom bolted closed. The fellows saw this massive hulk coming at us and there was a small panic trying to get the bolt open. Most of the fellows went over the top and clear out the other galley door. No one was hurt."

Ernie Pain of Cornwall, Ont., a *Louisburg* seaman, says: "The ramming was something else. I was lying on a messdeck locker when all of a sudden the ship lurched and I thought I could hear guns firing. But it was not guns, it was our rivets popping when *Bideford* dropped anchor on us."

* * *

Skinny Hayes assesses the struggle at sea in late 1942: "Life was tedious, uncomfortable, monotonous and frightening. The German U-boats had developed their wolf-pack tactics very effectively and sinkings reached new highs. The weather that winter was particularly bad and we still had little air cover in mid-Atlantic. *Trillium* with her new RN 271 radar set should have been most effective, but it seems to me that we had no more success than anyone else. Ships were torpedoed, the escorts carried out the prescribed searches, fired star shell, dropped depth charges on every promising contact and, as far as *Trillium* was concerned, only succeeded in picking up survivors."

There can be no doubt Germany was winning the battle at sea. Allied and neutral merchant ship losses in the Atlantic theatre averaged 510,000 tons per month in the second half of 1942 when the toll was an amazing 550 ships. This contributed to the horrendous average of 512,500 tons per month for the calendar year.

But there was some hope. The November 1942 Allied invasion of North Africa caused Hitler to order U-boats back into the Mediterranean, once again contrary to the advice of Admiral Dönitz, causing shipping losses in the Atlantic to drop sharply in December.

Christmas 1942 aboard corvettes ran the gamut. Doug Clarance, *Regina* sub-lieutenant, recalls: "We left Londonderry on December 23, 1942. We went down off Gibraltar, turned around and arrived back in Ireland

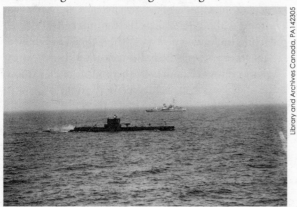

The corvette *Moncton* trains with a Royal Navy sub near Halifax in 1942.

In the *Louisburg* wheelhouse in November 1942 are Doug Decle (left), Gord McDonald, Mike Regan.

January 6, 1943. We missed Christmas, New Year's and I, my 21st birthday. A rather drab and dreary way to spend one of the most significant birthdays of one's life. But that was the way it was and that was the way we took it."

Sandy Brown of Thunder Bay, Ont., an *Agassiz* stoker, says: "We arrived in St. John's at 8 a.m. December 24, 1942, after a 16-day crossing in a bad storm, so everybody thought we would be in [port] for Christmas, but to our dismay we got sailing orders for Christmas morning at 8 a.m. I was on watch in the boiler room, but they didn't forget us. They sent down a beer each."

By late 1942, Ron Burton of Blind Bay, B.C., was an acting leading seaman in *Vancouver*: "My first Christmas, 1941, I didn't know the score in barracks and I was a little late getting to the mess hall. There wasn't much turkey left, except a few bones. My second Christmas, our ship was in port and four of us were on leave in Victoria. We made a visit to the Sally Ann [Salvation Army] and found out that a lady had left a cheque for 20 dollars there for some sailors to have a Christmas dinner. We obtained the money and went to a restaurant. We got a small turkey with all the trimmings and enjoyed our own private Christmas dinner."

William Wainio in *Trillium* recalls: "Before setting out for Ireland on the trip prior to Christmas 1942, someone came up with the idea of having a party for children from an orphanage in Londonderry. A committee went ashore in St. John's and purchased a pile of gifts for little children. On reaching the other side, arrangements were made for a party for our little guests a few days before Christmas. All they needed was a Santa Claus.

"The officers and crew got together to select someone and I noticed that they were all looking at me. As I was a bit rotund in appearance, I suppose they thought I would fill the bill admirably. Being a little on the bashful side, I had some second thoughts. However, while they were getting me rigged out in the Santa Claus suit, complete with beard and all, the navigating officer handed me a glass with about four fingers of rum. No more problem! Passing out the gifts was an experience I will never forget. To see the looks on those cute little faces was something to behold. In return, we were rewarded with songs from those little children who were happy to perform for us."

* * *

At sea, things were still grim. Rod Kendall of Thunder Bay, Ont., was HSD in *Napanee*:

Our westbound trip with ONS 154 was different from the start. To begin with, we headed almost due south after clearing the Irish headland. We altered course to the west just off the Azores, so you can see how far south we went. In contrast to our usual weather, we were now basking in a subtropical climate.

Napanee went alongside a tanker to refuel: When we finally got the fuel hose aboard ship, we discovered the threads on the standpipe to our tanks and the threads on the hose from the tanker were different. Luckily there were manholes for access to clean the tanks, so off came the retaining nuts and the hose went directly into the tanks. It was a tricky and sloppy job as it was impossible to keep both ships a constant distance apart. It took pretty well all the off-watch ratings spelling each other to pull the lines in when the ships came close and pay them out when we separated.

The date was December 27. Says Rod Kendall: Towards midnight I stepped out on the wings of the bridge for a breath of fresh air. One of the merchantmen fired a star shell and there dead ahead was what I first took for one of our escorts. It turned out to be a sub on the surface, facing the convoy. The captain [Stuart Henderson] ordered full ahead to ram. Our 4-inch gun fired a star shell and I could see the sub going into a crash-dive. I ran back to the asdic set, but as the operator had good contact with the sub, I let him operate.

We dropped a full pattern of charges and opened to the customary 1,000 yards before turning back to run another attack. The ratings manning the depth charge throwers on the starboard side could see the disturbed water caused by the sub's crash-dive. That's how close we were.

According to routine, the leading torpedo operator dropped a calcium flare over the side with the last of the charges to mark the spot in the event we lost contact by asdic. It was the leading torpedo operator's job to keep his eyes on the flare and he told us later that after the charges had all gone off, a huge bubble rose from the surface. As we were ordered to maintain our station, we couldn't turn back to investigate. We heard later that an aircraft reported a damaged sub on the surface in that area.

The slow convoy was attacked continuously for five days. Emergency changes of course were made. Fourteen of 47 merchant ships were lost. Late in the crossing, the senior officer of the escort, Lieutenant-Commander Guy Windeyer in the destroyer *St. Laurent*, broke down and was put under a doctor's care. One U-boat was believed damaged. Postwar examination of German records indicated that *U-356* was actually lost the night of December 27, 1942.

Though some feel *St. Laurent* got the kill, several escorts made promising attacks. No one can say with certainty which attack damaged or finished the U-boat. The credit was officially given to the destroyer and three corvettes, *Battleford*, *Chilliwack* and *Napanee*.

When asked about the sinking of *U-356*, Jack Shirley of *Chilliwack* replied: "I have no recollection of believing that we had sunk the U-boat. At that time, life in the mid-Atlantic was rather hectic and U-boat attacks were rather routine, escorts so few and not allowed to be away from the convoy for very long. In retrospect, the object had to be to keep the sub down and prevent another torpedo attack until the convoy moved on."

ONS 154 can only be regarded as a disaster. The convoy illustrated that without adequate air cover in the middle of the Atlantic, an escort group could be overwhelmed by concentrated attacks from a sizable U-boat pack. There was also no doubt that the escort group lacked strong leadership, as well as group training and cohesion.

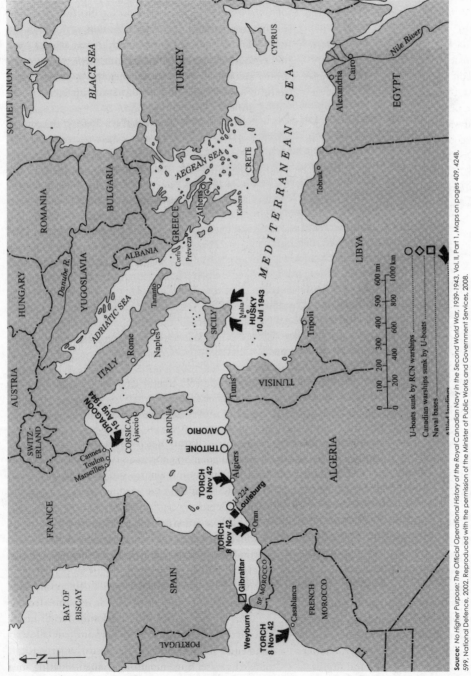

RCN Operations in the Mediterranean 1942-1945.

Source: *No Higher Purpose: The Official Operational History of the Royal Canadian Navy in the Second World War, 1939-1943*, Vol. II, Part 1, Maps on pages 409, 424B, 599, National Defence, 2002. Reproduced with the permission of the Minister of Public Works and Government Services, 2008.

CHAPTER ELEVEN

"FROM THE BRIDGE ABOVE CAME THE CAPTAIN'S COMMAND — 'ABANDON SHIP!'"

"WE WERE TOLD TO PICK UP six months' supplies, everything imaginable: light bulbs, gloves, rags, paint, you name it," recalls *Calgary* stoker petty officer Don Prentice of Hamilton, Ont. "The canteen got cigarettes, soap, razor blades, chocolate bars, candy, toothpaste. We filled every storeroom space with canned food, dehydrated fruit and vegetables, and lots of biscuits and corned beef."

A *Port Arthur* seaman, Ron Batchelor of Maxville, Ont., says: "No one knew where we were going until large sheepskin duffel coats were brought aboard. This had to indicate that we were heading for the Murmansk Run."

Ville de Quebec leading stoker Paul Morse says: "When we left Halifax for overseas there was an extra issue of heavy winter wear. The buzz was that we were being trained for the Murmansk Run."

Preparations included quick refits to install the latest radar and beef up the corvettes' anti-aircraft defence with a new setup of six Oerlikon 20mm guns. *Regina* ERA Bill MacLeod of Sydney, N.S., says: "We knew we were going to a bad place. We thought it was to Russia, but it wasn't."

Indeed, the clothing ploy worked. The actual task was to support the Allied invasion of North Africa, dubbed Operation Torch. The RCN provided 17 corvettes, including *Nasturtium*, an RN ship that had been part of a Canadian escort group. The corvettes left Halifax between mid-September and late October 1942. In order of departure, the RCN ships were: *Louisburg, Prescott, Woodstock, Lunenburg, Weyburn, Baddeck, Port Arthur, Camrose, Alberni, Calgary, Kitchener, Summerside, Ville de Quebec, Algoma, Moose Jaw* and *Regina*.

The invasion by British and American troops went in on November 8, 1942, at Casablanca in French Morocco, as well as Oran and Algiers in Algeria. The German *Afrika Korps* was already fighting the British 8th Army in Libya, immediately east of Algeria, so the invasion increased the seriousness of the Allied challenge to German control of North Africa. Thus the German and Italian air forces and navies targeted the Allied supply lines.

The extra corvette anti-aircraft guns were to protect against the significant threat from German and Italian land-based aircraft in the Mediterranean theatre. Harvey Burns in *Port Arthur* says: "I was a leading seaman gunner and in charge of a 20mm gun. I had a crew of two. I had two days' training before I took over this gun." His shipmate, Signalman Percy Warner of Saskatoon, says: "There was very limited training for the Med. Gunnery practice at drones on the way over."

One Torch duty was to escort convoys from the United Kingdom to Gibraltar, situated beside the southern tip of Spain on the north side of the narrow Strait of Gibraltar that links the Mediterranean Sea and the Atlantic Ocean.

Able Seaman Gib Todd of Winnipeg remembers that first trip well because Regina encountered a fierce storm: "We lived on King Oscal Sardines — a tin for breakfast, a tin for dinner and a tin for supper. I haven't eaten a sardine since, and never will." The upshot was repairs in Belfast before *Regina* made it to the Med.

Port Arthur coder Bruce Crickmore recalls his introduction to Gibraltar: "The harbour gate allowed us to enter and we tied up at the destroyer jetty. Right beside us was a huge monitor, a cement floating ship

131

with massive guns. Every time our signal lamp passed a letter, the ray of light would cut across these massive guns above us. A plane came over. The whole Rock seemed to lift into the air, with guns from all over streaking their tracer bullets into the sky and searchlights streaming up and converging on the target. It was quite a mesmerizing event."

* * *

After the Allies' successful landings in North Africa, the Canadian corvettes became part of the escort effort to ensure the land forces were resupplied through ports in northern Algeria. Batchelor explains: "From Gibraltar we convoyed full merchantmen to Oran, then on to Algiers, then to Bougie, Philippeville and finally Bône. It was like delivering milk, dropping off the full ones, then on the way back picking up the empties."

These ports were a culture shock. Bruce Crickmore recalls that as part of the destination deception, *Port Arthur* crew were issued "pusser dung-hampers — long, woolly underwear with a convenient flap on the backside." By the time they reached Algiers, "we realized that the dung-hampers were no good to us in the Med. So, when we tied up, quite a number of crew members threw them on the jetty, which was lined with ragged young kids and scruffy men in Bedouin clothing. The next day the jetty was filled with the same mass of humanity, but a bunch of them were fully clothed in the pusser dung-hampers — some with the flap in the back half undone!"

Port Arthur stoker Laurie Manuel says: "It was sad to see people fight like animals over mouldy bread we discarded one trip to Bône. It surprised many of us and also added to thoughts of how fortunate we were in so many ways to live in a place like Canada."

The Allies were not embraced by the populace and shore leave was quite limited, with curfews such as 8 p.m. in Algiers and 6 p.m. in Bône. *Camrose* leading seaman Donald McDiarmid says: "It wasn't exactly safe in the evenings in Bône, so we would go ashore after lunch. With wine at two francs a glass, and a franc worth two cents, we could afford to be big spenders."

Camrose leading signalman George Van Tassel comments: "After the usual sightseeing, there wasn't a great deal to do in Gibraltar. Runs ashore were mostly confined to the 'local' drinking beer with a plate of steamed periwinkles

and vinegar, or going aboard one of the RN destroyers or cruisers and playing tombola, what we call bingo."

Living conditions in the Med were not great. *Kitchener* stoker Moose McGill of Courtenay, B.C., comments: "Lovely bananas, oranges, beautiful Spanish onions and so on were available in stalls in Gib and Bône. The navy in its wisdom never provided us with any of this fresh produce. In fact, food on that run was lousy."

Ron Batchelor recalls Christmas 1942 in *Port Arthur*: "We were at sea in the Mediterranean. The day was bright sunshine and very warm, the sea was as calm as a lake. The menu was pork chops, the dessert, I forget. It is the custom for the youngest man aboard to become captain for the day and for all officers to serve the supper to the lower deck men. Bill Frith of London, Ont., age 19, was our youngest. The revelry was phenomenal, with the officers, including our captain, taking lots of guff from all the crew, all in good fun. Indeed, they were good sports and let their hair down on this day. Naturally, our young Bill Frith gave them lots of orders."

John Parker spent Christmas Eve in Gibraltar in the sergeants' mess of a British regiment, but he has a more vivid memory: *Algoma* crew members did not get their Christmas mail until they went alongside the wharf in Bône on March 6, 1943!

* * *

For most Canadian corvette crew members, the Med offered a new dimension — air raids in port. Doug Clarance in *Regina* says: "I remember returning to Philippeville about four o'clock one afternoon that bombers came over. When I heard the alarm sirens, I went up to the bridge to see what was going on. We were secured alongside a British destroyer and I noticed an officer on the other bridge drinking a spot of tea. When I saw some of the aircraft coming in over the barrage balloons, I called to him in great excitement, 'Look, there they are.' He calmly looked back and said, 'Yes, yes, I see them,' as he proceeded to sip his tea. It is odd what one remembers. Subsequently I learned it was common practice for the Germans to disturb the British navy at tea time."

Port Arthur able seaman Jack Bagnell says: "Bône was a hell of a place. We would sometimes get two air attacks per day. One day we were tied up to the jetty with a big freighter next to us. She was loaded with heavy gear on the back end and that's where they got her with two bombs. She was loaded with ammunition in the front end. If they had gotten her there, I guess we all would have been gone."

His shipmate, Ron Batchelor, recalls another air raid at Bône: "They were after the merchant ships in the harbour while we and a few empty merchantmen were outside the harbour waiting for other empties to join us. Bombing inside and firing outside were intense. Our Bill Green of Montreal was wounded in the arm, in all probability not by enemy aircraft but by small arms and anti-aircraft fire coming from every direction. No ships were hit outside the harbour. One ship was damaged badly inside the harbour."

John Parker in *Algoma* remembers March 12: "Arrived Bône — unfortunately! Experienced three heavy air raids. Returned fire with an extensive anti-aircraft barrage from all ships in the harbour. All kinds of flak — lots of shrapnel fell all around us on our ack-ack platform. Luckily, no one was injured, even though some were fighting in their jockey shorts. At least three airplanes were shot down. This was the worst blitz I had experienced. The wharf where we were moored was completely loaded with ammunition to be transported to the desert army."

There was aerial action at sea, too, of course. *Ville de Quebec* leading stoker John Wilson of St. Thomas, Ont., recalls being strafed by aircraft: "I had just relieved Richard Crable from White Fox, Sask. He started to go out of the engine room and had just got his hand by the gangway when he had a finger shot off. He came back down and I heard him say, 'I'm not going up there for they are shooting at us.'"

Percy Warner in *Port Arthur* remembers one encounter: "When planes flew over us, the convoy opened fire and hit our ship, wounding Charlie Steen, a gunner, in the arm."

Doug Clarance in *Regina* has a vivid memory: "I remember one occasion when there was a very distinct phosphorescence in the wake of the ship. We were at action stations when we heard a bomber diving at us hard up the stern, aiming at the end of the wake. At the last possible moment the captain ordered hard a-port and, to our great delight, the bomb missed on the starboard side, although it certainly came damn close. This is another occasion when [Lieutenant-Commander] Harry Freeland won my admiration for his calmness and coolness under fire. After the bomb went off, most of us had picked ourselves up off the

Nyassa, a Portuguese neutral carrying contraband, was seized on the Atlantic by the corvette *Regina* on February 18, 1943.

deck to find the captain still standing there looking straight ahead doing his business. He was quite a man."

A number of *Regina* crew members recall a special assignment in February 1943 that was unusual for a Canadian corvette. *Regina* was dispatched from Gibraltar to intercept a Portuguese liner. *Nyassa* was encountered about an hour's distance from Lisbon, Portugal.

"With four or five ratings, [Sub-Lieutenant] Ross Stewart and I boarded her to take her to Gibraltar under contraband control," recalls Clarance. "It was a bit of a vacation from reality. The ship had recently come from Brazil and the Argentine. It had wine and all kinds of steak and good foods, which were served in a sumptuous way in a very pleasant restaurant setting. For our boarding-party members who had been enjoying the questionable benefits of hardtack, it was a complete and delightful change. We took her to Gibraltar and I recall her captain gave us a bottle of wine called 'Lachrema de Christi' [the Tears of Christ] for our skipper, which pleased Freeland immensely.

"It was not until about two years later, while crossing the ocean by troopship to another appointment, that I heard what had happened to the *Nyassa*. Among the six officers in our cabin during the crossing, one had served in contraband control in Gibraltar. He informed me that they had known exactly where to go to find industrial diamonds being smuggled for the German war effort. They simply confiscated the diamonds and let the *Nyassa* continue her way to Lisbon."

* * *

The Canadian corvette duty in the Med will best be remembered for events that occurred during a six-week span in early 1943.

On the afternoon of January 13, the 15-ship convoy TE 13 was eastbound in the Mediterranean about 90 miles west of Algiers under the escort of four Canadian corvettes and two British *Bangor* minesweepers, with the senior officer being *Ville de Quebec* under Lieutenant-Commander A.R.E. Coleman of Montreal, Que. Records at the National Defence Directorate of History and Heritage indicate that *U-224* was coming in for an attack on the convoy when *Ville de Quebec* asdic operator Stanley Miller of Saskatoon, Sask., reported a sub contact on the starboard bow. The corvette responded immediately with a shallow pattern of 10 depth charges. Within minutes, the damaged U-boat surfaced, with her bow shooting perhaps 20 feet out of the water. The corvette's Oerlikon guns opened up, preventing the Germans from manning their deck gun. After turning to ram, the corvette continued to rake the U-boat's hull and conning tower.

Ville de Quebec struck the sub about eight feet ahead of the conning tower. John Wilson relates: "I was in the boiler room and we all braced for a shock, but there was none, just a grinding noise on our hull as we passed over the sub and then a loud explosion to our stern."

The ramming settled the matter and *U-224* went down by the bows. This sequence took only nine minutes. Then came an underwater explosion, followed by debris and oil coming to the surface. There was one survivor. First Lieutenant Wolf-Dietrich Danckworth was emerging from the conning tower hatch to assess the depth charge damage when the Type VII C boat was rammed. Thrown clear, he was rescued by a seaboat from the Canadian corvette *Port Arthur*. The U-boat captain, *Oberleutnant zur See* Hans-Karl Kosbadt, approaching at periscope depth, had so concentrated on the convoy that he did not notice the escort until it was too late.

Two forward compartments were ripped open in *Ville de Quebec* and the asdic dome was knocked off. Damage control measures were undertaken to reduce the pressure on forward bulkheads, which held. Civilian ships blew their whistles in tribute as *Ville de Quebec* rejoined the convoy to proceed to Algiers, where temporary repairs were made.

The victory became a newsworthy item. It was announced on January 25 in Montreal by the chief of the naval staff, Vice-Admiral Percy Nelles. The next day in Algiers, the ship's company was inspected by the high brass, including the First Sea Lord, Admiral of the Fleet Sir Dudley Pound; the commander-in-chief of the Mediterranean, Admiral Sir Andrew Cunningham; the chief of Combined Operations, Vice-Admiral Lord Louis Mountbatten; and the chief of the Imperial General Staff, Sir John Dill. Once back in the United Kingdom, *Ville de Quebec* was inspected by the King and Queen. Among the awards that followed was the Distinguished Service Order for captain Coleman, a 45-year-old, Royal Navy veteran of World War I, and Mention in Dispatches for Able Seaman Miller.

* * *

Port Arthur soon shared centre stage. On the afternoon of January 19, 1943, five Canadian corvettes were among the 10 escorts for the 29-ship convoy MKS 6 in the Mediterranean Sea. Near Bougie, *Port Arthur* obtained a contact that was definitely classed as a submarine at 1,400 yards. The corvette increased speed and four minutes later let loose a pattern of 10 depth charges. "When we dropped our charges, mine didn't throw out for about a minute after the rest," recalls Bruce Crickmore. "My firing lanyard was stuck and I had to stand upon the thrower with both feet and pull with all my force before it got unstuck and fired."

Records at Library and Archives Canada and the National Defence Directorate of History and Heritage show that the sub had been lying in wait at a depth of about 33 feet to attack the westbound convoy. At the last minute it tried unsuccessfully to get underneath *Port Arthur* to avoid the depth charges, which found their mark and sent the sub down to 250 feet with severe damage. Surfacing in desperation, the sub was down at the stern. Ordered to man their guns, some of the crew seized the opportunity to jump out of the conning tower into the water.

The depth charge explosions knocked out *Port Arthur*'s asdic and she lost contact with the sub. *Port Arthur* signalled a sister escort, the RN destroyer *Antelope*, which was moving in. *Port Arthur* turned to ram, but the sub had come up closer to *Antelope*, which opened fire with 4.7-inch guns, Oerlikons and her 2-pounder pom-pom, scoring several direct hits and killing some of the sub's crew. The sub captain gave the order to scuttle and abandon ship. The sub sank about two minutes after surfacing. Four sub officers and 24 ratings were lost. The destroyer picked up three officers and 22 ratings while the corvette responded to another asdic contact, which proved to be non-submarine.

The sub captain had been trying to attack despite damage from an earlier American air assault. Credit went to *Port Arthur* since it was felt the sub would have sunk without *Antelope*'s intervention. The prize was not a U-boat, but the 950-ton Italian sub *Tritone* on her first patrol. Foremost among the awards for the sub kill was the Distinguished Service Order to *Port Arthur*'s captain, Lieutenant Ted Simmons, who had earned the Distinguished Service Cross for leading *Chambly*'s boarding party in the September 1941 sinking of *U-501*.

British Prime Minister Winston Churchill sent congratulations to his Canadian counterpart, Mackenzie King, for the successes by *Ville de Quebec* and *Port Arthur*. But it was *Port Arthur*'s crew who earned a rare tangible reward — a $1,000 purse raised by public subscription in that Ontario city after it adopted the corvette in 1942.

* * *

On February 6, 1943, convoy KMS 8 was eastbound about 60 miles past Oran with an escort of eight Canadian corvettes and two British destroyers. As a routine precaution, the corvette *Louisburg* went to action stations at dusk and depth charge crews began some practice drill.

"We were about eight miles off the North African coast, when off our starboard bow the next escort ship [HMS *Laforey*], maybe a mile away, started shooting," recalls Cook W.R. Ransome. "Three great plumes of water went up behind them. We thought they were depth charges, but they were bombs from high-level bombers and action started everywhere. I ran for the galley to get my steel helmet, leaving my life belt hanging there. I think my excitement said you don't need a life belt in an air raid."

Suddenly there was a new threat — a formation of three dive bombers. Able Seaman Ernie Pain of Cornwall, Ont., a loader on an Oerlikon gun aft, says: "They came from over the mountains. The sun was setting fast and we had a hard time zeroing in on them because of the sun glaring in our eyes. They came in low just above the sea and as soon as one was close enough, he let a torpedo go. We were at a disadvantage because we could not lower our guns below the guard rails. They were very cunning."

Able Seaman Budd Parks recalls:

From the crow's nest above, the lookout's warning came too late. I saw the torpedo's track racing towards us at the same time the torpedo plane rose above the horizon. The tracers from our Oerlikon guns were missing, going beneath the plane as it banked across our bow. With a blinding flash the torpedo exploded, ripping into the ship's engine room. The concussion, smoke and flames roared up from directly below. I was lifted and dropped. I tumbled and stumbled down the bridge-deck ladder to the boat deck below, hitting my head and shoulders against a steel ammunition locker. From my sprawling position, I could see the engine room skylights were blown out. Belching steam blowing across the boat deck blocked my view of the after section of the ship.

From the bridge above came the captain's command — 'Abandon Ship!' I moved onto a float ramp a few feet away. Four seaman were already there. I had a clear view of the stern settling beneath the water. Panic shook me. The ship was sinking fast. I turned to the Carley float. It was held in place with two wide cross-straps. A blake slip held each strap to the ramp. One strap was off. Someone was trying to loosen the other blake slip with his fingers. The ship was newly painted and using one's fingers would take too long. Using my right boot, I kicked blake slip, fingers and all. The Carley float lay free.

Taking a grip on the rope running around the edge of the float, I lifted and stepped towards the end ramp. The four seamen decided to do the same. A sudden surge of power sent the Carley float over the side, pulling me behind it. The float hit the water on its edge and toppled away astern. I missed the float by inches, plunging into the water in a crouched position. The impact against my chest and face straightened my body, sending me deep. Swimming to regain the surface, I realized my saturated greatcoat was holding me back. Reaching down with both hands, I pulled the two ends apart and the coat fell away. With lungs burning for oxygen, I raced to the surface and gulped in air.

The stench of crude oil greeted my nostrils. My head, face and upper body were covered in thick, black oil. One quick look told me the ship's company was plummeting into the oil-covered water all around me. Their oily features made recognition impossible. Without a life preserver and treading water, I slowly made my way through the panic-stricken scene and away from the sinking ship. When I looked back, the darkening shadow of the ship's bow, pointed skyward, slipped away with the sound of belching air, leaving a blackened, oily sea of seamen struggling for survival against time and the elements as darkness settled around us.

A deep rumble from an underwater explosion sent a shock wave through the survivors on the surface, killing many. I felt the sting of the blast from my heels to the back of my neck, making me flinch severely. Approximately six minutes had passed since the torpedo struck. The cries from the darkness were fewer now. As each minute passed, I found myself frequently fighting panic. With the realization that my body muscles needed support, I swam towards the sound of voices. Voices meant a group. A group could mean a Carley float and a float would give me the required support for survival.

The direction of sounds across darkened waters is often deceiving. My tired body told me there would be no margin for error. Using the sounds as a guide, stopping often to get a true bearing, and with my luck still holding, I eventually swam into a laden Carley float. Feeling my way in the darkness, I moved between two startled seamen. Hooking my left arm into the webbing of the float, I relaxed for the first time in about 10 minutes.

I climbed onto the edge of the float, disregarding the shouts of anger. I then began to remove my boots and pants. From the conversation around me, I learned that the centre webbing of the float carried the weight of an officer with two broken legs, a petty officer in severe shock and a seaman who had swallowed a mixture of crude oil and salt water. The Carley float had lost its buoyancy and lay about two inches below the surface due to being overweight. Many of the ratings clinging to the outer edge of the float were also without life belts.

A leading hand had taken charge of the small group of survivors and was trying desperately to unify their cries for help. Time passed. Then, from the darkness, a clear, calm voice with a British accent was saying, "All right chaps, stand by to be taken aboard." A cry of joy ushered forth from the float as the British destroyer [*Lookout*] slowly moved alongside. We could hear the British sailors issuing instructions to each survivor being helped up over the side.

The Carley float had regained its buoyancy as I eased my way across the centre webbing to the inside edge. Strong hands gripped my wet jumper and held me in close to the rope netting. With help, I climbed the netting to the deck above, took a few steps and fell to my hands and knees. My body shook with relief. My eyes were flooded with tears as I felt my strength slowly coming back. Refusing further help, I pushed off the deck to an upright position and staggered towards the hatch leading below, anxious to join the rest of the survivors.

In the meantime, W.R. Ransome made it back to *Louisburg's* main deck with his steel hat: "The stern was settling fairly fast. The bow was raising up and men were jumping overboard amidship, maybe six or seven feet off the water. I did not want anyone to jump on top of me in the water as I cannot swim, so I moved about 15 feet forward where it was clear. I learned a lesson right there — you do not jump into the water with the strap of a steel helmet under your chin! When I surfaced, there was a float close by and I was the third man to reach it. There were underwater explosions from our depth charges and possibly a boiler exploded. When we were rescued this eight-man float held up 13 survivors."

Ernie Pain was knocked out by the initial blast. "After recovering I could not find anyone around, so went to the life jacket locker and grabbed two jackets," he says. "I proceeded to the quarterdeck, which was underwater and sinking fast. I waded into the sea rather than jump from a higher deck. I was too scared to jump into the unknown, being that it was now pitch dark. I knew she was going down fast and that I could be drawn down with her. By fate I was entangled in the signal halyards of the mast, but by some miracle I was blown to the surface by underwater explosions. I heard voices and started to call out for help. To my surprise, not too far distant was a mate by the name of [Joseph] Gauvin from Montreal who put his hand out and pulled me aside of a damaged Carley float.

"Sometime later we were picked up by HMS *Lookout* who put men over the side to haul us out of the water. I had taken a lot of oil into my stomach and was very sick for a few days, but then I was more fortunate than many who died on the messdeck tables with the bends. We were laying on messdeck lockers just above the ammunition locker and when I heard guns going off, I asked one of the British tars, 'Do you have to keep us here above the ammunition locker?' He replied, 'Don't worry, mate, you won't feel a thing.'"

Able Seaman Gordon MacDonald of Moncton, N.B., says: "I was standing behind the 4-inch gun with a 4-inch projectile in my hands when the torpedo hit. I was lifted off the deck. I came down on my back with the projectile on my shoulder. Everything is sort of blurred then. I knew I couldn't swim much and our life jackets were the ones you tied around your waist and blew up. There was no time for that and I knew there were other types of jackets, with a cushion front, in the lifeboats. Back I ran for the lifeboats that were amidship. By the time I got there, the water was to my knees. The ship just went and me with it.

"I remember thinking I was gone, but whether the ship filled with water, or maybe the boilers blew, but somehow I was on the surface and a Carley float was only maybe 20 or so feet away. I was a very lucky man. A bunch of us hung on to that float until a British destroyer stopped. The captain told us not to make so much noise and hurry to get aboard because he couldn't stop long. It was dark, or maybe they wouldn't have been able to stop at all. They took us to Algiers the next day. I spent a week in the hospital there with a broken shoulder, but I sure didn't feel that in the water."

Lieutenant Hall Tingley remembers: "The torpedo exploded in the engine room just under my position directing the 20mm Oerlikon fire from the after-bandstand. I went head over heels and suffered a broken knee joint and a cracked heel bone. I observed a Carley float about 100 feet away and, in company with an officers' steward named [John] McCauley, took off to swim to it. McCauley [from Windsor, Ont.] said he couldn't swim, but he did darn well and made the Carley float with only a little encouragement from me. We were picked up by HMS *Lookout* and taken to Algiers. I spent a full month there in a British army field hospital."

Nearly 50 years later, Doris Nickerson of Clarks Harbour, N.S., summed up the experience of her husband, Able Seaman Ed Nickerson, who was by then in a Halifax veterans' hospital with Alzheimer's disease: "Ed was strapped to an anti-aircraft gun trying to shoot down an aircraft. After the torpedo hit, he remembers nothing, until he found himself in the water covered in oil. How he got the straps off, he does not know. Maybe the explosion did it, maybe a buddy. But I think the will to live probably caused a reaction to get out of the straps and jump into the sea. No one will ever know. After a long time in the water, he was picked up and put into a hospital in Algiers. He was later transferred to an American hospital in Londonderry. He was discharged on May 1, 1943, medically unfit."

Leading Sick Berth Attendant James Cornell of Oliver, B.C., recalls:

We did not have much time to get off the ship. There was not much time to even feel any fear. I was below deck when she was hit and I was the last to scramble up to the main deck, which was awash with water by then. The captain [Lieutenant-Commander William Campbell] grabbed me and asked if there was anyone left below. I said I didn't think so. He advised me to get off the ship and went below to check on his crew. He never made it back up.

She seemed to break in two and reach for the sky with her bow before she sank. I swam, but was no match for the pull of the ship as she sank. I was haunted for years with that memory and tormented with nightmares. I kept trying to break the surface. I could see it above me like a window of light, but the ship would not let me go upward. The light grew smaller and smaller and I thought my lungs would burst. I had a sense of resignation to death and was about to let go and try a breath of water when a great swooshing sound hit my ears and the pressure propelled me upward to the light and through to the surface. I think the boilers blew up. I have a feeling a lot of the crew who died were caught by the ship and the blast. How I survived is a mystery when so many others died around me. I was vaguely conscious of others struggling around me.

I don't remember too much about my time in the water. I clung to a piece of matting that had been blown off the ship and I kept vomiting. I swallowed a lot of oil and my eyes burned — but being sick meant being alive and I was filled with a sense of elation on that score. I remember a ship, a destroyer

I think, passing by and a voice calling out, "Cheer up matey, we'll send help for you." I believe I was in the water about four hours, but I'm not sure. I do remember that when the rescue ship did arrive, I was able to paddle to the netting they threw over, but was too weak to climb. One of the crew climbed down and threw me over his shoulder. When he placed me on the ship's deck I think I cried. I was grateful then for the oil that reddened my eyes for I did not want anyone to see me weep. The relief on rescue is joyous and indescribable. We cling to life with such tenacity even when the circumstances are brutal.

Leading Stoker Jim Willett recalls:

The after-half of the ship was upending and sinking. I was standing on the forward section, in a daze at what was happening before my very eyes. The captain, or someone on the bridge, was shouting, "Abandon ship! Away with Carley floats!"

I realized there were no life jackets within my reach. An officer rushed by me, saying "Is everyone up from below?" Not waiting for my reply, he rushed into the seamen's mess, hollering, "Everybody out!"

Just then I saw my friend Hugh Merryweather in the water and he called to me to jump. "Come on, Willie," he said, and held up a life buoy. Without further thought, I jumped. Hugh swam towards me and gave me the cork life preserver. Of course, the water was by then polluted with heavy bunker oil from the tanks and the air was filled with cries of "Help!", "Over here!", and "Oh God!"

Someone in our vicinity kept repeating over and over, "Get away from the suction," but it was too late for some of us. Within another 30 seconds the forward half of the ship slid under the water, drawing Hugh, myself and countless others down with her. Down, down and over and over I went, hanging on for dear life to the life buoy, thinking this was the end. Suddenly there was a tremendous explosion and I found myself on top of the water again, although in much pain.

Several hundred feet from where I surfaced was a Carley float with a number of sailors on it. Eventually I was able to get onboard also. The tail end of the convoy and escorts were rushing past us and we could see a British destroyer picking up some of our crew from the water. But darkness was fast approaching and in a very short time complete darkness enveloped us.

The water was comparatively warm and fairly smooth. By this time I was deaf — could hear absolutely nothing. The left side of my head was bleeding and I thought I had a fractured skull. As well, I was vomiting blood and oil, and was in considerable pain. We were destined to spend the night in our misery before being picked up by a British flying boat very early the next morning. We were taken to a British hospital in Algiers. I never saw my friend Hugh and later, back in Halifax, I learned he was one of the casualties.

Four crew members were awarded Mention in Dispatches. The CO, William Campbell of Toronto, Ont., "was responsible for the saving of many lives, due to his rapid summing up of the situation and his prompt action. His bravery, in the face of the enemy, cost him his own life."

The citation for Coder Hugh Merryweather of Edmonton, Alta., reads: "This rating lost his own life by sacrificing his life belt to another rating when HMCS *Louisburg* was sinking. His gallantry was worthy of the highest traditions of the service."

Ordinary Seaman Joseph Guersette of Sherbrooke, Que., was named for helping "several semi-stunned ratings" over the side. One of them was the fourth man decorated, Leading Seaman W.M. Ritson-Bennett of Edmonton, Alta., who says: "I was in the bandstand, which the explosion toppled. I was knocked unconscious. Guersette stopped to release me from my gun and I stopped to release someone else from their gun. I ended up in hospital in Algiers with a concussion."

There was a fifth award, a higher one. The Distinguished Service Cross was awarded to Sub-Lieutenant William Richard Wright of Montreal, Que.: "For conspicuous gallantry and leadership. When the ship was fatally hit by an enemy torpedo, this officer, though seriously wounded and having lost the sight of one eye, continued to assist in the work of rescue. He himself was the last of the ship's company to be rescued from the water." In October 1944, Wright, too, was discharged as medically unfit.

Louisburg sank in four minutes. The torpedo itself apparently only killed a small number of sailors. Most of the crew actually made it into the water, but many died there, either by being sucked down with the ship or when the boilers and some depth charges exploded. Several men died in hospital in Algiers, after being listed as survivors. Not surprisingly, various casualty and survivor counts do not correspond. However, in preparing a softcover book for *Louisburg* families as a memorial to the casualties, crew member William John Quinsey of Mississauga, Ont., did extensive research and I think it likely he has the numbers right: 45 survivors (44 Canadian plus 1 Royal Navy passenger) and 42 dead (37 Canadian and 5 Royal Navy passengers). Newspapers of the day reported there were two other victims — the ship's mascots, an Irish terrier named Looie and a black kitten.

The official operational history of the Royal Canadian Navy in World War II says that "confusion remains as to whether the aircraft were German or Italian." However, I encountered no doubt in the minds of those *Louisburg* survivors with whom I talked and corresponded. Ernie Pain speaks for them when he says the planes were Savoia-Marchetti 79s, meaning the Italian Savoia-Marchetti SM.79, which served as a land-based torpedo bomber as well as in the normal bombing role.

James Cornell puts the sinking in a larger perspective: "It is my understanding that *Louisburg* had the somewhat dubious distinction of being the first Canadian warship sunk by enemy action in the Mediterranean as well as being the first [and so far only] Canadian warship destroyed by aerial action. I recall being somewhat embarrassed by the fact that we lost our ship through the action of an Italian bomber crew. At the time, the Italian air force was not considered much of a threat. They were considered better lovers than flying eagles.'"

Louisburg survivors had one final item to address. Ernie Pain explains: "When we got back to Canada, we all decided to send *Louisburg*'s remaining canteen funds, a couple of thousand dollars, to HMS *Lookout*'s canteen fund because they were so good to us. There were no uniforms for us, but they even gave us their underwear."

* * *

On February 8, 1943, the corvette *Regina* and the minesweeper HMS *Rhyl* were east of Algiers, escorting two merchant ships that formed a second section of convoy KMS 8 to Bône. Records at Library and Archives Canada and the National Defence Directorate of History and Heritage show that at 2310 *Regina* able seaman Joseph Saulnier of Meteghan River, N.S., detected a faint radar contact at a distance of three and a half miles. Course was altered to investigate.

The radar contact soon disappeared, but an asdic contact was obtained at a range of 1,000 yards. It was a sub and it had dived to escape. *Regina* raced in and attacked with a pattern of 10 depth charges, went out 1,000 yards, turned and came back. With his rudder jammed and boat badly damaged, the captain of the Italian sub *Avorio* [Ivory] chose to surface.

Depth charge damage prevented use of the sub's forward torpedo tubes and her main surface armament, a 3.9-inch deck gun. Also unable to maintain a straight course because the steering gear was jammed, the sub executed a series of S-turns and used her machine-guns to hit the bridge and wheelhouse of the zigzagging corvette. Sub-Lieutenant Doug Clarance recalls: "I remember standing on the bridge alongside one of the Oerlikons and seeing the tracer going out and seeming to come back, when I realized they were shooting back at us. All of a sudden I was six feet taller than I needed to be."

Able Seaman Gib Todd says: "I was captain of the two-pounder, or pom pom, located above the quarterdeck. We got our licks in, managed a few hits and were more or less shielded from the sub's firing in as much as we were in the stern. Mind you, that machine-gun sprayed us pretty good and came awful close. Everything happened so fast — too fast to be scared. I did everything as we were trained to do. I think I was more scared after it was all over, when I thought of what could have happened."

In this duel in the dark, *Regina* had the upper hand from the start. She expended eight rounds of 4-inch shells, 20 rounds of pom pom and 635 rounds of Oerlikon ammunition. The sub's conning tower was holed and the captain and first lieutenant were among those killed. Some crew members began to abandon the sub and the corvette turned away to avoid an unnecessary ramming.

Lieutenant-Commander Harry Freeland, the corvette captain, ordered the Italians to keep the submarine afloat or else. *Regina* searched the area for 15 minutes to ensure there wasn't another sub about, then sent over a boarding party to assess the damage and see if the sub could be salvaged.

Regina's commanding officer, Lieutenant-Commander Harry Freeland, on April 30, 1943.

Able Seaman Vic Martin recalls: "We lowered a boarding party in our lifeboat. I was one of a three-man boat crew — two oars each for [Able Seaman Byron] 'Big Fish' Nodding and myself. Six of our men were put on the sub and we started taking prisoners back to our ship. *Regina* never stopped moving. If she did, she would have been a sitting duck. We made several trips back and forth from ship to sub. It took some time for our ship to find us as it was a very dark night."

Stoker Petty Officer Raymond Alexander of Winnipeg, Man., was in the boarding party. "Italians were standing on the bow of the sub as the stern was sitting low in the water," he recalls. "Her bow had been opened up by the depth charges. One of our crew spoke Italian so that helped. Our men had a couple of pistols and they gave me a submachine-gun and told me if there was any trouble I only had to press the trigger. We got the prisoners off, but kept the engineer and a petty officer aboard as we wanted to try to start the engines and drive the sub into shore. They gave me a hand gun and told me to take the petty officer and go down to the engine room to see if anything could be done. The water was up to our knees and since I couldn't talk to him I motioned for us to go back up to the upper deck. I found a nice pair of German binoculars and put them around my neck. When we got back to the upper deck, the sub was getting lower in the water."

As it turned out, the sub's crew hadn't been able to scuttle the boat because the depth charges had caused flooding of the magazine where the scuttling charges were stored. The boarding party's exploration indicated that the sub could not proceed under her own power. Captain Freeland did not attempt to take the sub in tow because his radar had been knocked out by the depth charge explosions and he was fearful of encountering another sub. Although salvage prospects looked poor, the sub was a tantalizing prize and he requested a tug. *Jaunty* arrived at 0345 on February 9 and towing commenced.

By 0500 the sub was taking on more water, so the corvette sent a seaboat away to bring back the boarding party and the two Italians. "The tug's crew cut the tow line," says Alexander. "We asked them to take us aboard as the sub was sinking and they said no way, and off they went. We were left standing on the upper deck and the water was around our knees. I told our party I was getting off as she was sinking. I dove off first and the rest followed. I looked around and her bow was straight up in the air and down she went. Our seamen in the lifeboat hollered to us that they were coming and shortly afterwards picked us up one by one. I kept the binoculars around my neck and took them home with me."

The sub had been surprised while cruising at about 7 knots recharging its batteries. Although the figures in several post-action reports do not agree, it appears 16 Italians died and 26 were taken prisoner. "The prisoners were surprised to have one of our ratings speak to them in their own language," says Coder Leonard Horne of Windsor, Ont. "They were cleaned up and fed the same as our own."

All accessible areas of the crippled *Avorio* were inspected by the boarding party and the survivors were questioned, which revealed some information about the boat's operational capabilities.

C.C. Williams, the mayor of Regina, sent captain Freeland a telegram: "Citizens of Regina very proud of achievement [of] corvette named after our city. Please convey to officers and crew our congratulations and hope this is the first of many similar victories. Good hunting and a safe return to port."

There were eight awards to *Regina* crew members, with Harry Freeland's Distinguished Service Order atop the list. Mention in Dispatches went to Joseph Saulnier, the radar operator whose alertness started the chain of events.

Courtesy Vic Martin

The corvette *Regina* brings prisoners of war from the Italian submarine *Avorio* to Bône, Algeria, on February 9, 1943.

But the enduring legacy in the minds of a number of *Regina* crew is a poem about the *Avorio* engagement. Comprised of 17 stanzas, each four lines long, it was written by Ted Latreille of Sudbury, Ont. The final four verses are:

Our boys were still aboard the sub,
They tried their best to keep her above.
Their efforts were futile; it was no use,
Her hull had taken too much abuse.

They waited too long to take their leave
As the bow took a dip and the stern a heave.
She started down on her last long dive,
They were lucky they all got off alive.

You must admit she'd have been a prize,
To be brought into port by a ship our size.
But after all, who are we to say,
We may get a chance another day.

Let's drink a toast to Canada's fleet.
We know it's small, but it's hard to beat.
Her men, no doubt, you all have met,
The ones who man our small corvettes.

Stoker Latreille, 32, did not survive long enough to share in that toast. On the trip from Ireland to Canada, the last leg of the long journey home, he suffered a ruptured appendix and succumbed, despite an emergency operation at sea by the doctor given to *Regina* for Operation Torch. The stoker was buried at sea March 25, 1943.

* * *

On the morning of February 22, 1943, the corvette *Weyburn* left Gibraltar and rejoined slow convoy MKS 8 bound for the U.K., records at Library and Archives Canada and the National Defence Directorate of History and Heritage indicate. The convoy was well to port within the swept channel about seven miles off Cape Spartel. On the way up the convoy's port side to assume her escort position, *Weyburn* struck a mine, which exploded amidship.

A large hole was blown on the port side. Steam and heat poured from the funnel, which had split in two vertically. Steam pipes inside the ship burst. Deck plates buckled and the engine room flooded, but the corvette remained afloat. As the crew recovered from the shock, Lieutenant Pat Milsom of Toronto, Ont., and Ordinary Seaman Daniel Tansey, a Royal Navy rating, removed the primers from

Library and Archives Canada, PA105907

The corvette *Weyburn* at Halifax in May 1942.

the depth charges. However, the primers could not be removed from two charges jammed in the twisted wreckage, but their firing mechanisms were set to safe.

When the listing *Weyburn* stopped moving, HMS *Wivern* decided she was not going to sink. While the sloop *Black Swan* provided a protective screen, *Wivern* positioned herself so that the wounded could climb directly onto the destroyer. This worked, although *Weyburn* First Lieutenant William Garrard of Victoria, B.C., suffered a crushed leg in the process. A seaboat from the destroyer also began picking up other survivors in the oil-covered water.

About 20 minutes after striking the mine, *Weyburn* suddenly reared and sank stern first. Within seconds the scene was rocked by two violent explosions, in all likelihood caused by the two depth charges that could not be disarmed. One blast sent one of *Weyburn*'s bow anchors over *Wivern*'s bridge and onto her deck. *Wivern* was seriously damaged. All was chaos.

Ordinary Seaman Wally Charbonneau of Gatineau, Que., recalls the tragedy:

I was sitting in the mess, right at the end of the bench, with my cup waiting for up spirits [distribution of the daily rum ration]. That's when the big bang happened. I went flying up and hit my head on the bulkhead [ceiling] and I came down and hit my side on the corner of the table, but that didn't bother me too much. But then, having been well brought up, I let everybody go by — until I realized that I was being too polite and I joined the crowd and got out.

The davits were broken, but the skiff, the lifeboat, was in the water. It was alongside the ship, so I said, "I'll jump into that" with three other fellows. The four of us we were trying to cut the line that was attached to the ship and before we managed, the ship started sinking stern-first. And that's when we saw the captain [Lieutenant-Commander Tom Golby] on the bridge with blood coming down his face. And then somebody mentioned that the captain was hanging on. And then Sub-Lieutenant

Courtesy Wally Charbonneau

Two *Weyburn* sailors in Oran, Algeria, on December 12, 1942, are Al Smith of Toronto, Ont., (left) and Wally Charbonneau of Gatineau, Que.

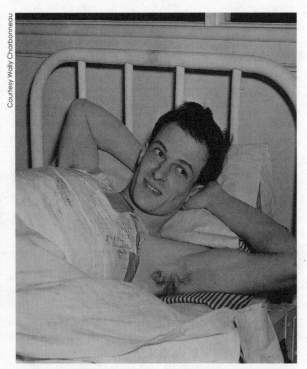

Courtesy Wally Charbonneau

Weyburn casualty Able Seaman John Peters recovers in a British hospital in Gibraltar in February 1943.

[Wilfred] Bark says, "I'll go for him." Just after he reached him, the stern went down and they both disappeared. Then the explosions took place. We're sure it was the depth charges astern that went off because water went sky high. And then it's a blank.

After that, I'm looking for a place, something, to hang on to. I saw a wooden board come by with a little brass plate on it, Communications Mess, so I grabbed on and hung on to that until I was picked up. The lifeboat that was picking me up was full. No room for me there, but they let me hang onto the chains inside and when I got ahold of that, I said to myself, "If they won't let me aboard and they want me to let go, they'll have to cut my hands off."

They rowed back to *Wivern,* which had [scramble] nets on the side. I couldn't climb, I was too weak. So then a British guy says, "Here, Jack, come on and grab ahold." I was in coveralls so I was soaked. He grabbed onto me and he heaved me over the railing. And that's when a big sigh came out. Then we were

stripped naked and given a grey blanket. We were shaking. We were covered in oil and cork and we sat there.

I didn't know it, but there was a guy or body lying there all wrapped up and I heard, "Charb, Charb!"

I said, "Who's calling me?" I looked down at my feet. "Are you calling me?"

"Yeah," he says. It was a fellow from Port Arthur [now Thunder Bay, Ont.], an Italian fellow. "Turn me over," he says. "I have to pee."

I didn't recognize him, he was so bad off.

Weyburn Able Seaman Frank Cleave of Georgetown, Ont., says: "I received a broken jaw from flying debris and as a result I wandered around like a punch-drunk boxer for several hours struggling to clear my mind and vision. Many of the happenings at the time of the sinking and for a few weeks previous are still very hazy and confused."

Courtesy John Parker

Crew members from *Algoma* perform a burial at sea from a Polish trawler in the Straits of Gibraltar for Able Seaman Dorn McGaw of Kincardine, Ont., a victim of the sinking of *Weyburn* in February 1943.

RCN, courtesy Wally Charbonneau

In Victoria, B.C., Pam Golby accepts the return of her pet Posh, the mascot that survived the sinking of the corvette *Weyburn* in the Mediterranean in February 1943. Her father, Lieutenant-Commander Tom Golby, *Weyburn*'s captain, was lost with his ship.

The many acts of bravery by crew members of both ships earned 10 gallantry awards — four of them post-humous, including Mention in Dispatches to *Weyburn* officers Tom Golby of Victoria, B.C., and Wilfred Bark of Montreal, Que., and Ordinary Seaman Tansey. The dazed captain, who probably had a fractured skull, was desperately trying to get a sailor off the bridge to safety, unaware that the man was likely already dead. Bark had rushed to help him and they both died in the process, along with *Wivern* Stoker Petty Officer Sydney Frank Day, who jumped over to *Weyburn* to assist.

Lieutenant Milsom and Executive Officer Garrard were each made a Member of the British Empire (Military Division) "for gallant rescue work." The *Wivern* medical officer, Surgeon-Lieutenant P.R.C. Evans, received the George Medal. Though suffering from two broken ankles, and passing out several times from pain, he lay on his back and directed the operation on Garrard's crushed leg while it was performed by *Wivern*'s sick berth attendant. Garrard, who served overseas with the Canadian Army in World War I, was certainly gutsy. There was no anesthetic and he is reported to have said, "Hack away, boys. I'm all in favour of it."

Wivern was eventually towed to Gibraltar by *Black Swan*. There was no board of inquiry, but it's believed the mine was laid by a U-boat, perhaps *U-118*. *Weyburn* had 68 survivors and nine fatalities, two of whom died in hospital in Gibraltar. Able Seaman John Parker comments: "When *Algoma* went back to Gib on one of our trips, we were the only Canadian ship in harbour and we were asked to bury one of *Weyburn*'s crew who had died there. I vividly remember going to the morgue in the dockyard at Gib. There were six of us. The body was wrapped in canvas and weighted. I put my hand under the victim's shoulders, between the body and the cold slab, an eerie feeling. We put the body on a stretcher and walked through the rain to a Polish trawler used to bury casualties at sea. We proceeded out to the Straits and with a brief ceremony deposited the body to the deep. I believe the boy [Able Seaman Dorn McGaw] was from Kincardine, Ont., and was severely wounded in the water when depth charges exploded."

Weyburn crew members had another duty to perform. It began when, despite a leg so seriously crushed it would have to be amputated, Stoker Thomas Baxter, of Penetang, Ont., carried the ship's mascot, a springer spaniel, off the sinking ship. Posh had swallowed a lot of oil and suffered other injuries, so while *Weyburn*'s crew was in hospital in Gibraltar, the mascot was treated in a veterinary hospital. Reports on his condition were issued daily.

When recovered, Posh returned to Canada with some of the crew. From there, a long train ride in a padded wooden crate took him to Vancouver and a reunion with five-year-old Pam Golby, the captain's daughter who had given her pet to her dad. A story and photos of the reunion appeared in newspapers across Canada. Many years later, Pam Golby and her mother Joan Golby attended a reunion of the *Weyburn* crew held in Victoria.

* * *

On March 13, 1943, while escorting northbound convoy MKS 9, the Torch corvette *Prescott* attacked two U-boats in the Atlantic northwest of Spain, or so her crew thought. In 1987, by comparing British and German records and signal logs, an Admiralty researcher concluded that *Prescott* had, in fact, attacked the same boat twice and deserved credit for a solo kill of *U-163*. The Type IX C boat did not answer German requests on March 15 and 16 to state its position. The U-boat was never heard from again and German authorities had been unable to determine its fate. They now accept the British reassessment.

A report by *Prescott* captain Lieutenant-Commander Wilfred McIsaac said that at 9:49 p.m. radar contact was made at 3,400 yards and course was altered to close. At 1,400 yards, the U-boat was seen diving. In all, the corvette fired three patterns of depth charges, totalling 23, and also took a couple of shots with her main four-inch gun at what was believed to be a second U-boat, before dropping single charges at three different points. After four hours and 21 minutes, the corvette returned to the convoy as directed.

U-163 had left its base in Lorient, France, on the Bay of Biscay for its third war patrol only three days earlier.

Before succumbing to *Prescott* with the loss of all 57 hands, *U-163* had sunk three merchant vessels and badly damaged an American warship, USS *Erie PG-50*.

Upon learning of the reassessment when reading an article in *Legion Magazine* in June 1998, Arnold Trask of Digby, N.S., an ordinary seaman in *Prescott,* said, "I checked my diary, and on March 13, 1943, we did attack a submarine. We dropped 20 depth charges during the attack and we were almost certain that we had sunk the sub, however, we could not find anything — no oil slick, no bodies or other debris whatsoever, so had nothing to prove that we had killed the submarine. Perhaps you can imagine my surprise to find out in 1998 that we had received credit for the sinking, not a long time later, only 55 years."

"We were on the way back to the U.K. from Operation Torch in the Mediterranean," Trask explained. "We were headed to Londonderry, then Halifax, then Liverpool, N.S., for refit. We were leaking quite badly. That was the main reason for the refit."

* * *

Eventually, of course, all the Canadian corvettes headed home by way of the United Kingdom. Bruce Crickmore remembers: "When we were leaving, a Spanish ship passed us at sea with all lights aglow in the middle of the night. We felt like sitting ducks as we were silhouetted between the liner and the sea. But what a sight it was. Almost none of us had been at sea in peacetime and this was the first ship we had ever seen with all lights on."

Arriving back in Canada "happy to be home and, of course, anticipating leave," *Port Arthur*'s crew was met by the naval brass and got a rude surprise, says a disappointed Jack Skinner. "They told us what a tough time our sailors had been having on the Atlantic runs while we had been on our yachting cruise in the Med and we were to replace these crews while they went home on leave. So away we went to spend the summer on North Atlantic convoy."

Courtesy Arnold Trask

Prescott crew member Forbes stands by one of the ship's four depth charge throwers.

Brantford is iced up in St John's, Newfoundland, after a severe spray storm on the Grand Banks during the winter of 1943-44.

CHAPTER TWELVE

"THE WINTER, THE SEA — THESE WERE THE ENEMY."

BELIEVING that the four Canadian escort groups were long on energy and short on the intricacies of anti-submarine warfare, the British government demanded in mid-December 1942 that they be pulled from the North Atlantic. As evidence, the British cited heavy losses in convoys assigned to Canadian groups. Offended and bitter, the Royal Canadian Navy resisted. Then, reeling from the disaster of convoy ONS 154 at the end of 1942, the RCN acceded early in 1943.

Skinny Hayes says: "We only did one round trip after I joined *Kenogami* as first lieutenant in January 1943, when we were suddenly informed that the whole group was to be given individual ship workups, and a group workup before further employment. Very confusing! It was nearly 40 years later that I found out this relatively violent hiccup in the employment of Canadian ships was as the result of a difference of opinion between the Canadian and British authorities regarding the steps necessary to improve the performance of Canadian escort groups."

Though the withdrawal of the Canadian groups wasn't widely known, this was the RCN's low point in World War II. In reality, the British had oversimplified the problem. There were many overlapping factors.

The RCN had forced its volunteers to take on too much. Individual crews were light on experience and training. Ships within each group lacked the proper training to function well as a team. Most of the Canadian mid-ocean escorts were corvettes, which were small and slow, and they drew the bulk of the slow convoys, which were the most vulnerable.

The RCN also had serious weaknesses in the field of technology. And while it unreasonably expected the RCN to shoulder a major portion of the escort load, the RN looked after its own technological needs first. As a result, the performance of Canadian escorts was inhibited by inferior equipment.

Further, there simply weren't enough escorts. To make up for the shortage in number, functioning ships were left at sea as long as possible. The standard of regular ship's maintenance suffered, which increased the risk of breakdowns at sea. It was also hard on men and morale, for their greater sea time was at the expense of rest and training, which could have improved operating efficiency.

Other major factors compounded these problems. The North Atlantic was the main focus of the German thrust in 1942. U-boat signal traffic was no longer being read regularly because British codebreakers had not yet cracked the improved German Enigma cipher machine. Meanwhile, the Germans were still reading British convoy routing messages. The Canadian groups also had to manage without adequate air cover. It was a calamitous mix.

A new commander-in-chief of Western Approaches, Admiral Max Horton, took firm control. The Canadian groups would finally be properly trained for the task at hand and their equipment would be upgraded. In the next short while, Canadian groups would also work the easier U.K.-Gibraltar Run where the air cover was better.

"*Kenogami*'s group only did one trip to Gibraltar, and as soon as we had crossed the Bay of Biscay the difference really became apparent," says Skinny Hayes. "Even though we had a busy trip, with both air and submarine attack, it seemed a little like a picnic to us. The weather was superb. We got out of our duffel coats and into shorts. There were flat seas and warm days and nights. Heaven!"

While on the U.K.-Gibraltar Run in March, *Morden* came to the aid of SS *City of Christchurch*, which was damaged by a bomb during a German air attack, a file at the National Defence Directorate of History and Heritage shows. When the freighter was abandoned, the corvette took in her crew of 102 and successfully salvaged one of three RN harbour-defence motor launches, costing more than $100,000, which had been deck cargo.

The U.K.-Gibraltar assignment was short-lived. Skinny Hayes says: "By the end of March 1943, we were back on the Newfie-Derry Run again. Back to the fight with the weather and the wolf packs."

There the Canadian groups rejoined a number of individual RCN warships, including corvettes, which had remained on the Newfie-Derry Run as part of RN or American escort groups.

* * *

"During the winter months on the North Atlantic it was a continuous contest between man and nature," says *Dauphin* signalman George Rickard. "Ocean spray froze, forming salt-water ice that covered every solid or moving object: the four-inch gun, depth charges, life rafts, wireless antennae — everything in the open."

Leading Seaman Archie Marsh, who served in *Regina*, *Matapedia* and *Nanaimo*, concurs: "Ice was one of the curses that plagued the small escort vessels. Even in just a moderate sea, the ocean spray would freeze solid on every part of an escort's superstructure. It would become impossible to walk or manoeuvre on the upper decks."

Arnold Trask of Digby, N.S., a seaman in *Prescott* and *Brantford,* says: "There was always the danger of capsizing if the accumulation of ice became too heavy. We would have to get rid of it by using steam hoses and anything we could to beat if off and then shovel it over the side to keep the ship from becoming top heavy — a risky job as the decks and everything else was very slippery, making it very difficult to stay on one's feet while the ship was moving about on the waves."

He remembers *Brantford* encountered a particularly "severe freezing spray storm" on the Grand Banks of New-

foundland during the winter of 1943-44: "The bridge was fully encased in ice. The depth charge throwers on both the port and starboard sides were also covered in ice. It was estimated that there was about 60 tons of ice on the forward part of the ship. This made it heavy in the bow and consequently every wave added a little more ice as the ship would dip a little deeper each time it hit another wave."

Ice buildup would cause a ship to become top-heavy and sluggish. While no Canadian corvette capsized in World War II, the auxiliary minesweeper *Bras d'Or* had simply disappeared in the Gulf of St. Lawrence in October 1940. Its exact fate has never been determined, but it is presumed she foundered. This undoubtedly increased the natural concern about ice making a ship so unstable she would capsize — "turn turtle," the sailors called it.

So, when ice accumulated, Jack Shirley in *Chilliwack* notes, "Everybody had to go out with fire axes, crowbars, hammers, anything solid metal, to knock the ice off. It was a very cold job and frequently you got iced up in the process."

Able Seaman Reid Sheppard, who served in *Cobalt* and *Strathroy*, says: "The climb to the crow's-nest in a rough sea on a winter's night was something to remember. I'm glad I was 18 when I had to do it."

Summerside lieutenant Don McGivern of Ottawa, Ont., says: "The lifeline from the foc's'le to the quarterdeck was an essential safety precaution in storms. There is no scary feeling like the pressure of the water on your seaboots as you hold onto the lifeline while making your way aft."

Water was everywhere, of course. George Rickard found it beneficial to tolerate the water that accumulated in his seaboots because it warmed a bit and eventually acted as a sort of insulation. "I learned this the hard way by dumping out the water in my boots and putting them back on again," he explains. "The result was a minor frostbite.

"Regardless of continuously being soaked to the ears in all kinds of weather, none of us seemed to suffer, or pick up a cold. This usually happened while in port."

Fennel leading signalman Bill Acheson sums it up: "The winter, the sea — these were the enemy. For all its unseen threat and terror, the U-boat was all but forgotten at these times. For it too, the sea was the real enemy, an enemy that immobilized and incapacitated its crew, reducing them to fellow sufferers buffeted by mountainous seas and shrieking winds.

Courtesy Arnold Trask

This side view of *Brantford* illustrates how iced up a corvette could become. The thick coating has incapacitated the 4-inch gun after a severe spray storm on the Grand Banks during the winter of 1943-44.

"Through it all, however, a semblance of good naval order and discipline prevailed and the convoys slowly but implacably moved on and made it through. Again and yet again, a new convoy but the same old sea. The new sailors, the new stokers, the new signalmen — now veterans all. Some might even say, now heroes all."

* * *

In February 1943, on the Newfie-Derry Run, convoy ON 166 was beset first by Atlantic gales and then U-boats while westbound from Northern Ireland with four Canadian corvettes in an escort group led by the U.S. Coast Guard cutters *Campbell* and *Spencer*. The convoy had 63 merchant ships, but weather forced 13 to return to the U.K. and an-

other to put in at Iceland. Nine more lost touch with the convoy and became stragglers.

On the night of February 21, seven U-boats attacked. *Rosthern* leading stoker John Dennis of Unionville, Ont., was at action stations at the corvette's stern depth charge rail when *Spencer* attempted to ram a sub. Trouble is, she picked the wrong vessel, Dennis says: "At about 500 yards from us and closing in at full speed preparing to ram, *Spencer* turned on her searchlight, fully illuminating *Rosthern*. At that moment two torpedoes passed by our stern, their fluorescent wake highly visible to myself and others. This was almost a double play by the U-boat. *Spencer* realized her error and both escorts took evasive action, with *Spencer* passing at full speed within yards of our stern."

On the Atlantic on February 23, 1943, the corvette *Trillium* is overloaded with 160 survivors from convoy ONS 166.

That same night the freighter *Empire Trader* was torpedoed. She took in water forward and her stern rose so much her single propeller could not bite water. George Rickard remembers the incident:

The *Empire Trader* crew took to the boats but, on realizing that their ship was not sinking, they reboarded and commenced moving cargo aft by hand to try to bring the stern down far enough into the water to allow her to go stern-first back to Ireland.

Being the stern escort vessel, it was now up to *Dauphin* to screen the old coal-burner. Around and around we went as the Old Man on *Empire Trader* attempted to trim ship. Finally our frustrated captain ordered him to abandon ship as we had to return to the convoy, which was now many miles ahead. The *Empire Trader* crew rowed over to *Dauphin*. As soon as everyone was aboard, we poured on the oil and headed for the convoy, leaving *Empire Trader* deserted with lights on deck still burning and a wisp of smoke rising from her funnel.

Now we had 106 extra mouths to feed, plus two cats. Our food supply began to dwindle. The bakers from *Empire Trader* made bread in the galley. We got about two slices each. To supplement our diet,

we borrowed a large baking pan from the cook and dumped in a couple of cans of red lead. We added crunched-up hardtack and had it heated in the galley to make it palatable.

Once after being on the bridge for a long time, I went below to climb into my mick for a few hours sleep. On glancing up I noticed a black leg sticking over the side. A Lascar coal trimmer had decided to use my sack!

Campbell rammed and sank a U-boat, but was badly damaged the night of February 22. The Polish *Burza* screened her while emergency repairs were undertaken, but the destroyer was low on fuel and ran for Newfie when *Dauphin* arrived on the morning of February 24. Finally a seagoing tug, *Tenacity*, towed *Campbell* in.

Meanwhile, *Trillium* came to the rescue after three merchant ships, *Empire Redshank*, *Expositor* and *Chattanooga City*, were torpedoed the night of February 22. "We burnt the paint off the side of our ship trying to get close to a torpedoed tanker. The water was burning with high-test gas all around her," recalls Harry Mann in *Trillium*. "We picked up 167 survivors and a cat from the sunken ships. We were very crowded and food was short. Two of the survivors died and we wrapped their bodies and lashed them down at the stern of the ship."

Courtesy RCN. WRN - 445.

Aerial view of North Atlantic convoy.

The attacks continued. Over the next three days, overcrowded *Trillium* was visited by *Spencer*'s doctor with medical supplies and fought three more U-boat actions while running low on food, water and fuel. In all, 12 ships were lost and only 28 reached Newfiejohn in convoy.

William Wainio in *Trillium* recalls: "The survivors we picked up took up a collection for us to have a drink on them. There was enough to rent a large room at the Lennox Hotel for a ship's party when we went to Boston for refit in April. A great time was had by all."

Moose McGill in *Kitchener* comments on merchant ship survivors in general: "If at all possible, most survivors returned to see us in port, bringing a well-received bottle. On the whole, when merchant seamen came on board, saw the type of armament we had and our old reciprocating engines, they went back to sea with an entirely different picture of us.

"But survivors were not always pleasant company even though we plucked them from the cold Atlantic. Our mess-

es were quite crowded and extra men made things almost unbearable. However, some of our merchant friends would complain about the food and the living conditions — 'We wouldn't live like this on a merchant vessel!' — and not help clean up or wash the dishes."

* * *

Over on the Gibraltar Run, on March 4, 1943, southbound convoy KMS 10 endured a German aerial attack. Soon after, the corvette *Shediac* detected a U-boat astern of the convoy and fired 38 depth charges in five attacks over three hours. The last two produced underwater explosions and brought oil and bubbles to the surface. No U-boat appeared, however, and the destroyer *St. Croix* followed up with 12 more depth charges. *Shediac* CO Lieutenant J.E. Clayton felt that the U-boat had sank after trying unsuccessfully to surface. It turns out that *U-87*, a Type VII B boat on its fifth war patrol, did indeed go down in this engagement in

A Hawker Sea Hurricane aircraft launches from a CAM (catapult armed merchant) ship in a North Atlantic convoy on July 22, 1942.

the Atlantic off Portugal with the loss of all 49 crew. *Shediac* and *St. Croix* shared the credit.

* * *

Back in the main theatre, the North Atlantic, the *U-boot-waffe* had introduced a new weapon, the *Federapparat Torpedo* (FAT). A steering device fitted to a standard torpedo allowed the projectile to run a wandering course with 180-degree turns and find its own target in a convoy. This added a new dimension to attack techniques.

Allied and neutral merchant shipping losses in the Atlantic averaged 260,000 tons per month in January and February before ballooning to 538,695 tons in March, but a number of factors were beginning to come together. Major decisions were made that month at the Atlantic Convoy Conference in Washington, D.C.

Control of the Atlantic theatre was simplified: North of 40 latitude, the RCN would take the western sector and the RN would have the eastern portion, with the dividing line being 47 west longitude. Canadian Rear-Admiral Leonard Murray became commander-in-chief Northwest Atlantic with control over all anti-submarine forces, both surface and air.

Out on the North Atlantic, the Allies had virtually no air power, relying largely on CAM (catapult armed merchant) ships. *Calgary* leading seaman Frank Moss recalls a 1943 crossing from Newfie to Derry: "We had a CAM ship which had a fighter aircraft on a launcher on the bow. In mid-Atlantic a German aircraft was shadowing the convoy and reporting our position to U-boats. Our fighter took off and shot it down, but the fighter had to ditch as he was too far from land.

"He flew by slowly and gave us a wave, then climbed astern of us and put his plane into a vertical dive. It never even made a splash as it hit the ocean. He parachuted down and we hastened to pick him up. The VA and the cook had blankets warming in the oven and a pot of hot rum on the burner. The ocean was sort of rough and we had a scramble net over the side. When we were only 25 yards from the pilot, he took off his life jacket and swam for our ship. He disappeared. All we got was his flying jacket. His name was on it — Bradford from Southern Rhodesia [now Zimbabwe]. What a letdown for our crew."

CAM ships were used against German long-range bombers, which both attacked convoys and directed U-boats to them. It was a primitive response. The merchant ship lacked a flight deck and the airplane could not be retrieved. The plane was almost certain to be lost — and the pilot's chances were not much better.

The need for greater air cover was addressed. Land-based VLR (very long range) Liberators would finally be provided in numbers to eliminate the mid-ocean gap, and some of these four-engine planes would go to RCAF operations in Newfoundland. Previously, the bulk of them went to the Royal Air Force for Bomber Command's offensive against Germany.

The events of May 13, 1943, are an example of the benefits of air cover. A land-based Sunderland Flying Boat of 423 Squadron, RCAF, attacked a surfaced U-boat that was closing in on convoy HX 237 in mid-Atlantic. The corvette *Drumheller* rushed to the attack and the RN frigate *Lagan* engaged also. The Sunderland and the two warships shared the credit for the kill. Research by the Admiralty now indicates the victim was *U-753*, a Type VII C boat, but for 46 years it was believed to be *U-456*.

The Allies also gave naval air a tremendous boost. It was agreed the U.S. would supply a number of escort carriers — small aircraft carriers. Support groups designed not to escort convoys but to hunt U-boats down and to come to the aid of beleaguered convoys had been created in September 1942. Now they would be augmented by escort carriers armed with fast fighters. This would immediately increase the striking power and range of the Allied navies.

Shipping losses in the Atlantic theatre dropped to 252,533 tons in April and 205,598 tons in May. U-boat losses rose dramatically and reached 41 in May alone. Submariner Karl Dönitz, by now Grand Admiral in charge of the German navy, recalled most of his U-boats from the Atlantic on May 24 to regroup.

At the end of May, the Allies introduced another defensive measure, MAC ships — merchant aircraft carriers — equipped with a flight deck. Before war's end, 13 of these ships were oil tankers carrying three Fairey Swordfish aircraft, while the remaining six were grain carriers with four of the bi-wing Swordfish aircraft, which could both take off and land. The aircraft conducted patrols to provide protection from U-boats and German bombers.

In June, shipping losses dropped all the way to 30,115 tons. The average for the first half of 1943 was 53 ships and 257,795 tons per month, down from 92 ships and 510,000

One of 13 oil tankers that doubled as a merchdnt aircraft carrier to protect Atlantic convoys.

One of six grain carriers that doubled as a merchant aircraft carrier to protect Atlantic convoys.

tons in the second half of 1942. U-boat losses in all theatres totalled 113 in the first six months of 1943, compared to 87 in all of 1942.

The tide had turned.

* * *

There was lots going on away from the Newfie-Derry Run in 1943. The corvettes *Dawson* and *Vancouver* participated in the American North Pacific campaign in the Aleutians from February to May. The Triangle Run escort force was beefed up with more RCN corvettes as new RCN frigates began to assume the mid-ocean escort role for which the corvettes were never intended. As well, in August there was a welcome name change to Western Escort Force. Gone was the stigma of the word "Local."

The Gulf of St. Lawrence remained closed to transatlantic shipping in 1943 and the Gulf Escort Force was on duty. It was not tested as the Germans did not wage a Gulf offensive, though two U-boats did pass through on other business. Quebec Force ran Quebec-Labrador convoys that summer and fall. Ordinary Seaman Rolf Tornblom of Thunder Bay, Ont., served in *Algoma* from June to November:

> *Algoma* and three other corvettes [*Alberni, Moose Jaw* and *Ville de Quebec*] convoyed merchant ships from the St. Lawrence River through the Gulf, the Strait of Belle Isle and up the Labrador coast to Hamilton Inlet. There the escorts anchored at Rigolet while the cargo vessels proceeded through Lake Melville to the RCAF base at Goose Bay. Once they were unloaded, in about three days, we took them back to Father Point [Rimouski] on the St. Lawrence, then we went to Quebec City until the next convoy was ready, about another three days. The ship was re-provisioned and got minor repairs while the crew cleaned and painted and got shore leave. That was a good place for relaxation and fun. I have many fond memories as an 18-year-old in Quebec City.
>
> We made 10 trips that summer and fall. There was no shipping in winter. These were small convoys — four or five merchant ships. A round trip would take two to three weeks, depending on ice, fog and mechanical problems. There was one small old coastal steamer that was forever slowing because of

breakdowns. On the first and last trips we had a government icebreaker and arctic supply ship that spent the summer in the north. We had a pretty easy time that year, contrary to the previous year when the U-boats were very active in the gulf, but the potential was always there. Every asdic contact with a school of fish, sighting of a fishing boat, whale, porpoise and so on had to be checked out. We had to be prepared at all times, so exercises were carried out.

> On our first voyage to Labrador we encountered miles and miles of ice floe with dozens of huge icebergs, so big that from two or three miles they made a corvette look like a fly speck. A very sharp lookout, visual and radar, had to be kept at all times, especially at night so that we could warn the other ships. These bergs were all along the Labrador coast and even into the Strait of Belle Isle. The ice floe wasn't a problem after the first trip, but the big guys were all through the summer and fall. I found the continuous use of binoculars for even a one-hour trick [shift] was tiring on the eyes.
>
> We encountered fog quite often, but one trip we were fogbound for a week. We couldn't proceed into Hamilton Inlet as the merchant ships did not carry radar, so we hove to. There was a heavy groundswell, which is a long, smooth swell that rebounds off the shore. This puts a ship broadside, when not under power and steering control, and tends to carry her towards shore. When we got too close, each corvette would shepherd a merchant ship to a safer distance off shore. Then we'd continue to wallow again. It was monotonous, but still stressful as a sharp radar and visual watch had to be kept. It must have been more so for the captain and navigating officer as they had to keep track of our position by radar and guesswork.

Alberni able seaman Elmer Phillips of St. Eleanor's, P.E.I., recalls his first trip, escorting two cargo ships and two tankers laden with aviation fuel: "Sailing along the Labrador coast we started to see icebergs for the first time and snow flurries. We saw a lot of whales with calves having fun all around us. To me this was exciting. Later we saw several whales, killed by harpoon or shot, floating on top of the water with a red flag dangling on top of a

RCN Photo, courtesy Frances O'Brien

The corvette *Snowberry* with convoy in 1943.

marker pole speared into them. There had to be a whaler nearby. We also saw fishing boats — Newfoundlanders spending the summer and drying their fish along the Labrador coast.

"At Rigolet, volunteers from our crew went along on the cargo ships to help with the unloading at Goose Bay — a little extra cash for the sailors. Some of the remaining crew spent a lot of time fishing cod over the side. I never saw cod so plentiful in all my life — and large. For our second voyage, someone aboard ship made a deal with a Quebec City restaurant owner for the cod that we caught at Rigolet. We would fish cod and put them in our cooler. The money we received we split among the few that participated. Then we would purchase a couple of bottles of rum at four dollars a bottle. These were sold to the dockworkers at Goose Bay for 25 dollars a bottle."

* * *

In early August 1943, the 5th Escort Group was assigned to patrol duty in the Bay of Biscay, which takes in the north coast of Spain and the west coast of France, including the U-boat ports of St. Nazaire and Lorient. EG 5 was a support group composed of the RN frigates *Nene* and *Tweed* and the RCN corvettes *Calgary*, *Edmundston* and *Snowberry*. Lieutenant Barry O'Brien, captain of *Snowberry*, prepared an account at the conclusion of the eventful month:

> Upon arrival in the U.K., we were sent to an exercise area for a three-day workup program to familiarize us with the details of the operation which had been established in the bay and entailed the vital co-operation of warships and aircraft. Our job now would be the detection and destruction of the enemy, as opposed to the safe and timely arrival of the convoy. This was the stuff that we had been waiting for.

The working-up was successful. *Snowberry* was fortunate in locating the sub during the radar exercise the first night, after the aircraft had homed the group to the diving position as per plan. The sub led us on a merry chase for 50 minutes at full speed, zigzagging and fishtailing until we had closed the range from 6,000 to 2,000 yards. She then signalled that we had made "a fair cop," adding: "We are practically on the Free State and your starshells are landing on it. I guess we gave the people ashore a thrill." We were then a mile and a half off the land.

This three-day training was extremely beneficial to myself, officers and crew. Upon completion, EG 5, minus *Nene* and *Calgary*, proceeded to the bay. *Nene*, defects repaired, joined us in a couple of days, but *Calgary* missed the first trip entirely. *Tweed* was senior officer until *Nene* returned.

Before leaving, our senior officer presented us each with a large envelope containing the latest information regarding the patrol areas: types of friendly and enemy aircraft we would encounter, names of the blockade runners that might be in the vicinity, Spanish and French tunny fishermen to be sunk, the whereabouts of four German *Narvik*-class destroyers on the prowl, merchantmen to be investigated and, of course, the positions of numerous U-boats on passage in and out. We anticipated a busy time.

Our trip down was uneventful except for a few shadowing aircraft. But as we dropped in latitude we gladly shed our connections with the northern convoy routes, particularly our duffel coats and seaboots. Hammocks appeared on deck at night while the first lieutenant and I made our home on the flag deck abaft the bridge.

Our original orders had been cancelled en route and we were now to rendezvous with EG 40 and patrol from the 100th fathom line in, on the Spanish coast between capes Villano and Ortigal. Nice work if you can get it.

At 2000 [hours] on August 22, as we approached at about 25 miles from the coast, we spotted two Spanish fishing vessels ahead. *Tweed* signalled "Let's go" and promptly left us behind at her 21 knots. *Tweed* fired a shot across the bow of one as she approached and they both stopped. We got permission from *Tweed* to take the near one.

Away boarding party to capture the *Volga*! After two trips by our dinghy, we had aboard the crew of 13. The captain was brought up to the bridge. A little grey-haired man about five feet tall, he smelled very much of his profession. Unfortunately, we had no one who spoke Spanish to act as an interpreter, and they had no one familiar with English. But the captain was very demonstrative — indeed, they all were — and by the use of gestures and facial expressions we gathered they were a pretty harmless lot.

At 0530 on August 23, we joined the RN escorts *Landguard*, *Bideford* and *Waveney* and commenced patrol. That afternoon we had a visit from four Ju-88s and two Focke-Wulfs. Nothing came of it, but it helped to put the boys on their mettle.

As we had been ordered to investigate every type of vessel encountered, we then spent a busy night chasing radar contacts and sightings, but in each case we were disappointed as there was no sign of the enemy. *Tweed* and *Snowberry*, being the innermost ships on patrol and practically on the coast, had steaming lights on to represent ourselves as Spanish merchantmen. But if there were U-boats around, we apparently did not fool them.

At 0700 on August 24, *Nene* rejoined and took over as senior officer, having been delayed an extra day in a successful hunt for six American airmen who had been shot down by Ju-88s.

Landguard passed us then, steaming in the opposite direction, off to investigate a blockade runner beached in one of the bays. We requested to be allowed to go with her. However, this proved impossible as she was going in on the pretense of landing valuable stores picked up at sea. A Focke-Wulf decided that he had better investigate this gathering and came in close. So, hastily hoisting our boat and ringing full ahead, *Snowberry* opened fire with her guns, all four of them, estimating a few hits with our starboard Oerlikon, but with no evident damage. *Landguard* was nicely arching her five-inch shells over us and getting very close to Jerry, while our four-inch was raising quite a disturbance among a group of fishermen. This was all taking place on the border of the three-mile limit.

At 1100 we set course to rejoin the group and, taking station, signalled *Nene*, "Never a dull moment. We nearly had a Focke-Wulf for you." *Nene* replied, "Too bad. There will probably be other chances." That was no lie. All was quiet until 1800 when three Focke-Wulfs appeared low on the horizon, seemingly more bent on reconnaissance than attack, although they hung around for about three-quarters of an hour while ships with long-range guns popped away at them.

At 1805 *Edmundston* signalled all ships, "Three unidentified warships coming up astern." Coming simultaneously with the appearance of the Focke-Wulfs, this gave all the evidence of an interesting session. At 1809 *Nene* signalled all ships, "Identified as Spanish, one cruiser and two destroyers." I had been caught for this action stations in underwear, shorts and tin hat as the weather during this whole patrol was ideal and everyone availed themselves of the chance to absorb lots of the old vitamin D.

Next day, August 25, we were greeted bright and early by our three Focke-Wulf friends, who kept coming and going all morning, usually out of range, but requiring continuous action stations on our part.

At 1320 a lone American Liberator appeared overhead going hell bent for leather towards Gibraltar, passing with a curt radiotelegraphy signal, "21 enemy planes heading this way," then ducking into the clouds. At 1342 they appeared ahead at 4,000 feet, all 21 of them — later identified as 14 Dornier 17s and seven Ju-88s. They proceeded to split into groups of three and we all fully expected a dive-bombing attack from ahead, but they fooled us and moved over the starboard side, giving evidence of a low-level job from beam-on. This, too, was not to be.

It was evident that this was not an ordinary high-level attack as each bomb appeared to shoot out from under the planes for a distance of 200 feet or so, leaving behind a trail of white vapour. First the bomb ran on a parallel course to the target ship, then it suddenly made a right-angle turn towards the

target and followed any evasive actions of the ship. Each Dornier dropped a bomb, but their homing technique was lousy. They caused damage only by two near misses.

At 1418, *Nene* signalled, "Speed 14 knots" and at 1425, "Flag 1," which means take individual avoiding action. At 1430, *Tweed* to *Snowberry*, "What is your best speed?" Answer, "15 knots." *Tweed* to *Snowberry*, "Don't give us that, we are doing 18 and we can't shake you." The chief ERA confessed afterwards to urging 10 more revs out of the old ice cream freezer than he ever had before. He claimed that by the time the news of the enemy planes reached the engine room, there were at least 50 around, so he figured that we needed all available juice. Heard from the four-inch-gun platform, "Guess these guys ain't fooling today." And from another, "Come on in you bastards, so we can get a decent crack at you." And on the bridge, "Boy this is the first time *Snowberry* has been in this kind of action." Then came a reply, "Yes, and I had to be here at the time."

At 1453 we secured action stations, paying little heed to the three Focke-Wulfs that were now considered to be very small fry. We signalled *Nene*: "No hits, no runs, no errors." The attack had been unsuccessful with two near misses, but this was the introduction of the glider bomb — 500 pounds of destruction with a wingspread of about eight feet. It was radio controlled, with the aircraft crew providing the directions by visual observation.

August 26 was calm and peaceful. At 1730, EG 5 was detached, with the RCN *Tribal*-class destroyer *Athabaskan* and the RN destroyer *Grenville* joining. The Admiralty sent a wireless message that the enemy had used a new weapon which had been nicknamed "Chase Me Charlie" because of its capability of homing in on a ship. You moved and it moved. The Admiralty also suggested two antidotes: Shoot it down with anti-aircraft guns or plug in all your electric razors because they might be on the same wavelength as the radio-controlled glider bombs. This we later tried, without positive result.

On August 27 the Dorniers were back. Unfortunately, their control of Charlie had improved.

The RN sloop *Egret* sank in 40 seconds with a direct hit, and our *Athabaskan* was hit and suffered severe wounds, but was able to make port due to the excellent seamanship and courage of all hands.

Our next patrol was uneventful as we had been moved out of Dornier range. *Calgary* was now back in the fold to complete our group. We did hunt a sub that the RN destroyer *Havelock* had flushed, but no luck. Now further from the coast to get outside the range of the land-based Dorniers, we couldn't do our intended job, so the group was withdrawn.

* * *

On the North Atlantic, things were warming up again. Reid Sheppard in *Cobalt* recalls an August incident: "We were at action stations most of the time for two and a half days. We sent a boarding party to put out a fire on a gasoline tanker. It was hoped that we could take it to harbour, but that was vetoed. Several of the crew were decorated."

Indeed, the navigating officer, Mate Alfred Bett of Toronto, Ont., won the George Medal. His citation reads: "This officer led a volunteer boarding party to SS *J.H. Senior*, an American tanker with a full cargo of gasoline, which was stopped and heavily afire after collision in a fog on August 18, 1943. In order to save this very valuable ship and her cargo, this officer and his party fought the fires for over two hours with hand extinguishers, although they knew the ship was in danger of blowing up at any moment. During this time, he showed complete disregard for his own safety, and his leadership was an inspiration and example of bravery and devotion to duty in keeping with the highest traditions of the service."

The ship and most of the cargo were saved. "We were to get prize money," says Sheppard. "At the time we had hoped to be rich — maybe one thousand dollars for an able seaman." *Cobalt* crew members did get salvage money, but not until 1959, and not very much — $9.95 for Able Seaman Sheppard, for example.

When the U-boats returned to the Atlantic in force, they had a new weapon and a new tactic. The RCN destroyer *St. Croix* was the first victim and the RN corvette *Polyanthus* the second, both on September 20, 1943. The RN frigate *Itchen* became the third on September 22 in the same battle over the combined convoy ON 202 and ONS 18. All three warships were hit in the stern because the new weapon was the *Zaunkonig* or acoustic torpedo, which homed in on sound and so sought out a ship's propellers.

"We were outer screen on convoy ON 202," says *Calgary* sub-lieutenant Mac Orr of West Vancouver, B.C. "There sure was a great deal of gloom amongst all of us when we arrived in St. John's. The bar at the Crow's Nest got a lot of use."

The new tactic was evident in the choice of its first victims and also in the name the Germans gave to the acoustic torpedo — "escort killer" — but the weapon had a weakness, an overly sensitive firing pistol. For example, on September 21, *U-584* took a shot at the corvette *Chambly*. While diving and retreating quickly, the U-boat crew heard the torpedo explode and so assumed and reported a hit. It was not so, however. The torpedo had exploded while crossing a ship's wake. There were other such incidents, too.

The RCN quickly introduced a counter-measure. "The gadget was simple enough," says Ray Burwash, HSD in *Agassiz* in 1943. It was a metal frame housing two steel bars that "vibrated or chattered when water was forced between them while being towed astern. The device was designed to create far more underwater noise than a ship's propeller and thus decoy the homing torpedo away from our stern area."

CAT gear, which stands for "Canadian anti-torpedo," became widely used, but it was strictly a defensive tool. In fact, the noise was so loud it rendered asdic ineffective, so a corvette couldn't hunt a submerged U-boat and cover its butt at the same time. The RN devised a different noisemaker called "Foxer." Among the Allies the acoustic torpedo, in turn, became known as the "Gnat."

Meanwhile, that age-old enemy the weather struck again on September 8, 1943, when the corvette *Matapedia* was rammed amidship in a thick fog off Halifax by the 4,800-ton British freighter SS *Scorton*. *Matapedia* Petty Officer John George Alerie earned Mention in Dispatches. His citation reads, "For coolness and expert seamanship and leadership in the face of trying circumstances following a collision, thereby setting a fine example to the upper deck crew. ...Petty Officer Alerie took immediate action in charge of all available hands in rigging the collision mat over the hole sustained. At the same time, he had various parties clearing away the wreckage making the job of rigging the collision mat possible. His quick action and expert leadership probably saved HMCS *Matapedia* from sinking."

In November, a running battle around a convoy pitted German planes and U-boats against Allied escorts and planes flying from Gibraltar and new bases in the Azores, which Portugal allowed Britain to use beginning in October 1943. Allied surface reinforcements were sent to the scene and, on November 20, 1943, three members of a support group — the RCN corvettes *Calgary* and *Snowberry* and the RN frigate *Nene* — combined to sink *U-536* in the Atlantic north of the Azoles.

Records at the National Defence Directorate of History and Heritage show that *Nene* and *Snowberry* dropped charges and when the sub surfaced, *Snowberry* opened fire, her first four-inch shot hitting the conning tower. *Nene* and *Calgary* also blasted away. *Calgary* leading seaman Frank Moss says: "The sub surfaced between us. A gun's crew raced out of the conning tower towards their gun. You could see our 20mm tracer bullets fanning behind them before they jumped over the side. Another crew immediately followed with the same fate."

At one point in the mêlée, *Nene* came uncomfortably close to *Snowberry*, and at another *U-536* just missed an attempt to ram and banged against *Snowberry*'s side. In all, 18 of the U-boat's 55-man crew were rescued. "The ones we took aboard and brought back to Portsmouth were friendly and had been away from their home base for months," says *Snowberry* leading telegraphist George Mackay. "They played cards with our crew and enjoyed the meals our cook dished up."

"In retrospect, it was very sad," says *Calgary*'s Mac Orr. "If she had not tried to fight the three of us and just surrendered, instead of saving 18 lives we probably would have saved the whole crew." But that's the way it was. That defiant fighting spirit helped make the *U-bootwaffe* such a formidable opponent.

On the Canadian side, there was a personal irony. Barry O'Brien, long at sea, did not get credit for a sub kill. He was home on leave and the skipper of *Snowberry* was J.A. Dunn of Montreal, Que., a spare commanding officer on his first trip in the corvette. Such are the vagaries of war.

* * *

Corvettes were essentially an anti-submarine vessel and depth charges were their main weapon. "Heavy canisters of explosives rolled off steel rails on the stern and were fired from throwers on each side, out 65 yards," says Acting Lieutenant-Commander Rodney Pike, CO of *Orangeville*. "The depth for the explosion was set on a pistol on each charge. The first corvettes fired a five-charge pattern. It was later increased to a 10-charge pattern."

Jack Skinner, leading torpedo operator in *Charlottetown* and *Port Arthur*, remembers: "We had two types of charges, light and heavy. All charges had the same amount of explosive, the only difference being a heavy charge had a weight on one end that caused it to sink faster, and it was usually set to go off deeper than a light charge. On the attack, the ship would be travelling at full speed. When shallow settings were used, the effect on the ship when the charges exploded was considerable. Power failures were common, fire extinguishers were often knocked about and delicate equipment damaged. This damage had to be repaired immediately so that the ship could continue the attack."

Long Branch ERA Harry Seip of Victoria, B.C., notes that to get clear of the explosions, "when a pattern of depth charges was to be fired we had to utilize every last bit of power we could muster. The engine is just a-rocking and shaking like it could come off its base. When the charges exploded, everything happened — lagging off pipes would shower down and pipe brackets broke loose."

Midland ERA George Hollins recalls: "The first depth charge attack I experienced was while on watch in the boiler room. When the charges detonated, the insulation around the boiler piping and steam lines showered down like snow and the deck plates lifted, as did the ship. You could feel an elevator sensation and it scared hell out of me, for one."

Stoker F.L. Taylor of Toronto, Ont., recalls an occasion in late 1943 in the western Atlantic when *Amherst* dropped a pattern of charges while he was in one of the two boiler rooms: "But someone forgot to give the signal full ahead to the engine room. Disaster followed. It felt like the ship lifted out of the water, the lights went out and the emergency lights came on. The dirt and lagging rained down on us, the boiler started to hum and I did a lot of praying that the boilers would stay together. The end result was a number of pipes ruptured in the engine room and the main shaft damaged. We limped into Newfoundland. Not one of the greater efforts of a good ship."

Leading Seaman Gerard Dube and Quartermaster Dutchy Roman of *Louisburg*.

Able Seaman Howard Abbott recalls when *Arvida* was escorting convoy ON 188 in June 1943: "One charge was not set properly. It went off too soon and loosened our rear plates. We sprung a leak and had to shut down the engines. The pumps had to be manned and we sat dead still in the North Atlantic. It was more than two days before a seagoing tug got out to us. Then we were towed into Iceland for repairs, which took a week."

Depth charges were quite a load to handle. *Oakville* able seaman George Kahan says: "On watch I dreaded to report depth charges loose, as the order would come back to go and secure them. Three hundred pounds of rolling garbage can — fight that and the rolling ship. Quite the feat. One time me and the VA had to do it. A big green one came over the side and dropped on us. We did not know where we were. I thought I was over the side and tried to swim. The wave threw me against the depth charge rack and just about put me out. The VA got a dislocated shoulder."

Trillium leading seaman Harry Mann recalls an incident while escorting an eastbound convoy: "Ron Niddrie and I were detailed to lash down a depth charge that had broken loose on the port side during a storm. We had just finished when a wave hit us, knocking us over. I remember being underwater and I thought I was over the side, then I felt something and I hung onto it. The ship rolled and the water went over the gunwales. l was about 50 feet from the depth charge we were lashing down. I looked for Ron but couldn't see him. Apparently the after lookout saw what happened. Ron had been washed between the after depth

charge rails and, unconscious, was hanging onto them. He had to be hit to get him to let go."

* * *

The RCN commissioned 11 of a new type of revised Flower-class corvette in the last quarter of 1943. Nine hundred and seventy tons, with extended foc's'le and water-tube boilers, they were labelled "increased endurance" and rated for 7,400 miles at 10 knots.

There was another difference, too. Nine were built in Canada, but two were constructed in the U.K. Since the war began, Canadian shipyards had produced 89 flowers, but they were now turning to other projects, notably River-class frigates that were superior to the corvette for anti-submarine warfare.

In Canada, *Athol*, *Frontenac* and *North Bay* appeared in October; *Lindsay*, *Owen Sound* and *Rivière du Loup* came in November; and *Louisburg (2nd)*, *Norsyd* and *Trentonian* followed in December. There was a twist to the U.K. pair: *Giffard*, a November newcomer, was laid down as HMS *Buddleia* and *Forest Hill*, a December arrival, started out as HMS *Ceanothus*.

When ships were commissioned in Central Canada late in the year there was still a rush to beat the freeze-up of the St. Lawrence River. Telegraphist Tom Farrell of San Diego, California, recalls: "I picked up *Trentonian* in Quebec City in December and we had to be broken out of the ice by an icebreaker so we could head down the St. Lawrence River. On arrival in Halifax, we had a bent bow caused by hitting a lot of ice floes in the river."

The total number of corvettes commissioned by the RCN now stood at 91. It was RCN policy to enlist the involvement of the community after which each ship was named. In addition to generating public backing of the Canadian war effort, this community sponsorship provided both moral support and tangible assistance for the ship's crew, while saving the navy money in the process.

Representatives of the namesake community were invited to appropriate ceremonies, whether they be the christening and launching or the commissioning.

The corvette *Oakville* was constructed on Lake Superior by Port Arthur Shipbuilding Co. Ltd. and launched June 21, 1941. Her fitting out followed and, on her way to Halifax, N.S., she proceeded through the Great Lakes chain to the city of Oakville on Lake Ontario just west of Toronto. There, on November 5, 1941, amid pomp and circumstance,

Courtesy Vic Martin

The Maritimes members of *Regina's* crew on April 30, 1943, are (front, from left): Patty Flanagan, Noble, Jack Winn, Camille Lanteigne, H.B. Moore, Ted Kieck, Jospeh Saulnier, John Howard; (rear) Bill MacLeod, Byron Nodding, Chandler, Eddie Boudreau.

a christening, parade, reception and banquet were held, with local dignitaries and students participating, as well as two very special guests, Angus L. Macdonald, minister of national defence for naval affairs, and Rear-Admiral Percy Nelles, chief of naval staff.

Among the many gifts *Oakville* received were: the ship's bell, a silk White Ensign [the RCN flag], a ship's library, a ship's clock, electric percolators, electric plates, four radios, windbreakers and ditty bags containing comforts knitted by the women of Oakville and district. The ship's commissioning came later in Montreal.

The Alberni District Historical Society in Port Alberni, B.C., provides a newspaper account of the christening and launching of HMCS *Alberni* at Esquimalt, B.C. Saying she slid "easily down the greased ways into the harbour," the report in the *West Coast Advocate* adds: "As she made a

great splash and floated easily, crowds at the dockyard and along the shore cheered and waved their caps and small boats screeched noisily."

Officials of Amherst, N.S., attended the commissioning of their corvette at Saint John, N.B., and presented the ship with a plaque bearing the town's crest. In his patriotic speech, the mayor of Amherst, M.J. Kaufman, noted the vessel was "commissioned for the purpose of aiding the destruction of that sinister force which threatens the very existence of mankind." He concluded: "As you now go forth on your great mission, each of us shall remember that somewhere on the high seas is a staunch craft bearing the crest of our town, manned by valiant sons of Canada who stand guard over all those ideals which the people of this Dominion and the British Empire hold so dear. May God give you strength and wisdom for the task."

Courtesy Vic Martin

Half the Ontario members of *Regina*'s crew on April 30, 1943, are (front, from left): Carmody, Trevor Martin, J. Keith Daubney, Bobo Johnston, Doug Tope, Doug McNaughton, Fred Heath; (rear) Jack Lynch, Vern Cavanaugh, Bill Neaves, Len Horne, R. Harper, Bill Walsh, Malcolm Cunningham.

Regina spent $135 on a plaque bearing the municipal crest and this was displayed in a downtown store before presentation to the ship. It became common for a municipality to present its ship with such a plaque and/or a silk White Ensign, the standard of the RN and of the RCN at that time. As well, photographs of the community and the ship were often exchanged.

The RCN took seriously its policy of creating goodwill and public support. The service encouraged visits by a ship's commanding officer to the namesake community. For example, after their return to Canada, the captain and officers of *Ville de Quebec* visited Quebec City for a reception in their honour to mark the corvette's destruction of a U-boat in the Mediterranean.

A ship's visit to her community was worked in if at all possible. *Louisburg* leading seaman Doug Lynn re-

calls: "After several days in Halifax, we sailed for the port of Louisburg, where we were welcomed by the municipal dignitaries and townspeople who threw a party for the ship and presented the skipper with the keys to the town."

The historic Nova Scotia town welcomed the ship despite Mayor M.S. Huntington's objection to the RCN's spelling of the ship's name. He considered the "burg" ending to be a corruption of the original spelling of the town's name — Louisbourg — in honour of Louis XIV, king of France. The mayor acknowledged that, "unfortunately at present the great majority, even in our town, use the 'burg' ending." In a polite reply, the RCN cited a number of examples to show that "by common usage" over many years the spelling had been changed to Louisburg.

A dinner and dance were held for the crew and the Louisburg Branch of the Red Cross Society became a solid supporter, providing a washing-machine, coffee urn and 20 subscriptions to *Reader's Digest.*

Presentations of gifts that made a tough life a little more bearable were often a feature of a ship's visit. HSD Reg Baker comments: "*Owen Sound* was commissioned at Collingwood, Ont., on November 17, 1943. A few days later we sailed for Owen Sound. We arrived around noon with the whole town and district on the jetty to greet us. What a day! This being a nautical town on Georgian Bay, they had compassion for the sailor as many of their own had made a career of sailing on the Great Lakes. They gave us an apartment-size piano, radios, toasters, irons, and a washing machine. We let groups of 50 or so at a time come aboard and tour their ship. We tried to tell them proudly all we were allowed to say. Of course, the captain, Manuel Watson, was from Owen Sound, as well as the chief ERA and a sub-lieutenant. The rest of us were a cross-section of the country."

Rivière du Loup, Que., on the St. Lawrence River east of Quebec City, welcomed its corvette. The Chamber of Commerce, Knights of Columbus, Rotary Club and Red Cross Society were involved in the presentation of gifts, which included ditty bags for crew members.

There was strong support in most communities. Sheila Brooks describes the situation in the former town of Bowmanville, now part of Newcastle, Ont.: "No local person ever served in *Bowmanville*, but at the time of commissioning the citizens held a street fair and street dance to raise funds to provide comforts for the crew. Two Beatty washers were provided through a local store and there are unconfirmed rumours a piano was also donated. The ladies of the community knit socks and navy turtlenecks to include in ditty bags given each crew member and containing personal supplies, candy, etc. There was good coverage in the local press."

Just a little further east, citizens of Trenton, Ont., banded behind their corvette, *Trentonian*, providing a washing machine, electrical appliances, musical instruments, cigarettes, Christmas parcels, socks and money for the ship's canteen.

Saskatoon, Sask., city council adopted the corvette *Saskatoon*. Crew members received a washing machine, washboards, four radios, writing materials, 22,700 cigarettes, ashtrays, sewing kits, cards and games.

Regina ERA Tom Baird comments on Regina's con-

tributions: "We did have one stoker petty officer from the home town of our ship. We were well looked after at all times with those extra comforts of life, even toasters and washing machines. You should have seen the thank-you letter he would send back. I am sure he must have gotten help to compose that letter."

In British Columbia, the communities of Port Alberni and Alberni split the cost of a washing machine for *Alberni.*

Kitchener, Ont., provided a washing machine, irons, toasters, sweaters, socks, mitts, books, soap and chocolate bars. Nearby Fergus backed its boys, too, says Able Seaman Howard Trusdale: "We were provided with a Beatty washing machine, which was made in the town, and a couple of galvanized washtubs, which made great bathtubs. Our ship's library was provided and we all received a ditty bag of practical things such as needle and thread for repairs."

St. Thomas, Ont., dispatched a washing machine, irons and personal items, says Sterling Ince, Curator of the Elgin Military Museum. There was also correspondence between crew members and the staff and students of St. Thomas Collegiate Institute.

Entertainment was sometimes a big part of the equation. *Kincardine* telegraphist Wes Johnson says: "The Town of Kincardine sent us a whole raft of musical instruments when the ship was commissioned. They even sent us a small pump organ which we lashed to the bulwark. I used to play it quite a bit. We also had accordions, which I played, and all the brass instruments, banjos and guitars. I'd like to thank the town for doing this. It certainly was nice of them."

The list could go on, and on. Smiths Falls, Ont., sent a vacuum cleaner. Dundas, Ont., sent a raft of things, including toasters, irons, coffee percolators, radios, a typewriter and sweaters. Belleville, Ont., sent jackets manufactured by a local firm and scarves.

Wool was purchased by the municipalities of Shediac, N.B., and Wetaskiwin, Alta., for local knitters who produced things like scarves and sweaters. *Orangeville* was also a recipient of homemade clothing and skipper Rodney Pike says: "The parcels of knitted goods from the ladies of Orangeville were most appreciated."

Guelph received a piano, some mitts, sweaters, tuques — and a mascot, a black cocker spaniel donated by a local breeder. The captain, Lieutenant Skinny Hayes, says: "After a short meeting of the men, I was informed that I had been elected as the dog's valet, since I had the least work to do in the ship! I pretended to be reluctant to take on such responsibility, but was secretly delighted. The dog was named Rags and lived in my cabin, although he wandered at will around the ship. When I left the ship a year later, they gave him to me as a farewell gift."

Still reeling from the Depression that devastated Saskatchewan's economy, the city of Weyburn was unable to provide material things like most other Canadian communities. Instead, the municipality sent a framed photo showing the main street with a banner strung between two light posts reading, "Welcome to Weyburn." The photo was displayed on the ship's bridge.

* * *

As the end of 1943 approached, the spirit of celebration prevailed in many venues. *Regina* ERA Tom Baird remembers: "After workups we arrived at Halifax the day before Christmas and were third ship out from the jetty. It looked like a very quiet Christmas until one of our petty officers got a brainwave. Wearing only his tiddly dress pants and nice white shirt — no coat or cap to give away his rank as only a petty officer — he went to the ship next to us and right down to their wardroom. He gave a hard-luck story

that we had just gotten in and had no liquor ration yet, so could he borrow a couple of bottles to be returned when ours arrived. It being so close to Christmas, they could not refuse him, so back he comes ready to treat the mess. Before long he was gone to another ship and lo and behold he did it all over again, so it was a very good party and merry Christmas after all."

Giffard SBA Howard Stark of London, Ont., says: "We spent Christmas at Tobermory, Scotland. We had the day off from workups, so we enjoyed turkey and the trimmings and all the rum we could drink."

The year ended with the Allied forces in firm control of the vital convoy routes. Shipping losses on the Atlantic averaged only 19 ships and 108,939 tons per month in the last six months. This was considerably better than the 53 ships and 257,795 tons per month in the first half of 1943, which in itself had been a considerable improvement over the devastating 1942 loss rates.

As U-boat sinkings increased, crew quality inevitably suffered, but the U-boat force's morale remained remarkably high. U-boat losses in all theatres climbed to 124 in the last six months, bringing the 1943 count to 237. In the first 40 months of the war, from September 1939 to December 1942, Germany had lost only 153 U-boats, which illustrates how decisive 1943 was for the Allies.

Posing on April 30, 1943, with *Regina*'s gun-shield logo painted by Jack Muir are the four-inch gun's crew. They are (on the platform, from left): Joseph Saulnier, George Ralph, Trevor Martin, Frank Roach; (in the turret) Fred Heath, Bill Walsh, Bob Williams.

CHAPTER THIRTEEN
"IT'S MORALE THAT'S IMPORTANT."

"CANADIANS make great naval ratings providing they are treated fairly in a consistent manner. They are intelligent, aggressive and can withstand almost anything. They will accept a firm hand but one must be consistent.

"The CO's job then," says Cliff Hatch, who commanded *Ville de Quebec* in 1944-45, "is to develop the crew into a cohesive machine which can sail and fight the ship. This is done through the officers and especially the chiefs and petty officers. A good CO will assess the strengths and weaknesses of each of the officers and, to a lesser degree, those of the NCOs. Where he sees a weakness he will buttress or shore it up, either himself or by moving certain responsibilities away from one officer to another whom he feels can better handle them.

"Developing the crew is a never-ending process. For this reason, the longer a crew is together the better it will become. Frequent changes of crew, such as losing ratings to courses ashore, make the job more difficult. Crews develop a great loyalty to the ship and to each other and the longer they are together, the deeper it becomes.

"The officers, especially the CO, must earn the respect of the crew. If they are professionally competent and consistent in their dealings with the men, then there are no problems. So much for the ship and its crew. Not too different than running a business."

Ted Best of Cambridge, Ont., formed a 1942-43 *Cobalt* leadership tandem with Colin Angus of Ottawa, Ont. Angus was the captain and sailor; Best the first lieutenant and manager. Best says: "If you want to relate it to business, the captain is the president and the Jimmy is the chief operating officer. The Jimmy ran the ship and the captain took the responsibility.

"It's morale that's important. You run a tight ship that's fair. You have to earn respect. You can't order it or buy it. It's nice to be liked, but it's more important to have respect. It's a funny thing, the two usually go hand in glove. There's one other thing — you must be consistent. You can't treat one bod different than another."

Kitchener stoker Moose McGill says: "A sailor becomes very attached to his ship if all goes well. He's very fond of his shipmates and most of the officers. A good captain always commands respect. A good Jimmy keeps in contact with the crew. He's the chap who runs a happy and a clean, efficient ship."

There was a clear definition between officers and men. It was rooted in the traditional military belief that familiarity would undermine responsibility: An officer was expected to make decisions that could imperil lives, a difficult task that ought not be influenced by friendship.

Pictou CO Tony Griffin comments: "During the war, the ancient principle still existed in all three branches of the service that there was an 'officer class' who were supposed to provide leadership. ...There was a deliberate social distance between officers and men, combined, however, with friendliness. There was a general acceptance of this principle by the other ranks of the service, subject to instant reaction to any perceived abuse of officers' privilege and status."

While the RCN did not have the type of class distinction found in the RN, post-secondary education was not widely available in Canada and the rich were much more likely to be educated than the middle class or poor. A university education virtually guaranteed a person a commission in the navy. Indeed, even the completion of high school often put one in position to become an officer.

After what could fairly be called a crash course, the navy's King's College in Halifax churned out many young officers without previous naval experience. These instant officers became collectively and derisively known as "90-day wonders."

Strathroy stoker Bill McCallum observes: "The Canadian navy expanded very rapidly during the war and as a result the selection and training of both men and officers left a lot to be desired. I think that this showed up most with the officers. There certainly were some good officers, but others were not capable of crewing a one-man rowboat."

On the other end of the scale were old hands like the 1942-43 *Oakville* CO, Lieutenant-Commander Clarence King, a World War I veteran. His training methods are recalled by Able Seaman Reg Adams: "Captain King was only aboard a short time when we heard the pipe 'Man overboard!' and everyone ran to the side to see who the silly bugger was who had fallen over the side. It had been a drill and, of course, we got hell from the captain for being stupid. The next drill was 'Fire in the galley!', but we were ready."

Favourable comments about officers far outnumber criticisms. Some remarks are brief, but glowing. *Regina* ERA Bill MacLeod says, "Harry Freeland was a good man and knew his job from A to Z." *Amherst* crewman Manuel Zlatin says of Louis Audette, "He became an excellent commanding officer." *Orangeville* leading cook Ivan McCabe says of Rodney Pike, "I tell you, he's one of the finest men alive." *Trillium* able seaman Slim Canning says, "I can't speak too highly of Barry O'Brien. He was a prince."

Two crew members comment on Commander Chummy Prentice, 1941-42 *Chambly* CO. Able Seaman Syd Moyle says, "Prentice read the Bible every day. He was a born-for-glory type. He had a strict ship but a happy ship. I had a lot of respect for him. He wouldn't ask his lower-deck men to do anything he wouldn't do." Able Seaman David Grimes says, "He was the kind of captain you would go anywhere with and feel safe."

Phil George, 1942-44 HSD in *Alberni*, says: "Our officers were excellent. Acting Lieutenant-Commander Ian Bell was our captain. He was a chartered accountant from British Columbia. He was a fearless man. He wouldn't ask anyone to do anything he wouldn't do himself."

Yeoman of Signals George Dollis sizes up the 1944-45 *Chambly* skipper, Acting Lieutenant-Commander Stephen Taylor: "A senior highly experienced Merchant Navy officer. Thoroughly knowledgeable and likable. A quiet, deep man, easily approachable. He exuded confidence in his quiet manner and instilled confidence in others."

Rolf Tornblom assesses his 1943 *Algoma* skipper, Acting Lieutenant-Commander J. Harding: "A quiet, competent, considerate officer, a good seaman except when coming alongside a jetty. He expected excellence from his crew, took an interest in their well-being and was quick to acknowledge a job well done."

Fred Stinson of Toronto, Ont., a 1942 *Halifax* able seaman asdic, recalls his captain, Lieutenant-Commander Charles Copelin: "She was a happy ship and we affectionately called the skipper by the nickname 'Gremlin,' without his knowledge, of course. He used to do rounds of the messdecks to make sure the men were fed properly and as comfortable as weather conditions would permit. When the food refrigeration failed one time, he insisted on going back to port for repairs before joining the convoy escort."

There were some characters in the corvette navy. One was the 1943-44 *La Malbaie* skipper, Acting Lieutenant-Commander J.S. (Foghorn) Davis, whose stomach sported a tattoo of a Plimsoll line, normally found on a ship's side to mark the limit of submersion. On his only ear, Foghorn wore an earring, which most of his crew copied.

Wetaskiwin HSD Allan McConney recalls another CO: "In 1942 our captain was Lieutenant-Commander Guy Windeyer, RN retired, ex-China Station with a black belt in judo. I once saw him lay out a couple of drunk stokers, each of whom was much bigger than he was." (Windeyer later became captain of the destroyer *St. Laurent* where he had a nervous breakdown during a very bad convoy battle.)

* * *

There was an informality about corvette life that particularly suited the RCNVR ratings. Able Seaman Reg Adams comments: "*Oakville* [in 1942-43] was not a pusser ship; by that I mean there was not too much navy routine. For instance, when entering or leaving harbour, all captain [Clarence] King demanded was that we wear our navy hats, whereas in some ships the crew would have to be in full uniform.

After all, we were just a bunch of guys who had joined up to fight a war — and not to make a career out of it. I guess by now you realize we loved captain King."

Summerside lieutenant Don McGivern says: "It was an accepted fact that the dress, discipline and relationships were less formal aboard small ships than in destroyers and above. At sea in a corvette the only distinguishing mark between the crew and officers was the officers' cap as all were turned out in turtlenecks, sweaters and duffel coats. That's why sea-going officers always had green cap badges, which were the envy of shore officers. Although the crew dressed warmly and somewhat unconventionally at sea, when they were in port and on leave they were turned out just as tiddly as their brother sailors on the more pusser ships."

Fergus able seaman Howard Trusdale gives a rating's overview of uniforms and dress regulations: "Most times at sea we wore our personal clothing — jeans, work shirts and rubber boots. It was more comfortable this way and we saved our issue clothing. Each man had his own kit and from time to time there'd be a kit inspection. This could cause problems as articles of kit had a monetary value and, if broke, you could sell something to get back on your feet. Shortages had to be replaced.

"We received four uniforms — two darks and two whites. They were rated No. 1s and No. 3s. No. 9s were your coveralls. No. 1s were your best uniform and saved for going ashore, though most of us bought our own tiddlys made of officers' serge and cut sausage-skin tight. Help was often needed to get the jumper on and almost always to get it off, especially in hot weather when the garment stuck to your hide. No. 3s were worn for non-duty jobs about the ship and always worn when entering harbour. It's a tradition that the crew would line the decks, standing at ease, as we sailed past other ships on our way to a mooring. The one piece of issue garb I disliked was the long johns. 'Twas good stuff — 100 percent wool — and itched like mad. I only wore it a few times. I'm convinced there was barbed wire in the fabric."

Strathroy stoker Bill McCallum says: "Life at sea in a small ship like a corvette was in many ways relaxed. Each person had a job to do and did it. Few orders were given and many of the rules were relaxed. Dress codes were not enforced. Life ashore was totally different. You were always in full uniform. All discipline was enforced. And your war was not with the enemy, but with the navy."

Agassiz signalman George Goodwillie sketches a typical corvette crew: "Most of us would be in our late teens or early twenties and it was our first time away from home. The engine room personnel were normally older, many having worked prior to the war and developed skills the navy could use. The rest of the crew were all pretty youthful. Probably because of our youth, we had a certain feeling of our own invincibility and immortality and I cannot ever recall any sense of panic or paralysing fear."

There were pivotal players in the mosaic. One perspective comes from *Cobalt*'s Jimmy, Ted Best: "You need a good coxswain and a good buffer who knows the capabilities of the men. They are really the Jimmy's two key guys." The coxswain was the senior rating of the seamen's branch. Usually a chief petty officer, he was in charge of discipline and the general running of the ship. The buffer, usually a petty officer, was responsible for the upkeep of the upper deck and regularly assigned jobs to seamen.

Regina ERA Bill MacLeod says: "I believe the coxswain had more to do with running the ship than the captain or officers. If you had a coxswain who was strict but fair, you had a happy ship."

The sprinkling of experienced seamen was important. *Sackville* telegraphist Jim Alward says: "I was 19 and had only an incomplete Grade 11 education. I knew practically nothing about the technical side of the job. My leading tel, Roy Adams, seemed to be a harsh taskmaster. In spite of extreme seasickness, I was obliged to carry on with a bucket between my knees. 'Don't miss a message you little b_____!' he'd growl. His bark was worse than his bite. After I adjusted to the job, he treated me in a more kindly fashion. After all, he was an older man — 25 years old."

Able Seaman Dick Swanson of Abbotsford, B.C., comments on the *Arrowhead* crew in 1942-43: "The ship was blessed with a nucleus of top seamen from P.E.I. and Cape Breton, guys who had been around the ocean forever. They taught us endlessly — anchors and cables, boat work, rigging and splicing. I can still picture them, the coxswain, buffer and killicks volunteering their time for us."

A corvette crew usually developed a sense of common cause. *Saskatoon* lieutenant Bill Winegard says: "Nothing brings people closer together than to serve under difficult physical conditions with apprehension, excitement and, from time to time, fear as constant companions."

Orillia able seaman Albert Baker says: "The kinship we built up in the messdecks was special. Over a period

Courtesy Hoot Gibson

It's mail time in a *Port Arthur* mess in 1944.

Courtesy Roy Bergren

Two *Frontenac* pals in 1944 are Doug Orr (left) and Harris. Orr would become the father of hockey great Bobby Orr.

of time you would get closer than your own family. You were in such close contact with one another. If a guy was cantankerous, it wouldn't take too long before he changed his ways as someone would be on his back all the time."

Mayflower able seaman radar Bob Hill says: "In many ways we were like a big family." *Arrowhead* ERA Glenn Martin adds: "We became a part of a lot of fellows' families. We knew the parents — where dad worked, what mom cooked at home, where and what brothers and sisters were doing. We got letters from home and shared with others in our mess the good news and some of the bad news. I had the opportunity to meet a few of these families since the war and, in some instances, surprised them with what I knew of their family."

Harold Fisher recalls his *Morden* service: "The captain, officers and men were great, a real family. It's a companion-

ship I shall ever cherish — all for one and one for all. You could always rely on your shipmates. My thanks and the best to them all."

Telegraphist Dave Thom of Kenville, Man., says: "I crossed the ocean nine times in *Orangeville* before I was sent on leave. I didn't like to go and leave behind that ship and crew, but there was no choice."

Ville de Quebec leading stoker Paul Morse says: "I have not been in touch with any of my shipmates, not that I haven't dreamed of these friends of which there is no equal. In my quiet moments I have often though of my mates, the laughter and the tears. From these came strength that has carried me through some of life's trials."

These bonds forged by closeness, shared conditions and a common enemy were usually evident in a common attitude. *Amherst* leading seaman J.E. Schumacher says:

Hamming for the camera in 1944 are *Frontenac* crew members (front, from left): unidentified, A.W. Smith; (rear) Wally Quigley and Monroe.

"There was very little sickness or illness on these vessels except for seasickness, and also very little grousing and grumbling. Anyone who wanted to moan and drip was very quickly put down. In fact, a very lighthearted approach to everything seemed to be the norm, except the serious business of war. Drills and so on were to be taken seriously, but not the discomforts. Someone could always be counted on to come up with something to laugh about."

There was play at sea. *Giffard* SBA Howard Stark says: "There seemed to be continual poker games going on in the messes in off-duty hours." *Algoma* able seaman Harry Connell says: "My hammock was slung right next to a table and some of the crew would play crib for hours. I would try to get some sleep amid continual chants of '15-2, 15-4, 15-6.' I have never played crib since." Poker and crib were easily the most popular card games; some euchre and bridge were also played.

Music was appreciated on many ships, whether it came from records, the radio, or a piano and other live instruments. *Calgary* stoker Howard Libbey says: "Swing music and the big bands were the vogue at that time and the whole crew loved it. *Calgary* was the jumping ship of the fleet as the electrician rigged up a loudspeaking system on the upper deck. In harbour all the old swing numbers were blasted out and the crew jazzed around the upper deck."

Trentonian telegraphist Tom Farrell says: "Eric Muff, Phil Kevins and I were the best of buddies and normally went on shore leave together. Muff was a real character and kept us amused by reciting numerous poems by Robert Service. Kevins had a wonderful voice and could sure sing those Irish songs. We'd go to a pub and I would more or less be the emcee and ask the folks if they would like to hear a poem or a song or two. We had many a free beer that way, especially when we were based in Londonderry."

The pursuit of fun was ongoing. *Collingwood* stoker William Anderson comments: "I don't think anyone who was not there can ever appreciate the fun and hellery we had. Our main interest was to beat the authorities and regulations, get ashore and have fun."

MTL.

* * *

Another dimension which corvette life encompassed was religion. In that era more than 60 years ago, regular church attendance was higher than it is today, and religion was a more integral part of Canadian society. The RCN certainly reflected the times in its steps to look after the spiritual well-being of its sailors, a duty which fell largely to the navy's chaplaincy service.

Canon Harold Graven of Bridgewater, N.S., says, "We were appointed according to denominational population; for example, for every 1,000 Anglicans, an Anglican padre; for every 1,000 Baptists, a Baptist padre, etcetera."

Reverend Orville Hossie of Don Mills, Ont., says: "Canadian naval chaplains continued the practice of the Royal Navy. One had only the rank Chaplain RCN (Temporary)." Harold Graven adds: "We wore an officer's uniform with no rank insignia. The theory was that when we took our caps off we were the equal of the men in the messdeck and likewise in the admiral's office." Orville Hossie concludes: "It was a good plan because it enabled us to have such easy contact with all, regardless of rank."

Reverend W. Grant MacDonald of Dartmouth, N.S.,

explains: "With the exception of the few chaplains who served afloat in a carrier or cruiser, our duties as chaplains centred around the shore establishments."

Reverend Bruce Peglar of Guelph, Ont., remarks: "Of the 90 or 100 men of a religious denomination, none was specifically assigned to corvettes. All corvettes were visited regularly, and where help was needed a chaplain was there."

Reverend D. St. Clair Campbell of London, Ont., recalls: "We would board corvettes when they pulled into the jetty at Halifax. Most of our personal contacts were on shore, in the chaplains' office near the dockside. No particular distinction was made between corvette ratings and others."

Harold Graven elaborates on the system in Halifax: "As Captain D Padre, I was responsible for the work on ships because D was in charge of all ships based in or coming to Halifax. Any problems with chaplains or services, and there were some, and D would call me in. We did the usual things such as baptisms, sometimes on board ship; marriages, often in a dockyard room fixed up as a chapel; and burials.

"I had four to six chaplains working with me because we would have as many as 100 ships at a time in harbour. In our office we had a large blackboard containing the names of ships and the dates on which they were visited. Each morning we met and decided what ships we would visit that day. We conducted a number of services on Sunday, both on jetties and on ships. We distributed signals to every ship in harbour on Saturday so that everyone would know where the services were.

"We also took turns as duty chaplains. Every person was required to see a padre before an operation, so there were lots of night calls.

"One of our main tasks was counselling. Because our offices were in the dockyard, it was not unusual to see 10 to 20 men with problems in a single day. There was also the unpleasant task of informing next of kin of the death of a loved one."

ERA George Hollins, who served in *Midland* on the Triangle Run, remarks, "Religion for seagoing corvette crews consisted of the bosun piping, in St. John's and Halifax, 'Roman Catholics to the wheelhouse.' An RC priest usually came on board immediately we were tied up. I can't recall hearing that pipe in Boston or New York. Anyway,

our bosun must have been a born comedian because he changed the pipe to 'Ring chasers to the wheelhouse.'"

Padre W. Grant MacDonald says: "In the messdecks and the wardrooms we talked with the men who were really fighting the war at sea and tried to share in their experiences. Many we came to know and to welcome back as their ships put in for a few days before heading out again. When we held church services in the messdecks every Sunday, a hymn that was always requested — and which we would try to sing even though we had no instrumental accompaniment — went, 'Eternal Father, strong to save … hear us when we cry to Thee for those in peril on the sea.' Of course, there were cases where ships did not return, and always on board were some men we had come to know, and whose return we had looked forward to."

If Halifax was action central, the second hub of RCN activity was Newfiejohn. Harold Graven was there in 1941-42: "In St. John's we visited the men in ships, in hospitals, in cells, in hostels. We did the usual church things like baptisms, marriages and funerals, as well as services on Sundays. These were general services and Anglicans had Holy Communion services as well. We tried to arrange them so that every man had a service to go to if he wished. On Easter Sunday, 1942, I well remember that I had 13 services, most of them Holy Communion, starting at 7 a.m.

"One of our main chores in those early days was at the Fleet Mail Office, censoring mail from ships as well as shore establishments. This onerous task was later taken over by Wren [Women's Royal Canadian Naval Service] officers. These were grim days when corvettes would often come in with double their complement, having picked up survivors from the icy sea."

Reverend Murray Armstrong of Petitcodiac, N.B., spent a lot of time in Newfoundland. One thing he recalls is counselling: "Some of the problems the boys sought help for were marital. Sometimes they were at fault, and sometimes it was the wife at home. A story reached one sailor that his wife was running around. This caused my friend a great deal of heartache, so much so I felt the best way to clear it up was to encourage the wife to come down to St. John's from Toronto. She came with their three-year-old boy. With face-to-face contact, they were able to straighten out their problems. The stories about her were grossly exaggerated by careless gossip. All problems were not that easily solved."

On visits to ships, Murray Armstrong offered the sailors copies of the New Testament: "The men were apparently glad to receive them. Sometimes they would ask me questions about the Bible, and thus an opportunity was provided to discuss the spiritual side of life."

The padres grew to realize, Murray Armstrong says, that they had to go to sea "if we were adequately to minister to men who had to endure the rigours of the sea and face the dangers of a tireless enemy." Approval was granted and his first crossing in a destroyer led Armstrong to some conclusions: "I was impressed with the fine quality of young manhood in the navy. The officers were keen, the men did their jobs efficiently and reaffirmed my conviction that man is made in the image of God. There was some grousing now and then, but above all there prevailed that fine spirit of comradeship that comes from facing common dangers, from having enlisted in a great cause, and in bending one's energies towards a great purpose, not a selfish one.

"I was impressed, too, with the cost of this fight for freedom. Truly, 'with a great sum we obtain this freedom.' Millions of dollars' worth of war materials were lost that trip, and lives too."

Precedent set, padres made occasional trips in destroyers, frigates and corvettes. "We tried to work it so that we would go over in one ship and return in another. Sharing the life of the men at sea surely made them feel the padre was one of them, truly a shipmate."

Of course, the padres were entering a different realm, in several respects. Chaplain Harold Graven remembers being sick in corvettes: "They had a horrible motion like a corkscrew, pitching and rolling at the same time."

George Hollins recalls one trip when *Midland* carried a Protestant chaplain: "We had action stations. The crews on the depth-charge throwers and the gun crew on the aft pom-pom frequently conversed, for emphasis, with the F-word. The minister heard all this, and some time later we had a clear-lower-decks pipe. We got a 'sermon' by the minister cautioning the offenders as tempting the wrath of God — to the cost of our souls, in this world or the next. No psalms, no hymns, no scripture reading, just a dressing down. There was also a rumour aboard that any warship carrying a man of the cloth was bound for bad luck."

Some overseas establishments also had RCN chaplains. Reverend Waldo Smith of Kingston, Ont., says, "At Glasgow, Liverpool and Londonderry, Canadian naval chaplains met sailors off Canadian ships."

And Reverend Harry Pike of Victoria, B.C., says: "Many a Sunday service I conducted aboard our corvettes while I was based at Portsmouth, England. On a Sunday morning, I would go aboard perhaps two or three Canadian ships for a short service. The captain would always read the scripture lesson and the ship's company would join me in offering a prayer for the navy. After the service, I would have nice visits with the fellows in their messdecks, looking at pictures from home."

At sea without a chaplain, the standard corvette practice is described by *Amherst* able seaman Thomas King: "Every Sunday, if weather and the U-boats would permit, our captain would lead us in prayer and we would sing 'The Navy Hymn.'"

* * *

Strain was ever present in the corvette navy, particularly in the peak period of 1942-43. *Sackville* telegraphist Jim Alward puts it this way: "When men and boys work under stressful conditions for prolonged periods, inevitably the best and worst traits will appear — the best predominating at sea and the worst in port. The boys and the men either survived this experience and became better men, or simply succumbed to disintegrative forces initiated by hardship and stress. In short, for the individual it was a war within a war."

Anecdotal evidence suggests the strain showed more in officers, hardly surprising given the weight of command. Sometimes individuals sought solace in the bottle, either on a spree or a long-term basis. Lieutenant Henry Campsie was briefly CO of *Trillium* in late 1941, before getting posted to another ship. When they cleaned out his cabin, they found 31 empty bottles, says a fellow officer. Campsie had been CO for 24 days.

Lieutenant H.G. Denyer, 1941-42 *Amherst* CO, is another example. Asdic operator Alf Cockburn comments: "Regrettably, Denyer had been heavily under the influence of liquor all the time in Newfie prior to sailing on SC 96 and was seldom seen for all of that convoy, or in Londonderry or all the way back on ON 127. When he did come to the bridge on some action stations, he could hardly stand up.

"On our return from ON 127, the whole crew gathered on deck in Newfoundland and made a presentation to the

Jimmy that we wouldn't sail again with Denyer and that if he wanted to prevent a mutiny if Denyer remained in command, then the onus would be on him. We had lost faith in a once-competent seaman and made the decision that we wouldn't sail with him again."

The message was conveyed to Captain D. A decision was taken to replace Denyer. He would not leave the ship, however, and finally was removed forcibly on September 19, 1942. The Judge Advocate General's (JAG) branch of the Canadian Forces says that Lieutenant Denyer resigned from the RCN on December 14, 1942, after being "the subject of a sea board of inquiry." It's not unlikely his resignation was requested.

The first definition of mutiny given by *The Concise Oxford Dictionary* is: "Open revolt against constituted authority, esp. by soldiers, etc. against officers." Officially, there wasn't a single mutiny in the RCN in World War II. It may be that failure to call certain incidents mutiny was face-saving for the RCN, or that it was a conscious humanitarian decision in cases where a charge would have serious repercussions for mutineers who clearly had reason for grievance. Certainly there were incidents in a few other corvettes and in other types of ships.

* * *

In the current era of individual rights, sexual attitudes are liberal and the key element is consent between participating adults. In the World War II era, the state prescribed against a wider variety of sexual practices. Under the Criminal Code segment of "Offences against Morality," buggery was an indictable offence. Also called sodomy, it applied primarily to anal intercourse between human beings, regardless if consent were granted and irrespective of gender, or even if the accused were husband and wife. Another offence, called gross indecency, covered a variety of acts, including oral sex. Through these and other provisions, homosexuals were particularly constrained by the law. In the RCN, homosexuals were not popular. Most tried to keep their sexual orientation secret. Although it often seemed slow to act, officialdom could sometimes respond when presented with the possibility of malfeasance.

Lieutenant-Commander A.K. Young was the first CO of *Amherst*, which was commissioned in August 1941 and began convoy escort duty in October. Young was replaced in November 1941 after many of the crew rebelled at the

manner in which they perceived their captain was expressing his sexual preference. It must be stressed that Young was never charged with any offence. He was, however, discharged from the navy in February 1943 at a time when experienced officers were in short supply.

Action was more severe in the case of Lieutenant L.F. Moore, *Algoma* CO from April until August 1944. The matter often comes up when *Algoma* crew members get together. Their captain was perceived to "like" certain young sailors. Leading Seaman Paul Poirier of Dalhousie, N.B., and Able Seaman Harry Connell of Trail, B.C., confirm that a young seaman accused the captain of plying him with booze and attempting to seduce him. The captain cleared lower decks. It's alleged that the captain then exposed himself to the crew in a bizarre attempt to provide physical evidence that he could not possibly have been the person said to have acted improperly. Some crew members previously had doubts about their captain, but this incident was the final straw. The crew refused to sail with him. "Call it mutiny if you wish," says Harry Connell, "but the end result was that the captain was sent ashore."

The Privacy Act precluded an examination of Moore's personnel file, and material relating to RCN disciplinary and court martial proceedings during World War II has been destroyed, the JAG says. The JAG does, however, confirm that Moore "was the subject of court martial proceedings held at Portsmouth, England, on 14 December 1944, and was dismissed from His Majesty's service."

* * *

Health care — the physical well-being of sailors — was a part of navy life, of course. As a rule of thumb, the bigger the ship, the better the medical care. Things were pretty crude at first in small ships such as corvettes, but they improved during the war.

Albert Baker, in *Orillia* in 1941, says, "In the early days we had no sick bay attendant and had to rely on what little first aid we knew."

Art Geizer in *Agassiz* harkens back to 1941, too: "One of my duties as coxswain was being the sick bay attendant. What I knew about being a 'Piss-Pot Commando' you could read from the bottles."

Laurie Simpkin says: "I was the victualling assistant in *Hepatica* when she was commissioned in November 1940, and served in her until August 1941. As the ship's small complement did not allow for a writer (clerk)/sick berth attendant, I was volunteered for that responsibility as well."

Coder George Hedden remembers injuring himself while *Chicoutimi* was outside the harbour at Sydney, N.S., in the summer of 1941: "The pinkie and ring finger of my left hand were just hanging on. We did not have any sick bay attendant, so the petty officer coxswain offered to stitch my injury. I declined in no uncertain terms. He then did what he thought was best, dumping a bottle of iodine into the laceration. I must say this seared it pretty good because when I was returned to port by a harbour craft, the 12 stitches required to close the laceration were not even felt, but the one stitch needed in my head did give me cause to wince. This little escapade gave me 12 days ashore, until my ship returned. Tough way to get shore leave."

George Hedden also recalls the time when *Chicoutimi* rolled in heavy seas and a swinging door chopped off one thumb of an officers' steward: "As the destroyer [the senior officer's ship] was the only one in the escort group with a doctor, and as it was far too rough to transfer the injured steward for treatment, he had to remain aboard with the injury bandaged. While sleeping in his hammock, he would hit the deckhead with the injured hand and would let out an ungodly scream. He was taken aboard the depot ship in Iceland for treatment."

Recognizing the benefit of even limited medical expertise in smaller ships, the navy trained a number of men as sick berth attendants (SBAs).

Howard Stark, *Giffard* SBA in 1943-44, says: "The sick bay on the starboard side of the main deck was a small cabin, roughly five feet by six feet. There was just room enough for me to stand up and my patient to sit on a padded bench. There was a deep sink, cupboards and one porthole. While at sea on the Newfie-Derry Run, after sick call at 0900 hours and my resulting report to the captain, I usually was assigned to help the cook or VA. This made sense as I was on 24-hour call as an SBA and my sick bay was opposite the galley.

"One time after tying up in Londonderry, I went to the RN base for medical supplies. All I was given was a box of bandages and bottles of iodine and castor oil. That's apparently all that was available in early 1944. I can't remember carrying any drugs other than aspirin and a bit of morphine, which the captain kept in his cabin."

James Cornell, who was in *Louisburg* from 1941-43 and became leading SBA, says: "I was in first year medicine at Queen's University in Kingston when war was declared. I enlisted in the navy, was trained as a sick berth attendant and assigned to *Louisburg*. As an SBA I was a good first-aid attendant.

"I never got to assist with any major trauma cases, with the exception of one crew member who had a serious fall while crossing from one ship to another while docked in Gibraltar. His name was Walter Pulsifer [of Powell River, B.C.]. That guy hurt! I remember feeling helpless in the presence of his pain. The painkillers I gave him didn't seem to help. I had neither the professional training nor the diagnostic skill to help him properly, but I suspected he had more than broken ribs. I had him transferred for medical help. That particular episode reinforced my desire to study medicine, and later I returned to Queen's and graduated with my medical degree in 1951.

"Mostly I bandaged, sutured or treated minor cuts and bruises. We had two crew members who were well over six feet in height. Periodically they knocked themselves out during action stations by hitting their heads on the bulkhead doors. I think they spent most of their time at sea suffering from mild concussions and thumping headaches."

William Oneschuk of Essex, Ont., *Regina* SBA in 1943-44, says: "My duties included the care of the sick and injured and the cleanliness of the ship. I was a munitions passer when required."

Harry Cole of Exeter, Ont., *Arrowhead* SBA in 1944-45, recalls: "The health of the crew is duty 24 hours a day. Soot particles in eyes were a problem for many when at sea."

The background of SBAs varied widely. In civilian life, Ed (Doc) Stiles of Lucknow, Ont., had been an ambulance attendant and then a funeral director. He relates:

Aboard *Orangeville* I found I was almost 10 years older than the majority of the crew. Since I was married and had a family, I was more quickly approached than the skipper, whom they had to request to see, and I soon became a father-figure.

My ambulance training was a help. I had watched and assisted while doctors sutured the injured, so was often called upon to sew up one of the crew, officers included. In my first three months on board, I was very seasick. Consequently, patient and doc would rush to the rail and I would upchuck, and then it was back to being a seamstress.

Most shipmates in the RCNVR were A-1 category, so my duties were mainly caring for cuts, bruises and infections. One time when the skipper was going on leave to London, he asked if I could do something for his pet corn on one little toe. Corn plasters as such did not exist in our medical supplies, so I built up one out of one-half-inch tape, layer upon layer, with holes cut out in the centre in the shape of a pyramid. On his return, I removed the creation and in the middle of it rested the corn. The skipper would have made me leading SBA on the spot, if he could have.

There were lighter moments, too. Robert MacDonald, a 1942-43 *Dundas* telegraphist, recalls:

I remember helping the SBA check off items on a list of supplies he had just received. I read off a certain item, 'one gross pouches, male.' Looking rather bewildered, the SBA said, 'I didn't see one mailbag, let alone 144 of them.' It was a cause for some hilarity when we finally realized male pouches was the navalese for condoms.

The SBA was an RCNVR rating, as were most of the crew. He had only received a crash course in medical mysteries and was quite young and inexperienced, both in things medical and in the ways of the world. One afternoon in Esquimalt harbour, some jokesters dredged up a quantity of miniature crabs from the bottom and put some in each of the heads, then reported to the SBA that the ship was infested with crabs.

Crabs or pubic lice were often the bane of those susceptible. The faked concern fooled the SBA who rushed to the toilets to behold the infestation. The disbelieving look of amazement on his face was priceless and well rewarded the perpetrators, as it took him a little time to realize he was being had. These crabs were less than the size of a dime, but certainly looked pretty scary when skittering around in the toilets.

As a leading telegraphist in *Orangeville* in 1944-45, MacDonald remembers certain forms of health protection:

Besides being issued with condoms, we had the prophylactic kit known as the "V packet." This package consisted of a soap-impregnated cloth requiring only moistening, two plastic tubes, one I believe of calomel salve, the other an antiseptic ointment, and a cloth bag with a drawstring.

According to the instruction sheet, after an unprotected sexual encounter, you were to thoroughly cleanse the entire pubic area and penis with the washcloth, then snip the ends off the tubes, inserting one up the penis and smearing the contents of the other over the entire area. You then tied the bag over the penis with a bow knot on top. This was supposed to be left on as long as possible. There were certainly some ridiculous sights seen in *Orangeville* after a run ashore.

Skinny Hayes describes a particular SBA from his stint as first lieutenant in *Kenogami* in 1943:

I guess the most unforgettable character in *Kenogami* was Tiffy, the SBA. His real name is Don Martin but, as in every ship, he was called Tiffy by everyone. He could do anything — and did! He was into everything, knew everything and everybody, knew what was going on everywhere and, most importantly, was trusted by everyone aboard.

As well as being an expert SBA, he could help in the galley, he knew about proper nutrition, he could write an official letter and sometimes kept watches on the bridge. A measure of his ability and willingness was the time I decided that the ship needed a filing system for correspondence. We found the "Correspondence Manual" and completely refiled all the correspondence into and out of the ship since she had commissioned two years before.

He has remained the melting-pot for *Kenogami* intelligence. He has kept track of many of the people and corresponds with them. Over the years, starting in about 1943, he began getting mythical promotions. He is now a surgeon vice-admiral, having spent unduly long as a surgeon rear-admiral!

The *Orangeville* crew in 1944.

Orangeville crew members J.W. Thorpe, Robert McClintock and Worthington appear to be airing a hammock at sea in 1944.

A check of the records shows that Donald Martin was awarded Mention in Dispatches for his three years at sea. The citation reads, in part; "He has taken a great interest in the health of the ship's company and has been greatly instrumental in keeping the spirit of HMCS *Kenogami* at a high level."

Health problems at sea could be a serious matter, *Arvida* ordinary seaman Jim Simpson found out in 1943 on the Newfie-Derry Run: "Three days out of Ireland with a westbound convoy, I suffered from severe stomach pains. Our tiffy relayed my symptoms to the doctor in the destroyer in our escort group. The doctor's instructions were to have the patient drink two gallons of warm salt water to induce vomiting. It didn't work, and the pain didn't get any easier. Finally, the doctor's diagnosis was suspected appendicitis. He ordered that I be transferred to an RN hospital ship that was in the convoy. Travel by seaboat [lifeboat] on the open ocean is not exactly my idea of a yachting holiday when, at the end of the voyage, you have to climb a Jacob's ladder up the side of a ship that looks higher than Mount Everest. Luckily I made it to the ship's deck before passing out. The RN doctors were kind enough not to operate at sea, saving me for the knife at the RCN hospital in Halifax."

Few corvettes ever had a doctor and, when they did, it usually was associated with a risky assignment. For example, *Port Arthur* and *Ville de Quebec* each got a doc for Operation Torch in the Mediterranean, while *Regina* got one for Torch and one for the English Channel in 1944.

Kitchener also had a doc, as Stoker Moose McGill notes:

Our doctor came from a small-town practice in Ontario. He was just what a corvette needed. He treated us for the everyday things a sailor encountered — scabies, dhobi rash and crabs we contracted from unclean toilets in drydock heads. He was a great guy. We often played cards in the stokers' mess and he never gave up trying to reform us incorrigible characters.

Fred the doctor was one of the few men I met in the navy who never uttered a word of profanity. One night down in the Mediterranean, he went rushing out the blackout curtain at the break in the foc's'le. He had to step a good 10 inches through a watertight door. The doctor was a tall man and as he rushed through the door, he struck his head. He fell flat on his back on the deck, his tin hat flying off. He picked himself up, retrieved his tin hat and said, "Oh my goodness." I remember a big gunner saying, "If the s.o.b. didn't cuss after that, he never will."

I felt sorry for Fred one day. On one of the merchant ships in the convoy, a chap was quite ill. We launched a seaboat and took the doctor over. The man had a ruptured appendix and consequently died. We sat playing cards and Fred said to me: "We're just like another mechanic, Moose. We don't know it all." He did his best under the circumstances, but it hurt him to lose a life. Fred was a real asset to us.

Normally, there was one doc in each escort group. He usually travelled in the senior officer's ship, often a destroyer, but sometimes a frigate as the war went on. Dr. Peter Playfair of Iroquois, Ont., was slated for a frigate, but until it was completed he made four or five 1944 crossings in *Orangeville*, a new Castle-class corvette. He comments: "There were no special problems in the corvettes. The beauty of the navy was the youthful men involved. Basically, they were keen and healthy so medical needs were minimal. So a tiffy was able to look after a corvette crew easily, with the group surgeon to back him up. …

"The SBA's setup, even in the old corvettes, was small but adequate. In *Orangeville* it was much better and almost the same as in the new frigates.

"There were never any major problems in *Orangeville*. Usually there were more damages to repair after a few days of shore leave than was the case at sea. We had our share of minor things like bruises and minor fractures, lacerations and occasionally teeth to remove, and the odd appendicitis, which was usually treated medically until we got to shore. The doctor occasionally made trips to other ships in the convoy, but more often the patient came to the doc."

* * *

Pets were another element of corvette life. People love pets and sailors are certainly no exception. The most common mascots in corvettes were cats and dogs, but the perceptions of their adaptability vary.

Kincardine telegraphist Wes Johnson says: "When we had pets aboard ship, the cats were able to survive, but dogs just couldn't hack it and they got seasick, especially young pups. You'd watch them go down the companionway and they'd be falling over. When the ship rolled, they couldn't stand up. They'd be completely disoriented. The cats would just roll with the ship itself and have no problem at all."

Forest Hill ERA Garry Flock remembers a cat: "The poor thing would meow so much in rough weather. I can remember it walking along the companionway and as the ship rolled it would lean to keep balance and its back would arch and it would meow so badly. Sad, but oh so comical to watch. It got worse. When the ship pitched down, the cat would be virtually weightless and then when it pitched up, the cat would be forced against the deck. Never actually saw the cat sick at any time, though."

Orangeville captain Rodney Pike says: "In January 1945 while escorting westbound convoy ONS 41 we rode out a hurricane. After a while we became accustomed to the

violent motion, the whistling wind and the background noise of surging and gurgling water. I remember looking one time at Ping the cat, rocking back and forth like one of those children's toys with a weight in the bottom to make it spring back up, and thinking, 'Are we really rolling that much?'"

Kincardine stoker petty officer Harold Miles says: "Our cat was brought aboard as a kitten and I guess bracing himself on the deck in rough weather caused his front legs to become bowed like those of a sailor. He sure looked weird."

* * *

One visible aspect of corvette life related to ship's identity. Jack Muir of Toronto, Ont., a telegraphist in *Amherst* and *Regina,* explains: "On almost every ship there was someone who did sketches." So sketch they did, creating a variety of gun-shield logos. Muir painted *Regina*'s logo in 1943. "I painted it right after we got that Italian sub. It was a picture of a cowboy on a sea horse lassoeing a sub."

Most of this art mingled humour with grim intent towards the enemy. The inspiration was often drawn from the ship's name. The best known work belongs to Burnie Forbes of Smiths Falls, Ont., on *Wetaskiwin*. Working from the sound of the town's name, he drew the Queen of Hearts sitting in a pool of water. Hence, the moniker "Wet Ass Queen" which became the standard way to refer to the ship. Usually the logos were painted on the steel plate of the gun shield. "As each year went by, and I painted the logo on again, I upgraded it, a little," Forbes explains. "I raised her skirt and gave her bigger boobs."

Drumheller's logo, one of the first, showed the devil beating a drum. *Moose Jaw*'s logo by Signalman Peter Younger of Toronto, Ont., depicted an enraged moose, with a U-boat in its antlers, taking a chunk out of the pants of a fleeing Adof Hitler.

George Rickard of London, Ont., explains his logo involvement: "I had noticed on approaching Job's Wharf in St. John's harbour that the four-inch gun-shield graffiti on one corvette had not been finished. I also did not realize that this was to be my ship. As soon as my history sheet was scanned by our captain, Lieutenant-Commander Robert McNeil, and another officer, both noted that I was an artist and designer by profession. Immediately they had me detailed to finish *Dauphin*'s gun-shield painting. It was a job that I was actually a little reluctant to do, as the portrayal of a Mountie with raised pistol astride a bucking and broken U-boat had not been very well drawn. However, on completion it satisfied our captain, who had been with the RCMP Marine Service prior to the war, as had the other officer. Ship's paint and modified paint brushes are not the best for rendering a good painting."

The Walt Disney Company offered to do free logos for American and Canadian army, navy and air force units, using Disney characters, Muir recalls. Few, if any, Canadian ships accepted, possibly because of the logistics. Still, some ship's logos sported buckshee versions of well-known cartoon characters. For example, *Amherst*'s logo featuring Pluto was drawn by Lieutenant Edward Winslow-Spragge of Almonte, Ont. Disney did not object to these drawings; it was all in support of the war effort.

* * *

Corvettes had a presence across the land because so many were named after Canadian communities. It's not surprising, then, that they played a part in the campaigns to sell war bonds and drum up public support for Canada's war effort. One example is the depiction of *La Malbaie* on the 1942 Canadian 20-cent stamp.

The National Film Board, founded in 1939, helped *Port Arthur* play a more prominent role. Able Seaman Lloyd MacDonald of Spryfield, N.S., explains: "While we were doing workups in the summer of 1942, we also did a short movie for the NFB called *Corvette Port Arthur*." An NFB promotional catalogue provides this description: "A film tribute to the Royal Canadian Navy. The stars: those men who sail the fighting ship *Port Arthur*, credited, shortly after the picture was completed, with sinking an Italian submarine in the Mediterranean. The film reaches a climax when a submarine is detected approaching the convoy and the signal for 'action stations' is sounded throughout the ship."

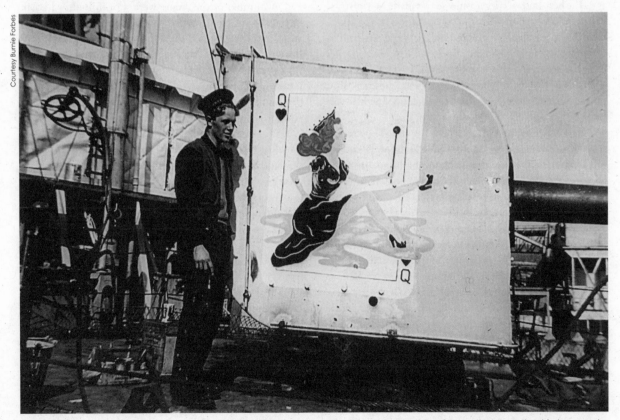

Burnie Forbes paints the *Wetaskiwin* gun-shield logo featuring the Queen of Hearts in a puddle of water that gave the ship her popular nickname, Wet Ass Queen.

In reality, a Dutch sub used for training RCN crews played the role of the enemy. *Port Arthur* ERA Leslie McLean says: "The only part I remember was where our captain went aboard the sub with several of the crew. A few minutes later they reappeared, jumped into the water and the sub then sank."

Jack Skinner, leading torpedo operator in *Port Arthur*, says: "It was probably one of the worst movies I ever saw. However, extracts have been shown in other movies and on television over the years. I had great difficulty convincing my children that the fellow dropping the depth charges over the stern was me, until I had a chance to tape the 1989 Remembrance Day ceremonies on TV, then slow down the segment to prove that it was dad dropping those charges."

The world premiere of *Corvette Port Arthur* took place at the Colonial Theatre in Port Arthur on May 3, 1943, amid tremendous fanfare and public ceremonies involving the army and air force as well as the navy.

The best-known corvette movie was made by Universal Picture Corporation with the co-operation of the RCN. With a recognizable star in Randolph Scott, it came out as *Corvette K-225*, the pennant number of *Kitchener*. Earlier it had at least two other names, *Corvette* and *Corvettes in Action*. Many of the shipboard and ocean scenes were shot during *Kitchener's* initial workups at Pictou, N.S., a period extended to six weeks in the summer of 1942.

Stoker Moose McGill says: "We never had any movie stars aboard. There were doubles for Randolph Scott and Ella Raines. They took a lot of still shots of the engine room, boiler room and so on, so that they could mock these up in the studio. Andy Devine was one of the stokers in the film, also Barry Fitzgerald.

"We did the usual workup things which they filmed: firing depth charges, the four-inch gun and our machine-guns, launching sea-boats, etc. Of course, the training sub was brought into play. We also had a Carley float in the water with men aboard to simulate survivors...At this point I went home on leave. *Kitchener* then made two trips to New York with the film crew aboard. They wanted to get some shots of rough weather and, from what I'm told, they got the weather okay, but were not in very good shape to film it."

Kitchener was assigned to Operation Torch for the invasion of North Africa before filming was completed. The short foc's'le corvette *Buctouche* was her stand-in.

Buctouche signalman Al Campbell says: "The dockyard carpenters fashioned a plywood extended foc's'le on one side of the ship and had K-225 painted on the bow on that side. K-179 was not altered on the stern of the ship nor on the port side. With two numbers showing, we confused the harbour master and had lots of signals to make while entering or leaving the boom gates at Halifax.

"A number of the scenes were shot in Bedford Basin. At the end of the picture we sailed past a number of cargo ships and they dipped their flags and *Buctouche* dipped the ensign. I was the sig assigned to this job and after the war when the film came to our theatre, I was very proud pointing this fact out to my wife and parents."

And although it was shot 65 years ago, *Corvette K-225* still turns up occasionally in the late movies on television.

But Moose McGill feels the movie wasn't entirely a blessing: "I think we original *Kitchener* people always resented the terms 'Hollywood ship' and 'movie ship' as we were bugged during the war. *Kitchener* gave a pretty good account of herself during the war in the Atlantic, the Med and the English Channel during the invasion. The movie *K-225* was probably the least of her achievements."

Fun was part of the picture for these *Regina* crew members with shaved heads. They are (front, from left): Lou Proietti, Jospeh Saulnier, Jim Peters; (middle) Vic Martin, Doug Tope, Bill Neaves; (rear) Bob Dunlop, Frank Roach, Len Horne.

The distinctive lattice mast of the Castle-class corvette is evident in *Kincardine*.

CHAPTER FOURTEEN

"THERE WAS NO FLASH — JUST A HUGE WALL OF WATER INTO THE SKY."

PERCY NELLES, chief of the naval staff, had taken into World War II a tiny navy which was unprepared because neither the politicians nor the public were willing to fund it significantly in peacetime. Nelles led the RCN through an unprecedented period of wartime expansion, but he was only able to take it so far. After acrimonious exchanges with Navy Minister Angus L. Macdonald, Nelles was removed as chief of the naval staff at the end of 1943.

It's true Nelles had a difficult task, but his performance warranted criticism. He was often overly willing to help the RN. He also wanted to be one of the big boys. Both attitudes contributed to the poor decision to close the Gulf of St. Lawrence in 1942 and send to Operation Torch corvettes that were badly needed on the North Atlantic.

His eyes were also set on the navy of the future — unfortunately at the expense of the war at hand. In 1942 he opted for four Tribal-class destroyers when mid-ocean escorts were the major need. Worse, he chose to build them in Canada, which had never produced such large, complex warships. Though begun in 1942, the four Tribals weren't completed in time to fight in this war. If Nelles had to have Tribals, he would have been far better off to get them from the U.K., as he did with four others.

But it was his neglect of Canada's fleet that led to his demise as chief of naval staff. He seemed not to appreciate the technical evolution of the war at sea, and RCN ships were perpetually behind their Allied counterparts in technology, none more so than corvettes. In fact, Nelles never really pushed hard to modernize his

ships and close this equipment gap. It finally caught up to him, but in the meantime the men of the RCNVR had to stand the gaff, many of them in ill-equipped corvettes.

Cliff Hatch, who served in *Napanee* and commanded *Ville de Quebec*, says: "I spent four of my five years in the navy at sea. Perhaps I'm biased, but our equipment was far inferior to that of the RN and we received it from six months to two years after they had theirs."

That feeling is widespread. Able Seaman Rick Collins, whose five ships included two corvettes, says: "It is common knowledge now that the RN and USN got all the latest equipment. I was in the asdic department and how we ever had any success against the U-boats with the sets we had is beyond me. It wasn't until March or April of 1943 that we started to get up-to-date radar and asdic equipment."

Canadian radar is a particular sore point. The National Research Council in Ottawa began work in 1941 on the infamous SW1C (surface warning 1st Canadian), which was fitted in RCN ships in 1942. Charlottetown lieutenant Dave Jeffreys comments: "The Canadian radar set fitted to early corvettes was a menace. A target presumably on the starboard bow could just as well be on the port quarter. This sort of erratic information does not lead to confidence." Because of poor liaison, the RCN never realized that the RN had already introduced a superior new generation of radar in 1941.

Another example was "hedgehog." Although the RN introduced this anti-submarine device in early 1942, only a few RCN corvettes had it by mid-1943 and it wasn't widely installed in RCN escorts until 1944. The beauty of hedgehog was that it fired 24 depth bombs in an oval pattern ahead of the attacking vessel while she was still in asdic contact with a submerged U-boat. Previously, when the escort got close enough to a submerged U-boat to drop depth charges, the asdic echoes ceased.

"Quite an apparatus," says *Oakville* able seaman George Kahan, "24 bombs on spigots to be fired [at] full speed ahead, then turn. Electric-impulse firing, lots of noise and we had to stand behind a plate for safety."

Though a major advance, hedgehog had drawbacks. At the time of firing, the attacking escort had to be pointed in the direction of the submerged U-boat, then turn sharply to avoid the target area. And each bomb containing 32 pounds of the explosive Torpex only went off on contact, so a high degree of accuracy was required. Close did not count.

Up to now, the norm for the overextended Canadian corvettes was piecemeal improvements during refits that usually occurred when overdue, which worked out to about once a year. Hedgehog was just one of a package of improvements needed to make them adequate mid-ocean escorts. The RCN brass dithered in making essential decisions. It didn't help that some of the equipment wasn't available in Canada and that East Coast shipyards couldn't handle the task alone.

Ray Burwash, HSD in *Agassiz* in 1943, comments: "Since being commissioned, *Agassiz* had a very good reputation as being one of the better corvettes, and as such she was continually kept at sea. This meant she still had her short foc's'le and older everything. Such was the penalty of being a good and seasoned ship — you could not be spared for the luxury of refit and modernization." Some examples illustrate this point: *Arrowhead*, *Chambly*, *Cobalt*, *Hepatica*, *Orillia* and *Wetaskiwin* were all commissioned in 1940, but not modernized until 1944. *Agassiz*, *Algoma* and *Battleford* were all commissioned in 1941, but not modernized until 1944.

The pace was slow and Canadian shipyard capacity already taxed. Over two years, the early corvettes were modernized in three countries — Canada, the U.K. and the U.S. Twenty-six were completed in 1943 and 39 in 1944. The emphasis was on navigation, electronics and weapons. They got new radar, new sonar, the gyro compass, hedgehog, a new bridge from which to command the action and other improvements. Not least, they also got an extended foc's'le.

Lieutenant Don Storey of Shediac, N.B., who became commanding officer of *Arvida* while she was being renewed in 1944, says: "Living conditions in the corvette were much improved with the extended forecastle. I can recall many drenchings for both crew and officers as well as the crew experiencing very poor and wet conditions in their messdecks when I served in *Rosthern* on the North Atlantic in 1941-42. With the extended forecastle, the bridge layout was also much improved, providing for better conditions in the sonar, radar and telegraphy areas. It also provided better conditions for fighting and conning [directing the steering of] the corvette."

The modernization program was so belated that five corvettes served for the duration of the war without being revamped. While they received some improvements, *Chicoutimi*, *Nanaimo*, *Rosthern* and *The Pas*, commissioned in 1941, and *Brantford*, commissioned in 1942, retained the short foc's'le and its deplorable living conditions.

* * *

The year 1944 started auspiciously at sea. On January 8, the Canadian corvette *Camrose* and the British frigate *Bayntun* were acting as a screen for the combined convoys OS 64 and KMS 38 when they made eight depth-charge attacks in two hours and sank *U-757*, a Type VII C boat, on the eastern side of the North Atlantic.

This was a period of change at sea. On the Allied side, new frigates went to support groups hunting U-boats, and to mid-ocean escort groups, where they were often joined by the newer revised corvettes with increased endurance. Instead of being under the control of the ranking officer among the escort captains, many mid-ocean groups now got a senior officer with the specific duty of directing the group. With greater numbers of proper mid-ocean escorts coming on, a number of the early corvettes were pushed to the coastal work for which they were originally intended.

On the German side, January 1944, marked the introduction of the *schnorchel*, or snorkel, in U-boats on combat patrol. The snorkel was a collapsible mast that brought air into the submarine, allowing it to run on diesel engines and, for the first time, recharge its batteries while slightly submerged. This development greatly reduced the vulnerability of U-boats to detection and destruction by long-range patrol aircraft, which had become their biggest concern. While the snorkel made U-boats much harder to detect, the device was not perfect. The snorkel head left a wake that could sometimes be seen, and with its diesels running, a U-boat's hydrophone listening device was ineffective. Unlike the RCN, the German navy wasted no time in refitting its fleet. By June, half the U-boats stationed in France had the device and no new U-boat put to sea without it.

The combination of improved Allied air cover, support groups and better escort performance led to high U-boat losses and the abandonment of the wolf-pack tactic by early 1944. Most U-boats would now hunt alone. While some U-boats remained in mid-ocean, they concentrated inshore, both in the U.K. and on the east coast of North America. It seems ironic that the new escorts encountered fewer U-boats than many of the older escorts had.

"Life, except for one isolated attack, was not memorable for the telling," says *Chambly* able seaman Howard Markle. "After the war, in fact, I noticed in the wrap-up accounts that nearly all of the U-boats had been either off-task completely or tasked away from the mid-Atlantic during most of my time aboard through August 1944. This would have been nice to know, especially at the twice-daily precautionary exercise of action stations, dawn and dusk, and when some poor sea creature was catching hell from maybe a less-than-accurate assessment of an underwater contact."

The slogging continued, sometimes with complications. *Summerside* lieutenant Don McGivern recalls refuelling at sea: "Once, with a good sea running, we came astern of a tanker, the crew did a commendable job of catching lines, heaving the heavy rubber fuel line aboard and making the hose connection on the foc's'le. When *Summerside*'s tanks were topped up, the signal was given to the tanker to stop pumping. Due to some misunderstanding, the oil continued to pour through the hose, so the captain ordered the coupling disconnected. Naturally that was the one time it got stuck, so the captain ordered the hose cut and a couple of able seamen flailed away with axes. It was a harrowing experience when the hose was severed and the oil poured out over the foc's'le, down the decks and scuppers and down the companionways to the alleyways and messdecks. The cleanup took several days."

Refuelling at sea could create more serious problems than a sticky mess. *Forest Hill* ERA Garry Flock recalls: "We had a warrant engineer officer. Somehow he got his foot caught in a loop of steel cable and broke his leg while we were taking on oil from a tanker. He was fortunate that he did not have his foot severed."

Courtesy Doug May

Kincardine refuels at sea from a merchant aircraft carrier called a MAC ship.

While escorting convoy SC 154 in early March, 1944, *Regina* attempted to refuel at sea. ERA Tom Baird says: "It was a continuous change of revs on the engine: Up five, down three, up five, down eight. Finally, these orders from the bridge let up. Then the engine ground to a sudden stop. Down comes the engineer officer and the officer of the day. In their excitement, they had run over the line and it was wrapped around the screw [propeller]. We were just a sitting duck floating in the breeze."

ERA Bill MacLeod says: "That evening a German reconnaissance plane spotted us. All night we expected a torpedo to come through our side any minute."

The stricken *Regina* was protected by the destroyer *St. Laurent*. When a tug arrived in the morning to tow the corvette to the Azores, *St. Laurent* departed to rejoin the convoy. "No sooner had the destroyer left us when she launched an attack on a sub which had been rather too close for comfort," Tom Baird notes.

While emergency repairs were undertaken at Horta in the Azores, *Regina*'s crew celebrated. Bill MacLeod says: "The liquor was dirt cheap. It was the first time I saw the crew having more than they could drink."

Tom Baird recalls: "We had quite an experience. The people there are Portuguese and many of the older ones never had shoes in their life. You should have seen their feet, almost as wide as long. They would trade liquor and watches for shoes and even empty tin cans from the galley. In fact, when we received orders to sail, the captain delayed for three or four hours to get some of his crew members sobered up. We also had several boys who traded off all their shoes, so they had to go to Ireland barefoot.

"When we left the Azores, we headed due north to pick up a freighter in distress. Her cargo had shifted, but she was still able to continue slowly and was waiting for a salvage tug to take her to Ireland. These merchant ships used to carry enormous deck-loads of lumber from Canada to Britain. You could hardly imagine how they would stack it up."

The Canadian Escort Group C 2 was composed of the RCN destroyers *Gatineau* and *Chaudière*, the frigate *St. Catharines*, the corvettes *Chilliwack* and *Fennel*, and the RN destroyer *Icarus*. These six and the RN corvette *Kenilworth Castle* combined to sink *U-744* in the North Atlantic in a prolonged drama on March 5 and 6, 1944, files at the National Defence Directorate of History and Heritage show. At 32 hours, this was the second-longest successful hunt of the war.

Chilliwack able seaman Ralph Chartrand recalls the action: "When the sub started to surface, everything that could shoot went into action and we fired all we could. While the crew of *U-744* was jumping out of the conning tower, *St. Catharines* was closing in, but our captain manoeuvred *Chilliwack* in front to make sure that this was our sub. He gave the order, 'Prepare to ram!' but soon the sub was empty, so we didn't ram. We lowered a lifeboat with a boarding party and they proceeded to *U-744*. While the lifeboat was tied to the sub, some members boarded the sub. Then a big wave hit our lifeboat and flipped the crew in the water with the German sailors. We took 17 prisoners on board and made them as comfortable as possible. We even shared our blankets."

It was almost a major coup. Three lifeboats reached the Type VII C boat. German code books and the cipher machine were seized, but all three sea-boats capsized in the rough sea and only one book was saved. All the Canadians were picked up. So, too, were 40 Germans. *Icarus* then dispatched the unsavable *U-744* with a torpedo. Eleven Germans died, including the captain.

Meanwhile, convoy SC 154 had encountered difficulties, so elements of Escort Group 9, a support group, were shifted to strengthen her protection. Thus on March 10, 1944, the new EG 9 corvette *Owen Sound* shared the kill of *U-845* with the RCN destroyer *St. Laurent* and frigate *Swansea* and the RN destroyer *Forester*.

The Type IX C-40 boat was spotted on the surface at 1624 hours and dived. *Owen Sound* HSD Reg Baker says: "We ran in and fired a pattern and all hell broke loose. We were travelling too slow."

Communications rating Len Leier says: "Our speed was not the greatest and I remember it seemed to me that, as well as dropping the depth charges, we almost blew ourselves out of the water. Anyway, I can remember there was a big gush of water all of a sudden. This was when I realized that we were not playing a game, but that it was for real and I was very frightened."

The asdic and electrical power were knocked out. Repairs were made rapidly. *Owen Sound* was *hors de combat* for about 10 minutes, then participated in more attacks. At one point, it appears the U-boat released a canister designed to simulate a sub and mislead the attackers' detection devices. The corvette's asdic operator was faced with two echoes. "The operator was confused and asked me what echo he should hold onto and I said the first one, which turned out okay for us," Reg Baker recalls.

With the destroyer *Forester* also in on the promising hunt, the slower *Owen Sound* was ordered back to assist a damaged freighter. Deliberate creeping attacks were made, then *Forester* had asdic problems and *Swansea* joined. Finally, the damaged U-boat surfaced at 2234, hoping to slip away in the dark. But *St. Laurent* and *Swansea* were ready and scored some immediate hits. *Forester* joined the one-hour gun battle that ended with the Germans abandoning the sinking *U-845*. She went under at 2338. *Swansea*, *St. Laurent* and *Forester* picked up 45 survivors. Months later, the awards for the U-boat kill included Mention in Dispatches for the corvette's captain, Acting Lieutenant-Commander

William Hamilton, Library and Archives Canada, PA14082

On March 6, 1944, a whaler crew from the corvette *Chilliwack* boards *U-744*.

Manny Watson, Chief ERA Richard Faulkner and HSD Reg Baker.

Also in March 1944 in the North Atlantic, Ordinary Seaman Roy Bergren of Melfort, Sask., was ready to go on duty at 0800 hours to stand a depth charge watch at the rear of the corvette *Frontenac*. "A stoker came up from the en-gine room and asked me to dump a pail of oily rags over the side. A wave hit me and the next thing I knew I was about 40 feet out in the water. The temperature of the water at that time was about 34 degrees Fahrenheit [1 Celsius]. After several attempts to rescue me, the ship having lost sight of me many times, I managed to grab onto a heaving line and the crew pulled me alongside the ship and then onboard. I was in the frigid water about 30-35 minutes. I was barely conscious when rescued. The crew stripped my clothes off and got me to sick bay where I remained for a few days. I suffered from numbness in my fingers for many months. When I went home in July, I couldn't handle a knife and fork, but I didn't let on to my parents so they wouldn't worry." Summarizing his ship's activity at this time, the CO, Lieutenant Eric Wennberg, wrote: "We've seen a lot of water and many a bitter storm, in one of which we lost a man overboard. Due to what our senior officers claimed was good seamanship and what I firmly maintain was good luck, I managed to pick him up again."

During the early months of 1944, the RCN progressively took on a greater share of the mid-ocean escort work. This coincided with declining RN involvement as the British and Americans, in particular, prepared their naval forces for the invasion of Normandy.

* * *

On April 9, 1944, the corvette *Dawson* collided with the minesweepers *Medicine Hat* and *Gaspé* in Halifax harbour. The damage was not serious, a file at the National Archives shows. *Dawson* "had too much way" — navalese for going too fast — and should have turned sharply to starboard and made a new approach to the berth rather than continue with her initial attempt, Captain D Halifax determined. His rebuke of *Dawson*'s skipper was mild, however: "More care and attention is to be paid to berthing in future, to avoid unnecessary accidents which may result in immobilizing an operating ship for no good reason."

To draw an analogy, putting a ship in a berth is quite unlike parking a car. The ship cannot stop, start or turn with such ease. As well, the ship must often contend with the tide, while the street beneath a car does not often move.

Departing isn't necessarily a cinch, either. Don McGivern of Ottawa, Ont., comments: "If you happen to be one of the inside corvettes when ordered to sail, it can be rather exciting getting untangled. One time there was great difficulty, because of the wind and the current, in getting the stern line released and as we drifted a few hundred feet away from the jetty, the captain ordered, 'Clear the decks!' He feared the line would become taut, then snap and whirl around out of control, killing or maiming the hands on duty. The happy ending to the episode was that the wharf

workers were able to free the line from the bollard [post] just as it was coming out of the water."

* * *

After turning a westbound convoy over to the local escort on the afternoon of May 6, 1944, C 1 escort group steamed for Newfiejohn in line-abreast formation about 3,000 yards apart, with the frigate *Valleyfield* in the centre flanked by the corvettes *Frontenac*, *Halifax*, *Giffard* and *Edmundston*. At about 2340, a lone torpedo from *U-548* struck *Valleyfield* in one boiler room, archival files indicate.

Giffard signalman Ken Hotston of Peterborough, Ont., recalls, "I was on the 8-to-midnight watch and when the explosion took place there was no flash — just a huge wall of water into the sky."

On a clear, moonlit night, she broke in two right away, with the bow section sinking first in about three minutes, then the stern about five minutes later.

While the other corvettes continued unawares, *Giffard* responded, but her captain, Acting Lieutenant-Commander Charles Petersen, took some time to comprehend what had happened. When it became clear *Valleyfield* had sunk, *Giffard* tried briefly to pick up survivors, but this was ineffective because she did not stop for fear of making herself a sitting target for a U-boat. Crewman Bud Carr says, "Many of her crew were in the water yelling and crying for help. Several were already floating face down. We had slowed *Giffard* down, but not fully stopped."

When he finally realized the sinking was caused by torpedoing, captain Petersen alerted the other corvettes and faced the perpetual dilemma: Should he save the freezing men in the water or go after the sub? He reluctantly turned away from the men and carried out a cursory search for the sub while the other corvettes were rushing back to the scene. *Giffard* able seaman Chuck McFadden relates: "We went after the sub but couldn't find it with our asdic, so we returned to pick up the survivors. The water was 32 degrees Fahrenheit in the afternoon, so a person can't last in that. Some of us were over the side on the rope ladders hoisting them up so others could reach down to pull them over the side."

At this stage, Bud Carr notes, "We were able to rescue a number of survivors, but a few of the crew from *Valleyfield* were actually sucked into our propeller."

Giffard leading seaman Scott Sanders recalls: "An officer called to me and gave me a long-handled net, much like a landing net for fish. It had a 15-to-20-foot tapered handle. He said, 'Get someone on this,' which I did. I tried to pull this man up, after reassuring him that he was going to be okay. The trouble was he may have weighed 200 pounds, plus all his wet clothing, making it impossible to raise him out of the water — much less all the way up the side! I was leaning out over the gunwale, which slanted out at the top. I could get no leverage so as the ship was going slowly forward the pole began to slip through my hands. Another rating jumped up on the rail to help, but it was no use. The last I saw was the pole disappearing under the ship's side near the stern. I'll always remember this: As soon as I got him in the net, it sealed his fate!"

All told, says Chuck McFadden, "We picked up 38 alive and five dead. We draped survivors in our blankets and proceeded on to St. John's." Indeed, only two of 15 officers and 36 of 148 ratings survived the *Valleyfield* sinking. It's clear that a great many died of exposure in the icy water. In fact, the last to be saved appear to be have been in the water nearly 90 minutes, making their survival amazing.

Ordinary Seaman Roy Bergren of Melfort, Sask., in *Frontenac* recalls: "We went back to the place where the ship had gone down and *Giffard* was already there picking up survivors. The water was extremely cold and covered with bunker fuel. We were ordered to screen *Giffard*. ... It was very traumatic to see our fellow sailors in the frigid and fuel-covered water. Our radar was broke down, but we stayed out for three days searching for the submarine with no luck."

During the intensive search, *Edmundston* dropped charges on a solid asdic contact, only to discover from the debris that came to the surface that she had bombed part of the sunken frigate.

It was an inglorious episode. A lone U-boat had prevailed even though other Canadian warships and aircraft had been searching for it for days. In fact, that night the C 1 ships had encountered two corvettes and a patrol aircraft searching for *U-548* in the area. Though the floe ice seemed to be behind them, the C 1 escorts were still steaming in a straight line, rather than zigzagging, and their CAT gear was not deployed, despite the fact that *Frontenac's* radar was out of commission and *Valleyfield's* radar was considered unreliable.

It would seem the escorts were complacent or overconfident. After all, there were five of them. Further, it was a big ocean and despite the reports of a sub in the area it was

unlikely they would encounter it. In reality, however, the escorts ran across *U-548*'s path about 50 miles southeast of Cape Race on Newfoundland's Avalon Peninsula and did not detect the surfaced U-boat, which dived, manoeuvred into an attack position and made the kill with one torpedo.

Finally, *Giffard* did not immediately alert the other escorts, so there was no quick, concerted counterattack. Though the rescue was not commenced swiftly because of circumstances, it was valiant and *Giffard* Lieutenant Ralph Flitton of Mount Royal, Que., was awarded Mention in Dispatches for "brave rescue work."

Lieutenant John Dyke of Cambridge, Ont., has his own reason to remember *Valleyfield*: "I was one of three Canadian engineer officers taking a course with the RN in London in the spring of 1944. Stan Howe and John Storey of Esquimalt, B.C., were the others. On completion, we received a signal to return to Londonderry to take passage to Canada. Wishing to spend our last weekend in London, Stan and I requested extension of leave till Monday as convoys were usually late. Permission granted. John Storey, being anxious to be sure of not missing the convoy, left on Friday.

"When Stan and I arrived Monday morn, the convoy was steaming up to leave and for the three of us there were two berths in *Valleyfield* and two berths in *Frontenac*. The frigate was more comfortable than the corvette and, naturally, we all wanted to make the trip in her. Thus, in navy tradition, we tossed a coin. As the coin hit the deck, I put my foot on it, saying to Stan that since we had had such a good time together in the last couple of weeks, why split up now? It was agreed we two would go aboard *Frontenac* and I put the coin in my pocket. When *Valleyfield* was sunk just off Newfoundland, John Storey never made it. But for the corvette, neither would we."

While the five *Valleyfield* fatalities brought in by *Giffard* were accorded a military funeral in St. John's, the circumstances of battle prevented funeral observances for their shipmates. In many cases of death at sea, burial was at sea, with the captain performing a brief ceremony following centuries-old tradition. *Giffard* crewman Bud Carr of Calgary, Alta., recalls one such occasion in June 1944: "We had a stoker [Thomas Langton of Belleville, Ont.] who also filled in as the ship's barber. One day he suffered a brain hemorrhage and passed away. They sewed his body up in canvas, weighed it down with a four-inch shell and we buried him at sea."

On June 8, Barry O'Brien of Ottawa, Ont., received recognition, Mention in Dispatches. His citation read: "For outstanding cheerfulness and devotion to duty, whilst serving as an officer in His Majesty's Canadian corvettes on escort duty in the North Atlantic since September 1940; Lieutenant O'Brien has at all times displayed the highest degree of initiative, energy and resourcefulness in encounters with the enemy. When promoted to command [HMCS *Snowberry*], his superior qualities of leadership, tact and unfailing good humour resulted in his having one of the happiest and most efficient ships in Newfoundland Command."

Allied control of the sea lanes continued in the first half of 1944. Shipping losses on the Atlantic averaged only 11 ships and 41,906 tons per month. U-boat losses in all theatres rose to 128 in the period and 518 for the war to date.

* * *

"We made a trip to Londonderry which was unremarkable except to say that it was the largest convoy crossing throughout the entire war — 167 ships delivered unmolested," says Stoker Bob MacIntosh, now in *Fennel*. Indeed, convoy HXS 300 left New York on July 17, 1944, with a close escort of seven RCN ships, one frigate and six corvettes. It also contained four MAC ships for air cover. The trip took 17 days. This was the zenith of the trend to larger convoys that allowed the Allies to concentrate their air cover and escorts. It also helped free up warships for hunting groups.

Changing roles affected some corvettes. The short-foc's'le *Rosthern* became a training ship out of Halifax. She was not alone. *Sackville* able seaman Jim Simpson explains: "*Sackville* continued on escort duty until July 1944, when she developed boiler problems and we were tied up in Londonderry for three or four weeks. We returned to Halifax in a convoy. Only a skeleton crew remained on board. We then began training officer cadets, sailing around the Nova Scotia coast doing gun shoots and navigational training. She was finally laid up in October for refit and the crew transferred to other duties."

Sackville's days as a fighting ship were over. She was converted to a loop-laying vessel. Later she was paid off, then recommissioned as a depot ship before finding a new career as a research ship, operated by the Department of National Defence for the Bedford Institute of Oceanography.

The RCN corvette *Hespeler* and frigate *Dunver* of Escort Group C 5 were credited with destroying *U-484* on September 10, 1944, after the Type VII C boat was located in U.K. waters near the Hebrides by an RCAF Liberator. The original credit was assigned soon after the war by the British Admiralty despite the C 5 senior officer's report that the contact was doubtful. That credit has now been reassigned to two British ships, the corvette *Portchester Castle* and the frigate *Helmsdale*, that were originally thought to have sunk *U-743*, which, in turn, is now assumed to have been lost to unknown causes.

On the evening of October 4, 1944, the RCN frigate *Chebogue* was struck in the stern by an acoustic torpedo while escorting convoy ONS 33 in mid-Atlantic. It became a case of corvettes to the rescue. *Arnprior* took off most of *Chebogue*'s crew, then transferred some to *Orangeville*. *Giffard* provided protection. *Chambly* then began a relay of sorts as a number of warships and an ocean-going tug towed the frigate to the U.K., where she later went aground off Wales in a gale and was so badly damaged she never fought again. Meanwhile, the convoy continued on its way to Newfoundland.

That excitement was the exception rather than the rule by October 1944. Coder H.J. Taylor, who served in *Agassiz* and *Tillsonburg*, comments: "By now the North Atlantic was a milk run, boredom our biggest problem. To some young sailors action stations was really something to get excited about, but to old hands it was a big change from the Battle of the Atlantic in 1942 and 1943."

There was something to get excited about on August 14, 1944. Petty Officer J.C. (Charlie) Hawkins of Stratford, Ont., tells the story:

I was the HSD in HMCS *Brandon*. While carrying out a depth charge attack in shallow waters north off Ireland, our electrical generator and switchboard were damaged by the explosion, forcing us back to Londonderry for repairs while the outward bound convoy we were escorting continued on its Atlantic crossing.

We left port three days later to proceed independently to St. John's, Newfoundland, to rejoin our group. South of Iceland we ran into very heavy seas, low visibility and rain squalls. As the ship

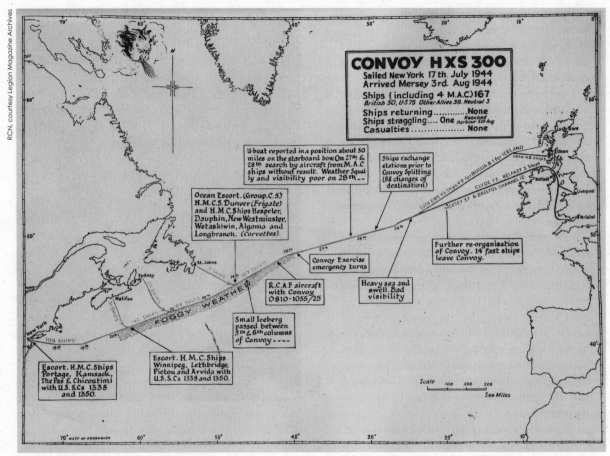

A chart of HXS 300, largest convoy of WWII.

was proceeding at the maximum speed that could be kept in such weather, the waves were breaking over the bow and foc's'le and smothering the upper decks. The water was entering the two air-intake ventilators forward of the anchor winch that went down to the chain locker and asdic compartment located in the bottom of the ship next to the bilge keel.

Being the HSD and responsible for the asdic compartment and its electrical and electronic equipment and realizing the damage salt water coming down the ventilator could do, I decided that the canvas covers for the ventilators should be installed at once. Leading Seaman Tom Dent and Able Seaman Tabernor and I dressed in rubber survival suits and seaboots and waited on the deck

between the wheelhouse and port railing for a subsided sea. I took off my lifebelt to be more agile for the short time we had to install the covers.

A lull came and Tabernor and I dashed out past the gun platform and proceeded to put on the covers. We had both covers on when suddenly the ship nosed into a tremendous wave. I yelled, "Hang on tight with your arms around the ventilator." We were buried under tons of water, which tore my grip from the ventilator, swept me past the starboard side of the gun platform and over to the starboard rail. I grabbed the rail but the water just slipped me over and my back hit the edge of the outboard deck as I was swept overboard. I looked and saw the ship sliding by. There were two off-duty stokers standing in the doorway at the break of the foc's'le and I shouted "Man overboard!" to them.

I was concerned right then that I would be drawn into the propeller but the huge seas took me clear. I saw the stern of the ship disappear in the distance and I realized I was all alone. I had a knife and a lanyard around my waist which, for a short time, trapped air in my rubber suit and helped keep me afloat. My suit filled with water so I lost all my buoyancy and had to swim hard to go through each wave and catch a breath in each trough. As I passed through waves which could have washed 30 to 50 feet of water over me, it was like entering a green cathedral and was very peaceful.

After fifteen minutes of this, I got mad. We were returning home and were scheduled for refit and leave. I had thoughts of just stopping swimming and letting myself drop into the two miles of water below me. A seagull changed this. I came out into a trough and found a great grey gull hovering a foot above my head. Knowing that they prey on the eyes of floating bodies, I was concerned that he would attack me, so I started to curse and scream at him after every pass through a wave. For me, it was a battle between the gull and me, never realizing that the gull would be my benefactor.

By this time the ship had travelled some distance and I had been reported overboard. The visibility was down to less than a mile. The captain, Lieutenant J.F. Evans, had taken the ship about and steered on a reciprocal course to search for me, knowing that in seas like this there would be only a small chance of finding me. The signalman on watch at last saw a seagull that flew up and down between the waves as if it had something to land on.

The captain altered course and found me. He let the ship drift down as it was too rough to launch a seaboat, and I was picked off the top of a wave that broached the funnel deck maybe twenty feet above the water. …Willing hands held on to me. Somebody started to give me artificial respiration and I was too tired to stop him. They took me down to the sick bay and tried to give me a double tot of Pusser's rum, but I did not have the energy to drink it. I think my friend Tom Dent drank it for

J.C. (Charlie) Hawkins in 1941 before he became a *Brandon* petty officer.

me and I heard someone remark, "Are you sure that was Hawkins we fished out of the sea? I've never seen him refuse a tot."

My friend the gull went off in the mist. My life was saved by a seagull.

Ron Batchelor, by now a *Brandon* leading seaman, remembers the event well. He was on watch on the starboard wing of the bridge:

What saved this lad was the appearance of a sole sea-bird. … I believe, however, that his salvation was attributable to an act of God. Without the intervention of the bird, he would have become too exhausted, gone under and we couldn't have found him. He treaded water for about 20 minutes. How he withstood the cold water was a miracle unto itself.

Charlie Hawkins, who died in 2000 at age 77, was touched by his miraculous escape, says his widow, June: "He did mention that it was just like a cathedral it was so quiet with that green wave going over him. He just felt his life was a bonus after that." Charlie is an example of the personal price some veterans pay as a result of their wartime experiences. June explains: "We got married in 1946. He had a lot of nightmares when he came home from the war. He was an asdic operator in cramped quarters and he was always claustrophobic after that."

* * *

With the U-boat threat diminishing and Canadian escort strength increasing, the Gulf of St. Lawrence was reopened to ocean-going traffic in the spring of 1944. The Battle of the St. Lawrence resumed when U-boats returned in September 1944.

The frigate *Magog* lost 60 feet of her stern to an acoustic torpedo from *U-1223* in the St. Lawrence River near Pointe-des-Monts, Que., on October 14 and was towed to Quebec. She was later scrapped. The Canadian grain carrier *Fort Thompson* was damaged by torpedo on November 2 in the same area.

The most significant casualty was the corvette *Shawinigan*, lost with all hands — seven officers and 83 men — on November 25, 1944, without getting off an emergency signal.

Files at Library and Archives Canada show that *Shawinigan* and a U.S. Coast Guard cutter, *Sassafras*, had escorted the ferry SS *Burgeo* on her regular run from Sydney to Port aux Basques on November 24, arriving at 1800 hours. The American ship was detached, leaving the corvette to escort the ferry alone on the return trip the next day.

Everyone was very conscious of the 1942 sinking of the ferry the *Caribou*, and instead of being allowed to put into port, *Shawinigan* was sent out alone on anti-submarine patrol overnight. This was a regular practice on the premise such a patrol would prevent a U-boat from lying in wait for the ferry the next morning. The practice was based on the questionable presumption a lone corvette could handle a snorkel U-boat in the gulf's difficult asdic conditions. *Shawinigan* took a route that had been cancelled, but it was similar to the intended course, so the shore authorities did not intervene, testimony at the board of inquiry revealed.

When *Shawinigan* did not show up next morning for the appointed rendezvous, Burgeo sailed to Sydney alone.

Thus it wasn't until the evening of November 25 that the corvette's absence was noticed. In the searches that followed, six bodies were recovered. Five were identified and each was buried in his home community. The unidentified sixth lies at Gaspé. The navy did not publicize this funeral for fear many families would think the victim was their kin.

The federal government sent a letter to Newfoundland's commissioner for public utilities complaining that the *Burgeo* committed "a serious breach" of standing orders, first by not reporting the corvette's failure to appear and second by proceeding alone. Signed by a deputy minister, W.G. Mills, the letter says, in part: "This action on the part of the master of the *Burgeo* may have cost the lives of any men who survived the destruction of HMCS *Shawinigan*; it might very easily have resulted in the destruction of SS *Burgeo* and her crew. ..." By the time *Burgeo* reached Sydney, few hours of daylight were left, "insufficient for a thorough search of the area in which the disaster occurred. If any of *Shawinigan*'s crew survived the loss of their ship during the night of the 24th to 25th, they may have lived through most of the day but hardly through the following night." The letter concluded: "The maintenance of regular steamship schedules, desirable and important as it is, must not be allowed to jeopardize the safety of ships and men of either Navy or Merchant Marine."

The board of inquiry couldn't establish the cause of the sinking, though it leaned towards a torpedo. Later, interrogation of the crew of *U-1228*, which surrendered to the U.S. Navy in May 1945, established that one acoustic torpedo did the job. The corvette sank quickly and there were further explosions, likely from some of her depth charges.

Long before she became Rose J. Murray of Calgary, Alta., she was Rose Lawrence of Saskatoon, Sask. She received a telegram and three letters from the naval secretary providing information about the fate of *Shawinigan* and her husband, Able Seaman Thomas Lawrence. The last letter, dated August 28, 1945, advised the widow that "the position of the sinking cannot be exactly ascertained, although from German evidence and the department's computation, it is estimated to be in the vicinity of the three-mile limit off Channel Head, near Port aux Basques, Newfoundland."

While November 25, 1944, has long been regarded as the date of the sinking, German records would make it November 24, at about 10:35 p.m. Atlantic Daylight Time. November 24 is the date the Canadian Agency of the Commonwealth War Graves Commission uses.

* * *

After World War II, the Commonwealth navies relied on the worldwide battle honours list created by the Royal Navy. The Battle of the Atlantic was prominent and several hundred Canadian warships qualified. In September 1992, the Governor General approved a new Canadian World War II battle honour — Gulf of St. Lawrence — to redress an oversight which stemmed from reliance on the British list. Recommended after a review by the Canadian Forces Honours Committee, the new honour recognizes convoy escort and patrol operations in the Gulf of St. Lawrence from Quebec City to the Cabot Strait and the Strait of Belle Isle, from May to October in 1942 and September to November in 1944.

There is no medal or other form of personal recognition involved. Battle honours are awarded only to named warships. They are designed to promote unit pride and *esprit de corps* among ships' companies, although they have the secondary benefit of commemorating worthwhile endeavours. Succeeding warships of the same name perpetuate honours. So, *Charlottetown* covers both the honour earned by the corvette *Charlottetown* in 1942 and the frigate *Charlottetown (2nd)* in 1944. Thus, 74 warships made the list, although 75 ships physically earned the gulf honour. Of the 75, 29 were corvettes, 29 minesweepers, 13 frigates and four armed yachts. As Canadian battle honours are only given to named ships, the smaller, numbered Fairmiles that served extensively in the gulf were not eligible.

The corvette list is:

1942 – *Brantford, Charlottetown, Hepatica, Kamloops, Kenogami, Kitchener, Lunenburg, Port Arthur, Trail, Ville de Quebec, Weyburn.*
1942 and 1944 – *Arrowhead, Lethbridge, Shawinigan, Summerside.*
1944 – *Agassiz, Amherst, Brandon, Camrose, Dawson, La Malbaie, Matapedia, Nanaimo, Norsyd, Prescott, Quesnel, Riviere du Loup, Snowberry, Wetaskiwin.*

The same review looked at Canadian naval operations on the Pacific coast, but declined to recommend a naval battle honour for that theatre. It noted that there was no engagement with the enemy, no Canadian ships were sunk and it was not necessary to form convoys there to protect shipping, as it was in the Gulf of St. Lawrence.

En route to Halifax, N.S., in 1944, *Fergus* passes through the Welland Canal linking Lake Erie and Lake Ontario.

* * *

In 1944, the RCN commissioned 20 increased endurance (IE) Flower-class corvettes rated for 7,400 miles at 10 knots. Eighteen of these 970-ton ships with extended foc's'le and water-tube boilers were built in Canada and two in the U.K. That completed the IEs at 31 vessels, with 27 built in Canada and four in the U.K.

The 1944 British-built RCN Flowers were laid down for the RN, so HMS *Candytuft* became *Long Branch* in January, and HMS *Bulrush* became *Mimico* in February.

The Canadian-built numbers were *Cobourg, Guelph* and *St. Lambert* in May; *Asbestos, Hawkesbury, Peterborough* and *Whitby* in June; *Parry Sound* in August; *Beauharnois* and *Stellarton* in September; *Belleville, Lachute* and *West York*

Courtesy Victor Large

Shipbuilder Henry Robb, Lady Darling and *Orangeville* captain Acting Lieutenant-Commander Rodney Pike display the ship's original crest presented by the builder.

in October; and *Fergus, Merrittonia, Smiths Falls, Strathroy* and *Thorlock* in November.

Crew members appreciated these ships. *Long Branch* captain Barry O'Brien says: "She was a great ship, larger and better equipped than the older corvettes. She was faster and required less fuelling at sea." An engine room view comes from *Strathroy*'s Bern Rawle: "She was a lovely ship. She was much roomier than poor old *Cobalt* and the mast was behind the bridge where it belonged. She also seemed better balanced and did not roll so badly."

These were the last of the RCN's Flowers. There were 111 RCN Flowers in all, with 107 built in Canada and four in the U.K. One hundred and one RCN Flowers were owned by Canada and 10 were on loan from the RN. Of the four distinct types, there were 65 at 950 tons with short

foc's'le and cylindrical boilers; five at 950 tons with short foc's'le and water-tube boilers; ten at 1,015 tons with extended foc's'le and water-tube boilers; and 31 at 970 tons with extended foc's'le and water-tube boilers.

Canada also got 12 Castle-class corvettes from the U.K. in 1944. These 12 Castles and the four increased-endurance Flowers built in the U.K. came to the RCN in exchange for Algerine-class ships designed as minesweepers and built in Canada.

The Castle-class was so named because the RN ships of this class were named after castles. Started for the RN, the dozen in question were no exception. Transferred to the RCN, each was commissioned in the name of a Canadian community, just like the 101 Flowers owned by the RCN.

Castle-class corvettes featured the 'squid' forward-throwing, anti-submarine weapon seen here in *Kincardine*.

The Castle-class corvette HMCS *Hespeler*.

Hespeler (formerly HMS *Guildford Castle*) was commissioned in February, *Orangeville* (*Hedingham Castle*) in April and *St. Thomas* (*Sandgate Castle*) in May. *Arnprior* (*Rising Castle*), *Huntsville* (*Wolvesey Castle*), *Kincardine* (*Tamworth Castle*), *Petrolia* (*Sherborne Castle*) and *Tillsonburg* (*Pembroke Castle*) came in June. *Copper Cliff* (*Hever Castle*) was a July arrival, followed by *Leaside* (*Walmer Castle*) in August and *Bowmanville* (*Nunney Castle*) and *Humberstone* (*Norham Castle*) in September.

Noting that his crew took across an American-built destroyer escort for the RN en route to collect *Orangeville* from her builder, Henry Robb Ltd. of Leith, Scotland, Acting Lieutenant-Commander Rodney Pike writes:

On April 24th the brass came from London and Niobe, and after a thorough inspection said they were pleased with Henry Robb's work. The padre arrived at 1530, followed by Ernest Brown, MP. Then Lady Darling, wife of the Lord Provost of Scotland, arrived in a big black Daimler car with an attendant in a red coat and top hat. The ship's company were fallen in on the quarterdeck, the padre blessed the ship and we sang "For Those in Peril on the Sea." Henry Robb presented us with the ship's badge and Lady Darling wished us "good hunting." The "still" was piped and the White Ensign was hauled up for the first time.

The Castles were a different nature of beast entirely. The early Flowers were 205 feet long, 33 feet across and displaced 950 tons. The Castles were 252 feet long, 36 feet across and displaced 1,060 tons.

The old Flowers had a World War I four-inch gun. *Louisburg* able seaman Gordon MacDonald describes its operation: "I was ammunition number on the foc's'le. I stood behind the gun and did the loading. First the projectile was rammed in, then a bag of cordite, then the breech was closed. The gun captain put in the cap and pulled the lanyard that fired the gun. It was obsolete then."

The Castles had a modern four-inch gun that took fixed ammunition — complete shells — and fired rapidly. It also elevated so it could be used against aerial targets in addition to surface ones. Ross Huffman recalls that *Bowmanville* would withdraw a bit from the convoy for gunnery practice: "On one occasion a buoy with its flag was dropped into the wake, then we sailed off smartly to open the distance for shooting. A smooth turn to port opened the target to the gun. Shoot! The first shot sunk the buoy. End of exercise."

Depth charges were the main weapon of the Flowers, which were equipped with four throwers and, at the stern, two rails plus storage racks, making for a cramped quarterdeck. The Castles had four throwers, but only one stern rail and carried far fewer charges, so the quarterdeck was uncluttered.

"The most significant difference from Flowers was 'squid,' a far more advanced anti-sub weapon than depth charges or 'hedgehog,'" says Lieutenant-Commander Mort Duffus, captain of *Bowmanville*. "A top-secret weapon at the time, squid could be trained on the target, in contrast to hedgehog where the ship had to be pointed at the target.

Kincardine looking fore.

The Castle-class *Kincardine* built in the U.K. had its own motor launch in which Wes Kaufman of Listowel, Ont., sits.

The combination of this with the latest asdic, which gave both distance and depth, was a great advance."

Hedgehog had twenty-four 32-pound bombs that exploded only on contact. Squid had three 100-pound bombs with adjustable depth settings, so the crew got the satisfaction of shaking up things every time. The firing was automated with the detection gear. It was a sophisticated weapon, arguably the best anti-submarine advance of the war. *Kincardine* stoker Morley Barnes says: "Man, this had force. Three columns of water would shoot up. Deck plates would lift, light bulbs would burst in their sockets. The ship would creak from one end to the other. When the squid was fired the job of the helmsman was to turn the ship hard to port or starboard, simply to avoid our own blast."

A distinctive lattice mast that bore a resemblance to a modern hydroelectric transmission tower went with the latest in radar. *Orangeville* radar operator Art Chinery comments: "One night in 1945, when my partner was Freddie Small, we scooped the escort group with a report of a ship that was on a collision course with the convoy. Our position was the stern sweep. This ship was well ahead of the convoy and a good eight miles nearer the lead escort than we were. Either they were asleep or our radar was working far better than theirs. I believe it was the latter because when we reported the contact it was at least 20 minutes before any other ship verified our contact. We made the headlines in the ship's newspaper."

Sleek in appearance, the Castles had a large bridge with wings and superior anti-aircraft mountings. Endurance was also great — 6,200 miles at 15 knots. Her top speed was 17 or 18 knots. Crew size was up to 112 — seven officers and 105 ratings, and living conditions were reasonable.

River-class frigates were superior to Castles as mid-ocean vessels in terms of size, length, crew complement, speed, twin-screw design and surface armament. The Castles, however, had the advantage in anti-sub capability with their squid.

* * *

The school of practical experience helped produce some beneficial change in another area. Bern Rawle comments: "When I look back to my *Cobalt* days in 1942, I realize how untrained and ill-equipped we were. Our training in many cases was learning on the job. We certainly were not provided with adequate, warm clothing and our life jackets were something like an oversized, canvas-wrapped sausage that was inflated by mouth. When I commissioned *Strathroy* in 1944, our life jackets were of a greatly improved type, a sort of flotation jacket with a triangular piece that passed between the legs and hitched to the top. This was to protect the intestines if you had the bad luck to have depth charges go off while you were in the water. Speaking of that, I'm not sure that keeping a man afloat in the North Atlantic was much of a kindness considering the water temperature. It probably would be kinder to let the poor bastard drown."

Alberni crewman Leo McVarish praises the new life jackets, noting that they also had a neck rest, lights and whistle. "They were the best in existence at the time," he says.

* * *

Archie Marsh of Abbotsford, B.C., survived service in three corvettes, but just barely: "The third corvette was HMCS *Matapedia,* K112. *Matapedia* was hit by a torpedo from *U-1231* on December 5, 1944, off the coast of Gaspe, but fortunately for those of us aboard, it did not explode." The corvette was escorting convoy QS 107 from Quebec to Sydney, N.S., when struck, but the torpedo — or at least its firing pistol — failed. Several days earlier, *U-1231* had three FAT torpedoes bounce of the hull of an unawares freighter. The torpedoes were duds.

On the morning of December 24, 1944, the RCN *Bangor*-class minesweeper *Clayoquot* was torpedoed and sank in the approaches to Halifax harbour. The corvette *Fennel* decided that because the water was cold, "rapid rescue was imperative," a file at the National Defence Directorate of

Christmas at sea aboard *Kincardine* in 1944.

History and Heritage indicates. While other RCN warships started to hunt for the U-boat, *Fennel* hauled numbed survivors aboard. Only four officers and four men were lost. "During the rescue operation, the corvette narrowly escaped sinking herself," the file notes. "Her CAT gear, streamed to protect her from acoustic torpedoes, exploded one." The heartbreaking incident did confirm that CAT gear could save lives and ships, and that looking for the killer before rescuing survivors was a sound practice.

Arrowhead, which reached Halifax on December 23, was one of the ships thrown into the search for *Clayoquot's* killer, *U-806*. Able Seaman Henry Kozlowski recalls: "Our ship spent Christmas and a few days afterwards hunting for the submarine. There was no leave coming because right afterwards we were sent out to escort another convoy. It was a long stretch at sea."

Norsyd stoker Tony Cebulski says: "On December 23 we had Christmas on board in Derry because we would be at sea on Christmas Day. On Christmas Day we sang carols on the upper deck. In the afternoon we had action stations four times, firing two patterns of hedgehog and 10 depth charges."

Owen Sound was in Derry and Signalman Charlie Bridle's log reads: "December 24 — Good old Sally Ann. Xmas dinner with all the trimmings. Just great to us. Over 50 of us at one sitting. Pub crawling later." And on December 25, he wrote: "Xmas in Londonderry. Decorated messdeck with signal flags. Presents of a sort exchanged. Slipped ashore at night. Pub crawling."

Being the youngest *Port Arthur* crewman, Ordinary Seaman René Gervais of Verdun, Que., upheld naval tradition: "Being Captain for a Day you splice the main brace and go around wishing everyone a Merry Christmas. You also inspect the ship. It only lasted about two hours because we were anchored waiting for orders to escort a convoy."

Aboard an eastbound *Chambly*, Yeoman of Signals George Dollis recalls Christmas Day in the Gulf Stream. The two youngest ratings exchanged positions with the captain and the first lieutenant for a brief spell. "This was done with great solemnity," then the officers were convicted of "some trumped-up misdemeanor, thus fulfilling the tradition."

Leading Cook Ivan McCabe was eastbound on the Newfie-Derry Run in *Orangeville*: "I had my 21st birthday on Christmas Day 1944. I remember cooking 24 chickens for Christmas dinner."

Rodney Pike, *Orangeville*'s skipper, says: "On Boxing Day the refrigeration of the MV *Samuel Chase* broke down and we went alongside and got tackle rigged to transfer sides of beef, lamb and chickens. I sent the master a bottle of whisky."

Orangeville leading seaman W. Leo Johnson remembers that transfer for another reason: "They shipped us across cases of Coca-Cola — enough for the whole crew and then some! Drinking Coke in mid-Atlantic — pretty nice, wouldn't you say?"

* * *

On the North Atlantic on December 27, 1944, at 0614, the Flower-class corvette *Edmundston* abandoned an asdic contact as non-sub. Coming along behind, the Castle-class corvette *St. Thomas* picked it up. Though classifying the contact as doubtful, she made two attacks with the for-

ward-throwing squid anti-submarine weapon within an hour. *St. Thomas* searched some more, but finally gave up and at 0819 she signalled her intention to return to eastbound convoy HX 327.

ERA Jim Shurrie recalls: "I was on the 4-to-8 watch in the engine room. Around 8 a.m. action stations were cancelled, so the 8-to-12 group took over in the engine room. We were just sitting down to breakfast when action stations were resumed."

The sub was sighted about 2.5 miles away at 0824. *St. Thomas* attacked immediately, firing her four-inch gun, but pulled up when it became clear the vessel was being abandoned by the crew, who launched two inflatable rafts. "My post was on the boarding party," Shurrie adds. "As we were lowering our longboat for the boarding party to go to the sub to try to salvage it, *U-877* gracefully sank. The most relieved man in the navy was me."

Stoker Petty Officer Don Cameron of Oromocto, N.B., recalls: "I finished my watch below in the boiler room and came topside just in time to see the sub come to the surface in two sections and then go below the surface. We had the scramble nets over the side and there were German sailors in the water and on life rafts."

All 55 U-boat crew members survived, *St. Thomas* picking up four officers and 30 ratings and the RCN frigate *Sea Cliff* collecting one officer and 20 ratings. Two heavy underwater explosions were heard at 0835.

Archival files show that subsequent questioning of survivors revealed the corvette's second squid attack caused severe leaks all over the hull of *U-877*. In what must have been anxious moments for the crew, the Type IX C-40 boat "sank stern first at an angle of about 40 degrees and went down to the unprecedented depth of 350 metres (previous maximum depth recorded 320 metres). Prisoners reported that at this depth the pressure hull could be heard bending. By going full speed ahead and blowing all tanks, the U-boat was able to come to about 160 metres where the captain attempted to maintain depth and proceed slowly ahead. This was found to be impossible. ..."

The engineer officer now reported that the only chance of survival was to surface, so the U-boat came up under the power of one electric motor, with the pressure inside rising steadily. When the hatch was opened, "the first two men were blown at least 50 feet into the air," says *St. Thomas* ERA Shurrie. Another report has four men being blown out of the sub. The German crew members were fortunate, suffering only relatively minor lacerations.

This was the RCN's first squid kill. It occurred in mid-Atlantic northwest of the Azores. *St. Thomas* continued on to the U.K. with her prisoners. "Our survivors ranged in age from 17 to 27, that one being the captain," says Don Cameron. They were very good prisoners except for one who was the youngest and who would not let anyone near him. He hid under the mess table." Don's widow, Georgie, observes: "Don didn't talk about the war much, but he did remark on how young the German sailors were. He said they were nervous that they would be walked onto one side of the ship and off the other. They were relieved when they saw that they would become prisoners."

ERA Dan McPhee of Sydney, N.S., has the last word on the incident: "I was the only engineer to survive the aerial torpedo attack on *Louisburg* in February 1943. Later I was aboard *St. Thomas* when she alone sank a German submarine. So, they put me in the water once and I helped put them in the water once. For me, the game evened out."

The Allies dominated the shipping routes in the second half of 1944. Losses on the Atlantic averaged only nine ships and 42,721 tons per month. U-boat losses in all theatres were 111 for the period, 239 for the year and 629 for the war to date.

Couresty Georgie Cameron

U-877 crew members are helped up scramble nets on the side of St. Thomas.

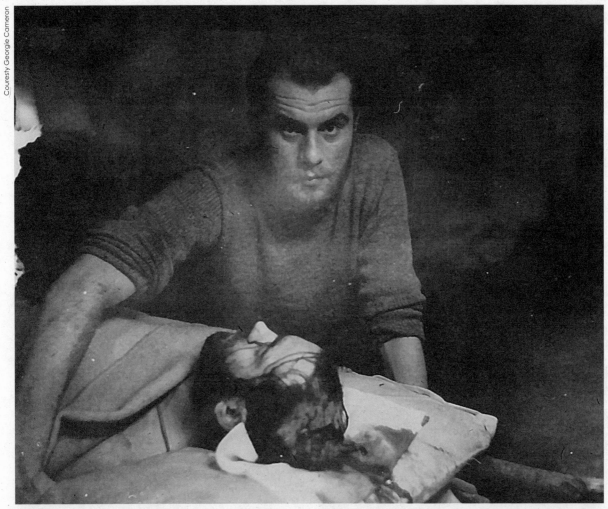

U-877 CO *Kapitanleutnant* Eberhard Findeisen was injured December 27, 1944, when his boat was sunk by the corvette *St. Thomas.*

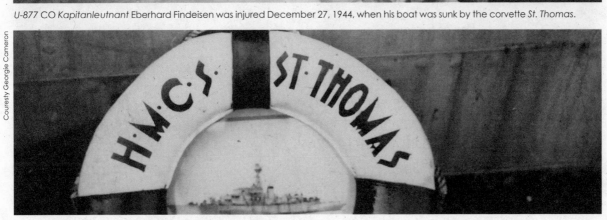

A certain corvette's life preserver.

Couresty Georgie Cameron

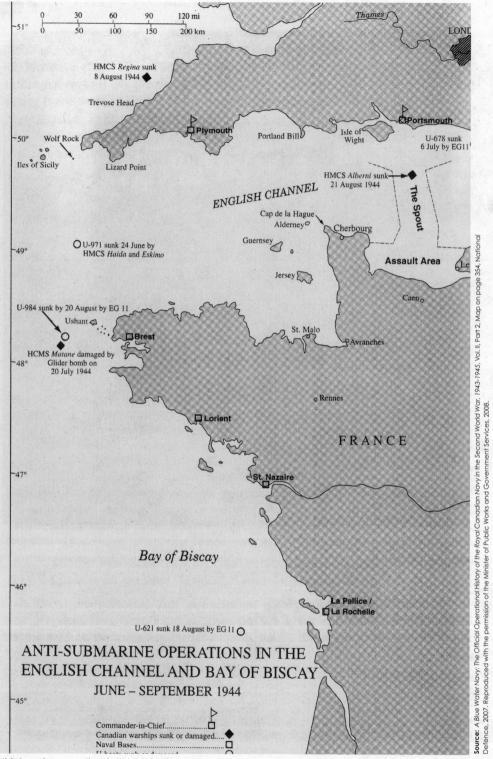

ANTI-SUBMARINE OPERATIONS IN THE
ENGLISH CHANNEL AND BAY OF BISCAY
JUNE – SEPTEMBER 1944

Anti-Submarine operations in the English Channel and Bay of Biscay, June-September 1944.

Source: A Blue Water Navy: The Official Operational History of the Royal Canadian Navy in the Second World War, 1943-1945, Vol. II, Part 2, Map on page 354, National Defence, 2007. Reproduced with the permission of the Minister of Public Works and Government Services, 2008.

CHAPTER FIFTEEN

"A FEW DAYS LATER WE LEARNED THAT WE HAD BEEN SEARCHING FOR GLENN MILLER.... NO WRECKAGE WAS EVER FOUND."

D-DAY IS synonymous with the year 1944 and Canada's corvettes played a role in the Allied invasion of Normandy and the run-up to it. "During the spring of 1944, we spent most of our time around the English Channel, convoying goods being gathered in southern England for the invasion of France," recalls *Regina* electrical artificer George Sims. "Our home port was Milford Haven in Wales, but we also ran out of Portsmouth, Plymouth, Southend on Sea and other ports in the Channel. Some nights we worked with a group of British destroyers, patrolling the Channel on the lookout for German surface craft or subs.

"We generally felt the invasion was not far off, but we did not know when we started out with our convoy on June 5, 1944, that this was it. Everything was put back one day because of the weather, so we started out again on June 6 to cross the Channel. All day long the sky was filled with Allied aircraft heading to France and returning to their bases in England. The first troops had landed on the continent. We arrived early in the morning of June 7 with our troops and supply ships, in the middle of what appeared to be organized confusion.

"It is not likely that we will ever see the number of ships gathered in one area as there were on June 7, 1944. From our position, I guess five or six miles offshore, to the horizon east and west it was a solid mass of ships of every description, from tiny minesweepers and corvettes to destroyers, cruisers, battleships and freighters."

Confusion indeed. Operation Overlord, the invasion of Normandy, created an unparalleled concentration of ships, men and aircraft. Operation Neptune was the codename for the naval plan. The RCN alone contributed a number of vessels for various tasks: 13 destroyers, 11 frigates, 19 corvettes, 16 minesweepers, two large landing ships and a slew of motor torpedo boats and infantry landing craft.

The Neptune corvettes were *Alberni, Baddeck, Calgary, Camrose, Drumheller, Kitchener, Lindsay, Louisburg (2nd), Lunenburg, Mayflower, Mimico, Moose Jaw, Port Arthur, Prescott, Regina, Rimouski, Summerside, Trentonian, Woodstock.*

Kitchener escorted landing craft, and appears to have been the sole Canadian corvette to reach the invasion beaches on June 6. The others were at sea with slow convoys or were earmarked for a subsequent wave. *Trentonian* able seaman Jack Scott says: "D-Day was something one would never forget. The amount of traffic was tremendous. A ship carrying Canadian soldiers passed us and recognized the maple leaf on our stack [funnel]. They waved and hollered at us. The Allied aircraft overhead were marked with black and white stripes on their wings. Flight after flight passed overhead at various levels. A British battleship was continuously firing, apparently being used for artillery support for the army. The shell casings piled on her deck looked like cordwood."

Mimico lieutenant George Angus recalls: "We moved off at 0400 on June 6 escorting 54 auxiliary landing craft carrying (field) kitchens, hospitals, machine shops, and so on. Seas were rough and we were only doing about 3 knots. We anchored offshore that night. We were near some of the big British battleships that were firing all night. I never saw a fireworks display like it — star shells and tracers all night." *Mimico* able seaman Ed Gaudet of

203

Mississauga, Ont., adds, "When all guns opened fire, it was very scary, gun flashes in all directions."

Louisburg (2nd) helped escort an unusual convoy, says First Lieutenant Murray Knowles: "We had 60 block ships — very old merchant ships and oil tankers including one pre-World War I French battleship. These old ships were manned with brave skeleton crews and each hulk fitted with special valves and seacocks to allow each ship to sink on even keel. We arrived without incident on June 7. The ships were sunk in line bow to stern in six to eight fathoms of water close in to the Normandy beaches. The main purpose was to create an emergency seawall to break the heavy seas. This was followed up by the placement of the famous mulberries — large concrete caissons that formed an artificial floating harbour."

Two mulberries were built to resupply the advancing Allied armies until ports could be captured and opened to shipping. A fierce storm destroyed one of the artificial harbours. The mulberries became famous as a feat of ingenuity and engineering. Some of their hulking remains are still very visible today during low tide at Arromanches in the American sector of Normandy.

Port Arthur stoker A.J. Ross of Regina, Sask., says: "We were the second wave, to escort Americans into Omaha Beach early the morning of June 7. We could hear the guns, see flashes and see dust rising above the shore as we sailed closer. The big battleships were sending shells miles inland. Small ships and landing craft were landing men and material on the beach. I saw bodies and equipment float by."

Prescott able seaman Sam Leslie of Rexdale, Ont., recalls:

We arrived on D plus one. The Allies had progressed inland and there wasn't too much to see from the ship. Some of the larger ships were still shelling inland. After dropping off our convoy, we tied up to a hospital ship and went on board to distribute cigarettes, candy and a word of cheer. Many of these young men had just arrived and were already heading back. Their war was over, but not their pain and suffering.

We found bodies floating in the Channel and picked up five to give them a proper burial. Being a gunner, it was my duty to help prepare them for burial. After removing their ID, which was turned

over to the proper authorities, we sewed the men up in hammocks which we weighted with practice shells from the four-inch gun. We then cleared lower decks and had a proper burial at sea. This was done as we sailed towards our next convoy which we were to meet in mid-Channel.

The preparation of these men for burial did not bother me during the fact because it was a job that had to be done. But when I returned to my watch station, I became quite shook up. The officer of the watch noticed me and told me to report to the quarterdeck to receive my pay for preparing these men for burial. The pay turned out to be a tot of rum, which certainly helped settle my nerves.

At about 2 a.m. on June 11, action stations sounded. USS *Partridge*, a sea-going tug towing a mulberry, had been torpedoed by a U-boat. We first started to chase the sub, but returned to rescue the tug's crew of about 100. We lowered a sea-boat and put a scramble net over the side. My mate and I were the first to go over the side on the scramble net. We were about waist deep in the water so that we could assist the survivors out of the water and up the net onto the ship. All the survivors were coated with oil. Most of them were in night attire. We picked up a total of 55 survivors while another corvette picked up about 40 more.

Five of the men we picked up died and had to be buried at sea. We headed for a hospital ship off the coast of Normandy where we dropped off those needing medical attention. Our SBA did a super job throughout the night taking care of the wounded. I spent the rest of the night looking after a man with a serious head wound. We discharged the balance of the survivors at Portsmouth. The action of our ship's company was something to be proud of and earned us a splicing of the main brace.

Trentonian telegraphist Tom Farrell recalls: "The lower decks were sealed off to everyone but the ones who had duty below. We were standing double watches — four hours on duty, four off — so it was tough to get a decent rest. On June 13, we were escorting a ship that was laying cable across the Channel to France. During the night we were fired on by an American destroyer and a number of fellows on the cable layer, the *Monarch*, were killed or wounded. I slept through the whole mess and was not aware of what had gone on till I lined up for breakfast and found a bunch of strange faces in line. I later found out that a few more of my shipmates had also slept right through the episode."

In 15 minutes the destroyer had fired 80 rounds of 5-inch shells. They went right over the corvette, which had a low profile, and destroyed the cable ship. At least four men died and more than 20 were badly injured. The corvette and the cable ship insisted they had followed proper procedures in identifying themselves, while the destroyer claimed she had received no reply to her challenge. No action was apparently taken against the aggressor. The friendly-fire incident seems to have been written off as one of those unfortunate things that happen in the fog of war. Indeed, friendly-fire incidents once again involving American and Canadian forces, this time in Afghanistan, have recently reminded Canadians of the dangers of the battleground.

Jim Elmsley of Toronto, Ont., CO of two Channel corvettes, *Louisburg (2nd)* and *Mimico*, analyses the theatre: "Like the Atlantic escort duties, this was also an anti-submarine function, but in addition protection from surface attacks by German motor torpedo boats, called E-boats, became important. We were fitted with additional 20mm cannons for surface action and anti-aircraft defence.

"E-boats usually attacked at night and could be detected with radar by their hydrophone effect. Once their course and speed had been plotted, the strategy was to create a pool of light in their path by firing an array of star shell. The enemy were usually unwilling to be exposed to whatever might greet them if they carried on, and would take off. They would also respond to live fire by dropping buoyant containers of gasoline, which would be ignited by timed explosive devices to create the impression the boat had been hit.

"*Louisburg (2nd)* was successful on a number of occasions in protecting convoys from attack. Because of our lack of speed, we had to play a defensive role and not expose our convoy to any end-run tactics."

Murray Knowles recalls the night of June 13 when *Louisburg (2nd)*, *Camrose* and *Baddeck* were escorting cement blocks for the mulberries. Asdic and radar crews identified two E-boats approaching:

Suddenly the captain ordered "Open fire! Fire star shell!" Immediately, two E-boats became visible in the illumination. We responded with continuous four-inch high explosive shells. Within a few minutes, *Camrose* opened fire, too.

We heard enemy aircraft overhead. Our ship was suddenly exposed as if in broad daylight when the enemy dropped a flare. An anti-aircraft gun fired rounds by the hundreds. Moments later, rockets and star shell from our gun exposed the E-boats crossing ahead, somewhat too close. Again all our firepower was directed on the targets. Suddenly a terrific explosion occurred close above in the air and not far from our stern. We assumed one of the enemy aircraft had been hit and exploded.

The action continued for 45 minutes and we met with a goodly amount of shellfire from both sea and air. Finally we put the naval attackers on the run and our aircraft dispersed the raiders from the sky. During the action the E-boats tried to get into position to fire torpedoes. The captain of *Camrose* claimed one torpedo had passed under his stern. Our 4-inch gun had fired 140 salvos, leaving dozens of empty shells lying all around the gun deck. We had to kick them over the side into the Channel. We also fired several thousand rounds from the Oerlikon guns and several hundred from our pom-pom gun.

Moose Jaw lieutenant Max Corkum recalls June for another reason: "The area just off the invasion beaches was littered with lost supplies which floated off ships that had been sunk. Our boys fashioned spears with hooks which they would throw and bring the cartons on board. All sorts of things were recovered. Food items or cigarettes were the real prizes. Frequently we sighted bodies. The first time we provided a proper burial. He was a German soldier. After that we simply reported the sighting and a specially equipped boat would follow up."

In late June, while towing a disabled landing craft, *Moose Jaw* had an aerial encounter, says Corkum: "I arrived at my action station on the bridge in the dark just in time to get a glimpse of what we all identified as a Junkers 88 flying over the ship. We did not get a shot away. The watch on deck said the torpedo bomber had come in low over the water and dropped two torpedoes which had gone under the tow line. The plane must have had a big target on radar and fired at the centre which, fortunately for us, was the tow line."

Things eventually settled down, *Calgary* lieutenant Mac Orr says: "The escort work became very routine. There were, of course, moments of action. One night a German destroyer sank an American sea-going tug a couple of miles ahead of us. We picked up all the survivors and took the injured to a hospital ship."

* * *

Traffic for France was organized into two major streams, one coming from the Bristol Channel and the other from the Thames Estuary. RCN corvettes escorted small convoys along the coast from Milford Haven in southwestern Wales to Sheerness in eastern England. Sometimes they stopped at ports along the way. Other times, merchant ships either joined or left the convoy, or there was a change in escorts. *Trentonian* able seaman Jack Scott says: "For several months we convoyed ships from Wales to France. As we sailed east along the south coast of England, ships would come out of ports and join our convoy. Eventually we would head across the Channel to France. Usually these trips were slow and uneventful."

Jim Elmsley says: "One of our greatest difficulties was terrible thick fogs. Not only did they obscure our convoy from the enemy, but also we could not see each other. The channels swept for the convoys [to clear mines] were heavily used, and ships did not always stay in the starboard half. It is hard to imagine the horror of picking up on our radar an approaching convoy on a collision course with our own. The procedure was to order course alterations by means of signal blasts in Morse code on our sirens. Such signals were often not understood by many of the ships' captains, and the chaotic situations which developed in the swirling fog were awful."

Detection of submarines was complicated by the existence of many shipwrecks on the sea bottom, particularly in the English Channel. Elmsley explains: "These would give our asdic a contact identical to that of a submarine. We had wreck charts which were accurate, but not up to date. To be safe, we would carry out a depth charge attack and subsequently make runs over the object using our echo sounder to see if the shape of the outline traced on the depth recorder paper could help in identifying the type of vessel. The fact that the contact was motionless did not rule out the possibility that it could be a submarine playing possum."

Al Keenliside on *Port Arthur's* Oerlikon gun in 1944.

Although he did not have a lot of Channel time, Barry O'Brien can attest to that from his 1944-45 term as CO of *Long Branch*: "We did pound hell out of a great contact in the Channel, oil slicks surfacing with considerable debris. We broke radio telegraphy silence to report to Admiralty, but our joy was somewhat contained when we received a terse signal, 'Check your wreck charts.' We had been attacking a U-boat victim lying on the bottom."

In addition to U-boats and E-boats, mines were a problem. Paths were cleared by minesweepers, but it was an ongoing concern because mines would be dropped regularly by German planes, fast attack boats or even U-boats. *Regina* ERA Tom Baird recalls: "One day we came across a floating mine, so the Oerlikon gunners all had a go at sinking it, but nothing happened. Then the pom-pom crew did not fare any better. Our head gunner on the four-inch gun was an Indian from B.C. He could hardly wait for his chance to show his ability. In order for him to get the range, we had to move away to the point you had to really get your eye on the mine to see it. Well, his first shell just went over the top. The second hit that mine dead-on."

Aircraft were not a constant threat, but a serious one. Asdic operator Leo McVarish relates one incident: "For *Alberni*, activity became monotonous until July 26 off the Normandy coast. The ship's radio crackled, 'Two Junkers 88 in your area laying mines.' Action stations were rung. One of the minelayers was off our starboard beam and the guns were spitting fire in no time. Within seconds, the *Alberni* gun crews had shot down a German plane. The 20mm Oerlikons and the 2-pounder pom-pom did the damage. There were no survivors. There was much rejoicing afterwards."

A report in the Directorate of History and Heritage confirming the aircraft kill also says: "Two nights later *Alberni* was near-missed by a mine dropped from aircraft." It notes the corvette also attacked an asdic contact that day and set off a mine 200 yards off her starboard beam. No damage was sustained.

In August, *Mimico* was assigned to Operation PLUTO (pipe laying under the ocean). To supply the Allied armies in Europe with fuel, 20 submerged pipelines were laid across the Channel, 16 from the Isle of Wight to Cherbourg and four from Dungeness to Boulogne. The job would start from the French coast. Albert Brooks says: "We were kept on this run for three or four trips. It was mainly uneventful with air support and plenty of warships on hand. Some of the pipes were laid from huge floating drums, and then from cable-laying ships." Able Seaman Ed Gaudet recalls one hitch: "One time while we were laying the pipeline, we dropped anchor and it got caught on the [submerged] pipeline. We had a difficult time to release it."

August 1944 was a black month for the Channel corvettes. On August 8, *Regina* was bound for the Normandy beachhead as the lone escort to EBC 66, a convoy of 11 ships. Eight miles off the Cornish coast, at 1930 hours, the merchant ship *Ezra Weston* suffered an explosion and reported it was caused by a mine. *Regina,* zigzagging about a mile ahead of the convoy, headed for the disabled vessel. An effort was made to beach the 7,200-ton American ship, but she began to settle by the bows. *Regina* stopped engines and stood near as *Landing Ship Tank 644* took off *Ezra Weston's* crew, save for four who would stay aboard. The LST then began to tow the merchantman towards shore. Suddenly there was a tremendous explosion and *Regina* went under just like that.

ERA John Reuvers of Las Vegas, Nevada, says: "The captain rang stop engines, which to me was odd because we were the only escort to the convoy. I went up the ladder and went aft. Standing on two depth charges, I could see men in the water from a torpedoed ship. The next thing I was blown perhaps 100 feet in the air, came down and landed on the propeller and went down with the ship for about 20 feet. After I surfaced, all I had on was my T-shirt and hat, almost in the proper rig of the day for heaven."

Leading Seaman Archie Marsh says: "I was standing on the stern with a number of mates. We were all thrown to the deck by the force. A wall of water immediately swept over us. I still recall vividly that I was being violently twist-ed and turned by turbulent water. How deep I had been dragged is impossible to say. My thoughts were strange. I was going to drown, but was not in panic. Suddenly I shot to the surface, wiping my eyes. Straight ahead I could see the bow of *Regina* standing straight up. With a loud roaring, hissing sound she plunged rapidly down. In a few seconds all that was left was the gurgling of air bubbles rising to the surface."

The sea was an oil slick. ERA Tom Baird comments: "I suppose most people have had a good sunburn in their day. Well, that is nothing compared to getting soaked in Bunker C oil for an hour or two. It takes days to get back to normal."

Electrical Artificer George Sims says: "As a true prairie sailor, I cannot swim a stroke and I had never been in the water with my life jacket. I consider that vest the best piece of equipment that the navy supplied me."

An air force crash boat was first on the scene, followed by *LST 644.* Though a sailor on each side of him was killed, *Regina* SBA William Oneschuk survived: "I was injured but carried on. An ERA by the name of [Lionel] Racker who joined the ship the previous day was injured. I heard his screams. I went to his assistance and to my surprise his left leg below the knee was severed to the hanging point. I was required to assist in the amputation of Racker's leg on the LST deck by Dr. Grant Gould, our ship's doctor."

Tom Baird says: "The doctor gave the ERA a healthy drink of rum supplied by the LST skipper. Then while three or four held the ERA, the doctor finished the job." Flashlights provided the only illumination during the amputation on the LST's quarterdeck, where other wounded were also treated. The operation was a success. Lionel Racker of Montreal did not pass away until 1992 at the age of 83. The doctor and the SBA, both injured themselves, were among those decorated for helping the wounded.

It's estimated *Regina* sank in 28 seconds. Amazingly the death toll was only 30; there were 63 survivors. A file at Library and Archives Canada notes the board of inquiry concluded that, on the evidence available, "it is not possible to form a decided opinion as to whether the *Ezra Weston* and HMCS *Regina* were torpedoed or mined." However, *Regina*'s captain, Lieutenant Jack Radford of Sydney, N.S., was officially informed that he "made a grave error of judgment" in permitting his ship to remain stopped in the vicinity of the damaged merchantman.

On a minute sheet attached to the report and memo of censure, a senior officer's handwritten note says: "A single escort under such circumstances is in a tough spot as he cannot possibly provide A/S [anti-submarine] protection for a convoy of 10 ships. It seems to me that the correct procedure would have been to remain in the vicinity carrying out a square search around the damaged ship on the assumption that she might have been torpedoed, not mined."

One of the cardinal rules of sea warfare is that, unless you have a protective screen, you do not stop your ship lest you become a sitting duck. That Radford was not subjected to a penalty more severe than censure was probably influenced by three factors: *Ezra Weston's* captain thought she had been mined; there was no prior evidence U-boats were operating in the Bristol Channel at that time; and a serious effort was underway to save the American ship.

Post-war examination of German records revealed that both *Regina* and *Ezra Weston* were sunk by *U-667*. The Type VII C boat soon shared *Regina's* fate. Returning to its French port, the U-boat struck a mine in the Bay of Biscay on August 25, 1944, and was lost with all 45 hands.

On August 21, *Alberni* was lost while steaming alone in the Channel southeast of the Isle of Wight. The explosion occurred on the port side by the engine room. She broke up and sank instantly, with 59 dead and only 31 survivors. Leading Seaman Bob Carson says: "I had just drawn my rum — never did get it down me. Bang. I grabbed my life jacket from an overhead rack. I stepped up on the gunwale and started to swim."

Able Seaman Leo McVarish of Winnipeg, Man., says the men were just changing shift at lunchtime. He was in the seamen's mess and recalls: "*Alberni*, was still short foc's'le. That's why I was able to get out. I would never have got out otherwise, I'm sure. Everyone is scrambling to get free. A couple of us move over to the port side and start up the ladder to the foc's'le. We go no further. We are drawn under into the sea. It's pitch black. My life jacket is lost. At first I don't feel the cold. It starts to get lighter and finally I reach the surface. I feel no pull as I hurriedly swim away. I'm afraid some depth charges might go off. My watch stopped at 1145. That's when I hit the water. The whole episode happened so fast. Any hesitation was fatal. She just went down like a shot. … I keep going over it in my head, timing it, and I think it was 12 seconds, that's all."

The survivors were in the water about 45 minutes before being picked up by two Royal Navy motor torpedo boats which were returning to their base in Plymouth. Whether the sinking was caused by mine or torpedo was not clear for some years. Eventually, post-war examination of German records identified the Type VII C *U-480*. That U-boat was in turn sunk in the Channel in February 1945, probably by a mine, although the kill was originally credited to two British frigates before reassessment.

* * *

In September 1944 *Algoma*, *Snowberry* and *Ville de Quebec* joined the RCN Channel corvettes. The weather struck *Algoma* leading stoker Art Kellythorne of Vancouver, B.C.: "One trip we could not carry on due to heavy fog and had to halt the convoy. Down below in the engine room and boiler room, we figured we were a prime target for enemy submarines. We were constantly on alert — and on edge! The main object was to keep the steam up, in case we had to move. Anyway, after about 24 hours the fog started to lift and we could see the mast-tops of the merchant ships. What a relief for all! We were soon on our way."

Also in September convoys being escorted through the Straits of Dover in daylight were being shelled from Calais. For protection, says *Mimico* lieutenant George Angus, "All escorts had to lay down smokescreens, and several low-flying aircraft dropped smoke flares."

Then came relief. Angus explains: "In late September while tied to our buoy we were rammed by a British destroyer coming downstream. Appears as if there was a mix-up between the captain and the helmsman. Quite a bit of structural damage, but all above the water line. Never saw such a happy crew, all yelling, 'Leave!' It was a good three weeks before we were back in action."

Not all was drama or drudgery. *Port Arthur* CO K.T. Chisholm of Oakville, Ont., says: "While in Portsmouth the fall of 1944, two of my enterprising crew captured a tethered goat on Southsea Common and brought it aboard ship. How they got it through the dockyard gate, guarded by Royal Marines, I will never know. However, the incident was reported and we received a visit from police. Our boys were, of course, charged and fined five pounds."

As the Allied armies moved inland on the continent, the destinations of convoys changed so that goods could be delivered as close to the front as safely possible. *Mimico*

Courtesy Hoot Gibson

Two crew members paint *Port Arthur* from a staging.

lieutenant George Angus says: "In late November we left Sheerness with a convoy for Flushing, Holland — the first convoy to go in there. We had two warnings to look out for three German destroyers and E-boats which were in the area, but luckily we never saw them. The town had taken quite a beating. It appeared as if every house had some damage and dockyard buildings were demolished. While we were at anchor, sweepers exploded four magnetic mines in the channel we had entered. I guess our degaussing equipment was working properly."

Snowberry leading telegraphist George Mackay of Victoria, B.C., recalls night runs escorting barges to Le Havre and Ostend, Belgium. He says: "These were dangerous waters. I can remember receiving a message one night saying we were in the centre of an area that had been laid with shallow oyster mines. Fortunately, we managed to get clear."

Max Corkum describes a *Moose Jaw* assignment a few weeks later: "On a return trip with a convoy of empties, we were detached to look for a downed plane between Dover and Le Havre. All we knew was that an important person in a small plane had not arrived at a destination in France and was presumed to have gone down in the Channel. It was a very dark night and there was a moderate sea running. We searched all night, firing star shell for illumination. A number of Royal Air Force planes also flew over and dropped parachute flares. We never saw a sign of anything. A few days later we learned that we had been searching for Glenn Miller, the well-known band leader. No wreckage was ever found."

Major Glenn Miller, United States Army, was a passenger in a single-engine Noorduyn Norseman which

disappeared the night of December 15, 1944, while en route from the U.K. to France. The legendary leader of the big band sound, he was going to Paris ahead of his service band to make plans for a big Christmas show. It's now believed the tiny plane was the victim of friendly fire — bombs from above. Their mission to Germany aborted, a wave of 139 Lancaster bombers returning to the U.K. released their payload over the English Channel because it would have been extremely dangerous to land with a full bomb load. Unfortunately, a bomb struck and destroyed the 32-foot Norseman, which seated a maximum of 10 passengers.

The crew of HMCS *Mimico* organized a special Christmas gift. "We had a Christmas party for 115 kids in a church hall in Sheerness," explains Able Seaman Ed Gaudet. We helped decorate the tree and we served the tables. We had clowns, puppets and presents for all. We had a good time." A heading in a local newspaper declared, "Blue Town Children in the Seventh Heaven of Delight!" The story painted a glowing picture of the sailors' generosity towards the children from the poorer part of war-damaged Sheerness, one of the corvette's regular ports of call.

Although there is agreement on credit for the vast majority of U-boat kills, confusion can reign when trying to sort out credit for kills when no tangible evidence is collected at the scene because neither the boat nor convincing debris surfaced. Even when reassessments are involved after a thorough search of both Allied and German records, there can be disagreement.

Take, for example, December 29, 1944. *Calgary* was one of two escorts for the Channel convoy TBC 21 with 20 merchant ships. After a merchant ship was sunk, *Calgary* carried out a depth charge attack on a suspected submarine. When another ship was sunk, *Calgary* picked up a good echo and attacked again. Three Royal Navy frigates took over the search and *Calgary* moved on with the convoy. That night, a Wellington aircraft from 407 Squadron RCAF sighted a snorkel and was credited with destroying *U-772* with six depth charges.

Now, however, based on the discovery of a U-boat wreck near the site of *Calgary's* second attack, the Naval Historical Branch of the Admiralty has awarded the kill to the Canadian corvette. Axel Niestle, a major German authority, does not accept this reassessment and continues to credit 407 Squadron.

At the same time, Chris Bishop, a British source

The corvette *Trentonian* enters a harbour in the U.K. on June 17, 1944.

specializing in German forces, has a third interpretation: *Calgary* actually sunk *U-322* on December 29 with all 52 hands; *U-322* had previously been credited to the British frigate *Ascension* on November 25, 1944. Bishop believes the British frigate *Nyasaland* sunk *U-722* on December 17; previously *Nyasaland* was thought to have sunk *U-400* that day. Bishop opines that *U-400* was probably sunk by a mine on or after December 15, and also that the 407 Squadron Wellington made an unsuccessful attack on *U-486* on December 29, rather than a successful attack on *U-772*. Do you get the picture? It's as clear as mud.

Max Corkum recalls New Year's Eve in *Moose Jaw*: "We were at sea. At midnight, there was a loud clatter from the engine room and boiler room. The new year was being rung in by the ringing sounds of tools being struck together."

Not long afterwards, *Moose Jaw* had a close call, Max

Corkum says: "We were coming up the north Cornish coast one dark night when the starboard lookout shouted, 'Dark object in the water dead ahead!' I picked it up in my binoculars immediately and saw it was a mine. I shouted 'Hard a-port!' to the quartermaster and pushed action stations at the same time. The mine was so close that after the bow swung clear, I had to go 'Hard a-starboard!' to swing the rest of the hull clear. By now all the ship's company had gathered at the starboard side to see the ugly mine with its shining horns passing down the side of the ship. Not a word was spoken. When clear, we sank it with gunfire. I still remember the starboard lookout's name — Nash — who was from Glace Bay, N.S. Had we hit that, the loss of life in the forward messdecks would have been heavy."

In February, *Trentonian* became the 10th and last RCN corvette lost in World War II. She was torpedoed by the Type VII C *U-1004* near Falmouth on February 22, 1945.

Six men died, 95 survived. Telegraphist Tom Farrell recalls: "I was on duty when our ship got hit and we were in touch with Falmouth as our convoy was under attack. When the torpedo struck, it hurled Phil Kevins my coder across the wireless shack and his knee smashed my nose. We managed to scramble up and get a message off that we had been hit. I'll always remember it: YSP in the particular code we were using meant that we were torpedoed astern."

Able Seaman Gordon Gibbins of Lindsay, Ont., says: "When the torpedo hit, I was thrown pretty hard up, then down on the deck, hurting my back quite severely. I managed to get up to my abandon ship station. When the skipper gave the word to abandon ship I, for some reason, very calmly took off my shoes and set them under the ammunition locker as if I was going to bed, and then jumped. I kept going down and down and thought I would never come up, but I did — with a rush like a cork. I was low in the water, hanging on to the end of a Carley float. My back hurt. I couldn't move too much. When they finally came and rescued us, they hauled everyone aboard except me. They did not see me. The Fairmile started to leave and if a seaman who was coiling rope on the quarterdeck had not seen my feeble wave one last time, I would never have made it. They soon came around and hauled me aboard."

The U.K. was hospitable to the Canadian corvette men. Food was the one big gripe. Max Corkum says: "Generally the food was poor. The quality and variety were far short of what was available in Canada. We had lots of beef, pork and as much mutton as we wanted. The beef and pork had been frozen for a long time and were always tough. The mutton was local, greasy and tough as well. We had poultry on two occasions — Christmas and the day we left to return to Canada. One thing we had was good, and that was soup. Often at noon, our big meal, I would have the soup and dessert and skip the main course. The dessert would usually be rice and raisins, or prunes. We made a deal to get milk and real butter from some of the farmers around Milford Haven."

Bonds were forged in some communities. In Milford Haven, for example, retired teacher Walter Ireland recalls his wartime days in the sea cadets: "*Quebec* adopted us actually and we used to go there after our parade on Thursday night. We used to have supper on board. We had no sweets — they were rationed — so they used to give us sweets."

On the eve of victory in Europe, *Moose Jaw* had a tragedy when a crew member fell overboard and drowned. The body of William Ernest Kruper, 21, was recovered three weeks later. He is buried in the war graves section of a Milford Haven cemetery.

The victory was official on May 8, 1945 — still known as VE-Day. *Moose Jaw* lieutenant Max Corkum recalls: "We had the wildest party imaginable on shore that night. VE-Day in the U.K. was a cause for service personnel and civilians joining together and having fun. All the pubs and bars threw their doors open and no one paid. All was on the house. When a pub went dry, you moved to another until the same thing happened."

Vernon Scott, long a reporter for the *Western Telegraph* in nearby Pembroke Dock, recalls the evening in May 1945 that the last of the Canadians left: "The four corvettes [*Kitchener*, *Algoma*, *Moose Jaw* and *Ville de Quebec*] sailed up Milford Haven harbour in line abreast with the crews lined up on deck. They were led out by *Kitchener*, and standing on the bow was a piper who played a lament as they headed out to sea in a deep purple haze. For the people on shore, it was very emotional. The Canadians were popular — very, very popular — here in the war."

Algoma able seaman Harry Connell of Trail, B.C., recalls it, too: "I think half of Milford Haven came down to the docks to see us off. I will always remember that."

The corvette *St. Thomas* transports a shipment of gold to Halifax from Londonderry, probably in 1944 or 1945.

CHAPTER SIXTEEN

"THE WAR IS OVER! SPLICE THE MAIN BRACE."

"CONVOY DUTY during the last year of the war was pretty uneventful," assesses *Kincardine* lieutenant Bill Taylor. Agreeing, *Bowmanville* lieutenant-commander Mort Duffus says, "I kept the hands at daily drill to prevent boredom. The only event of note was a terrible hurricane we experienced in mid-Atlantic with winds up to 87 knots."

Wes Johnson in *Kincardine* appreciated one regular occurrence: "On convoy duty we used to have air cover. Sunderland Flying Boats out of Milford Haven in Wales would fly about halfway across the Atlantic and meet the convoy. We would get a message on the radio the day before to send out a homing signal at a certain time. We'd press the radio keys, but we were told just to leave them for a few seconds. That was about the only time we could break radio silence without special cause. About half an hour later, these Flying Boats would come right in under the overcast, right on top of the convoy — dead on. It was a wonderful thing to see when you realized you were part of it. They would flap their wings and then head back out and sweep in front of the convoy course."

The tedium was occasionally lifted by an unusual event. Mort Duffus says: "When I came to the bridge early one morning, an odd-looking shape was on the horizon. After signalling the senior officer, I made best speed to investigate. The object turned out to be a section of a landing craft. We lowered the whaler and a party boarded it. They returned with a wire-haired terrier suffering no ill effects except that of being extremely thirsty. It was learned that the landing craft section was lost by a freighter that had passed by this point three days earlier."

Humour helped sailors cope. *Fergus* able seaman Howard Trusdale says: "Our good friends in the senior ship of our group, *Penetang*, seemed to get an inordinate number of submarine contacts — at least one asdic sounding each trip. We quickly changed her name to 'Pingatang!'"

In late March 1945, *Louisburg (2nd)* was in refit in Saint John, N.B., Telegraphist Don Lindberg recalls: "The four-inch gun was removed, complete with outer protective cover, to be sent out for repairs. It was loaded onto the back of a heavy truck, which proceeded out of the dockyard. As the truck turned to go up the street, the gun slid off the vehicle, landing on a parked car and flattening it. I imagine some explanation was necessary from the movers."

The last RCN warship loss of the war occurred on April 16, 1945. *Strathroy* stoker Bill McCallum says: "We were with the *Bangor* minesweeper *Esquimalt* when she was torpedoed off Halifax. We spent a lot of time and depth charges going after the U-boat [*U-190*], but no success. We were not part of the rescue operation."

The war was coming quickly to a close. *Saskatoon* lieutenant Bill Winegard recalls: "It was clear by early May that the war was about to end and there was a spirit of jubilation everywhere on the ship. The spirit of jubilation turned to spirits of another kind. Even before we left harbour to pick up another convoy off the coast of Halifax, the spirits were flowing freely. Later that day, as officer of the watch, I had reported to me an object off our starboard quarter. The report was definitely non-pusser in nature and went something like this: 'Shur, there is something up there. Right over there.

The explosion of a depth charge released from the stern rails of *Fergus*.

Courtesy Bev Bate

The flags on the corvette *Orangeville* tell the story: "The war is over! Splice the main brace." This means give an extra tot of rum to the sailors in celebration.

It unleashed in the sailors deep-seated resentment of what they perceived to be generally poor treatment by the navy, the merchants, the city and the citizenry. The result was the infamous Halifax riots with two days of looting and destruction downtown. Sailors, airmen and soldiers were all involved, along with many civilians, particularly looters, but Halifax was the major Canadian naval base and the sailors were blamed. It gave the navy a gigantic black eye and it cost Rear-Admiral L.W. Murray his career.

May 8 was VE-Day, but Allied warships were instructed to remain alert in case the surrender message was not received by all U-boats, or a U-boat commander chose to defy the order. Warships were also to be ready to accept the surrender of U-boats and, in fact, two U-boats did surrender to RCN ships.

Saskatoon lieutenant Bill Winegard says: "It was on May 10 that *U-889* surrendered to our escort group. All of our directions to the submarine were given in high school German and we ordered her to steer a given direction at a given speed. She went in the right direction but much more rapidly than we had indicated and we had to tell her to slow down or we would open fire. Corvettes were not the fastest ships on the North Atlantic.

"At dusk on the same day, after much signalling back and forth in laborious German, the captain signalled back to us using perfect Canadian naval procedure, 'And so to bed. Good night and pleasant dreams.' He was lucky we did not sink him on the spot."

On May 11, the corvette *Thorlock* and the frigate *Victoriaville* were detached from westbound convoy ON 300 to locate a U-boat which had radioed that it had surfaced and was flying the black flag of surrender. *Thorlock* signalman trained operator Gord Stoutenburg of Kelowna, B.C., was there:

It was late afternoon when we began our search, and after about two hours of seeing nothing, the skipper of *Victoriaville* signalled us that since it would be dark fairly soon, they would utilize their superior speed and scout ahead on their own for a while. They sent one final signal, "So long little buddy, we'll bring you back a U-boat."

During the second dog watch, with the waters calm and sun disappearing, we believed this would be a fruitless search. The bridge crew consisted of the

See?' What could one do but acknowledge the report in the best way possible?"

At war's end, ships were instructed to "splice the main brace" as a token of appreciation to the entire crew. It was a welcome toast and a time for celebration after nearly six years of war.

Newfiejohn was a scene of joyous celebration. Not so Halifax. In fact, the cheap RCN brass hadn't taken good care of their sailors in overcrowded Halifax; for example, they did not build adequate recreational facilities or amenities. Unprompted comments indicate many veterans consider that Halifax "was not a friendly place for sailors," as George Hollins puts it. The RCN brass also didn't bother to plan a celebration and the city was shut down for VE-Day. These thoughtless acts showed neither respect nor appreciation for the sailors who had *earned* a victory party.

U-889 off Shelbourne, N.S., in May 1945 after surrendering to a Canadian escort group. Overhead is a Consolidated Canso "Flying Boat" of 161 Squadron.

skipper, the officer of the watch, two lookouts and myself as signalman. We were all scanning the horizon. I heard the clatter of feet coming up the ladder to the bridge and turned to see one of our off-watch stokers, Andy Houde. He received permission from the officer of the watch to stay on the bridge, and was told to keep his eyes open.

Andy was the only one of us without binoculars. We were all very busy scanning the horizon when Andy asked me if we were close to Newfie. I said, "Hell no, we are at least 100 miles from land." He then said, "Oh, I thought that light over there was a lighthouse." I asked, "What light?" He pointed

off to starboard and I swung my binoculars to find a light blinking.

I reported, "Light flashing green 70," and ran to my starboard signal lamp. The skipper said, "Send the challenge of the day and find out who that is." I signalled the three-letter challenge. There was no reply. I sent it again and again. Still no reply. Meanwhile, action stations were sounded and gun crews were all closed up. Finally, I was able to discern a reply. The signal was "*U-Boot 190, U-Boot 190.*"

Thorlock sent over a boarding party which took charge of the U-boat. A German operating crew remained in the

Edward Dinsmore, courtesy Library and Archives Canada. PA145580

The corvette *Thorlock* and other RCN units escort *U-190* in Bay Bulls, Newfoundland, after its surrender.

sub under guard and the rest of the crew were taken to the corvette by sea-boat. Course was set for Bay Bulls, Newfoundland, at Captain D's instruction. "Strangely enough," says Stoutenburg, "most of the prisoners got seasick from the rolling and pitching of our corvette!" The next morning, a number of U-boat officers and crew were transferred to the frigate en route to Newfoundland.

Meanwhile, *Kincardine* was heading the other way. Wes Johnson says: "When we went back to Londonderry with the last convoy, there were more than 45 German subs tied up outside Londonderry at the mouth of the Foyle River. These were all different kinds of subs, old ones and new ones. I had the opportunity to go down into some of

them. I was very taken back by the conditions that these poor men had to serve in."

Kincardine able seaman Alfie Reid of Millville, N.B., says: "Many of us were assigned to clean all the equipment and guns off these subs. There was no way we could get Lugers, jackets, etc. past the Irish guards, but many things came aboard *Kincardine* and were hid away. When a search of the ship was ordered on our trip back to Halifax, most of these souvenirs were thrown out the portholes. What treasures are on the bottom of the Atlantic."

On June 4, the U-boat war officially ended. The lights went on again on the North Atlantic. The convoy system was quickly disbanded. The final figures showed that Allied and

Courtesy Doug May

A rear view of surrendered U-boats tied up at Lisahally, Londonderry, in May 1945.

neutral merchant shipping losses on the Atlantic crept up in 1945, averaging 11 ships and 73,354 tons per month from January through May. U-boats losses in all theatres were 153, making a total of 782 for the war. In six years, the U-boats sank 2,600 merchant ships in the Battle of the Atlantic, where shipping losses, to all causes, totalled 14 million tons.

"No story of corvettes, or any other ships, can be told without paying tribute to the men of the Merchant Navy, mostly British, on two counts," says Jim Elmsley of *Louisburg (2nd)* and *Mimico*. "Firstly, the merchant ships were the targets, not the escorts. The men who manned them were the real heroes of the war at sea. Secondly, our Canadian navy, which was so small at the outset, grew to be the third largest Allied navy. It was the retired merchant service officers who provided the nucleus of experienced sea-going commanding officers and provided us dry-land volunteers

with training and guidance on the job until we could carry some level of responsibilities."

Without fanfare, on June 4, 1945, *Strathroy* crew members signed a letter of best wishes and enclosed a cheque for Gerry Reinhart of Langley, B.C., a shipmate until a steel cable severed a leg while the ship was leaving Halifax harbour one dark night.

U-190 and *U-889*, both Type IX C-40 boats, were commissioned into the RCN for testing. During the summer of 1945, *U-190* was even taken on a ceremonial tour of the Gulf and St. Lawrence River all the way up to Montreal. In the post-war Allied division of spoils, *U-889* was allocated to the U.S., delivered by the RCN in early 1946 and sunk by the U.S. Navy in 1947.

In June 1945, without knowledge of *Prescott*'s 1943 destruction of *U-163,* Wilfred McIsaac got his reward, being

Courtesy Doug May

A frontal view reveals several different types of surrendered U-boats tied up at Lisahally, Londonderry, in May 1945. Number 802, a larger Type IX C-40 (second right), is flanked by two Type VII C boats, the most common sub in the Atlantic theatre.

made a Member of the British Empire. His citation reads: "This officer has served at sea during the last five years of war in escort vessels engaged in the Battle of the Atlantic. He has always displayed qualities of courage and endurance under arduous conditions, and by his unbounded zeal, cheerfulness and devotion to duty has set an outstanding example to all those with whom he has come in contact. His exemplary services, in keeping with the traditions of the Royal Canadian Navy, are worthy of the highest recognition."

Within a month of the end of the war in Europe, the RCN began the process of winding down the corvette navy. Corvettes on their way home for the last time often got rid of their ammunition — one way or another. Lieutenant Max Corkum recalls when *Moose Jaw* came home in a group of four corvettes: "We had been told to dump all of

our ammunition before we got back to Halifax. We decided we might as well have some fun with our pyrotechnics, so every night after dark we would take turns trying to outdo each other in our displays. We fired off parachute flares, parachute rockets, star shell, snowflake and the odd depth charge. This was more fun than throwing the stuff over the side."

Corvettes continued to return home. On their final westward trip, some corvettes played a small role in supplementing the limited supply of troop transports. *Bowmanville*'s Mort Duffus says: "We embarked about 200 shore-based naval personnel at Greenock to give them passage back to Canada. Needless to say, we were very crowded."

Lunenburg paid a visit to its namesake Nova Scotia town. Council minutes show that the municipality held a

The officers' wardroom in *U-190* after its surrender to the RCN in May 1945.

Albert Tigerstedt, courtesy Library and Archives Canada, PA137699

dinner for the ship's company, the Board of Trade organized a "motor ride" and the Legion held a dance.

The small ships would not have a place in the Canadian fleet being readied for the war against Japan in the Pacific. The eight surviving Flower-named corvettes on loan from the RN were turned back over in the U.K. Over a period of several months, the vast majority of the RCN corvettes went to Sydney, N.S., for removal of stores, weapons and equipment. Then, with skeleton crews, they went on to Sorel, Que., where they were "paid off" as navy vessels.

Lieutenant Mac Orr, now commanding *Calgary*, says: "When we arrived in Sorel, I felt happy that finally the war was over for most of us, but very upset to lose such a wonderful crew — the finest men I ever met."

Jim Bessey, commissioned from the lower decks to become a lieutenant in *Lethbridge*, says: "I cried like a baby when we had to leave her at the boneyard in Sorel. They were great ships, corvettes! Great people!"

Coxswain Hoot Gibson of Strathroy, Ont., reflects: "The captain [K.T. Chisholm] and I were the last two members off the ship. ... To say goodbye to *Port Arthur* and to the captain I had served under was very memorable. They had both taken us through bad times and brought us home safely."

At Sorel the mothballed ships awaited whatever fate could be arranged by the War Assets Corporation. It varied considerably. Nearly 50 Canadian corvettes were sold eventually. They were converted for a variety of tasks and sailed under a range of national flags. Some became whale catchers, particularly for Dutch and Honduran owners. A number served in the navies of Argentina, Chile, Uruguay, Venezuela, Israel, the Dominican Republic and the two Chinas, Nationalist and Communist.

A small number of corvettes stayed in Canada, among them *Hespeler*, *Leaside* and *St. Thomas*, which became passenger ferries on the West Coast. In fact, Union Steamships Ltd. of Vancouver paid $75,000 for *Hespeler* and apparently spent another $400,000 on her conversion. *Hespeler* was more or less typical when she went on to have several owners and several uses.

Except for those who signed on again for a Pacific campaign that never came to be, the navy discharged the wartime RCNVR sailors as quickly as it could manage administratively. *Louisburg (2nd)* crewman Don Lindberg says: "On discharge in September 1945, they noted I had not been paid for passing a telegraphist trained operator course. Some time later I received a cheque for $18 — five cents a day for nearly a year."

A *Barrie* leading seaman, or junior foreman in civilian terms, Roy Pallister got a rude shock: "When I joined the navy in June 1942, I was a boy. I found out 38 months later that I was still a boy. As soon as I took that blue uniform off, I was not even allowed to go in and enjoy a beer until December when I turned 21! And presumably became a man."

There were a large number of surplus ships as major navies scaled back to their peacetime requirements. When no takers could be found for many Canadian corvettes, particularly the early ones, over 40 of them were cut up for scrap, most at Hamilton. John Isbister of Stoney Creek, Ont., a 1943-44 *Sherbrooke* able seaman, remembers it well:

In 1940 I started to work at Stelco, one of Canada's largest producers of basic steel products. A good percentage of the Canadian navy's smaller ships in World War II were made from Stelco steel. I worked on the shipping floor of the plate mill and can remember loading hull plate for various Canadian shipyards building naval vessels: Burrard and Yarrow in British Columbia, Collingwood and Midland in Ontario, Marine Industries and Vickers in Quebec, and Saint John in New Brunswick. I joined the navy

in 1942 and my first ship was HMCS *Sherbrooke*. She was built by Marine Industries and I have the nagging thought I could very well have loaded her hull plate.

Immediately after the war, I returned to my job at Stelco. Some time later, word got around that the plant was cutting up naval ships for scrap. One day in 1947, I finally mustered enough courage to walk down to the yard where this operation was taking place. Secretly, I was hoping *Sherbrooke* would not be among them. She was literally my home for the best part of my war. Never once did she let us down. The pounding and beating we took on the North Atlantic was a testament to the excellent workmanship and quality of Canadian steelworkers and shipbuilders.

I discovered that some corvettes and minesweepers had been attacked by cutting torches. I recognized the pennant numbers of ships with which we had sailed. I stopped dead in my tracks as emotion overcame me. *Sherbrooke* was there. K-152 had followed me home. She was still intact. She still looked trim and seaworthy as I remembered her. I stood for several minutes and fondly recalled the better days spent aboard her.

It would have been very easy for me to go aboard *Sherbrooke*, but I could not bring myself to do it for this last time. I would be the only person aboard and somehow it would not be as I really remember her. *Sherbrooke* was a ship, yes, but what really made her was her crew and the comradeship we had with each other. The crew was now scattered, God knows where. Finally, I turned and walked away. I never went back. Over the years, I sometimes criticize myself for not going aboard that day. I would have been the very last crew member to board her. Had there been another shipmate, I could have boarded *Sherbrooke*. Alone, I just could not do it. It was a very sad, sad day.

In that period right after the war, there was much activity building oil refineries in southern Ontario. To this day, I often pass them when I drive between Hamilton and Toronto. When I behold the big steel storage tanks, I cannot help but think some of HMCS *Sherbrooke* is still there right before my eyes. Fantasy, perhaps, but the thought still persists.

* * *

Early in World War II, Allied governments and media — including Canada's — had been quick to depict the U-boats as evil instruments of the Nazi scourge. In the end, Karl Dönitz, who had gone on to head the German government in the last days of the war, was convicted of three charges in the Nuremberg war crimes trials and given a 10-year sentence, but there were no widespread consequences for the surviving men of the U-boat arm.

There were probably a number of reasons. There is something to the concept that technology dictates our perception of morality. As we become accustomed to the existence of a particular technology, we grow to accept that it has a place. In contrast to World War I, this had been a high-technology war: at sea with the evolution of submarine warfare and development of naval air power; on land with mechanized warfare featuring tanks and armoured vehicles; and in the air with massive long-range bombing, rockets and, ultimately, the atom bomb. Often when the targets were military there was what is now euphemistically called "collateral damage." And the targets were not always military. Thus, in this "modern" warfare, more civilians perished than combatants.

The Allies were also secure in the knowledge they had vanquished Germany and inflicted a heavy toll on the German submarine arm. In all, 696 or 84 per cent of the 830 U-boats that went on operations were destroyed. In human terms, the toll was grim: 25,870 men were lost and 5,000 were taken prisoner from a force of 40,900. That's a fatality rate of 63 per cent and a casualty rate of 83 per cent. In comparison, operating principally in the Pacific theatre, the U.S. deployed 288 submarines and lost 52 or 18 per cent, with a crew fatality rate of 22 per cent.

The German U-boats came to be known as "steel coffins" and their crews were not the object of our spite. In fact, the men won grudging respect. Norm Simpson, of Alliston, Ont., the 1944-45 *Bowmanville* Jimmy, concurs: "Until the very end the U-boat arm fought with discipline and efficiency. There was no relaxation of effort or hesitation to incur risks." Wes Johnson simply says: "I take my hat off to these men. They were very brave."

Tony Griffin in *Amherst* observes: "I should like to pay my respects to the enemy. ... These men served in conditions which were, at the best of times, physically demanding. At the worst of times, in midwinter, under

A bow view of *Orangeville* in drydock at Levis, Que., in 1946 for removal of all military gear before her sale to Chinese interests.

Courtesy Victor Large

attack, conditions became simply unspeakable. Yet there was, throughout, a high state of morale in the U-boat crews, even in the latter part of the war when the Allies got the upper hand and the number of U-boat sinkings skyrocketed. The standard of bravery knows no parallel. ..."

The submarine war paled by comparison with revelations of the horror on a grand scale that was the Holocaust, the great evil of the Nazi regime. As well, in the West attention was already shifting further east to the Soviet Union and soon there would be another major conflict, the Cold War.

* * *

After using *U-190* for testing and anti-submarine training, the RCN finally sank the sub in a heavy-handed display of

Courtesy Victor Large

A stern view of *Orangeville* in drydock at Levis, Que., in 1946 for removal of all military gear before her sale to Chinese interests.

symbolism and British heritage. The event involved a number of Canadian warships and naval aircraft. It took place off Halifax near the spot where *U-190* sank *Esquimalt* in April 1945. The date chosen was October 21, 1947 — Trafalgar Day, the anniversary of the 1803 defeat of Napoleon's fleet by Admiral Horatio Nelson, the most renowned British seaman.

This military display notwithstanding, the harbour and downtown of St. John's, Nfld., remain under U-boat surveillance to this day for *U-190*'s attack periscope has found a home in the Crow's Nest Officers' Club.

* * *

While 113 RCN corvettes commemorated 112 Canadian communities, in seven instances the corvette name was not an exact copy. The community name was deemed too close to an existing Allied warship or shore establishment in most cases; in the remainder, local preference won out. Thus from Ontario we have the following circumlocution: *Frontenac* for Kingston, *Merrittonia* for Merritton, *Thorlock* for Thorold, *Trentonian* for Trenton and *West York* for Weston, and in the Maritimes we have *Atholl* for Campbellton, N.B., and *Norsyd* for North Sydney, N.S.

Some of the 112 corvette communities, such as Giffard, Que., and Dunvegan, N.S., are not well known nationally. Some Ontario communities are no longer known by their former name. Galt and Hespeler are components of Cambridge, Humberstone is now part of Port Colborne and Merritton is part of St. Catharines. In addition,

Forest Hill, Leaside, Long Branch, Mimico and Weston have largely lost their identity in the urban mass that we know as the GTA [Greater Toronto Area].

During World War II, communities in all nine provinces and one of the two territories were represented by the 113 corvettes. The ships' geographical breakdown was:

British Columbia (9) — *Agassiz, Alberni, Chilliwack, Kamloops, Nanaimo, New Westminster, Vancouver, Quesnel, Trail*

Alberta (5) — *Calgary, Camrose, Drumheller, Lethbridge, Wetaskiwin*

Saskatchewan (7) — *Battleford, Kamsack, Moose Jaw, Regina, Rosthern, Saskatoon, Weyburn*

Manitoba (4) — *Brandon, Dauphin, Morden, The Pas*

Ontario (51) — *Algoma, Arnprior, Barrie, Belleville, Bowmanville, Brantford, Cobalt, Cobourg, Collingwood, Copper Cliff, Dundas, Fergus, Forest Hill, Frontenac, Galt, Guelph, Hawkesbury, Hespeler, Humberstone, Huntsville, Kenogami, Kincardine, Kitchener, Leaside, Lindsay, Long Branch, Merrittonia, Midland, Mimico, Napanee, North Bay, Oakville, Orangeville, Orillia, Owen Sound, Parry Sound, Peterborough, Petrolia, Port Arthur, Prescott, St. Thomas, Smiths Falls, Strathroy, Sudbury, Thorlock, Tilsonburg, Timmins, Trentonian, West York, Whitby, Woodstock*

Quebec (17) — *Arvida, Asbestos, Beauharnois, Chambly, Chicoutimi, Giffard, Lachute, La Malbaie, Levis, Matapedia, Rimouski, Riviere du Loup, St. Lambert, Shawinigan, Sherbrooke, Sorel, Ville de Quebec*

New Brunswick (7) — *Atholl, Buctouche, Edmundston, Fredericton, Moncton, Sackville, Shediac*

Nova Scotia (10) — *Amherst, Baddeck, Dunvegan, Halifax, Louisburg, Louisburg (2nd), Lunenburg, Norsyd, Pictou, Stellarton*

Prince Edward Island (2) — *Charlottetown, Summerside*

Yukon (1) — *Dawson*

RCN warships were involved in 33 submarine kills in World War II. Corvettes played a role in 17 kills — pretty good for such small ships that were most often limited to a purely defensive role. In all, 20 RCN corvettes — one in six — earned solo or shared credit for a submarine kill. They were *Battleford* (*U-356*), *Calgary* (*U-536* and either *U-772* or *U-322*), *Camrose* (*U-757*), *Chambly* (*U-501*), *Chilliwack* (*U-356* and *U-744*), *Drumheller* (*U-753*), *Fennel* (*U-744*), *Moose Jaw* (*U-501*), *Morden* (*U-756*), *Napanee* (*U-356*), *Oakville* (*U-94*), *Owen Sound* (*U-845*), *Port Arthur* (*Tritone*), *Prescott* (*U-163*), *Regina* (*Avorio*), *Shediac* (*U-87*), *Snowberry* (*U-536*), *St. Thomas* (*U-877*), *Ville de Quebec* (*U-224*), *Wetaskiwin* (*U-588*).

During World War II, 24 RCN named warships were sunk and five others were severely damaged in action and didn't fight again. Ten of the 24 were corvettes, six were destroyers, four were *Bangor* minesweepers, one was an auxiliary minesweeper, two were armed yachts and one was a frigate. The causes were many: 15 by torpedoing, four by collision, one each by mine, aircraft, explosion/fire, storm and unknown, but suspected to be foundering.

For the 10 corvettes sunk, seven were lost by torpedoing, and one each by collision, aircraft and mine. By theatre, three corvettes each were lost in the Atlantic (*Levis, Windflower, Spikenard*) and the English Channel (*Regina, Alberni, Trentonian*), and two each in the Gulf of St. Lawrence (*Charlottetown, Shawinigan*) and the Mediterranean (*Louisburg, Weyburn*).

* * *

Corvettes have long since ceased to have a high public profile, but there are still signs across the land of our corvette heritage.

Right after the war, the RCN showed its appreciation to communities that supported a Canadian warship by presenting to the municipality or an appropriate local organization the ship's bell. These bells, often accompanied by a framed photo and plaque, are on display. For example, they're in the council chamber in Summerside, P.E.I., the courthouse in Baddeck, N.S., the mayor's office in Rimouski, Que., the city museum in Quebec City, the council chamber in Dundas, Ont., a military museum in Cobalt, Ont., the Legion hall in Moose Jaw, Sask., the mayor's reception room in Saskatoon, Sask., and the Kamloops, B.C., Museum and Archives.

There are many other mementoes, too. For example, *Orangeville*'s beautiful hand-carved wooden crest is now in the town hall at Orangeville, Ont. And, a museum in Dawson City, Yukon, has a collection of a ship's photo, ditty bag, commissioning pennant and tattered White Ensign, all courtesy of *Dawson* coder Al G. King. Other tributes can be found here and there. For example, in 1989 the town of Oakville, Ont., erected a cairn in a lakeside park. In 1990, the city of Trenton, Ont., unveiled a memorial stone.

And from Bowmanville, now part of Newcastle, Ont., Sheila Brooks writes: "Our local sea cadet corps is 279 Bowmanville, so named for the ship, not the town. Framed pictures and memorabilia from the ship are prominently displayed in the quarters. We have received from Jack McCurdy his complete wartime service uniform, which we have on a mannequin. Every cadet is familiarized with the history of HMCS *Bowmanville*."

A federal agency was once responsible for all Canadian geographic names, but responsibility has since devolved to the provinces and territories. Toponymist Kathleen O'Brien of the Canadian Permanent Committee on Geographic Names says that "in the neighbourhood of 9,000 to 10,000 features" in Ontario, Manitoba, Saskatchewan, Alberta, British Columbia, the Yukon and the Northwest Territories are named for World War II dead from the army, navy, merchant navy and air force. The naming process continues to commemorate the war dead in Manitoba, Saskatchewan and British Columbia.

Corvette veterans are included, of course. Two features in British Columbia are a case in point. In 1956, Milthorp Point was named after *Spikenard* victim Patrick Milthorp. In 1990, Shadforth Creek was named after her skipper, Bert Shadforth. Each year British Columbia announces a list on Remembrance Day. Selections are made for previously unnamed features in areas of importance to the individual or his family, or in remote locations where geographical names are required for reference or administrative purposes.

The Northwest Territories has two geographical features which commemorate Canadian corvettes lost in World War II — Windflower Lake and Lac Levis. A third name, Spikenard Point, was proposed by the Canadian Hydrographic Service in 1956, but it lost out to Ocean

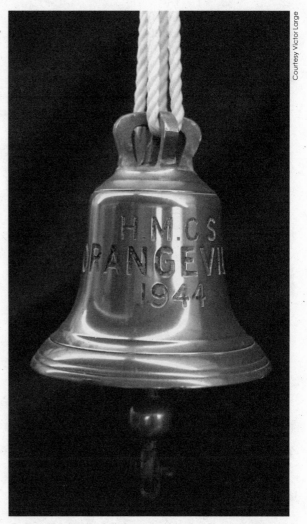

Orangeville's bell is now in her namesake Ontario community.

Eagle Point named after the tug *Ocean Eagle*, which operated in that area.

Continuing the tradition of re-using ships' names, seven of Canada's 12 patrol frigates perpetuate the name and carry the battle honours of a World War II corvette — *Halifax, Vancouver, Ville de Quebec, Regina, Calgary, Fredericton* and *Charlottetown*. In fact, Maritime Command included a number of corvette veterans in the commissioning ceremonies for their namesake ship, which the veterans greatly appreciated. As well, the crew of the current *Regina* conducts a memorial service each year on August 8 to commemorate the loss of her namesake corvette.

Maritime Command also remembers in another way. In the 1980s, it extended to the Halifax Memorial a certain mark of respect carried out by all warships in commission as they pass one another. Commemorating those lost at sea, the memorial in Point Pleasant Park must be passed by ships on their way in or out of Halifax harbour. Commander Phil Lebel explained: "When ships enter or leave harbour, for every ship they meet along the way, they receive or give the salute depending on the captains' seniority. The most junior pipes the 'still' bringing his company to attention. The saluted ship does the same and then pipes the 'carry on.' The saluting ship then pipes the carry on. The same is done at the sailors' memorial monument. Of course, there are no return pipes. It is similar, if you want, to the minutes of silence carried out at certain public functions."

* * *

Only one Canadian corvette lives on — HMCS *Sackville* in Halifax. Designated Canada's Naval Memorial by the federal government, she is maintained and operated by the Canadian Naval Memorial Trust, a non-profit society composed of more than 1,100 trustees from across Canada. The trust's mandate is "to preserve and maintain the Last Corvette in her 1944 configuration as Canada's naval memorial to all those who served in the naval service and to operate the ship as a naval museum for the benefit of all Canadians." In the summer, she is alongside Sackville Jetty in downtown Halifax. She winters in the Halifax naval dockyard.

Sackville's restoration was long and costly. It involved the efforts of many dedicated volunteers as well as corporate contributions of money, materials and labour. Thousands of naval veterans chipped in. So did a number of municipalities, examples being $500 from the Nova Scotia town now spelling its name Louisbourg and $1,000 from the city of Belleville, Ont. Assistance also came from Maritime Command. The corvette trust is always in need of supporters. You can become a trustee or a member of the ship's company for a modest annual fee. For more information, check out www.canadiannavalmemorial.org.

The corvette evokes many memories. Norman Stirling of Penticton, B.C., who served in *Sorel* and *Hawkesbury*, made a tour of Eastern Canada with his wife: "The highlight of the trip was going aboard HMCS *Sackville*. What

a blessing they have managed to save her for the coming generations. It was just like walking back all those years — a thrill, really."

Sackville has become a minor movie star. She was the star of the National Film Board film *The Last Corvette*. And she also played the part of HMCS *Fireweed* in the TV movie *Lifeline to Victory* produced for the CanWest Global System. Though fictional, the film had some basis in fact and was a tribute to the RCN's role in the Battle of the Atlantic.

There has also been a recent TV documentary on the sinking of HMCS *Regina*. Titled *Fatal Decision,* it has appeared on the History Channel as part of a three-hour series titled *Deep Wreck Mysteries.* The *Regina* hour includes underwater footage of the wreckage, which is in two main parts. The website is www.deepwreckmysteries.co.uk.

* * *

The bonds of service are so strong they have forged the desire for reunions. The big one is held by the Royal Canadian Naval Association, which in 2007 had 30 active clubs and about 4,500 members. The annual RCNA meeting for all naval vets is held at a different site each year. Despite the passing of the majority of World War II naval vets, the 2008 reunion, slated for Brantford, Ont., is likely to attract 500 or more people. Former crew members of specific ships try to hold mini-reunions at these gatherings.

Giffard signalman Ken Hotston says: "Periodically some of the chaps I sailed with get together at naval reunions and talk about our days in the service. A lot of people today have trouble wondering why we do this, but it was a part of our lives that we shall never forget and we thank God that we survived and cemented some good friendships."

A number of corvette crews have held their own ship's reunion, some a number of times. Able Seaman Jack Scott says: "After 45 years I finally got my medals mounted, bought a blazer and an airline ticket and attended my ship's reunion. This was a very memorable occasion and the hospitality of Trenton and its Legion branch were very much appreciated. Many of the men who attended the reunion were in this ship when they were in their late teens and early twenties. Despite their sometimes wild antics and experiences, I found that when they returned to civilian life they became solid Canadian citizens. I was proud to march with them and very proud to have been a crew member of HMCS *Trentonian.*"

Regina ERA Tom Baird says: "After the war was over, in fact about 30 years after, some of our more energetic boys got their heads together and arranged a reunion at the Royal York Hotel in Toronto. Some of the wives were just a bit leery about this after the war-years stories they'd heard. You would never have believed how these fellows had settled down. It really was a grand old weekend talking over old times."

One reunion often led to others. *St. Thomas* may well be the corvette that has had the most reunions — at least 10. *Strathroy* has had eight. Strathroy mayor Thomas Wolder travelled 600 kilometres to Ottawa to address the 1985 reunion: "Strathroy council authorized the official recognition of your reunion because we want to keep in contact with the men of our ship. The bell from HMCS *Strathroy* is in our town museum. A picture of the crew is in our council chamber. I brought it with me. The bell was too heavy.

"Strathroy has 9,000 citizens. As of this day, the number increases by almost 100 because Strathroy council has also authorized me to appoint you all honourary citizens. And to make this official, I have certificates made out to you personally.

"Now hear this, crew of HMCS *Strathroy* and honourary citizens of Strathroy. This is your mayor speaking. I order you to enjoy yourself this weekend and maintain the friendship of your shipmates. Thank you for permitting me to come aboard and smooth sailing."

* * *

In the final analysis, Canada has never been a military-minded country. Indeed, for a century we have been more or less locked in a cycle: Ignore the military, build up as rapidly as possible when a war of some scale breaks out, dismantle quickly when war ends, and ignore again.

In World War II, the RCN overextended itself by expanding from 2,000 full-time sailors to 100,000, a ratio of 50 to 1. The corresponding American ratio was 20 to 1 and the British ratio 8 to 1.

There were problems, some of them serious. There was a price — 2,000 RCN and 1,600 Canadian and Newfoundland Merchant Navy dead. But the bottom line was that the goods got through — 180 million tons of equipment, weapons, supplies and food reached the U.K. Thanks in no small part to the sailors of the RCNVR and our fleet of corvettes. In an understated Canadian way, Doug Clarance sums it up: "There are those who would guide the naval history of the Canadian effort during World War II with some criticism of a great degree of inefficiency, etc. I look upon it as a major accomplishment. The growth that it achieved in a relatively short time was remarkable. It accomplished a great deal in protecting the convoys and helping the fight for freedom."

THE END

BIBLIOGRAPHY

Audette, Louis C. *War Diary* (unpublished).

Bishop, Chris. *Kriegsmarine U-Boats 1939-45*. London: Amber Books, 2006.

Boutilier, J.A., ed. *The RCN in Retrospect*. Vancouver: UBC Press, 1982.

Brown, David. *Warship Losses of World War Two*. London: Arms and Armour Press, 1990.

Curry, Frank. *War at Sea: A Canadian Seaman on the North Atlantic*. Toronto: Lugus Productions Ltd., 1990.

Douglas, W.A.B., ed. *The RCN in Transition*. Vancouver: UBC Press, 1988.

Douglas, W.A.B., Roger Sarty, Michael Whitby et al. *No Higher Purpose*. St. Catharines: Vanwell Publishing Limited, 2002.

Douglas, W.A.B., Roger Sarty, Michael Whitby et al. *A Blue Water Navy*. St. Catharines: Vanwell Publishing Limited, 2007.

German, Tony. *The Sea Is at Our Gates*. Toronto: McClelland & Stewart Inc., 1990.

Griffin, A.G.S. *Footfalls in Memory*. Toronto: Privately published, 1998.

Hadley, Michael L. *U-Boats against Canada*. Montreal: McGill-Queen's University Press, 1985.

Lamb, James B. *The Corvette Navy*. Toronto: Macmillan of Canada, 1977.

— *On The Triangle Run*. Toronto: Macmillan of Canada, 1986.

Macpherson, Ken, and John Burgess. *The Ships of Canada's Naval Forces 1910-1981*. Toronto: Collins Publishers, 1981.

Milner, Marc. *North Atlantic Run*. Toronto: University of Toronto Press, 1985.

— *Battle Of The Atlantic*. St. Catharines: Vanwell Publishing Limited.

— *Canada's Navy: The First Century*. Toronto: University of Toronto Press, 1999.

Nieslte, Axel. *German U-Boat Losses During World War II*. U.S.: Naval Institute Press, 2005.

Paterson, Lawrence. First U-Boat Flotilla. Barnsley, U.K.: Leo Cooper, 2002.

Paterson, Lawrence. Second U-Boat Flotilla. Barnsley, U.K.: Leo Cooper, 2003.

Paquette, Edward R., and Charles G. Bainbridge. *Honours and Awards: Canadian Naval Forces World War II*. Victoria, B.C.: Project Gallantry, 1986.

Schull, Joseph. *Far Distant Ships*. Toronto: Stoddart, 1987. Originally published in 1950 by the Queen's Printer, Ottawa.

Tucker, Gilbert. *The Naval Service of Canada*. Vols I and II. Ottawa: Queen's Printer, 1952.

INDEX